Practical Data Structures Using C/C++

James L. Antonakos
Broome Community College

Kenneth C. Mansfield Jr.
Broome Community College

Prentice Hall

Upper Saddle River, New Jersey   Columbus, Ohio

Library of Congress Cataloging-in-Publication Data

Antonakos, James L.
    Practical data structures using C/C++ / James L. Antonakos,
Kenneth C. Mansfield Jr.
      p. cm.
    Includes index.
    ISBN 0-13-280843-9
    1. C (Computer program language) 2. C++ (Computer program
language) 3. Data structures (Computer science) I. Mansfield,
Kenneth C. III. Title.
QA76.73.C15A5363 1999
00.7'3—dc21

    97-46895
    CIP

Editor: Charles E. Stewart, Jr.
Production Editor: Alexandrina Benedicto Wolf
Production Coordinator: Custom Editorial Productions, Inc.
Cover Design Coordinator: Karrie Converse
Cover Photo: © Westlight
Cover Designer: Rod Harris
Production Manager: Deidra M. Schwartz
Marketing Manager: Ben Leonard

This book was set in Times Roman by Custom Editorial Productions, Inc., and was printed and bound by R. R. Donnelley & Sons Company. The cover was printed by Phoenix Cover Corp.

© 1999 by Prentice-Hall, Inc.
Simon & Schuster/A Viacom Company
Upper Saddle River, New Jersey 07458

Printed in the United States of America

10 9 8 7 6 5 4 3 2 1

ISBN: 0-13-280843-9

Prentice-Hall International (UK) Limited, *London*
Prentice-Hall of Australia Pty. Limited, *Sydney*
Prentice-Hall Canada Inc., *Toronto*
Prentice-Hall Hispanoamericana, S. A., *Mexico*
Prentice-Hall of India Private Limited, *New Delhi*
Prentice-Hall of Japan, Inc., *Tokyo*
Simon & Schuster Asia Pte. Ltd., *Singapore*
Editora Prentice-Hall do Brasil, Ltda., *Rio de Janeiro*

To Norma and Vince,
Turner says "Open the garage!"

James L. Antonakos

To Donny Rieber,
Life is what you make of it.
You can do whatever you want!

Kenneth C. Mansfield Jr.

Preface

Introduction

Using the C/C++ programming language to create data structures is finding its way into more and more curriculums and schools every day. Typically, a textbook on C/C++ programming does not provide enough detail for an extensive treatment of data structures. This book was created to fill that need. The fundamental data structures and their applications are presented in the C/C++ environment, for the beginner with no prior data structure experience.

Each new data structure is presented, with attention paid to the following:

- The storage method used.
- How the individual elements are accessed.
- How the structure is modified (elements added/deleted).
- When it should be used.

Whenever possible, structures are compared with each other in order to provide a method for choosing one strucure over another for a particular application. Factors such as storage requirements and search time are considered.

This book is suitable for students in any technological field, particularly students studying computer science and technology.

Chapter Topics

Chapter 1 introduces the general concept of a data structure and identifies many commonly used data structures and their associated operations. Both static and dynamic structures are explained.

Chapter 2 illustrates how character strings are handled. String initialization, passing a string as a function parameter, and built-in string handling functions are explained.

Chapter 3 provides the details of numeric arrays, both one- and two-dimensional. Many different array-sorting applications are included to show how arrays are accessed, partitioned, and passed between functions.

Chapter 4 covers the basic techniques of structuring data using `enum` and `typedef`. Structure tags and structures within structures are also discussed.

Chapter 5 introduces the concept of a node and shows how to connect many nodes together into a linked-list. Typical operations, such as add, delete, and search, are presented. Dynamic storage allocation is also covered.

Chapter 6 explains the operations of stacks and queues, and their data structure implementation.

Chapter 7 shows how a hierarchy of nodes can be organized into a data structure called a tree.

Chapter 8 discusses another data structure, the graph. Different methods of representing graphs are presented, along with the common graph operations.

Chapter 9 illustrates the unique characteristics of the hash table. Collisions, hash functions, and storage requirements are all examined.

Chapter 10 explores several other data structures such as heaps, sets, lookup tables, and both files and directories as data structures.

Chapter 11 ties many of the data structures together into a real-time virtual reality application called Virtual Maze. The data structures representing the game world, wall patterns, precomputed trig values, and player information are discussed.

For those students requiring a review of C/C++, Appendix A provides a detailed reference.

The Companion Disk

The companion disk contains the C/C++ source code files for all of the programs presented in the book. The files are grouped into subdirectories according to chapter.

The root directory contains an executable file called README.COM that explains the disk contents in detail.

Acknowledgments

We would like to thank all of the students who contributed many helpful comments during preparation of the manuscript.

We would also like to thank our editor, Charles Stewart, for his guidance and patience, and his assistants, Kate Linsner and Kimberly Yehle, for their attention to detail. Many thanks to our Project Editor at Custom Editorial Productions, Jim Reidel, who managed the book through production.

James L. Antonakos
antonakos_j@sunybroome.edu
http://www.sunybroome.edu/~antonakos_j

Kenneth C. Mansfield Jr.
mansfield_k@sunybroome.edu
http://www.sunybroome.edu/~mansfield_k

Brief Contents

Contents

1 Introduction to Data Structures

Objectives

This chapter gives you the opportunity to learn:

1. What constitutes a data structure.
2. The differences between static and dynamic data structures.
3. How to choose a data structure.
4. About the many different kinds of data structures.
5. The unique capabilities C++ offers in data structure usage.

Key Terms

Data Structure
Variables
Static Data Structure
Dynamic Data Structure
Node
Static Allocation
struct
Linked-List
Link Field
Dynamic Allocation
Stack
LIFO
Queue

FIFO
Hash Table
Hash Function
Collision
Tree
Child
Parent
Post-Order
Depth-First Search
Breadth-First Search
Graph
Class Declaration

Outline

Introduction

Many times, a novice programmer will begin to write code before thinking through what the requirements of the program really are. Some programs will use a lot of memory, while others will need to access data stored on disk. In both of these cases and many others, a **data structure** is used to access the memory and disk in a way that saves or retrieves information efficiently. Most programs will require many data structures to solve a typical programming problem.

In this chapter and throughout this book, we will explore many different types of data structures. Some of these data structures are built-in to the language, such as strings and arrays, and some are user-specified functions. The data structures that are user specified are created by the programmer to meet the needs and requirements of the program. If we know in advance we are going to sort a group of 25 numbers, we might choose to use an array. If, however, we do not know in advance how many numbers, are to be sorted, it is not practical to use an array because we do not know how large to dimension it. Even setting aside thousands of locations just in case is not a good solution. There can always be one more data item than you have reserved room for. Also, if there are only a few data items, you have wasted a lot of storage space by preallocating a large block of memory.

Furthermore, exactly what type of data are we trying to structure? Individually, we can create one-element structures (called **variables**) that store a single value (such as the char, int, and float data types in C/C++). More importantly, many times we need to group individual variables together to represent an entire block of information. For instance, we might group a string variable, a character, an integer, and two floats together to represent a person's name, gender, age, height, and weight.

We have only touched the surface of the topics and issues involved with data structures. Let us now take a closer look.

1.1   What Is a Data Structure?

A data structure is a predefined arrangement of one or more pieces of data. For example, the individual ASCII characters 'c,' 'a,' and 't' could be grouped together into a data structure called a *string*, which would read as "cat." In another data structure, called a *two-dimensional array*, we might store the distances between four different towns, as indicated in Figure 1.1.

Do you see the relationship between the town-to-town map of Figure 1.1(a) and the numbers stored in the two-dimensional distance array shown in Figure 1.1(b)? The distance of zero is used to indicate the distance from a city to itself.

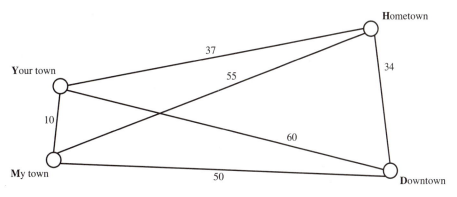

(a) Distance map of four towns

	From:			
	H	**D**	**Y**	**M**
H	0	34	37	55
D	34	0	60	50
Y	37	60	0	10
M	55	50	10	0

To:

(b) Two-dimensional distance array

Figure 1.1   Two Different Representations of the Distance Between Four Cities

So, a data structure contains data that may be arranged in a particular fashion (string, array, etc.). The data can be one or more items of the same type, such as eight characters, or 100-floating-point numbers, or it can be a mixture of many different types. A data structure designed to keep track of temperature measurements may contain the following elements:

- A 16-character string that contains the identification information for the temperature probe, such as "Inlet Port 2."
- A single character variable that specifies the temperature scale ('C' for Celsius, 'F' for Fahrenheit). Note that even when a variable stores only a single piece of data (such as one character or one integer) it is still thought of as a data structure.
- An integer variable that stores a count of the number of samples taken.
- A floating-point variable that stores the average temperature for all readings.
- A 100-element array of floating-point numbers that store the last 100 samples.

You should see by this example that a data structure might become very complicated with the mixing of many different data types.

The reason different data types can be thought of as different data structures has to do with how the data type is stored in memory. One difference between types (structures) is the number of bytes required for each data element. A character string may need 32 bytes, whereas an array of floating-point numbers might need 300 bytes.

Even when a single integer or a single floating-point number is being stored, there is still an underlying structure to the data. Typically, an integer in C/C++ uses two bytes for storage and a floating-point number uses four bytes. These two numbers must be accessed differently due to their predefined format. Other issues, such as which byte is least significant, must also be addressed.

In general, the standard data types provided by C/C++ (`char`, `int`, `float`) can be thought of as the simplest data structures possible. Other, more complicated structures, including strings and arrays, are constructed by combining several simpler data structures (or types) together.

Conclusion

In this section you were introduced to the notion of a data structure. Test your understanding of this material with the following section review.

1.1 Section Review

1. What is a data structure?
2. What are the different data structures mentioned in this section? Include different types of data as different structures.
3. Assume that a character requires one byte of storage, an integer two bytes, and a floating-point number four bytes. How many bytes are required for the temperature probe data structure?
4. Can you determine the shortest route possible that allows you to leave one town in Figure 1.1(a) and travel to the other three towns? You may not use the same path more than once.

1.2   Static and Dynamic Data Structures

A *static* **data structure** has the property that its allocated memory size is fixed at compile time. A character, or a `float`, or a 20-element integer array only needs to be allocated its total memory space once (at the beginning of execution). *Dynamic* **data structures** start out empty, and grow until they occupy as much space as they need to. For example, a data structure designed to keep track of the components of a mathematical expression varies in size as the complexity of the expression changes. Let us look at a few examples to illustrate these differences.

The `adder()` function shown here uses static allocation to reserve room for the local variables `k` and `sum`.

```
int adder(int a, int b)
{
     int k,sum;

     sum = 0;
```

```
    for(k = a; k< b; k++)
        sum += k;
    return(sum);
}
```

In this example, four bytes of memory are reserved for the local variables. This size is determined at compile time, since the compiler knows that each `int` requires two bytes of storage.

Dynamic allocation typically involves the allocation, on demand, of a block of storage called a **node.** The structure of a node may look like this:

```
typedef struct node
{
    char name[32];
    int age;
    float height;
    struct node *link;
} employee;
```

Note the use of the pointer variable `link`. This pointer is used to connect nodes together by storing the address of the next node in the data structure. The size of a node is fixed (determined by using the `sizeof()` function), but the size of the data structure is variable, since it may contain zero or more nodes.

It is common to use a pointer when dealing with a dynamic data structure. This is because we never know where the first allocated node will come from. Nodes are allocated with the `malloc()` function, which returns a pointer to the allocated block (or NULL if no memory could be allocated). The size of a dynamic structure is only limited by the amount of free memory available in the system.

Conclusion

Depending on the application, there may be reasons for choosing static allocation over dynamic, and vice versa. If you know in advance the number of pieces of data used by the application, static allocation is acceptable. In the following sections and chapters we will see that dynamic data structures require algorithms to create, add, delete, and search groups of nodes. For now, test your understanding of the material with the following section review.

1.2 Section Review

1. Why is an array of integers considered a static data structure?
2. Why do node structures contain pointer variables?
3. What is the size of the `employee` node?

1.3   Why Do We Need Data Structures?

It may seem odd to say that we need data structures because they *simplify* our programming chores, but they do. Imagine writing a program that works with several hundred pieces of data (a spreadsheet for three months of activity at a typical small business). What programmer would have the time or patience to create and use hundreds of different variables in a single program? Just trying to remember all their names would be a formidable challenge. A data structure allows you to group one or more pieces of data together, and then connect the groups of data together (into arrays or lists) that can be accessed with a *single variable*, a pointer to the beginning of the data structure.

Imagine trying to pass fifty or sixty data elements between functions. The hefty amount of typing involved is just the beginning. The task becomes trivial when a pointer to the data structure containing the fifty or sixty elements is passed instead of the data itself. If a programming task does not make sense, or is difficult to code, it is likely to be a data structure that comes to the rescue to simplify the job and make sense of the difficulties encountered earlier.

A data structure in the most simple form is a character, a string, a number, an array, a pointer, or a dynamically allocated node. Using the rich set of features available in the C/C++ language, some very elaborate and complex data structures can be developed from the basic building blocks. When we go to the trouble to create data structures, C/C++ will perform all of the required operations on the data. The time invested up front in the design of a good data structure will be rewarded with a simplified coding process, efficient use of resources (such as the run-time stack or memory), and a good understanding of exactly what is happening with the computer's resources.

Instead of asking "Why do we need data structures?" we might ask ourselves "When don't we need a data structure?"

Conclusion

In this section we discussed some of the reasons why data structures simplify some of the chores a programmer must perform. Test your understanding of this section by trying the following section review.

1.3 Section Review

1. How does a data structure simplify the task of coding?
2. Explain how a single variable can allow access to a data structure.
3. What happens if we do not use data structures when coding a C/C++ program?

1.4   Typical Data Structures

The simplest data structures supported by C/C++ are the `char`, `int`, and `float` data types. Here we have data structures that store a single element. It is more practical to store groups of numbers (or elements) together, and provide a mechanism to access an individual item in the data structure. In this section we will examine several common data structures, and see how they store their information and how all the elements are connected. In Section 1.5 we will see how each data structure is accessed and modified.

Figure 1.2 shows a wide variety of data structures. Let us discuss each one and see how it compares with the others.

Character strings and numeric arrays are shown in Figure 1.2(a). These data structures are **static,** their lengths determined at compile time. Individual elements are easily accessed using an index value into the array, as in:

```
value = array[index];
```

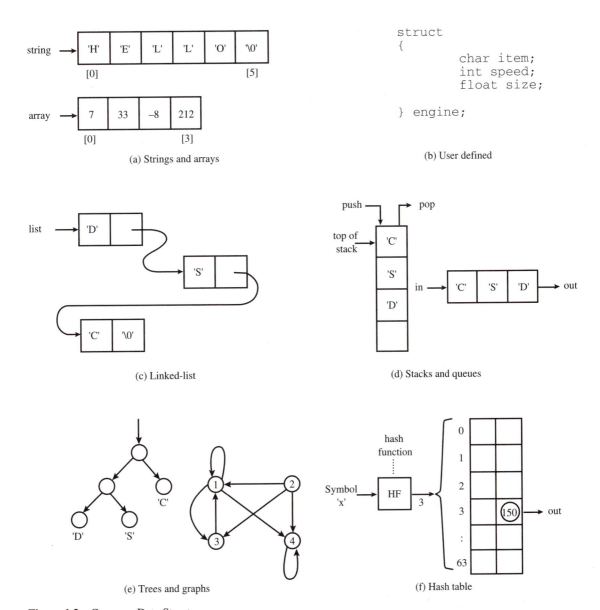

Figure 1.2 Common Data Structures

Figure 1.2(b) illustrates the use of the **struct** keyword to create a user-defined data structure. This powerful aspect of C/C++ allows us to create *any* kind of complicated structure we might need. The struct is also a static data structure, its size based on the storage requirements of each element. Individual elements are accessed using a simple syntax:

```
engine.item = 'A';
engine.speed = 1200;
engine.size = 3.3;
```

The **linked-list** detailed in Figure 1.2(c) extends the static `struct` into the dynamic arena by connecting individual `struct` variables together (which we now refer to as *nodes*). This is accomplished by including a special **link field** to the node's `struct` definition. The link field will contain a pointer to the next node in the linked list (or to NULL for the last node in the list). Nodes are allocated as they are needed, as many as free memory will support. This is the great advantage of **dynamic allocation.** Unfortunately, we must now search the list whenever we want to get at a specific node, a possibly time-consuming chore when the list is large.

The next two data structures are stacks and queues. Both are shown in Figure 1.2(d). These structures may be implemented as arrays or linked-lists (or some other data structure). The important aspect of these two data structures is the *order* in which they process data. The **stack** is also called a Last-In-First-Out **(LIFO)** data structure. The **queue** is a **FIFO** (First-In-First-Out). Stacks and queues have many practical applications and are easy to maintain. Individual functions are required to add and remove elements from each structure (`push()` and `pop()` for the stack, `en_queue()` and `de_queue()` for the queue).

Figure 1.2(e) illustrates two related structures, the tree and the graph. These data structures are very useful for representing dependent information (the hierarchy of mathematical operations in a complex arithmetic statement, state transitions in a machine, distances between a set of cities). Linked-lists with two or more link fields can be used to represent either structure. A graph can also be represented by a two-dimensional *connectivity* matrix.

No matter how either structure is implemented, it will still be necessary to search through them (traverse the tree, find a subgraph), so the method of implementation should be thought through carefully.

The last data structure, the **hash table,** is pictured in Figure 1.2(f). Hash tables require the use of a **hash function** to generate an index into the hash table. If the hash function is poorly designed, many different inputs will hash to the same index, resulting in a **collision.** This, however, is a small price to pay when getting the real benefit of the hash table: quick access time. Only the execution time of the hash function determines how long it takes to find the desired element (assuming there are no collisions). So we use a hash table when we want fast access to our stored data.

We will explore each of these data structures in detail. In addition, we will introduce other data structures such as Files, Heaps, Sets, and Lookup Tables.

Conclusion

The nine data structures just described will go a long way towards solving our data storage needs in most programming applications. The remaining chapters are devoted to detailed coverage of each structure. For now, test your understanding of the material with the following section review.

1.4 Section Review

1. Which data structures from Figure 1.2 have a fixed size?
2. What does FIFO stand for? LIFO?
3. Which is easier to access, an array or a linked-list?
4. What is the difference between a tree and a graph?

1.5   Operations on Data Structures

In Section 1.4 we were exposed to many different data structures (refer to Figure 1.2). In this section we will see what operations are performed on each of them. In addition to the initialization code required for each data structure, we make use of several functions to access and modify each structure.

Strings

Many different operations are possible with the string data structure. We can find the string length, search a string for a specific character, attach a second string to the end of the first, and compare strings (helpful during sorting), among other operations.

Arrays

Single and multidimensional arrays, like strings, require sorting, searching, and modification. Several examples of sorting will be presented to show you how array information is processed. One point to remember is that we might need to use a number to represent the last item in the array that is different from all the other numbers in the array.

User Defined (via `struct`)

The power of this data structure is its ability to store a wide variety of information as a single block of data. Sorting, searching, and other modifications are possible, assuming that a group of blocks is operated on. One way to implement the group of blocked data is by defining an array of structures, as in:

```
typedef struct
{
    char name[32];
    int age;
    float height;
} employee[20];
```

Now, individual employee information is accessed by using variable references such as:

```
employee[index].name
```

Another way to group the individual structures together is to use a linked-list. Let us see how this is done.

Linked-List

Two simple additions to the user-defined data structure will allow a linked-list to be created:

```
typedef struct node
{
    char name[32];
    int age;
```

```
        float height;
        struct node *link;
} employee;
```

As the new `struct` definition shows, a tag called `node` has been added, along with a structure pointer variable called `link`. The `link` pointer is loaded with the address returned by `malloc()` when a node is created. In this fashion, a linked-list of nodes is maintained. We use functions to add, delete, and search nodes. Searching a linked-list is more time consuming than searching an array, since the pointer to the next node must be continuously updated. The same is true for adding/deleting a node.

Stack

The stack uses a `push()` function to store an item, and a `pop()` function to read the last item pushed. An `empty()` function is also useful, and is used in conjunction with `pop()` to guarantee that we do not `pop()` data from an empty stack.

Queue

Queues use `en_queue()` and `de_queue()` functions to store and retrieve data. The first data item to enter the queue is the first to leave. An `empty()` function is useful for preventing false dequeues.

Tree

The hierarchical structure of a **tree** lends itself to search and traversal algorithms that either loop until all nodes have been processed, or use recursion to accomplish the same thing. Trees normally have a certain number of *levels*. The next level in any tree contains the **child** nodes of the current level's **parent** nodes.

We might traverse a special tree called a *binary tree,* which stores the various sequence of operations in an expression, and generate a **post-order** mathematical expression. The post-order expression is then easily evaluated with a stack.

Trees are often searched so that the bottommost node is found first. This is called a **depth-first search.** Trees are also searched so that all nodes at a particular level are examined before going to a deeper level. This is called a **breadth-first search.**

Other operations performed on trees are balance, add, and prune. A balanced tree has its node positions adjusted so that a minimum number of levels are needed.

Graph

A **graph** is similar to a tree except there is no concept of a level anymore. A node in a graph can connect to any other node in the graph, or even itself. The connection can be one way or two way. In a tree, a node connects to one or more nodes at the next level. Because of these differences, graphs require different search algorithms than trees do. A queue can be used to perform a search of a graph.

It is often possible to represent a graph using a two-dimensional matrix (as already shown in Figure 1.1(b) as a distance matrix). Then, using successive matrix multiplies, it is possible to determine if paths of length two, three, or more exist between two nodes in the graph. So, matrix multiply is a required function to implement.

Table 1.1   Data Structures and Their Operations

Data Structure	Operations
String	compare, sort, catenate, etc.
Array	sort, search, map
User Defined	depend on structure
Linked-List	add, delete, search
Stack	push, pop, empty
Queue	enqueue, dequeue, empty
Tree	search, balance, traverse, add, prune
Graph	search, spanning tree, find cycle, find subgraph
Hash Table	hash symbol, resolve collision

Since graphs are also used to represent control information (state transitions in a logic circuit or finite-state machine), it is also necessary to include a traversal function that can navigate through the graph one node at a time.

Hash Table

Hash tables require a `hash()` function that returns an index into the hash table based on the contents of an input string. Another function may be used to resolve collisions (when more than one input string hashes to the same index).

All of the operations are summarized in Table 1.1.

Conclusion

In the remaining chapters, we will take a detailed look at the operations just described. For now, test your understanding of the material with the following section review.

1.5 Section Review

1. What are two methods used to search a binary tree?
2. Describe the features of `struct`.
3. What operations can be performed on a linked-list?
4. When does a collision occur in a hash table?
5. Why do we use graphs?

1.6   Choosing a Data Structure

What influences our decision when choosing a data structure? It is possible that a mismatched data structure will actually lower the performance of a program (increased execution time, fewer calculations per second). Here are a few questions to consider:

- *Is memory being used efficiently?*

   It is possible to use data structures improperly. For example, using an array to store 100 `ints` takes 200 bytes. If a linked-list were used to store the same 100 `ints`, 400 bytes would be required, 200 bytes for the data and an additional 200 bytes for the pointer fields. In general, when we know how many data items there are in advance, we can use static allocation (as in the array of integers). When the amount of data is unknown at compile time, dynamic allocation is better (as in the linked-list of integers).

- *What is the search time?*

Search time is an important consideration when selecting a data structure. If you search an array for a particular value, you may have to search the entire array to find it. Searching through an array of 10, or even 100, elements may not be a problem. But looking at 1,024 elements during a search could be very time consuming. If we use a binary tree to store the same 1,024 elements, the entire tree can be searched with 10 or fewer comparisons.

- *How easy is it to use the structure?*

When we use a particular data structure, it should be easy to access and/or modify it from the application utilizing the data structure. For example, a stack's `push()` and `pop()` functions are straightforward, only having to add/delete a single node from the beginning of a linked-list. On the other hand, a binary tree storing a sorted group of numbers may have to be rearranged when a new number is inserted into its proper position.

- *Can the access method be tested?*

It is important to test underlying assumptions made about a particular data structure. For example, a poorly designed hash table may be more inefficient than an array, if the number of collisions is significant. For this reason, it is essential to test any functions with a large variety of sample data. The objective is to determine how the software operates under "normal" conditions. A program that uses pointers should be thoroughly tested to guarantee that no pointer references go off into uncharted memory areas.

- *What are the tradeoffs?*

We rarely can get everything we want out of a single data structure. Many times, our choice will depend on just a single factor that is important to us. For instance, if quick access time is really important, the hash table or binary tree would be acceptable choices. We may overlook the fact that it is time consuming to modify the binary tree, or that the hash function may generate a few more collisions than we would like. It could be that we will rarely add or delete nodes to the tree, or symbols to the hash table, once they are initialized. So we do not mind the overhead associated with these data structures because we can access them so fast. Another important consideration is time. If a good hashing function has already been written, it may be convenient to use it again as a need arises instead of taking the time to develop a custom structure for each application.

Conclusion

In this section we covered a number of points to ponder when choosing a data structure. Test your understanding of the material with the following section review.

1.6 Section Review

1. Why would one data structure be chosen over another?
2. How does the type of data structure affect its search time?

3. What are the consequences of choosing the wrong type of data structure?
4. Why settle for one particular data structure? Why not design a custom structure every time you need one?

1.7   A Note About C++

The programmers who already know C++ understand what kinds of features are built-in that support data structures. For those unfamiliar with C++, a short example will clue you in to the power available in C++.

The structure shown here is a C++ **class declaration.** The name of the class is ARRAY, and it contains the variables *and functions* needed to work with an array object.

```
class ARRAY {
public:
     int index;
     int data[16];
     int search_array(int item);
}
```

The variables and functions contained in the class definition are *members* of the class (search_array() is a member function).

The beauty of the class declaration is that we can completely change the way class objects are used by making one simple change:

```
class ARRAY {
     int index;
     int data[16];
public:
     int search_array(int item);
}
```

The difference in this new class declaration is that the public keyword has been moved after the two member variables. This automatically makes index and data *private* members, which can only be accessed by member functions instantiated from ARRAY. This means that trying to use index or data in main(), or some other function that is not a member function of ARRAY, will cause a compilation error. This feature of C++ classes allows the programmer to control who is allowed access to various member variables and functions.

Another benefit of using C++ to create and manage your data structures is that, through *instantiation,* multiple copies (multiple objects) of a data structure can be utilized. Do you need three stacks? Four binary trees? Six hash tables? The underlying C++ programming environment takes care of all the details. The programmer uses the same push() function for each stack, or the same index variable for each array or string. The specific stack, array, or hash table object is referred to by name, along with the operation, as in:

```
stack1.push();
tree2.traverse();
table6.hash();
```

The compiler *reuses* code between multiple copies of the same object, and maintains individual pointers to each object, all automatically.

If these features appeal to you, or fit the requirements of your programming assignment, use C++ to implement your data structure object. If you would rather use C, that is OK as well, since everything we can do in C++ we can do in C, with a little extra code and data.

Conclusion

Using the object-oriented capabilities of C++ adds a new dimension to the creation and use of data structures. Check your understanding of the material with the following section review.

1.7 Section Review

1. How is access to a member variable or function controlled by the `public` keyword?
2. What is meant by instantiation?
3. What is meant by this statement:

```
my_string.get();
```

Study Questions

General Concepts

Section 1.1
  1. Can a data structure contain different types of data?
  2. How did you choose the paths you used when checking for the shortest path between towns in Figure 1.1(a)?
  3. Why is something as simple as an integer considered a data structure?

Section 1.2
  4. What are some of the differences between static and dynamic data structures?
  5. How does the compiler handle static data, as in:

```
char abc;
int a,b,c;
float ave;
```

  6. How is a dynamic data structure limited in its storage capacity?

Section 1.3
  7. Why is the coding process simplified when we use a data structure?
  8. When does it make sense to use a data structure?
  9. What rewards does a data structure offer a programmer?
 10. Why is it inefficient to not use a data structure?

Section 1.4
 11. What is the difference between a string and an array?
 12. What is the difference between a stack and a queue?
 13. Which is easier to search, a linked-list or a hash table?

Section 1.5
 14. What types of operations can be performed on a queue?
 15. Describe the differences between trees and graphs.
 16. What is a distance matrix used for?

Section 1.6

17. Why bother worrying about how much memory a data structure uses?
18. Explain why a hash table might be used instead of a binary tree.
19. Explain why a binary tree might be used instead of a hash table.
20. What are the consequences of inadequate testing?

Section 1.7

21. What are the advantages of using C++ to implement a data structure?
22. What is the difference between `public` members and `private` members?
23. How are multiple objects of the same type managed?

Program Design

For a basic review of C/C++ and for practice using your compiler, load, compile, and execute all of the programs in Appendix A. Be sure you understand how each program operates.

2　Strings

Objectives

This chapter provides you the opportunity to learn:

1. How to use simple data structures consisting of strings.
2. The relationship between characters and pointers.
3. Methods of putting characters in memory to form strings.
4. The use of strings in C/C++.
5. How string functions manipulate strings.
6. Methods of sorting string data.

Key Terms

String
Array
NULL Character
Elements
Pointer

Initialization
Rectangular Array
Bubble Sort
Ragged Array

Outline

Introduction

In this chapter you will see the relationships among characters, pointers, and strings. Understanding how these are related will help you in developing programs that are capable of many powerful operations, including sorting.

With the information in this chapter, you will have a solid foundation for the development of programs that will solve a wide variety of complex problems using many different types of data structures.

2.1   Characters and Strings

Discussion

This section presents the relationships among characters, pointers, and strings. Here you will see how pointers are used to store characters in memory. You will receive your first introduction to arrays using characters and strings.

The use of strings is an important part of any technology program. Understanding how to use strings in your programs opens another dimension of technical programming. The ability to use the names of objects, people, and data is a powerful addition to your programming skills. This section introduces this important tool using simple built-in data structures.

Storing Strings

A character can be thought of as a single memory location that contains an ASCII code. A **string** is nothing more than an arrangement of characters. The word **array** means arrangement; therefore, a string can be thought of as an array of characters. How a string is stored in memory is illustrated in Figure 2.1.

Such a sequential arrangement of data within memory is also referred to as an array. Note that the last character of the string array in Figure 2.1 consists of the **NULL character** (represented by '\0'). All character strings require the NULL character to let the compiler know where the string ends. The NULL character is automatically placed at the end of the string when the string is defined.

To create a string (an array of characters), you must use the brackets [] immediately following your string identifier. This is demonstrated in Program 2.1.

Program 2.1

```
#include <stdio.h>

char string[] = "Hello";

main()
{
        printf("The string is %s.",string);
}
```

| 'H' | 'e' | 'l' | 'l' | 'o' | '\0' |

Figure 2.1   String Storage in Memory

When Program 2.1 is executed, the output will be

```
The string is Hello.
```

Note that the format specifier is %s for a string variable.

Program Analysis

The statement char string[] = "Hello"; reserves enough consecutive memory spaces to hold the string of characters: H e l l o. The variable string is now an array variable because it represents an arrangement of information in memory, not just one memory location.

The %s as the format specifier is used to display the array variable as a string of characters.

An Inside Look

An array is said to be made up of **elements.** As an example, in the string array "Hello," each character is an element of the array. Elements in a string array are numbered beginning with zero, so the zero element of this array is the letter H. To represent any single element of an array, simply place the element number inside the square brackets of the array variable; string[0] in this case is the letter H. This is illustrated by Program 2.2.

Program 2.2

```
#include <stdio.h>

        char string[] = "Hello";

main()
{
        printf("The string is %s.\n",string);
        printf("The characters are:\n");

        printf("%c\n",string[0]);
        printf("%c\n",string[1]);
        printf("%c\n",string[2]);
        printf("%c\n",string[3]);
        printf("%c\n",string[4]);
        printf("%c\n",string[5]);
}
```

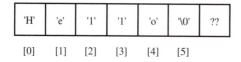

Figure 2.2   String Storage in Memory with Element Numbers

Execution of Program 2.2 yields

```
The string is Hello.
The characters are:
H
e
l
l
o
```

This shows some interesting facts about string arrays. First, they all start with the 0 element of the array. Second, all string arrays requires a NULL terminator as the last element of the array. This terminator is necessary so that the program knows when the string array ends. This concept is illustrated in Figure 2.2.

Program Analysis

Program 2.2 again uses the statement

```
char string[] = "Hello";
```

to define the string array `string`. The individual characters are then displayed by the `printf()` function using the character specifier `%c` along with a single array element:

```
printf("%c\n",string[0]);
```

This statement, for example, causes the first element (the 0 element) of the string array to display its contents as a character, and hence the capital letter H is displayed. In a like manner, the other `printf()` statements cause each of the other individual array elements to be displayed.

Where Are the Elements?

In a string array, each element is a character and represents a single memory location of one byte. As with other data, a **pointer** can also be used to access any element of the array. Consider Program 2.3. It defines the same string array and also a pointer (of type `char`). It then uses the `*ptr` to access each individual element of the array (each memory location).

Program 2.3

```
#include <stdio.h>

char string[] = "Hello";

main()
```

```
{
        char *ptr;

        ptr = string;

        printf("The string is %s.\n",string);
        printf("The characters are:\n");
        printf("%c\n",*ptr);
        printf("%c\n",*(ptr + 1));
        printf("%c\n",*(ptr + 2));
        printf("%c\n",*(ptr + 3));
        printf("%c\n",*(ptr + 4));
        printf("%c\n",*(ptr + 5));
}
```

Execution of Program 2.3 yields

```
The string is Hello.
The characters are:
H
e
l
l
o
```

As you can see, the output of Program 2.3 is identical to that of Program 2.2. This means that the following are exactly equal:

```
*ptr = string[0]
*(ptr + 1) = string[1]
*(ptr + 2) = string[2]
*(ptr + 3) = string[3]
*(ptr + 4) = string[4]
*(ptr + 5) = string[5]
```

The reason for this equality is because the variable string is declared as an arrayed variable (it was followed by the square brackets []). When the statement

```
ptr = string;
```

is used, this automatically places the address of the first string element (string[0]) in ptr. Thus, if you add 1 to the value contained in ptr (as with *(ptr + 1)), you are adding 1 to the address contained there, which is the memory location of the next character. This concept is illustrated in Figure 2.3. Note the use of sample memory addresses (5321 through 5326).

It's important to observe the difference between

```
*(ptr + 1)
```

and

```
ptr + 1
```

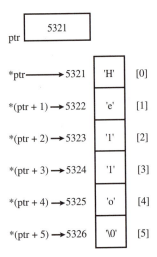

Figure 2.3   Using a Pointer to Access String Characters

In the first case, the program will be directed to the address that follows the address stored in `ptr`. In the second case, the value stored in `ptr` will have the number 1 added to it. This is illustrated by Program 2.4.

Program 2.4

```
#include <stdio.h>

        char string[] = "Hello";

main()
{
        char *ptr;

        ptr = string;

        printf("The string is %s.\n",string);
        printf("The characters are:\n");

        printf("Address => %d | %c |\n",ptr, *ptr);
        printf("Address => %d | %c |\n",ptr + 1, *(ptr + 1));
        printf("Address => %d | %c |\n",ptr + 2, *(ptr + 2));
        printf("Address => %d | %c |\n",ptr + 3, *(ptr + 3));
        printf("Address => %d | %c |\n",ptr + 4, *(ptr + 4));
        printf("Address => %d | %c |\n",ptr + 5, *(ptr + 5));
}
```

When Program 2.4 is executed, the output is

```
Address => 5321   | H |
Address => 5322   | e |
Address => 5323   | l |
```

```
Address => 5324   | l |
Address => 5325   | o |
Address => 5326   |   |
```

This demonstrates three things. First, the addresses of the character array are contiguous. Second, `ptr + 1` is a value that is 1 larger than the value contained in `ptr`. Third, `*(ptr + 1)` represents the character stored in the memory location whose address is 1 larger than the address stored in `ptr`.

Conclusion

This section introduced you to the use of strings. You were also introduced to the concept of an array as a contiguous set of data elements in memory. Here you saw that the first element number of an array is 0. You also saw that a string array must be terminated with the NULL character `'\0'`.

The relationship between arrays and pointers was also demonstrated. Check your understanding of this section by trying the following section review.

2.1 Section Review

1. State what is meant by a string.
2. Explain how you indicate a `char` string.
3. For a string consisting of five characters, how many array elements are required? Explain.
4. What is the element number of the first character in a string array?
5. Explain the relationship between pointers and string array elements.

2.2   Initializing Strings

In this section we will examine a number of ways a string of characters may be **initialized.** Recall from Section 2.1 that the statement

```
char string[] = "Hello";
```

automatically reserves the correct number of memory locations to store each element of the string, including the final NULL character `'\0'`. The same thing is accomplished with this new statement

```
char string[] = {'H', 'e', 'l', 'l', 'o', '\0'};
```

which you might agree is more cumbersome than a simple matching pair of double quotes.

When it is necessary to specify the length of a string, an integer length value must be placed between the `[]`s. For example, in the statement

```
char string[5] = "Hello";
```

the actual length of the string (5) is specified between the square brackets. Note that the NULL character is not counted as part of the string's length. It is thus possible to create a string of zero length by writing the NULL character into element 0's position, as in

```
string[0] = '\0';
```

Note that specifying more characters for the string than are required is common and relieves the programmer of the burden of counting the string characters while writing the program. So the statement

```
char string[80] = "Hello";
```

is also acceptable and allows more string characters to be added at a later time, if desired. Keep in mind that the extra character locations may contain random numbers that may not be correctly interpreted as valid characters without initialization.

In some cases we only wish to allocate memory for the string at the beginning of a program and stuff characters into the locations at a later time, as shown in the following code:

```
char string[5];

string[0] = 'H';
string[1] = 'e';
string[2] = 'l';
string[3] = 'l';
string[4] = 'o';
string[5] = '\0';
```

Note that it is necessary for us to place the NULL character into memory as well. This is required so that the compiler knows where the string ends. If we were to forget to do this, our string would not merely be "Hello" but "Hello" followed by all characters in memory following the 'o' until a NULL character was found. Also note the difference between using a single quote (as in 'x') and a double quote (as in "x"). Single quotes define a *single character,* whereas double quotes define a *string.* Thus, 'x' represents the single ASCII character 'x', and "x" represents a string containing the two characters 'x' and '\0'.

Another way to initialize a string is to reserve storage for it and then use scanf() to read the string in. Consider the following code:

```
char string[20];

printf("Enter a string => ");
scanf("%s",string);
```

Notice that the & character is not used before the variable name (e.g., &string) as it usually is when scanf() is used to read in a number. This is because the string's variable name automatically represents the starting address of the string, and that is what scanf() requires.

During execution, suppose that the user enters

```
Enter a string => Hello
```

The characters stored into memory by scanf will be 'H', 'e', 'l', 'l', and 'o' followed by the NULL character. However, scanf() has its limitations. For instance, if the user instead enters

```
Enter a string => Hello there.
```

scanf() will only load the same five characters, because it terminates scanning when it encounters the blank character between "Hello" and "there." This is unfortunate, because we would like to be able to enter strings containing blank characters (as in a word-processing application). The solution to this situation lies in the `gets()` function. The `gets()` function will read the entire line of text entered by the user, up to the carriage return. So, a better technique for reading a string into memory is as follows:

```
char string[20];

printf("Enter a string => ");
gets(string);
```

The `gets()` function only requires the name of the string to be supplied, and is included in `<stdio.h>` as a standard input function. If we enter

```
Enter a string => Oh, I get it!
```

the `gets()` function will store all 13 characters entered (including the blanks), plus a NULL character to terminate the string.

So there are many options available to a programmer when it comes to initializing strings. One last point deserves mention. It is often necessary to fill an entire string with blanks (or some other character). This is easily accomplished as follows:

```
char string[80];
int i;

for(i = 0; i < 80; i++)
    string[i] = ' ';
string[80] = '\0';
```

Once again, note the importance of writing the NULL character into memory to complete the string definition.

Conclusion

In this section you were introduced to several methods used to initialize strings. We examined the operation of the NULL character and discussed why it is important to have a NULL character in the definition of every string.

Check your understanding of this material by answering the questions in the section review.

2.2 Section Review

1. How many characters are placed into memory by the following statement?

   ```
   char string[] = "abcdefghijklmnopqrstuvwxyz";
   ```

2. What would be stored in memory by `scanf` if the following text were entered?

   ```
   "Oh, I get it!"
   ```

3. What is the difference between `"\0"` and `'\0'`?

4. Why use the statement `char string[80] = "Hello"` instead of `char string[] = "Hello"`?

2.3   Passing Strings Between Functions

Because strings are nothing more than character arrays, you can pass strings between functions by passing only a pointer to the first element of the string. This is demonstrated by Programs 2.5 and 2.6.

Program 2.5

```
#include <stdio.h>

void function1(char name[]);

main()
{
        char string[20];

        printf("What is your name => ");
        gets(string);

        function1(string);
}

void function1(char name[])
{
        printf("Hello there %s!",name);
}
```

Program 2.5 illustrates the passing of a string to a called function. Execution of the program produces

```
What is your name => Joe Smith
Hello there Joe Smith!
```

Program 2.6 shows the string being passed back to the calling function.

Program 2.6

```
#include <stdio.h>

void function1(char name[]);

main()
{
        char string[20];

        function1(string);
        printf("Hello there %s!\n\n",string);
}

void function1(char name[])
{
        printf("Enter your first name => ");
        gets(name);
}
```

The output of Program 2.6 is identical to that of Program 2.5. Note that only the starting address of the string is passed between function1() and main().

To pass multiple strings between functions you need only to include all string names in the function header. For example, Program 2.7 contains a function called equal_size() that compares the lengths of two strings passed into it. If both strings have the same number of characters before the NULL character, they have the same length. The starting addresses of both strings are passed into equal_size(), which returns a value of 1 if the strings do have an equal number of characters, and 0 if they do not.

Program 2.7

```
#include <stdio.h>

int equal_size(char s1[], char s2[]);

main()
{
        char str1[] = "One";
        char str2[] = "Two";
        char str3[] = "Three";

        if(1 == equal_size(str1,str2))
                printf("\"%s\" and \"%s\" are equal in length.\n",str1,str2);
        else
                printf("\"%s\" and \"%s\" are not equal in length.\n"
                        ,str1,str2);
        if(1 == equal_size(str1,str3))
                printf("\"%s\" and \"%s\" are equal in length.\n",str1,str3);
        else
                printf("\"%s\" and \"%s\" are not equal in length.\n"
                        ,str1,str3);
}

int equal_size(char s1[], char s2[])
{
        int i = 0, j = 0;
        while('\0' != s1[i])
                i++;
        while('\0' != s2[j])
                j++;
        if(i == j)
                return(1);
        else
                return(0);
}
```

An important point to remember concerns the passing of a string *back* from a function. It is necessary for the storage space for the passed string to be contained within the *calling* function. Otherwise, the memory contents of the string may be lost when the function terminates and its local storage is returned to the storage pool.

Conclusion

In this section we introduced the concept and a method to pass strings between functions. This involves simply passing a pointer to each string being passed.

Check your understanding of this material by trying the following section review.

2.3 Section Review

1. Would Programs 2.5 and 2.6 work the same way if `gets()` were replaced by `scanf()`?
2. Why is it not necessary to specify the string size when passing a string to a function?
3. In Program 2.7, what would happen during the execution of `equal_size()` if one or both of the strings were missing a terminating NULL character?

2.4   Working with String Elements

In this section we examine a number of built-in functions that allow us to input string elements, examine them, and even convert them from one form to another. Each operation is useful in a program that accepts text from a user.

One Character at a Time

One useful built-in function that gets one character at a time from the input is called `getchar()`. As you will see, the advantage of doing this is that each individual character may be tested. Doing this will determine if a character is a letter of the alphabet, a number, or some other kind of input such as a punctuation mark. The use of this function is illustrated in Program 2.8.

Program 2.8

```
#include <stdio.h>

main()
{
        char ch;

        printf("Give me a single input => ");
        ch = getchar();

}
```

The function `getchar()` reads a single character from the input. For example, a string of characters may be entered by the program user until a newline marker is encountered (meaning the program user has pressed the carriage return). This is demonstrated in Program 2.9.

Program 2.9

```
#include <stdio.h>

main()
{
```

```
        char ch;

        printf("Give me a number => ");

        while((ch = getchar()) != '\n');
}
```

In Program 2.9, the program user will be able to continually input characters from the keyboard until the return key is depressed. When this happens, the `while()` will terminate.

Checking Characters

There are several different types of built-in functions that will check the type of character that is entered into a program. Table 2.1 lists them.

Program 2.10 illustrates an application of one of the built-in character checking functions.

Program 2.10

```
#include <stdio.h>
#include <ctype.h>

main()
{
        char ch;

        printf("Give me a sentence => \n");

        while ((ch = getchar()) != '\r')
                printf("%d",isalpha(ch));
}
```

Execution of Program 2.10 produces

```
Give me a sentence =>
<Learn C>   — entered by user but not printed
 1222201    — displayed as user enters characters
```

As you can see from this output, the `isalpha()` function returns a 0 when the character is not a letter of the alphabet (such as the blank space). It returns a 1 for any uppercase character and a 2 for any lowercase character.

More Character Checking

Just as Program 2.10 checks for alphabetical characters, you can also check for numerical characters or any other type of character presented in Table 2.1.

Program 2.11 asks for a string of text from the user and prints out the string minus any punctuation or numerical digits. Lowercase alphabetical characters are converted to uppercase as well. This technique is useful in a word-processing application where spell checking is required and it is necessary to eliminate all nonalphabetical characters. Getting

Table 2.1 C Character Classifications in `<ctype.h>`

Function	Meaning (Returns a nonzero value if character meets the test, otherwise zero.)	Example (ch is character being tested)
`isalnum()`	Alphanumeric	`if(isalnum(ch) != 0)` `printf("%c is alphanumeric\n",ch);`
`isalpha()`	Alphabetical	`if(isalpha(ch) != 0)` `printf("%c is alphabetical\n",ch);`
`iscntrl()`	Control character	`if(iscntrl(ch) != 0)` `printf("%c is a control ch\n",ch);`
`isdigit()`	Digit	`if(isdigit(ch) != 0)` `printf("%c is a digit.\n",ch);`
`isgraph()`	Checks if character is printable Excludes the space character	`if(isgraph(ch) != 0)` `printf("%c is printable.\n",ch);`
`islower()`	Checks if character is lowercase	`if(islower(ch) != 0)` `printf("%c is lowercase\n",ch);`
`isprint()`	Checks if character is printable Includes the space character	`if(isprint(ch) != 0)` `printf("%c is printable.\n",ch);`
`ispunct()`	Checks if character is punctuation	`if(ispunct(ch) != 0)` `printf("%c is punctuation.\n",ch);`
`isspace()`	Space	`if(isspace(ch) != 0)` `printf("%c is a space.\n",ch);`
`isupper()`	Checks if character is uppercase	`if(isupper(ch) != 0)` `printf("%c is uppercase.\n",ch);`
`isxdigit()`	Hexadecimal digit	`if(isxdigit(ch) != 0)` `printf("%c is hex digit.\n",ch);`

all characters into uppercase provides for easier searching and comparing with the spell check dictionary.

Program 2.11

```
#include <stdio.h>
#include <ctype.h>

main()
{
        char string[80];
        int i = 0;

        printf("Enter a string of text including punctuation and numbers: \n");
        gets(string);

        while(string[i] != '\0')
        {
                if ((0 == ispunct(string[i])) && (0 == isdigit(string[i])))
```

```
        {
                if(0 != islower(string[i]))
                        string[i] = string[i] & 0xdf;
                printf("%c", string[i]);
        }
        i++;
    }
}
```

A sample execution of Program 2.11 is as follows:

```
Enter a string of text including punctuation and numbers:
Hello agent 99, this is Max! Where's the chief?
HELLO AGENT  THIS IS MAX WHERES THE CHIEF
```

Looking for Numbers

When the user enters a numeric string from the keyboard, the digits of the number are stored as ASCII character codes, not actual numeric digits. This makes it necessary to scan the string and convert each numeric ASCII code into its associated decimal value and combine all digits into a single number. Program 2.12 does just this for signed integers. The format of the signed integer is as follows:

```
[+ or -] [digits]
```

where the + or – sign is optional (with no sign indicating a positive integer). There must be at least one digit in the [digits] portion. Other types of numbers have similar, although more detailed, formats, as in

```
[+ or -] [digits] [.] [digits]     (real numbers)
[+ or -] [digits] [.] [digits] [e or E] [+ or -] [digits]  (scientific numbers)
```

Program 2.12 asks the user to enter a signed integer and then proceeds to examine the input string and build a resulting integer value based on the ASCII characters entered. Note that no error checking is provided to enforce the required format.

Program 2.12

```
#include <stdio.h>
#include <ctype.h>

main()
{
        char string[10];
        int i = 0;
        int sign = 1,number = 0;

        printf("Enter a signed integer => ");
        gets(string);
        if('-' == string[0])
        {
```

```
                    sign = -1;
                    i++;
          }
          if('+' == string[0])
                    i++;
          while(string[i] != '\0')
          {
                    number *= 10;
                    number += string[i] - 0x30;
                    i++;
          }
          number *= sign;
          printf("You entered %d.",number);
}
```

An alternative way to convert a string-based integer is through the use of the atoi() (ASCII to integer) function found in <stdlib.h>. This function provides an easy way to perform ASCII-to-integer conversion. Program 2.13 demonstrates the use of atoi().

Program 2.13

```
#include <stdio.h>
#include <stdlib.h>

main()
{
          char string[10];
          int number;

          printf("Enter a signed integer => ");
          gets(string);
          number = atoi(string);
          printf("You entered %d.",number);
}
```

Other related functions in <stdlib.h> are:

- atof() ASCII to float
- atol() ASCII to long

Although these built-in functions make it easy to perform necessary conversions, it is still a good programming challenge to write the conversion code yourself (with the added benefit of additional error checking).

Conclusion

In this section we examined a number of built-in functions that allow us to input strings. Some of these methods allow us to examine each character being inputted. We also examined the different types of character classifications.

Check your understanding of this material by trying the following section review.

2.4 Section Review

1. Explain the operation of `getchar()`.
2. What is meant by the character classifications? Give examples.
3. Will Program 2.11 output any characters besides alphabetical ones?
4. Can Program 2.11 be rewritten with a different `<ctype.h>` function and still output only alphabetical characters?
5. What happens if the user enters 40000 during execution of Program 2.12?

2.5 String Handling Functions

The programming examples covered so far in this chapter have dealt with operations on character strings on a character-by-character basis. From a different standpoint, what are the operations we might need to perform on an *entire* string? A few examples might be:

- Find the length of a string.
- Combine two strings.
- Compare two strings.
- Search a string for a character (or substring).

These operations, and many more, are provided through the functions found in the `include` file `<string.h>`. A subset of the available string handling functions is shown in Table 2.2. In this section, we will examine the operation and use of all functions shown in Table 2.2. In many cases, two example programs will be used to illustrate a function. The first program will show how the string function is used, and the second program will show how the string function can be implemented.

Table 2.2   String Functions Available Through `<string.h>`

Function	Meaning
`strlen()`	String length
`strcat()`	String concatenation
`strncat()`	String concatenation of *n* characters
`strcmp()`	String comparison
`strncmp()`	String comparison of *n* characters
`strchr()`	String has character
`strrchr()`	String has character (search from end)
`strstr()`	String has substring
`strpbrk()`	String pointer break
`strtod()`	String to double conversion
`strtol()`	String to long conversion
`strtoul()`	String to unsigned long conversion

strlen()

The `strlen()` function determines the length of a string. The length of a string is an integer value indicating the number of characters in the string up to, but not including, the NULL character. For example, a string defined as

```
char alpha[] = "abcdefghijklmnopqrstuvwxyz";
```

will cause

```
strlen(alpha)
```

to return a value of 26. Program 2.14 illustrates how `strlen()` is used.

Program 2.14

```
#include <stdio.h>
#include <string.h>

main()
{
        char alpha[] = "abcdefghijklmnopqrstuvwxyz";

        printf("The string \"%s\" contains %d characters.",alpha
                ,strlen(alpha));
}
```

It is important to use the `#include <string.h>` statement to make the `strlen()` function available during compilation. Program 2.14 outputs the following message:

```
The string "abcdefghijklmnopqrstuvwxyz" contains 26 characters.
```

Keep in mind that the double quotes (″) are output because of the `\″` used in the `printf()` statement, and not by `%s` itself.

To implement the `strlen()` function it is necessary to count the number of string characters, beginning with element `[0]`, until the `'\0'` is found. If element `[0]` contains the NULL character, the string length is zero. Program 2.15 shows how a function can be written to perform the same operation as `strlen()`.

Program 2.15

```
#include <stdio.h>

int lenstr(char text[]);

main()
{
        char alpha[] = "abcdefghijklmnopqrstuvwxyz";

        printf("The string \"%s\" contains %d characters."
                ,alpha,lenstr(alpha));
}

int lenstr(char text[])
```

```
{
        int ccount = 0;

        while (text[ccount] != '\0')
                ccount++;
        return(ccount);
}
```

Notice that `lenstr()` is used as the name of the function to avoid confusion with the name of the string handling function.

strcat() and strncat()

The `strcat()` and `strncat()` functions are used to *concatenate* two strings. When two strings are concatenated, the contents of the second string are copied to the end of the first string, as shown in Figure 2.4. In this case, `strcat()` is used to combine the two strings. It is important for the first string to have a predefined length that is long enough to hold the characters of the concatenated string. As Figure 2.4 shows, the `strcat()` function requires two arguments—the names of the strings to concatenate. The first string named will be the destination for the new string.

When it is not necessary to concatenate the entire second string, the `strncat()` function should be used. This function concatenates only the first *n* characters of the second string. Because the value of *n* must be supplied, `strncat()` requires three arguments, as follows:

```
strncat(str1,str2,n)
```

Suppose that `str1` and `str2` are defined as follows:

```
char str1[20] = "Where is ";
char str2[] = "Kenneth?";
```

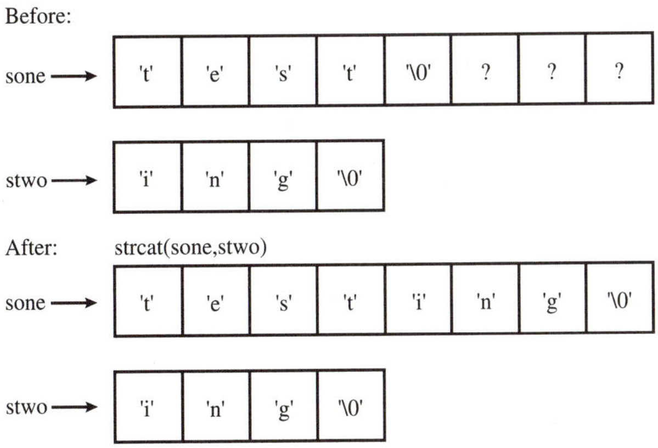

Before:

sone ⟶ | 't' | 'e' | 's' | 't' | '\0' | ? | ? | ? |

stwo ⟶ | 'i' | 'n' | 'g' | '\0' |

After: strcat(sone,stwo)

sone ⟶ | 't' | 'e' | 's' | 't' | 'i' | 'n' | 'g' | '\0' |

stwo ⟶ | 'i' | 'n' | 'g' | '\0' |

Figure 2.4 Concatenating Two Strings

What does `str1` look like after `strncat(str1,str2,3)` is executed? Because the value of *n* is 3, only the first three characters of `str2` will be concatenated, giving `"Where is Ken"` as the resulting string.

Program 2.16 shows how the `strcat()` function is used.

Program 2.16

```
#include <stdio.h>
#include <string.h>

main()
{
        char astring[80] = "C programming";
        char bstring[80] = " is fun";

        strcat(astring,bstring);
        printf("The new string is \"%s\".",astring);
}
```

Notice that the string size in Program 2.16 is defined as 80 characters, even though each string actually contains a much smaller number of characters. This advance planning helps to avoid problems later on, when multiple concatenations might possibly lead to large string lengths. Program 2.16 outputs the following message:

```
The new string is "C programming is fun".
```

Program 2.17 shows how the `strcat()` function is implemented.

Program 2.17

```
#include <stdio.h>
#include <string.h>

int catstr(char str1[], char str2[]);

main()
{
        char astring[80] = "C programming";
        char bstring[80] = " is fun";

        catstr(astring,bstring);
        printf("The new string is \"%s\".",astring);
}

int catstr(char str1[], char str2[])
{
        int aptr,length,j;

        aptr = strlen(str1);
        length = strlen(str2);
        for(j = 0; j < length; j++)
        {
```

```
                str1[aptr] = str2[j];
                aptr++;
        }
        str1[aptr] = '\0';
}
```

Once again, the name has been changed (to `catstr`) to avoid confusion. The `catstr()` function uses `strlen()` to determine the ending position of the first string. It then uses `strlen()` again to get the length of the second string and proceeds to copy characters from the second string to the end of the first string. It is necessary to place the NULL character at the end of the first string to guarantee its ending position.

strcmp() and strncmp()

The `strcmp()` and `strncmp()` functions are used to *compare* two strings. The comparison is performed on a character-by-character basis. Each function returns a value based on the result of the comparison. The integer value returned is:

- 0 if the strings are identical (same characters *and* length)
- < 0 if the first string alphabetically precedes the second
- > 0 if the second string alphabetically precedes the first

For example, consider this short list of last names:

"Doe"
"Morris"
"Morrison"
"Smith"

The four names are listed in alphabetical order. Thus, "D" comes before "M," and "M" comes before "S." Negative values will be returned by `strcmp("Doe","Morris")` and `strcmp("Morris","Smith")`. In the case of "Morris" and "Morrison," both names match for the first six characters. "Morrison" comes second because it contains more letters than "Morris." A negative value is returned by `strcmp("Morris","Morrison")` and a positive value by `strcmp("Morrison","Morris")`. When strings are listed in this fashion, they are said to be in *lexicographic order*. Thus, `strcmp()` returns a value related to the lexicographic ordering of its two arguments.

The `strncmp()` function requires a third argument, *n,* which specifies the number of characters to compare. Thus, "Morris" and "Morrison" look identical when `strncmp("Morris","Morrison",6)` is used.

Program 2.18 shows how the `strcmp()` function is used. Four strings are defined and compared in three different ways to illustrate what `strcmp()` does.

Program 2.18

```
#include <stdio.h>
#include <string.h>

void compare(char str1[], char str2[]);
```

```
main()
{
        char astring[] = "shopper";
        char bstring[] = "shopping";
        char cstring[] = "shopper";
        char dstring[] = "howdy";

        compare(astring,bstring);
        compare(astring,cstring);
        compare(astring,dstring);
}

void compare(char str1[], char str2[])
{
        int value;

        value = strcmp(str1,str2);
        if (value == 0)
                printf("\"%s\" is 'equal to' \"%s\".\n",str1,str2);
        else
        if (value < 0)
                printf("\"%s\" is 'less than' \"%s\".\n",str1,str2);
        else
                printf("\"%s\" is 'greater than' \"%s\".\n",str1,str2);
}
```

The output of Program 2.18 is as follows:

```
"shopper" is 'equal to' "shopper".
"shopper" is 'less than' "shopping".
"shopper" is 'greater than' "howdy".
```

Program 2.19 uses the function cmpstr() to emulate the operation of strcmp(). If the two strings have unequal length, the longer string length is used to drive the comparison loop. Comparisons continue as long as the two strings have identical characters in each position.

Program 2.19

```
#include <stdio.h>
#include <string.h>

int cmpstr(char str1[], char str2[]);
void compare(char str1[], char str2[]);

main()
{
        char astring[] = "shopper";
        char bstring[] = "shopping";
        char cstring[] = "shopper";
        char dstring[] = "howdy";
```

```
        compare(astring,bstring);
        compare(astring,cstring);
        compare(astring,dstring);
}

int cmpstr(char str1[], char str2[])
{
        int a,b,length;
        int j = 0;

        a = strlen(str1);
        b = strlen(str2);
        length = (a > b) ? a : b;
        while((str1[j] == str2[j]) && (j < length))
                j++;
        if ((str1[j] == '\0') && (str2[j] == '\0'))
                return(0);
        else
        if (str1[j] < str2[j])
                return(-1);
        else
                return(1);
}

void compare(char str1[], char str2[])
{
        int value;

        value = cmpstr(str1,str2);
        if (value == 0)
                printf("\"%s\" is 'equal to' \"%s\".\n",str1,str2);
        else
        if (value < 0)
                printf("\"%s\" is 'less than' \"%s\".\n",str1,str2);
        else
                printf("\"%s\" is 'greater than' \"%s\".\n",str1,str2);
}
```

strchr() and strrchr()

Both the strchr() and strrchr() functions search a string for a specified character. Two arguments are required. The first is the string to be searched. The second is the character to search for. Both functions return a pointer to the character's position within the string if found, or NULL if not found. The position of the first occurrence of the search character is returned by strchr(). The position of the last occurrence of the search character is returned by strrchr(). Program 2.20 shows how strchr() is used. The search() function uses strchr() to determine the position of the search character and then tests the position for a NULL value to see if the search was successful.

Program 2.20

```
#include <stdio.h>
#include <string.h>
#include <ctype.h>

void search(char text[], char letter);

main()
{
        char alpha[] = "abcdefghijklmnopqrstuvwxyz";

        search(alpha,'e');
        search(alpha,'E');
}

void search(char text[], char letter)
{
        int position;

        position = strchr(text,letter);
        if (position == '\0')
                printf("The letter %c is not in the string.\n",letter);
        else
                printf("The letter %c is located at address %X in memory.\n"
                        ,letter,position);
}
```

Execution of Program 2.20 results in the output

```
The letter e is located at address E0E in memory.
The letter E is not in the string.
```

This indicates that `strchr()` is *case sensitive*. Thus, lowercase characters and uppercase characters are not equal to each other. This makes sense, because lowercase and uppercase characters have unique ASCII codes assigned to them.

strstr()

The `strstr()` function searches for the first occurrence of a substring within a string. If the substring is found, `strstr()` returns a pointer to the beginning of the substring. If the substring is not found, `strstr()` returns NULL. For example, `strstr("yes indeed","in")` returns a pointer to the `"in"` substring within `"yes indeed"`, whereas `strstr("yes indeed","huh?")` returns NULL, because the substring `"huh?"` is not found anywhere.

Program 2.21 uses `strstr()` to find all occurrences of the word `"the"` in a sample of text.

Program 2.21

```
#include <stdio.h>
#include <string.h>

main()
{
        char text[] = "It is important for this block of text to "
                      "contain the word 'the' as many times as "
                      "possible, since the function strstr() will "
                      "count the number of times 'the' is seen. "
                      "This is a simple mathematical operation. "
                      "How many times does 'the' appear?";
        char *ptr;
        int thecount = 0;

        ptr = text;
        do
        {
                ptr = strstr(ptr,"the");
                if(ptr != '\0')
                {
                        thecount++;
                        ptr++;
                }
        } while(ptr != '\0');
        printf("The word 'the' appears %d times.",thecount);
}
```

Each time `strstr()` is called and a substring is found, the pointer returned is used to indicate where the next call to `strstr()` should begin searching. This process continues until the NULL value is returned.

Can you think of how `strstr()` might be useful in a word-processing spell checker?

strpbrk()

The `strpbrk()` function searches for the first occurrence of any character of a substring within a string. For example, `strpbrk("good morning","time out")` will return a pointer to the first `'o'` in `"good morning"`, because that is the first character in `"good morning"` that is also in `"time out"`. This function is useful when it is necessary to determine quickly if a string contains a specific character. For instance, if the supplied string represents a mathematical expression such as `"5*(2 - 3)"` it may be necessary to find the positions of all numbers in the formula. The statement

```
ptr = strpbrk(expr,"0123456789")
```

is a simple way to do this. Performing the same chore with `strchr()` would require multiple statements.

Program 2.22 shows how `strpbrk()` is used to remove all standard punctuation from an input string.

Program 2.22

```
#include <stdio.h>
#include <string.h>

main()
{
        char text[80];
        char *ptr;

        printf("Enter a string containing punctuation:\n");
        gets(text);
        ptr = text;
        while(ptr != '\0')
        {
                ptr = strpbrk(ptr,".,!;'\"?-");
                if(ptr != '\0')
                        *ptr = ' ';
        }
        printf("\n%s",text);
}
```

The punctuation searched for in Program 2.22 is `".,!;'\"?-"`. When it is found, it is replaced by a blank character. A sample execution is as follows:

```
Enter a string containing punctuation:
It's really sunny today! Don't you think so?

It s really sunny today  Don t you think so
```

This technique is useful when we wish to strip off meaningless or unimportant information, or data that we do not want to process at a particular time. If we were encrypting a text string, the punctuation would most likely be removed, because it might give clues about the lengths of words or sentences.

strtod(), strtol(), and strtoul()

The string functions `strtod()`, `strtol()`, and `strtoul()` provide the means for converting strings into double- and long-value numbers. This use is similar to that of the `atoi()` and `atof()` functions covered in the previous section. These functions simply allow larger numbers to be converted.

Conclusion

In this section we examined a number of built-in functions that allow us to manipulate strings after they have been entered. The string data structure is capable of storing a variety of information in many forms. It is very useful to have a good understanding of all the various methods used to manipulate a string.

Check your understanding of the material in this section by trying the following section review.

2.5 Section Review

1. What `include` statement is needed to make string functions available?
2. List the common string operations.
3. Why is it necessary for `strlen()` to encounter the NULL character?
4. What would a string *substitution* function require? For example, `strsub("abcde","bc", "howdy")` would result in the string `"ahowdyde"`.
5. What is the length requirement of the first string argument supplied to `strcat()`?
6. What does it mean that `strchr()` is *case sensitive?*
7. Which string functions are case sensitive? You may need to try examples to answer this question.

2.6   Sorting and Processing Strings

In this section we will begin with one way a collection of strings can be sorted into alphabetical order. The collection of strings is stored in memory as a *two-dimensional* array of characters. A two-dimensional array of five names with each name containing up to seven characters (the eighth position is reserved for the NULL character) is defined as follows:

```
char names[5][8];
```

This type of array is also referred to as a **rectangular array.**

Initializing the two-dimensional array is straightforward and can be accomplished in the following way:

```
char names[5][8] = { {'s', 'u', 'e'},
                     {'m', 'i', 'c', 'h', 'e', 'l', 'e'},
                     {'k', 'e', 'n', 'n', 'y'},
                     {'j', 'a', 'm', 'e', 's'},
                     {'k', 'e', 'n'} };
```

Notice that each individual string in the array is surrounded by a matching pair of braces `{}`, and that the entire array is also enclosed in braces. When a name has less than seven characters, this method of initialization automatically fills the remaining character positions with NULL characters, as shown in Figure 2.5.

As Program 2.23 shows, a single name from the list of names is referenced by using a single subscript, as in `names[j]` or `names[k]`. For example, the `strcpy()` function requires only a single subscript in this fashion to access the entire name.

Program 2.23

```
#include <stdio.h>
#include <string.h>
#define NUM 5

main()
{
        char names[5][8] = { {'s', 'u', 'e'},
```

```
                              {'m', 'i', 'c', 'h', 'e', 'l', 'e'},
                              {'k', 'e', 'n', 'n', 'y'},
                              {'j', 'a', 'm', 'e', 's'},
                              {'k', 'e', 'n'} };
       char swapname[8];
       int j,k;

       printf("The original list is:\n");
       for(j = 0; j < NUM; j++)
               printf("%s\n",names[j]);
       for(j = 0; j < NUM - 1; j++)
               for(k = j + 1; k < NUM; k++)
                       if(strcmp(names[j],names[k]) > 0)
                       {
                               strcpy(swapname,names[j]);
                               strcpy(names[j],names[k]);
                               strcpy(names[k],swapname);
                       }
       printf("\nThe sorted list is:\n");
       for(j = 0; j < NUM; j++)
               printf("%s\n",names[j]);
}
```

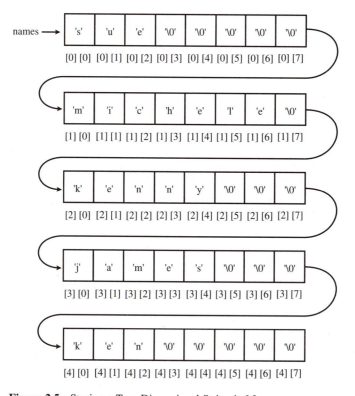

Figure 2.5 Storing a Two-Dimensional String in Memory

The technique used to sort the list of names in Program 2.23 is called *bubble sorting*. A **bubble sort** is actually a nested loop that performs $n - 1$ passes over a list of n items, swapping item X with item $X + 1$ during each pass if item X is "greater" than item $X + 1$. For example, the list of names defined in Program 2.23 begins with `"sue"`. Because `"sue"` is lexicographically greater than the other four names in the list, at the end of the first pass, `"sue"` will be the last name in the new, sorted list. Sample execution of Program 2.23 is as follows:

```
The original list is:
sue
michele
kenny
james
ken

The sorted list is:
james
ken
kenny
michele
sue
```

The bubble sort is one of the most simple sorting techniques, and one of the most inefficient. Consider a list of 100 names. A bubble sort of the list will require, unfortunately, almost 10,000 comparisons. In Chapter 3 we will examine other, more efficient, sorting techniques.

An alternative way of defining the two-dimensional array of characters for the sorting program is as follows:

```
char *names[5] = { {"sue      "},
                   {"michele"},
                   {"ken      "},
                   {"james   "},
                   {"kenny   "} };
```

This method of initialization also defines a rectangular array but requires the user to insert the correct number of blanks after each name to guarantee that each string in the array occupies the same amount of storage space. If this were not the case, the built-in string functions (`strcpy`, `strcmp`) would give unpredictable results. Program 2.24 shows how this new array is sorted. There is no change in the sorting code, only in the way the array is defined.

Program 2.24

```
#include <stdio.h>
#include <string.h>
#define NUM 5

main()
{
        char *names[5] = { {"sue      "},
                           {"michele"},
                           {"kenny   "},
```

```
                             {"james   "},
                             {"ken     "} };
            char swapname[8];
            int j,k;

            printf("The original list is:\n");
            for(j = 0; j < NUM; j++)
                    printf("%s\n",names[j]);
            for(j = 0; j < NUM - 1; j++)
                    for(k = j + 1; k < NUM; k++)
                            if(strcmp(names[j],names[k]) > 0)
                            {
                                    strcpy(swapname,names[j]);
                                    strcpy(names[j],names[k]);
                                    strcpy(names[k],swapname);
                            }
            printf("\nThe sorted list is:\n");
            for(j = 0; j < NUM; j++)
                    printf("%s\n",names[j]);
}
```

When the trailing blanks are not used, as in

```
char *names[5] = { {"sue"},
                   {"michele"},
                   {"kenny"},
                   {"james"},
                   {"ken"} };
```

the result is called a **ragged array.** This is illustrated in Figure 2.6. As you can see, the ragged array is not rectangular. It requires only 28 storage locations, whereas the rectangular array defined with names[5][8] requires 40. Thus, a ragged array is a more efficient storage method than a rectangular array, but it is also harder to work with. Consider the swap code from Program 2.24:

```
strcpy(swapname,names[j]);
strcpy(names[j],names[k]);
strcpy(names[k],swapname);
```

During the very first swap of "sue" with "michele", we get this unfortunate result:

```
names[0] = "michsue"
names[1] = "sue"
```

This results from the fact that the internal pointers for names[0], names[1], and so on, are defined when the array is initialized. Thus, the individual lengths of each string within the ragged array are fixed to specific values (4 for "sue" including the NULL character, 8 for "michele", etc.). Overwriting any of these strings may result in one string running over into another string's location, as we can see with names[0] becoming "michsue". A good programmer should remember the strengths and weaknesses of using one array definition over another.

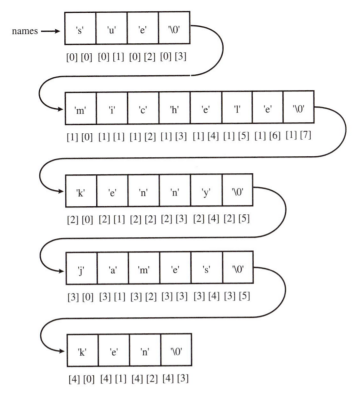

Figure 2.6   A Ragged Array of Characters

In addition to sorting, let us examine several programs to show you how to do many interesting and useful things with character strings. You are encouraged to study them to gain a full understanding of how they work.

ISBN Checker

Program 2.25 checks a user-supplied ISBN (International Standard Book Number) code to determine if it is a valid sequence.

Program 2.25

```
#include <stdio.h>

main()
{
        char input[10];
        int total = 0;
        int i,rem;

        printf("Enter the first 9 digits of an ISBN code => ");
        scanf("%s", input);
```

```
        for(i = 0; i < 9; i++)
                total += (input[i] - 0x30) * (i + 1);

        rem = total % 11;
        printf("The last character should be ");
        if(rem != 10)
                printf("%c",(rem + 0x30));
        else
                printf("X");
}
```

The format of an ISBN code is as follows:

- Group code (1 digit)
- Publisher code (4 digits)
- Book code (4 digits)
- Check character/digit (1 character/digit)

As an example, the ISBN code for a typical book is

$$0\ 6\ 7\ 5\ 2\ 0\ 9\ 9\ 3\ 5$$

The check character/digit is found in two steps. In step 1, the first nine digits of the code are multiplied, respectively, by the first nine integers, and their products are added together:

0	6	7	5	2	0	9	9	3
× 1	2	3	4	5	6	7	8	9

$$0 + 12 + 21 + 20 + 10 + 0 + 63 + 72 + 27 = 225$$

In step 2, the sum is divided by 11, and the integer remainder is saved. Division of 225 by 11 gives a remainder of 5. This is the computed check digit, which matches the check digit in the original ISBN code. If the remainder turns out to be 10, the character X is used instead. Thus,

$$0\ 6\ 7\ 5\ 2\ 0\ 7\ 7\ 2\ X$$

is also a valid ISBN code.

    Sample execution of Program 2.25 produces

```
Enter the first 9 digits of an ISBN code => 067520772
The last character should be X
```

Note that Program 2.25 converts each ASCII input digit into its associated numeric value by subtracting 0x30 (30 hexadecimal) from it. This is possible because the ASCII codes for '0' through '9' are 0x30 through 0x39.

    Try Program 2.25 with the ISBN codes from your textbooks.

Vowel Counter

Program 2.26 counts vowels (a, e, i, o, or u) found in a text string. Because uppercase and lowercase vowels are identical, they must both be counted. A five-element integer array is used to keep track of the vowel counts. To reduce the number of comparisons required, each character from the input string is converted into uppercase before the comparison is made. Lowercase ASCII characters in the range 'a' to 'z' are easily converted into uppercase by ANDing their codes with `0xdf`.

Program 2.26

```
#include <stdio.h>
#include <string.h>
#include <ctype.h>

main()
{
        char text[] = "OUR instructor SPEAKS clearly in EACH class.";
        char vstr[] = "AEIOU";
        static int vowels;
        static int vcount[5];
        int j;

        printf("The input string is => \"%s\"",text);
        for(j = 0; j < strlen(text); j++)
        {
                if (isalpha(text[j]) != 0)
                        text[j] = text[j] & 0xdf;
                if (strchr(vstr,text[j]) != '\0')
                        vowels++;
                switch(text[j])
                {
                        case 'A' : vcount[0]++; break;
                        case 'E' : vcount[1]++; break;
                        case 'I' : vcount[2]++; break;
                        case 'O' : vcount[3]++; break;
                        case 'U' : vcount[4]++; break;
                }
        }
        printf("\nThe input string contains %d vowels.\n",vowels);
        printf("There are %d A's,  %d E's,  %d I's,  %d O's, and  %d U's",
                vcount[0],vcount[1],vcount[2],vcount[3],vcount[4]);
}
```

Execution of Program 2.26 produces

```
The input string is => "OUR instructor SPEAKS clearly in EACH class."
The input string contains 13 vowels.
There are 4 A's,  3 E's,  2 I's,  2 O's, and  2 U's
```

Count the vowels for yourself to verify correct program operation.

Palindrome Checker

A *palindrome* is a string of symbols that reads the same forward and backward. Palindromes play an important role in the study of languages. Some sample palindromes are:

mom   radar   otto   11011011

Even entire expressions can be palindromes. Ignoring punctuation,

a man, a plan, a canal, panama

is also a palindrome.

Program 2.27 allows the user to enter a string of symbols. The program then deter-mines if the string is a valid palindrome by checking symbol equality beginning at each end of the string.

Program 2.27

```
#include <stdio.h>

main()
{
        char palstr[80];
        int lchar,rchar,stopped;

        printf("Enter a string => ");
        gets(palstr);
        lchar = 0;
        rchar = strlen(palstr) - 1;
        stopped = 0;
        while((lchar <= rchar) && !stopped)
        {
                if(palstr[lchar] != palstr[rchar])
                        stopped = 1;
                lchar++;
                rchar--;
        }
        if(!stopped)
                printf("\"%s\" is a palindrome.",palstr);
        else
                printf("\"%s\" is not a palindrome.",palstr);
}
```

A few sample executions are shown to illustrate the operation of Program 2.27.

```
Enter a string => radar
"radar" is a palindrome.

Enter a string => 11011011
"11011011" is a palindrome.

Enter a string => howdy
"howdy" is not a palindrome.
```

Note that Program 2.27 does *not* ignore punctuation.

A Tokenizer

The structure of a *compiler* program is shown in Figure 2.7. A compiler takes a source file (any .C text file, for example), breaks each line of the source file into individual *tokens,*

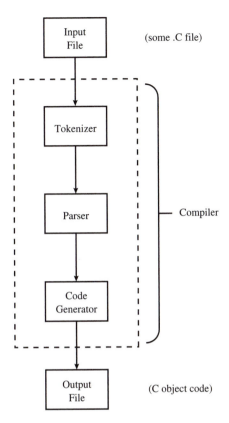

Figure 2.7   Structure of a Compiler

passes the tokens to a *parser,* which checks and enforces correct syntax, and finally builds a file of object code representative of the original source program. Because the study of compilers is an advanced topic, we will not go into any detail on their operation. Instead, we will examine the basic operation of the first part of a compiler, the *tokenizer.*

Consider this sample statement:

```
char string[] = "howdy";
```

This single statement is composed of the following tokens:

1. `char`
2. `string`
3. `[`
4. `]`
5. `=`
6. `"howdy"`
7. `;`

You can see that the purpose of a tokenizer is to break the input statement down into the smallest parts of a language (in this case, of the C language).

Program 2.28 is a limited tokenizer. It will not correctly tokenize any C statement that you enter, but only those statements that contain the defined token symbols shown in the *singles* and *doubles* arrays.

Program 2.28

```
#include <stdio.h>
#include <string.h>
#include <ctype.h>

main()
{
        char singles[] = ";{},=:()[]*?'\"\\";
        char doubles[] = "*= /= %= += -= || && == != <= >= << >> ++ --";
        char ch,input[80],ds[3];
        int pos = 0;

        printf("Enter a C statement => ");
        gets(input);
        while (pos < strlen(input))
        {
                printf("Token: ");
                do
                {
                        ch = input[pos];
                        pos++;
                } while(ch == ' ');       /* Skip blanks. */

                /* Do we have a symbol name? */
                if(isalpha(ch) != 0)
                {
                        printf("%c",ch);          /* Print first letter. */

                        /* Print remaining letters/digits. */
                        while(isalnum(input[pos]))
                        {
                                printf("%c",input[pos]);
                                pos++;
                        }
                }
                else

                /* Do we have a number? */
                if(isdigit(ch))
                {
                        printf("%c",ch);          /* Print first digit. */

                        /* Print remaining digits. */
                        while(isdigit(input[pos]))
                        {
                                printf("%c",input[pos]);
```

```
                                pos++;
                        }
                }
                else

                /* Check for a single token. */
                if(strchr(singles,ch) != '\0')
                {
                        printf("%c",ch);        /* Print token. */

                        /* String or character token? */
                        if((ch == '\"') || (ch == '\''))
                        {
                                do      /* Print remaining token text. */
                                {
                                        ch = input[pos];
                                        printf("%c",ch);
                                        pos++;
                                } while((ch != '\"') && (ch != '\''));
                        }
                        else

                        /* Check for == token. */
                        if((ch == '=') && (input[pos] == '='))
                        {
                                printf("=");
                                pos++;
                        }
                }
                else

                /* Check for double token. */
                {
                        ds[0] = ch;             /* Load double token. */
                        ds[1] = input[pos];
                        ds[2] = '\0';
                        if(strstr(doubles,ds) != '\0')
                        {
                                printf("%s",ds);        /* Print it. */
                                pos++;
                        }
                        else
                                printf("%c",ch);
                }
                printf("\n");
        }
}
```

The basic operation of Program 2.28 is as follows: If an input character is alphabetical, assume the beginning of a variable or function name. Otherwise, scan the singles and doubles arrays for a match. If no match is found, the unmatched input text is simply out-putted as an undefined token.

A sample execution is as follows:

```
Enter a C statement => a = max(values,n)*25;
Token: a
Token: =
Token: max
Token: (
Token: values
Token: ,
Token: n
Token: )
Token: *
Token: 25
Token: ;
```

As you can see, even a simple assignment statement is composed of many individual to-kens. You are encouraged to think of ways to improve the tokenizer. For example, how would hexadecimal or float numbers be tokenized?

Encoding Text

In the interest of security, many organizations now encode their computer data to keep prying eyes from gathering information. Many techniques exist for encoding (or en-crypting) text, some of which have been around for hundreds of years.

One of the simplest encoding techniques is called *transposition* encoding. In this technique, the input text is written as a two-dimensional array of characters. Then the array is transposed (rows and columns reversed) and the characters read out. Consider this sample input:

c programming is fun

Not including the blanks between words, we have 17 characters. Writing the input string down in matrix form, we have:

```
c p r o g
r a m m i
n g i s f
u n
```

Now, reading the characters out of the matrix a column at a time (ignoring blanks), we have:

crnupagnrmiomsgif

which is the transposition-encoded string. Blanks are ignored, because their positions might give away information about where words begin or end.

Program 2.29 performs transposition encoding by creating a square matrix whose di-mensions are based on the length of the input string. Unused matrix elements are filled with blanks to eliminate the possibility of stray characters appearing in the output.

Program 2.29

```c
#include <stdio.h>
#include <string.h>
#include <math.h>

main()
{
        char input[80];
        char encoder[9][9];
        int r,c,p,n,i;

        printf("Enter a text string to encode => ");
        gets(input);
        i = 0;
        for(n = 0; n < strlen(input); n++)
                if(input[n] == ' ')
                        i++;
        n = 1+sqrt(strlen(input) - i);
        for(r = 0; r < 9; r++)
                for(c = 0; c < 9; c++)
                        encoder[r][c] = ' ';
        p = 0;
        r = 0;
        c = 0;
        while(input[p] != '\0')
        {
                if(input[p] != ' ')
                {
                        encoder[r][c] = input[p];
                        r++;
                        if(r == n)
                        {
                                r = 0;
                                c++;
                        }
                }
                p++;

        }
        printf("Transposition encoding: ");
        for(r = 0; r < 9; r++)
                for(c = 0; c < 9; c++)
                        if(encoder[r][c] != ' ')
                                printf("%c",encoder[r][c]);
}
```

Running Program 2.29 with the sample string previously used gives the following results:

```
Enter a text string to encode => c programming is fun
Transposition encoding: crnupagnrmiomsgif
```

Reverse transposition encoding gives the original string back. It is up to you to figure out how this is done.

Conclusion

This section presented a variety of string applications. Test your knowledge of this material by trying the following section review.

2.6 Section Review

1. How many storage locations are required by a rectangular array defined as follows: `char array[7][10]`?
2. How many comparisons are required by the bubble sort in Program 2.23?
3. Show the entire `names` array after each complete pass of the outer `for()` loop in Program 2.23.
4. Why does the bubble sort make approximately n^2 comparisons for n items?
5. What are the strengths and weaknesses of rectangular and ragged arrays?
6. How are lowercase string characters converted to uppercase?

2.7   Application Program: Text Formatter

Discussion

String handling is such an important part of many programming applications that we now choose to devote this section to a string-based application. The application presented here takes the form of a text formatter. Text formatters are commonly available with most word-processing programs. The purpose of the text formatter is to adjust the way a block of text is displayed or printed by inserting the correct number of blanks between words on any given line in such a way that all lines exactly fit between the predefined left and right margins. For example, consider this block of input text:

```
The microcomputer is an important part of any engineering
curriculum. The machine itself can be used to teach many
hardware-based course topics, such as interfacing, memory
design, and microprocessor fundamentals. The software packages
now available offer the student a wide variety of
applications, including graphics, word processing,
spreadsheets, programming, and analog/digital design. All in
all, the microcomputer represents a valuable teaching and
productivity aid.
```

It may be necessary to reformat the text so that each line of text contains no more than 45 characters—possibly because of a printer requirement (the width of special paper loaded into the printer) or some other personal preference. When the block of text is reformatted to 45-character lines, we get:

```
The microcomputer is an important part of any
engineering  curriculum.  The  machine itself
can  be  used  to  teach  many hardware-based
```

```
course  topics,  such  as interfacing, memory
design,  and microprocessor fundamentals. The
software  packages  now  available  offer the
student  a  wide  variety  of  applications,
including       graphics,      word processing,
spreadsheets, programming, and analog/digital
design.  All  in  all,  the  microcomputer
represents   a    valuable   teaching   and
productivity aid.
```

Notice how lines (such as the third line from the bottom) that contain fewer than 45 characters are expanded with multiple blanks inserted between every two words. This block of formatted text certainly looks neater than the previous one, where each line ended at a different position.

    The application program developed here creates this type of output format.

The Problem

The problem with this type of formatting is twofold. First, how do we determine how many words will fit on a single line of text, and second, each line of displayed text may require a different number of blanks to be inserted to completely fill the margins. For example, consider the third line from the bottom. Its original form, before expansion, looked like this:

```
-->design. All in all, the microcomputer          <--
```

Why was the next word in the block of text being formatted ("represents") not included? The answer is simple. The $-->$ and $<--$ are used to signify the desired 45-character margins. The line of text contains 37 characters, which leaves $45 - 37 = 8$ blanks needed for expansion. The next word ("represents") requires ten character positions and there are only eight remaining. Thus it is necessary to expand the line as it currently looks (and place "represents" at the beginning of the *next* line). The problem then becomes this: How do we insert the blanks between words in the line of text? One solution is to advance through the line of text until a blank is found and then insert a new blank, then advance again until the end of the next word is found and insert a blank there. This process is repeated until the desired number of blanks have been inserted. The third line of text is expanded in the following way:

```
-->design.  All in all, the microcomputer          <--
-->design.  All  in all, the microcomputer         <--
-->design.  All  in  all, the microcomputer         <--
-->design.  All  in  all,  the microcomputer        <--
-->design.  All  in  all,  the  microcomputer       <--
-->design.  All  in  all,  the  microcomputer      <--
-->design.  All  in  all,  the  microcomputer <--
-->design.  All  in  all,  the  microcomputer<--
```

Although there may be other techniques for performing this expansion, this is the one used here.

Developing the Algorithm

The steps in the text formatting application are as follows:

1. Load new words into output buffer until no more words fit.
2. Expand the output buffer to fill the margins.
3. Display the output buffer.
4. Repeat steps 1 through 3 until no more words are left.
5. Do not expand the last line of text stored in the output buffer.

Each step requires examination of the input text and output text buffer. The built-in string handling functions will be used as necessary.

The Overall Process

The text formatter works in the following way: For each line of text that will be formatted, we must:

1. Start with an empty output buffer (buffer filled with NULLs).
2. Determine the length of the next word of text.
3. If there is room in the output buffer for the next word, copy it in and go back to step 2.
4. If there is not enough room for the next word, expand the output buffer, display it, and start the new output buffer with the next word.
5. Repeat steps 1 through 4 until there are no more words available.
6. If the output buffer is not empty when the end of the input text is reached, simply display the output buffer without expansion.

This process is implemented by a number of functions called from `main()`, which are:

`initbuff()`	Initialize empty output buffer.
`get()`	Get next word from input text.
`loadword()`	Load next word into output buffer.
`expand_line()`	Expand output buffer.

The code for `main()` is as follows:

```
main()
{
    spaceleft = WIDTH;
    where = 0;
    initbuff(buffer);
    do
    {
        next = get(text, where, nextword);
        if(spaceleft >= strlen(nextword))
        {
            loadword(buffer,nextword);
            where = next;
        }
        else
        {
            expand_line(buffer,EXP);
```

```
                              initbuff(buffer);
                              spaceleft = WIDTH;
                        }
                } while(0 != strlen(nextword));
                if(0 != strlen(buffer))
                        expand_line(buffer,NOEXP);
        }
```

The value of WIDTH is predefined to be the number of spaces between the margins. The where variable points to the current position in the input text, which is saved in the string text. The output buffer is called buffer and is utilized by initbuff(), get(), loadword(), and expand_line(). EXP and NOEXP stand for *expand* and *no-expand* and are used to control what expand_line() does with the output buffer.

Program 2.30 shows how the text formatter is implemented.

Program 2.30

```
#include <stdio.h>
#include <string.h>
#define EXP 1
#define NOEXP 0
#define WIDTH 45

void initbuff(char buff[]);
int get(char data[], int ptr, char word[]);
void loadword(char buff[], char word[]);
void expand_line(char buff[], int how);

        char text[] = "The microcomputer is an important part of any"
                        " engineering curriculum. The machine itself"
                        " can be used to teach many hardware-based"
                        " course topics, such as interfacing, memory"
                        " design, and microprocessor fundamentals."
                        " The software packages now available offer"
                        " the student a wide variety of applications,"
                        " including graphics, word processing,"
                        " spreadsheets, programming, and analog/digital"
                        " design. All in all, the microcomputer represents"
                        " a valuable teaching and productivity aid.";
        char buffer[80];
        char nextword[80];
        int spaceleft,where,next;

main()
{
        spaceleft = WIDTH;
        where = 0;
        initbuff(buffer);
        do
        {
                next = get(text, where, nextword);
                if(spaceleft >= strlen(nextword))
                {
```

```
                        loadword(buffer,nextword);
                        where = next;
                }
                else
                {
                        expand_line(buffer,EXP);
                        initbuff(buffer);
                        spaceleft = WIDTH;
                }
        } while(0 != strlen(nextword));
        if(0 != strlen(buffer))
                expand_line(buffer,NOEXP);
}

void initbuff(char buff[])
{
        int z;

        for(z = 0; z <= WIDTH; z++)
                buff[z] = '\0';
}

int get(char data[], int ptr, char word[])
{
        int i = 0;

        /* Skip blanks between words. */
        while((data[ptr] == ' ') && (data[ptr] != '\0'))
                ptr++;

        /* Copy characters until blank or NULL found. */
        while((data[ptr] != ' ') && (data[ptr] != '\0'))
        {
                word[i] = data[ptr];
                i++;
                ptr++;
        }
        word[i] = '\0';        /* Fix string end. */
        return ptr;
}

void loadword(char buff[], char word[])
{
        strcat(buff,word);                /* Copy new word to buffer. */
        spaceleft -= strlen(word);        /* Adjust remaining buffer space. */
        if(WIDTH > strlen(buff))          /* Is buffer full? */
        {
                strcat(buff," ");         /* Add blank after word if not. */
                spaceleft--;
        }
}

void expand_line(char buff[], int how)
{
```

```
int n,k,exp;

if(how == NOEXP)                    /* Do not expand buffer? */
        printf("%s\n",buff);
else
{
        /* Fill end of buffer with NULLs */
        n = WIDTH;
        while((buff[n] == '\0') || (buff[n] == ' '))
        {
                buff[n] = '\0';
                n -= 1;
        }

        /* Determine number of blanks to expand. */
        exp = WIDTH - strlen(buff);

        n = 0;
        while(exp > 0)     /* While there are blanks to insert... */
        {
                do                 /* Skip current word. */
                {
                        n++;
                } while((buff[n] != ' ') && (buff[n] != '\0'));

                /* Reset buffer index if end is reached. */
                if(buff[n] == '\0')
                        n = 0;
                else
                {                       /* Otherwise, insert one. */
                        do      /* New blank into buffer. */
                        {
                                n++;
                        } while(buff[n] == ' ');
                        for(k = WIDTH - 1; k > n; k--)
                                buff[k] = buff[k-1];
                        buff[n] = ' ';
                        n++;
                        exp--;  /* One less blank to insert. */
                }
        }
        printf("%s\n",buff);    /* Print expanded buffer. */
}
}
```

Conclusion

The text formatting application requires us to really understand how to use and manipulate strings. You are encouraged to think of a different way to achieve the same goal. For example, instead of loading one word at a time, you may choose to scan the input text until you know that you have reached the format width and then load the entire block of text at that point. You may also perform the expansion in a different way, by keeping track of the number of words on any given line and using the word count to mathematically compute the required number of spaces between words.

Check your understanding of this section by trying the following section review.

2.7 Section Review

1. Why is text formatting desired?
2. How is the length of the next word in the input text determined?
3. What happens if the output buffer is completely filled with text?
4. What happens when the WIDTH value is changed?
5. What happens if the WIDTH value is changed to 10?
6. Should restrictions be placed on the value of WIDTH?
7. How are blanks inserted in expand_line()?
8. Can ragged arrays be utilized to make the formatting work more easily?

Study Questions

General Concepts

Section 2.1

1. What is the index of the first character in a string?
2. State how many array elements are required in a string consisting of eight characters. Explain.
3. Explain the format of a character string.
4. How are character string variables declared?

Section 2.2

5. What are three ways of initializing the string "Data"?
6. Why dimension a string variable with a number larger than that required? For instance, why use char string[80] = "Hello"; instead of char string[] = "Hello";?
7. What are the differences between scanf() and gets() in relation to string input?

Section 2.3

8. What is actually passed between functions when one is dealing with strings?
9. Where must storage space for a string be reserved when strings are passed between functions?

Section 2.4

10. Why make the function isprint() available? What value does it have?
11. Does getchar() echo characters to the display?
12. Why write our own conversion functions when atoi() and atof() exist?

Section 2.5

13. If the NULL character is missing from the end of a character string, what does strlen() do?
14. What happens to each string used in a strcat() operation?
15. Why does it make sense that "Harris" has a smaller value than "Harrison"? How would you determine this?
16. How could strchr() be used to scan a string for math symbols +, -, *, and /?
17. What other string operations might be useful? Explain how they might be implemented.

Section 2.6

18. What is a rectangular array of characters? How is it stored in memory?
19. What are braces {} used for in a string declaration?

20. What are the different ways of defining a two-dimensional character string?
21. What is a ragged array?

Section 2.7

22. How is a very long character string defined?
23. What is the technique used to expand a line of text?
24. Why is the last `if` statement needed in the `main()` routine of Program 2.30?

Program Design

For each program you are assigned, document your design process and hand it in with your program. This process should include the design outline, process on the input, and required output as well as the program algorithm.

25. Write a program that will ask the user to enter a number in scientific notation and check the number for validity. If valid, convert the number into the appropriate floating value.
26. Write a program that will generate and display a random 10-by-10 array of letters from the alphabet.
27. Modify the program of problem 26 so that the array is scanned row by row and column by column for any of the following words:

one	two	three	four	five	six
seven	eight	nine	ten	help	see
saw	boy	girl	fast	slow	up
down	left	right	top	go	stop

28. Write your own `expand_line()` function for the text formatter (Section 2.7).
29. Write a function that scans the two-dimensional tic-tac-toe matrix TICTAC[3][3] for three 'X's in any row, column, or diagonal. Return 1 if three 'X's are found and 0 otherwise.
30. Write a program that checks a user-supplied binary string to determine if it is of the form WW, where W is any binary string. For example, 110110 is accepted, because W is 110. 10111011 is also accepted, because W must be 1011. However, 100001 is not accepted, because 100 does not match 001.
31. Improve the tokenizer developed in Program 2.28 so that more standard operators are identified.
32. Write a program that decodes a transposition-encoded string.
33. Create a program that will give the program user the color of an area of the grid system shown in Figure 2.8. The program user must enter the row and column numbers.

Column

	1	2	3	4
1	Red	Green	Blue	White
2	Violet	Amber	Brown	Black
3	Orange	Pink	Magenta	Yellow
4	Silver	Gold	Slate	Pink

Row

Figure 2.8   Grid System for Question 33

3 Numeric Arrays

Objectives

This chapter provides you the opportunity to learn:

1. What a numeric array is.
2. How to create and initialize an array.
3. Applications of arrays.
4. How to pass arrays between functions.
5. The basic concepts of sorting with arrays.
6. How to merge two sorted arrays.
7. Matrix algebra.
8. How to search an array.

Key Terms

Numeric Array
Dimension
Array Initialization
Array Passing
Array Index
Comparisons
Bucket Sort
Merge Sort
Quick Sort

Pivot
Multidimensional Arrays
Matrix
Rows
Columns
Row-Major Order
Field Width Specifier
Search Algorithm
Backtracking

Outline

Introduction

You will note some similarities between the operation of string variables (covered in Chapter 2) and the operation of numeric array variables. Both utilize multiple elements accessed with an index, and both must be dimensioned or initialized beforehand to work properly. In this chapter, we will concentrate on the use of numeric arrays in new applications and examine the methods used to access, partition, sort, merge, and search them.

3.1   Initializing Numeric Arrays

Discussion

In this section you will learn about **numeric array** data structures. You will discover how to dimension a numeric array and learn more about the relationship between array elements and pointers.

Basic Idea

To **dimension** a numeric array, you simply place a number inside its brackets. As an example, int array[3]; means that an array of three elements has been declared. These elements will consist of array[0], array[1], and array[2].

Program 3.1 shows the relationship between array and &array[0].

Program 3.1

```
#include <stdio.h>

main()
{
        int array[3];

        printf("array = %X\n",array);
        printf("&array[0] = %X\n",&array[0]);
}
```

Execution of Program 3.1 produces the same value for each of the two variables:

```
array = 7325
&array[0] = 7325
```

What this means is that the name of the array variable and the address of the first element of the array have the same value. This is the memory location of the first element of the array. This is illustrated in Figure 3.1.

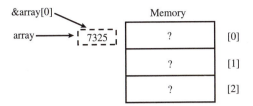

Figure 3.1   First Address of the Array

The Type int Array

Note that Program 3.1 uses an `int` as an array. Recall that on a personal computer an `int` uses *two* 8-bit memory locations (a `char` uses one). To illustrate this, the same array will be looked at again in Program 3.2. The difference this time is that the address of each array element is displayed.

Program 3.2

```
#include <stdio.h>

main()
{
        int array[3];

        printf("address array[0] => %d\n",&array[0]);
        printf("address array[1] => %d\n",&array[1]);
        printf("address array[2] => %d\n",&array[2]);
}
```

Execution of Program 3.2 yields

```
address array[0] => 7325
address array[1] => 7327
address array[2] => 7329
```

Note from the output that each address is two larger than the previous one. This is because the arrayed variable is a type `int`, which allocates two bytes per location. What is going on here is illustrated in Figure 3.2.

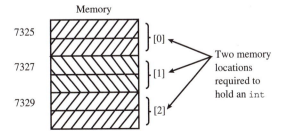

Figure 3.2   Address with Type `int` Arrays

What this means is that the compiler will automatically designate the required memory space depending on the data type you are using in the array. However, the fact remains that the elements of the array are contiguous in memory (unlike other structures we will examine later, such as linked-lists).

Inside Arrays

In Program 3.2, you saw the address of each array element. What is inside each of these elements (what is stored at these addresses)? Program 3.3 gives you an idea of what is there.

Program 3.3

```
#include <stdio.h>

main()
{
        int array[3];

        printf("contents of array[0] => %d\n",array[0]);
        printf("contents of array[1] => %d\n",array[1]);
        printf("contents of array[2] => %d\n",array[2]);
}
```

Execution of Program 3.3 produces

```
contents of array[0] => 0
contents of array[1] => -5672
contents of array[2] => 58
```

Where did these values come from? They are just what happened to be in those memory locations at the time the program was executed. What has happened is that the program has set aside memory space for the three-element array, but it hasn't put anything in these memory locations. Now consider Program 3.4, which is a slight variation of Program 3.3. This time, however, the array is being declared as a global variable.

Program 3.4

```
#include <stdio.h>

        int array[3];

main()
{
        printf("contents of array[0] => %d\n",array[0]);
        printf("contents of array[1] => %d\n",array[1]);
        printf("contents of array[2] => %d\n",array[2]);
}
```

Look at what happens when Program 3.4 is executed:

```
contents of array[0] => 0
contents of array[1] => 0
contents of array[2] => 0
```

Now all of the elements of the array have been set to zero. Setting the elements of an array to a known quantity is called **array initialization.**

The only difference between the last two programs is that in Program 3.3 the array was declared automatic (local), whereas in Program 3.4 the array was declared global (external). This illustrates an important point. Arrays declared global are initialized to zero by default, whereas local arrays are not.

When it is necessary to initialize a local numeric array to zero, an alternative technique that may be used is as follows:

```
main()
{
    static int array[3];
    .
    .
    .


}
```

Notice the use of the word `static` in the array declaration. A static integer array is automatically initialized to all zeros the first time the program is executed. However, because `static` has other features, such as control over the variables' lifetime, it is best to use the initialization technique described in the next section.

Putting in Your Own Values

You can place your own values into an array. One method of doing this is shown in Program 3.5.

Program 3.5

```
#include <stdio.h>

main()
{
        int array[3];

        array[0] = 10;
        array[1] = 20;
        array[2] = 30;

        printf("contents of array[0] => %d\n",array[0]);
        printf("contents of array[1] => %d\n",array[1]);
        printf("contents of array[2] => %d\n",array[2]);
}
```

Execution of Program 3.5 produces

```
contents of array[0] => 10
contents of array[1] => 20
contents of array[2] => 30
```

As you can see from Program 3.5, each element of the array now contains a value entered by you. You could also have used pointers to get the contents of each of your array elements. Program 3.6 shows how to do this.

Program 3.6

```
#include <stdio.h>

main()
{
        int array[3];
        int *ptr;

        array[0] = 10;
        array[1] = 20;
        array[2] = 30;

        ptr = array;

        printf("contents of array[0] => %d\n",*ptr);
        printf("contents of array[1] => %d\n",*(ptr + 1));
        printf("contents of array[2] => %d\n",*(ptr + 2));
}
```

Execution of Program 3.6 yields exactly the same results as did Program 3.5:

```
contents of array[0] => 10
contents of array[1] => 20
contents of array[2] => 30
```

This demonstrates the following equalities:

```
array[0] is equal to *ptr;
array[1] is equal to *(ptr + 1);
array[2] is equal to *(ptr + 2);
```

Note that *ptr is declared as type int. This lets the compiler know that every increment of *ptr is to be two bytes and not one (because type int uses two memory locations on a personal computer).

Conclusion

In this section we examined how to work with numeric arrays. The concepts of how an array is stored in memory, how much memory it takes, how to initialize and store your own values in it, and how to access the values using pointers were also examined. Test your understanding of this material by trying the following section review.

3.1 Section Review

1. How do you let the compiler know how many elements an array will have?
2. What is always the index of the first element in an array?
3. If the variable int value[5]; is declared in a function, what is the relationship between value[0] and &value[0]?

4. What is the difference between declaring a local array and a global array?
5. Why do `char abc[3];` and `int def[3];` reserve different amounts of memory?

3.2   Passing Arrays Between Functions

It is a common practice to pass an array to functions in a program. It is necessary to pass an array when we define it locally within a function and still want to use it in other functions. When you pass an array, the address of the array in memory is actually passed to a called function. It is not necessary to pass the whole array. Let us examine this process in more detail.

Passing Numeric Arrays

You can pass numeric arrays from one function to another. **Array passing** is shown in Program 3.7.

Program 3.7

```
#include <stdio.h>

void function1(int nums[]);

main()
{
        int array[3];

        array[0] = 10;
        array[1] = 20;
        array[2] = 30;

        function1(array);
}

void function1(int nums[])
{
        printf("contents of array[0] => %d\n",nums[0]);
        printf("contents of array[1] => %d\n",nums[1]);
        printf("contents of array[2] => %d\n",nums[2]);
}
```

Execution of Program 3.7 again produces

```
contents of array[0] => 10
contents of array[1] => 20
contents of array[2] => 30
```

Program Analysis

Program 3.7 declares a function prototype of type `void` that contains an array argument:

```
void function1(int nums[]);
```

Notice that the array is called `nums[]`. The indirection operator `*` is not used (it could have been) because `nums[]` is a pointer that will point to the first element of the array.

The function `main()` also defines an array type consisting of three elements; then it initializes each element:

```
int array[3];

array[0] = 10;
array[1] = 20;
array[2] = 30;
```

After this initialization, the function `function1()` is called:

```
function1(array);
```

Note that the actual argument does not use the `&` operator. (It could have used `&array[0]`.) However, `array` is the beginning address of the array. This is what is passed to `function1()`.

Next, `function1()` receives the value of the address of the first array element and then proceeds to display the values of the first three elements.

```
printf("contents of array[0] => %d\n",nums[0]);
printf("contents of array[1] => %d\n",nums[1]);
printf("contents of array[2] => %d\n",nums[2]);
```

What is happening is shown in Figure 3.3.

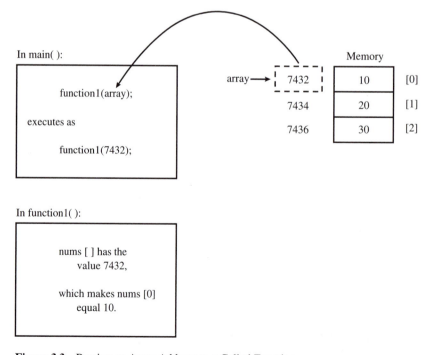

Figure 3.3 Passing an Array Address to a Called Function

Program 3.8 illustrates the passing of an array from a called function.

Program 3.8

```
#include <stdio.h>

void function1(int nums[]);

main()
{
        int array[3];

        function1(array);

        printf("contents of array[0] => %d\n",array[0]);
        printf("contents of array[1] => %d\n",array[1]);
        printf("contents of array[2] => %d\n",array[2]);
}

void function1(int nums[])
{
        nums[0] = 20;
        nums[1] = 40;
        nums[2] = 60;
}
```

Passing Numeric Arrays Back

Passing a numeric array back from a called function implies that the entire array is passed, although in actuality nothing is passed back. What really happens is that the called function uses the starting address of the array passed to it by the calling function to write new data into the memory locations reserved for the numeric array. Program 3.8 demonstrates this principle by having main() pass the starting address of the array to function1(). During function1()'s execution, the array elements are initialized (*passed back*) by the fact that function1() knows the address of the array elements and can access the actual memory location for each element.

The output of Program 3.8 is

```
contents of array[0] => 20
contents of array[1] => 40
contents of array[2] => 60
```

Again, the starting address of the array is passed to the called function by function1 (array); in main(). Because the starting address is known by function1, each element of the array can be initialized. Figure 3.4 illustrates the process.

As you can see from the preceding programs, arrayed variables can be easily passed between functions.

Conclusion

In this section we introduced how to pass an array between functions. Test your understanding of this material by trying the following section review.

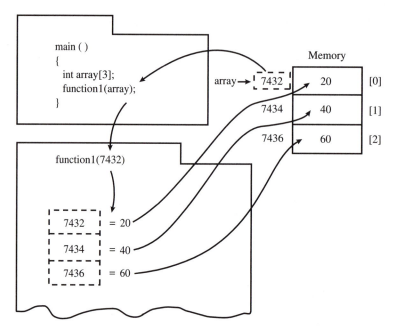

Figure 3.4   Process of Initialization in a Called Function

3.2 Section Review

1. When a numeric array is passed between functions, what is actually passed?
2. When a called function passes back an array, what is actually passed?
3. Can a function declared as `void` pass back values in an array that had been passed to it?
4. Are there any differences between an array called `numbers` and the element `&numbers[0]`?

3.3   Operations on Numeric Arrays

Discussion

This section introduces you to the fundamental concepts of applying arrays. Here you will see how to use arrays to rearrange a list of numbers. This will be developed into a program that will then be able to find the smallest value from a list of user input values. Other programs are presented to show how arrays are applied. The material presented here lays the foundation for the information in the next section of this chapter.

Working with the Array Index

The basic idea behind array applications is the ability to work with the index of the array. It is important not to think of the value of the **array index** as a fixed number. These values can be manipulated in any manner you choose. Program 3.9 illustrates this concept.

Program 3.9

```c
#include <stdio.h>

main()
{
        int number_array[7];
        int index;

        /*    Place values in the array.   */

        number_array[0] = 0;
        number_array[1] = 2;
        number_array[2] = 4;
        number_array[3] = 8;
        number_array[4] = 16;
        number_array[5] = 32;
        number_array[6] = 64;

        for(index = 1; index <= 5; index++)
        {
                printf("number_array[%d] = %d",index,number_array[index]);
                printf("number_array[%d + 1] = %d",index,number_array[index + 1]);
                printf("number_array[%d - 1] = %d\n",index,
                        number_array[index - 1]);
        }

}
```

Execution of Program 3.9 produces

```
number_array[1] = 2 number_array[1 + 1] = 4 number_array[1 - 1] = 0
number_array[2] = 4 number_array[2 + 1] = 8 number_array[2 - 1] = 2
number_array[3] = 8 number_array[3 + 1] = 16 number_array[3 - 1] = 4
number_array[4] = 16 number_array[4 + 1] = 32 number_array[4 - 1] = 8
number_array[5] = 32 number_array[5 + 1] = 64 number_array[5 - 1] = 16
```

As you can see from this output, changing the array index value causes a corresponding change in the program output value. In Program 3.9, values are assigned to each element of the array. Then the output of the array elements is displayed. However, to demonstrate the effect on the output of changing the index values, each index value is increased by 1 and then decreased by 1. This is done in order to demonstrate the resulting output. Thus, `number_array[3]` contains the same value as `number_array[2 + 1]` and `number_array[4 - 1]`.

Changing the Sequence

Program 3.10 further illustrates the manipulation of the array index. This program allows the program user to enter nine numbers. The program will then display the numbers in the order opposite to that in which they were entered.

Program 3.10

```c
#include <stdio.h>

#define maxnumber 9     /* Maximum number of array elements. */

void run_backwards(int user_array[]);

main()
{
        int number[maxnumber];
        int index;

        printf("Give me nine numbers and I'll print them backwards.\n");

        for(index = 0; index < maxnumber; index++)
        {
                printf("Number[%d] = ",index);
                scanf("%d",&number[index]);
        }

        printf("Thank you...\n");

        run_backwards(number);
}

void run_backwards(int user_array[])
{
        int index;

        printf("\n\nHere are the numbers you entered displayed\n");
        printf("in the reverse order of entry:\n");

        for(index = maxnumber - 1; index >= 0; index--)
                printf("number[%d] = %d\n",index, user_array[index]);
}
```

Assuming that the program user enters the numbers 10 through 90, by tens, execution of Program 3.10 will produce

```
Give me nine numbers and I'll print them backwards.
Number[0] = 10
Number[1] = 20
Number[2] = 30
Number[3] = 40
Number[4] = 50
Number[5] = 60
Number[6] = 70
Number[7] = 80
Number[8] = 90
Thank you...
```

```
Here are the numbers you entered displayed
in the reverse order of entry:
Number[8] = 90
Number[7] = 80
Number[6] = 70
Number[5] = 60
Number[4] = 50
Number[3] = 40
Number[2] = 30
Number[1] = 20
Number[0] = 10
```

Program Analysis

The program first defines the maximum size of the array with a `#define`:

```
#define maxnumber 9  /* Maximum number of array elements. */
```

A function prototype that uses an array in its formal argument is then declared:

```
void run_backwards(int user_array[]);
```

Next a `for()` loop gets input from the program user. Note that in this loop, the array index is being incremented, and it goes from 0 (first array element) to 1 less than `maxnumber` (last array element). This is an efficient method of getting array element values from the program user:

```
printf("Give me nine numbers and I'll print them backwards.\n");
for(index = 0; index < maxnumber; index++)
{
   printf("Number[%d] = ",index);
   scanf("%d",&number[index]);
}
```

The program then calls on the function that will now display the array in reverse order. Note that the pointer of the starting address of the array is used in the actual parameter.

```
run_backwards(number);
```

The called function uses another `for()` loop, but this time the loop starts the array index at `maxnumber - 1` (the maximum index value for the array) and ends at 0, doing a `--` on the variable `index`.

```
for(index = maxnumber - 1; index >= 0; index--)
   printf("number[%d] = %d\n",index, user_array[index]);
```

In each case, the value of the variable is printed out.

Finding a Minimum Value

Program 3.10 illustrates the changing of the order in which an array is displayed by reordering the array index. This concept will be developed further in Program 3.11, where the smallest value from a list of numbers is extracted. The program user enters the numbers, and the program searches through the list and extracts the smallest value and displays it on the screen.

Program 3.11

```
#include <stdio.h>

#define maxnumber 9  /*  Maximum number of array elements.   */

int minimum_value(int user_array[]);

main()
{
        int number[maxnumber];
        int index;

        printf("Give me nine numbers and I'll find the minimum value:\n");
        for(index = 0; index < maxnumber; index++)
        {
                printf("Number[%d] = ",index);
                scanf("%d",&number[index]);
        }
        printf("Thank you...\n");

        printf("The minimum value is %d\n",minimum_value(number));
}

int minimum_value(int user_array[])
{
        int index;
        int minimum;

        minimum = user_array[0];
        for(index = 1; index < maxnumber; index++)
                if(user_array[index] < minimum)
                        minimum = user_array[index];
        return(minimum);
}
```

Assuming the program user enters the following series of numbers, execution of Program 3.11 yields

```
Give me nine numbers and I'll find the minimum value:
Number[0] = 12
Number[1] = 21
Number[2] = 58
Number[3] = 3
Number[4] = 5
Number[5] = 8
Number[6] = 19
Number[7] = 91
```

```
Number[8] = 105
Thank you...
The minimum value is 3
```

Program Analysis

Program 3.11 is different from Program 3.10 in the called function. First, Program 3.11 does a function prototype for the new function:

```
int minimum_value(int user_array[]);
```

The function `main()` still gets nine values from the program user in the same manner as before. The difference is function `minimum_value()`. This function defines a variable called `minimum`. This will hold the minimum value of the array. First `minimum` is initialized to the value of the first element of the array:

```
minimum = user_array[0];
```

This is done so that the variable `minimum` has a value from the array with which to compare the other values. This comparison is done in a `for()` loop.

```
for(index = 1; index < maxnumber; index++)
    if(user_array[index] < minimum)
        minimum = user_array[index];
```

What happens is that the next element of the array is compared with `minimum`. If this element is less than `mininum`, then `minimum` is given this value. If this is not the case, minimum retains its previous value. It is in this manner that the smallest value of the array is selected. This value is then returned to the calling function:

```
return(minimum);
```

Swapping Elements of an Array

There are times, especially when sorting an array, that two elements of an array must be swapped. Figure 3.5 demonstrates how a swap is performed. The key to the swap operation is the use of a temporary variable to hold one of the elements being exchanged. Program 3.12 uses a function called `swap_elements()` to perform the element exchange.

Program 3.12

```
#include <stdio.h>

#define ASIZE 8

void swap_elements(int array[], int a, int b);
void display_array(int array[]);

main()
{
        int nums[ASIZE] = {1, 9, 4, 3, 7, 10, 8, 6};

        printf("This is the initial array: \n");
        display_array(nums);
```

```
        swap_elements(nums,2,5);
        printf("The final array is:\n");
        display_array(nums);
}

void swap_elements(int array[], int a, int b)
{
        int temp;

        temp = array[a];
        array[a] = array[b];
        array[b] = temp;
}

void display_array(int array[])
{
        int index;

        for (index = 0; index < ASIZE; index++)
                printf("%4d", array[index]);
        printf("\n");
}
```

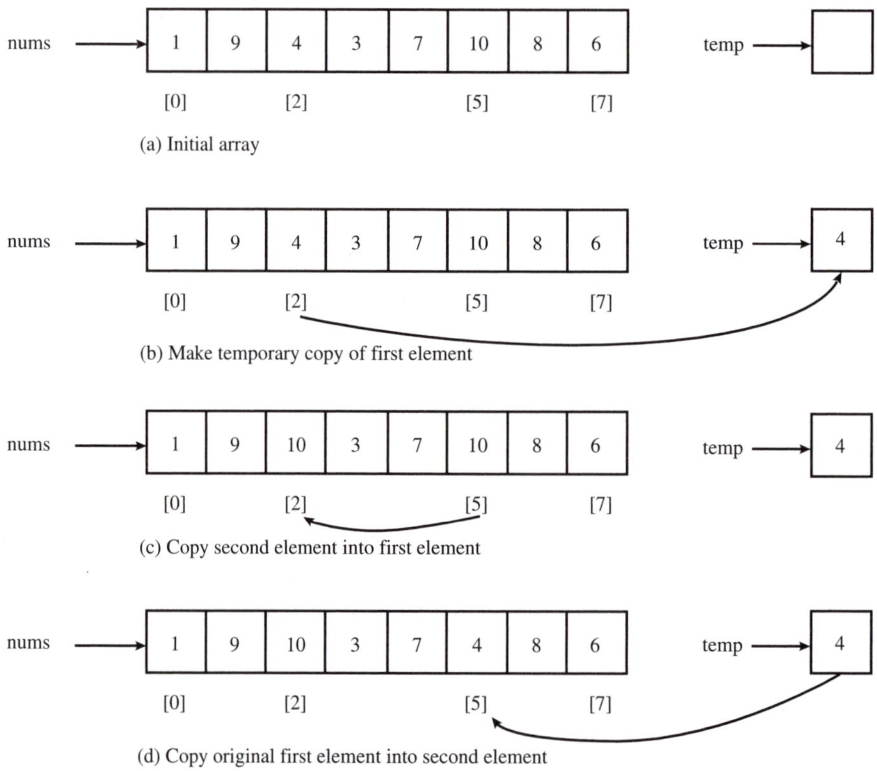

(a) Initial array

(b) Make temporary copy of first element

(c) Copy second element into first element

(d) Copy original first element into second element

Figure 3.5   Swapping Two Elements of an Array

The three-step procedure outlined in Figure 3.5 is implemented with these statements in `swap_elements()`:

```
temp = array[a];
array[a] = array[b];
array[b] = temp;
```

When Program 3.12 executes, we get the following results:

```
This is the initial array:
   1   9   4   3   7  10   8   6
The final array is:
   1   9  10   3   7   4   8   6
```

The results match the sample array used in Figure 3.5.

Searching an Array

Previously in this section we examined a technique to find the minimum value stored in an array (Program 3.11). We conclude this section with a more generalized search method that determines whether a specific element is stored in an array.

There are only two possible outcomes to our search:

1. The element is not in the array. Return –1 (an invalid index value).
2. The element is in the array. Return the index associated with the element.

How do we know when an element is *not* in the array? We must examine every location before saying the element is not present. So, the search function must, in the worst case, examine every element of the array. On the other hand, if the element is found, we do not want to continue searching, since the array might be very large.

The `search()` function shown here uses a `while()` loop rather than a `for()` loop so that it can exit when either of the two conditions arise.

```
int search(int array[], int item)
{
    int index, found;

    found = FALSE;
    index = 0;
    while ((index < ASIZE) && !found)
    {
        if (array[index] == item)
            found = TRUE;
        else
            index++;
    }
    if (found)
        return(index);
    else
        return(-1);
}
```

Note that the `while()` loop will terminate if the `index` variable reaches the size of the array, or when the search element has been found.

Look at Program 3.13 to see how search() is used.

Program 3.13

```c
#include <stdio.h>

#define FALSE 0
#define TRUE  1
#define ASIZE 8

void display_array(int array[]);
void find(int array[], int value);
int search(int array[], int item);

main()
{
        int nums[ASIZE] = {1, 9, 4, 3, 7, 10, 8, 6};

        printf("This is the initial array: \n");
        display_array(nums);
        find(nums, 7);
        find(nums, 5);
}

void display_array(int array[])
{
        int index;

        for (index = 0; index < ASIZE; index++)
                printf("%4d", array[index]);
        printf("\n");
}

void find(int array[], int value)
{
        int where;

        printf("The value %d was ", value);
        where = search(array,value);
        if (where == -1)
                printf("not ");
        printf("found in the array ");
        if (where != -1)
                printf("at index %d", where);
        printf("\n");
}

int search(int array[], int item)
{
        int index, found;

        found = FALSE;
        index = 0;
        while ((index < ASIZE) && !found)
```

```
            {
                    if (array[index] == item)
                            found = TRUE;
                    else
                            index++;
            }
            if (found)
                    return(index);
            else
                    return(-1);
}
```

The `find()` function calls `search()` and uses the `return()` value to display one of the two possible results. A sample execution is as follows:

```
This is the initial array:
   1   9   4   3   7   10   8   6
The value 7 was found in the array at index 4
The value 5 was not found in the array
```

With a little effort, you can verify that 7 is indeed stored at index 4 of the `nums` array.

Conclusion

In this section you were introduced to the concept of accessing arrayed data. Here you saw how to modify the index of an array in order to accomplish this. This section presented a method of rearranging how an array is displayed to show a minimum value from a list of values entered by the program user. We also examined techniques to swap two elements and search an array for a specific element. Test your understanding of this section by trying the following section review.

3.3 Section Review

1. State the basic idea behind array applications.
2. Explain the programming method used in order to get arrayed values from the program user.
3. State the method used to cause a series of entered values to be displayed in the opposite order from which they were entered.
4. What method is used in order to extract a minimum value from a list of entered values?
5. How can the maximum value be extracted from a list of values?
6. How are elements of an array swapped?
7. How many swaps are required to sort the array in Figure 3.5?

3.4   Sorting with Numeric Arrays

Several different sorting techniques will be examined in this section. These techniques go by the interesting names *bubble sort, bucket sort, merge sort,* and *quick sort.*

One measure of a sorting algorithm's efficiency is the number of **comparisons** it makes while sorting. Because the methods used in each technique are fundamentally different, some sorting techniques are more efficient than others (with bubble sort generally regarded as the least efficient). We will examine each technique and see how an array of integers is sorted by each one. The number of comparisons made will be computed in each case for efficiency evaluation.

Bubble Sort

The bubble sort technique gets its name from the fact that individual numbers in the array being sorted are *bubbled* to the top of the list as the sort progresses.

As an example, consider the following list of numbers:

$$6$$
$$3$$
$$6$$
$$8$$

Suppose it is your job to arrange this list in ascending order (smallest number first, largest last). Assume that you are to use the bubble sorting technique to accomplish this. Here are the rules you would use:

Bubble Sorting Rules (to sort in ascending order):

1. Test only two numbers at a time, starting with the first two numbers.
2. If the top number is smaller, leave as is. If the top number is larger, switch the two numbers.
3. Go down one number and compare that number with the number that follows it. These two will be a new pair.
4. Continue this process until no switch has been made in an entire pass through the list.

To sort in descending order, simply change rule 2 as follows:

2. If the top number is larger, leave as is. If the top number is smaller, switch the two numbers.

To sort the example list of data, start with the first rule. Test only two numbers at a time, starting with the first two numbers:

$$6$$
$$3$$

The top number is larger, so using rule 2, switch the two numbers:

$$3$$
$$6$$

The list now looks like this:

$$3$$
$$6$$
$$6$$
$$8$$

Go down one number and compare it with the number that follows (a new number pair):

$$6$$
$$6$$

These numbers are both the same. Because they are equal, it makes no difference what you do to them.

Go to the next new number pair:

6

8

Because the smaller number is already on top, leave them as is. You have completed the list, but a switch was made on this pass through the list; therefore, you must make another pass through the list:

Testing the first two numbers

3

6

no switch is necessary. Now the next two:

6

6

Again, no switch is necessary. The next two:

6

8

Still no required switch. Because there were no switches in this pass through the list, the sorting is completed and the resulting list is

3

6

6

8

Sample Program

A sample program that implements a bubble sort is shown in Program 3.14.

Program 3.14

```c
#include <stdio.h>

#define maxnumber 9      /* Maximum number of array elements.  */

int bubble_sort(int user_array[]);
void display_array(int sorted_array[]);

main()
{
        int number[maxnumber];
        int index,compares;

        printf("Give me nine numbers and I'll sort them:\n");
        for(index = 0; index < maxnumber; index++)
```

```
        {
                printf("Number[%d] = ",index);
                scanf("%d",&number[index]);
        }

        compares = bubble_sort(number);

        display_array(number);
        printf("\nThe number of comparisons is %d",compares);

}

int bubble_sort(int user_array[])
{
        int index;
        int switch_flag;
        int temp_value;
        int valtest = 0;

        do
        {

                switch_flag = 0;

                for (index = 0; index < maxnumber; index++)
                {
                        valtest++;
                        if((user_array[index] > user_array[index + 1])
                                && (index != maxnumber - 1))
                        {
                                temp_value = user_array[index];
                                user_array[index] = user_array[index + 1];
                                user_array[index + 1] = temp_value;
                                switch_flag = 1;
                        }
                }
        } while (switch_flag);
        return(valtest);
}

void display_array(int sorted_array[])
{
        int index;

        printf("\n\nThe sorted values are:\n");

        for (index = 0; index < maxnumber; index++)
                printf("Number[%d] = %d\n",index,sorted_array[index]);
}
```

Assuming that the program user enters the numbers as shown, execution of Program 3.14 produces

```
Give me nine numbers and I'll sort them:
Number[0] = 6
Number[1] = 7
Number[2] = 5
Number[3] = 8
Number[4] = 4
Number[5] = 9
Number[6] = 3
Number[7] = 0
Number[8] = 2

The sorted values are:
Number[0] = 0
Number[1] = 2
Number[2] = 3
Number[3] = 4
Number[4] = 5
Number[5] = 6
Number[6] = 7
Number[7] = 8
Number[8] = 9

The number of comparisons is 72
```

Program Analysis

After the `#define maxnumber 9`, which is used to set the maximum size of the array, the program defines two function prototypes:

```
int bubble_sort(int user_array[]);
void display_array(int sorted_array[]);
```

The formal parameters of both functions declare `int` arrays. The declaration `user_array[]` is a pointer, just as `*user_array` is a pointer. It will be used to store the address of the first element (`[0]`) of the array. The first function `bubble_sort()` will be used by `main()` to do the actual sorting. The next function `display_array()` is used to display the sorted array.

Function `main()` simply gets nine numbers from the program user:

```
int number[maxnumber];
int index,compares;

printf("Give me nine numbers and I'll sort them:\n");
for(index = 0; index < maxnumber; index++)
{
    printf("Number[%d] = ",index);
    scanf("%d",&number[index]);
}
```

The program excerpt defines an array `number` consisting of `maxnumber` elements. This means that the first element of the array will be `number[0]` and the last element `number[8]`. When the program user has entered all nine numbers, the program calls the two functions—one to sort the given numbers, and the other to display them. Note that the actual parameter passed is the address of the first element. Recall that this contains the address of the first element of the array. It is the same as using `&number[0]` as the parameter.

```
compares = bubble_sort(number);

display_array(number);
```

The function `bubble_sort()` declares three variables: `index`, `switch_flag`, and `temp_value`. The variable `index` will be used as the index for each of the array elements, `switch_flag` will let the program know when the sorting of the array is completed, and `temp_value` will temporarily store the value of one array element while it is being switched with another array element. You can think of a flag as a variable that is either up (ON) or down (OFF). Thus, for this example, `switch_flag` has just one of two values.

```
int index;
int switch_flag;
int temp_value;
```

In the body of the `bubble_sort()` function, a `do()` loop is used to repeatedly go through the array to check if a switch is needed between array elements. The loop starts by setting the `switch_flag` to 0 (thus making `switch_flag` false).

```
do
{
    switch_flag = 0;
```

Next there is a nested `for()` loop that causes a scan through each element of the array.

```
for (index = 0; index < maxnumber; index++)
```

Inside the `for()` loop, a comparison of each array element is made, and a check is made to ensure that no more than the maximum number of array elements is tested (`user_array[8]` is the largest array element).

```
if((user_array[index] > user_array[index + 1])
        && (index != maxnumber - 1))
```

If a switch is needed, the following then takes place:

```
{
    temp_value = user_array[index];
    user_array[index] = user_array[index + 1];
    user_array[index + 1] = temp_value;
    switch_flag = 1;
}
```

Notice how the variable `temp_value` is used. If a switch is made, then `switch_flag` is set to 1 (making it true). This means that the outer `do` loop will have to be repeated

```
} while (switch_flag);
```

Recall that the way of ensuring that the sorting of the loop is completed is by not having a switch on a comparison through the loop.

The display function simply uses an index counter in a `for()` loop to cause the now-sorted values to be displayed on the monitor:

```
for (index = 0; index < maxnumber; index++)
    printf("Number[%d] = %d\n",index,sorted_array[index]);
```

Notice that the number of comparisons made (72) is almost equal to the number of items squared ($9^2 = 81$). Thus, bubble sorting of 50 numbers might require almost 2,500 comparisons.

Bucket Sort

Unlike the bubble sort, which can sort any amount of numbers, a **bucket sort** requires the amount of numbers to be within a predetermined range. For example, consider the same numbers used in the execution of Program 3.14:

$$6 \quad 7 \quad 5 \quad 8 \quad 4 \quad 9 \quad 3 \quad 0 \quad 2$$

None of these numbers is larger than 9. In addition, none of the numbers is duplicated. These are both important requirements for the bucket sort. Knowing in advance that we will be sorting nonduplicated numbers less than or equal to 9 allows us to initialize a ten-element *bucket array,* as shown in Figure 3.6. As you can see, each element of the array is initialized to 0, which is used to represent an *empty bucket.*

The process of bucket sorting is now very straightforward. For each element in the input, we set the associated element in the bucket array equal to 1 (or any nonzero integer), signifying a *full* bucket. For example, Figure 3.7 shows the bucket array after the first input element (6) has been processed. Notice the 1-value in element position [6].

After all nine input elements have been processed, the bucket array contains the element values shown in Figure 3.8. The lone remaining zero indicates that we did not see the value '1' in our input list.

To display the sorted array, it is only necessary to start at the beginning of the bucket array and display each index number that contains a value of 1.

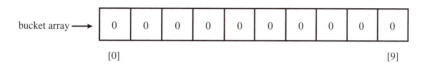

Figure 3.6 Initializing the Bucket Array

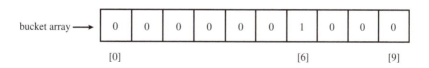

Figure 3.7 Bucket Array After Processing First Element

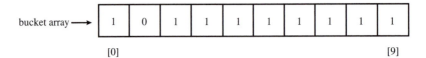

bucket array ⟶

1	0	1	1	1	1	1	1	1	1

[0]   [9]

Figure 3.8   Final Bucket Array

Program 3.15 shows how a bucket sort can be implemented. Because the input numbers are the same as those used in Program 3.14, the user is saved the trouble of having to enter them, since the program initializes the input array to these numbers.

Program 3.15

```c
#include <stdio.h>

int bucket_sort(int in[], int k, int out[]);


main()
{
        int inarray[20] = {6, 7, 5, 8, 4, 9, 3, 0, 2};
        int n = 9;
        int outarray[20];
        int i,compares;

        printf("Unsorted array => ");
        for(i = 0; i < n; i++)
                printf("%4d",inarray[i]);
        printf("\n");
        compares = bucket_sort(inarray,n,outarray);
        printf("Sorted array   => ");
        for(i = 0; i < 20; i++)
                if(outarray[i] != 0)
                        printf("%4d",i);
        printf("\nThe number of comparisons is %d",compares);
}

int bucket_sort(int in[], int k, int out[])
{
        int j;

        for(j = 0; j < 20; j++)
                out[j] = 0;
        for(j = 0; j < k; j++)
                out[in[j]] = 1;
        return(k);
}
```

The execution of Program 3.15 is as follows:

```
Unsorted array =>   6   7   5   8   4   9   3   0   2
Sorted array   =>   0   2   3   4   5   6   7   8   9
The number of comparisons is 9
```

The number of comparisons is misleading, because no comparisons are actually made. Instead, we should think of "comparisons" as "steps" in the bucket sort application. Recall from the bubble sort (Program 3.14) that 72 comparisons were required. If you think of these comparisons as 72 "steps," then the bucket sort is clearly more efficient. Do not forget, however, that the bucket sort can be used only in limited sorting situations.

Merge Sort

The **merge sort** technique has an efficiency that falls somewhere between those of the bucket and bubble sorts. Unlike the bucket sort, merge sort can work with numbers of unspecified size and unlimited duplication. The savings in the number of comparisons comes from the fact that the entire list of input numbers is divided into smaller lists, which require fewer comparisons to sort and merge back together. Figure 3.9 shows the first step in the process. The array of input numbers is identical to that of Program 3.15.

In step 1, the middle of the initial array is determined to be the element at position [4]. The array is broken into two subarrays containing elements 0 through 4 and elements 5 through 8.

In step 2, each subarray is split into two parts. Notice now that three of the subarrays contain only two elements. At this point a single comparison is performed on each of the three two-element subarrays to determine the order of each element.

In step 3, the subarray consisting of elements 0 through 2 is split again, resulting in the arrays shown in step 4. The resulting subarrays have two and one elements each. A single comparison is performed on the two-element array, and no comparison is necessary on the one-element array. So, even though we started with nine numbers, we have made only four comparisons so far to determine relative ordering.

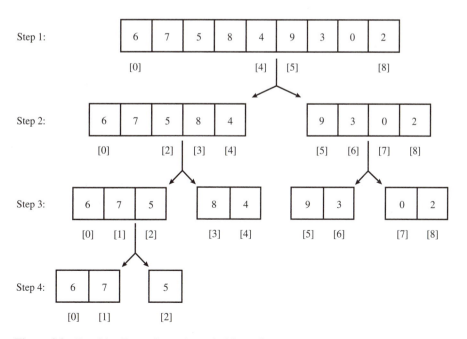

Figure 3.9 Breaking Down Input Array in Merge Sort

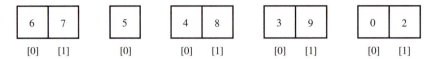

Figure 3.10   Subarrays Prior to Merging

Figure 3.10 shows all five subarrays prior to the beginning of the merge process. The numbers in the third and fourth subarrays have been switched as a result of their comparisons. So, each of the five subarrays contains elements that are in numeric order.

Merging two ordered arrays is a straightforward task. Elements in each array are compared one at a time. The smaller element is written to the result array and its associated index pointer is advanced. If the end of either array is reached, the remaining numbers in the other array are simply copied to the result array. For example, suppose the initial ordered arrays (and their index pointers) are as follows:

$$17 \quad 22 \quad 25 \quad \text{and} \quad 15 \quad 19 \quad 21$$
$$\wedge \qquad\qquad\qquad\qquad\qquad \wedge$$

Because 17 is larger than 15, 15 is written to the result and its array index is advanced, giving

$$17 \quad 22 \quad 25 \quad \text{and} \quad 15 \quad 19 \quad 21$$
$$\quad\; \wedge \qquad\qquad\qquad\qquad\qquad\qquad \wedge$$

Now, 19 is larger than 17, so 17 is written to the output and its index pointer is advanced. Now we have

$$17 \quad 22 \quad 25 \quad \text{and} \quad 15 \quad 19 \quad 21$$
$$\qquad\; \wedge \qquad\qquad\qquad\qquad\qquad\qquad \wedge$$

Comparison of 19 and 22 causes 19 to be written to the result and its index pointer to be adjusted. This gives us

$$17 \quad 22 \quad 25 \quad \text{and} \quad 15 \quad 19 \quad 21$$
$$\qquad\; \wedge \qquad\qquad\qquad\qquad\qquad\qquad\qquad \wedge$$

Comparing 22 and 21 sends 21 to the result. Because the pointer in the second array is now at the end, the remaining elements of the first array (22 and 25) are simply copied to the result.

When this merge technique is applied to our sample set of numbers, we get the result shown in Figure 3.11. The subarrays are merged back into the original arrays from which they were split, except that the elements are now in order. The final array contains all nine elements sorted into numeric order. Program 3.16 shows how the merge sort is implemented.

Program 3.16

```
#include <stdio.h>

void merge_sort(int in[], int a, int b, int out[]);
void showarray(int in[], int k);
void merge_array(int in1[], int in2[], int n1, int n2, int out[]);
```

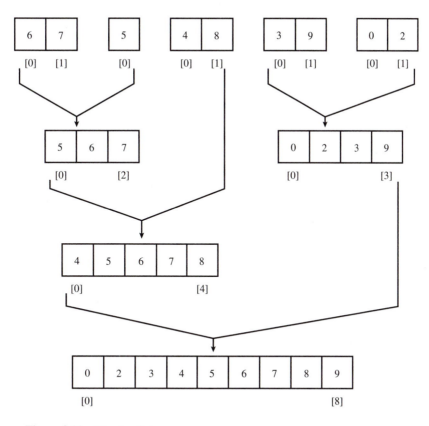

Figure 3.11   Merging Subarrays

```
        int compares = 0;

main()
{
        int inarray[20] = {6, 7, 5, 8, 4, 9, 3, 0, 2};
        int n = 9;
        int outarray[20];

        printf("Unsorted array => ");
        showarray(inarray,n);
        merge_sort(inarray,0,n-1,outarray);
        printf("Sorted array   => ");
        showarray(outarray,n);
        printf("\nThe number of comparisons is %d",compares);
}

void showarray(int in[], int k)
{
        int i;

        for(i = 0; i < k; i++)
```

```
                    printf("%4d",in[i]);
        printf("\n");
}


void merge_sort(int in[], int a, int b, int out[])
{
        int m;
        int out1[20], out2[20];

        /* Does array contain a single element? */
        if(a == b)
                out[0] = in[a];             /* Return single element. */
        else

        /* Does array contain only two elements? */
        if(1 == (b - a))
        {
                if(in[a] <= in[b])          /* Do not swap elements. */
                {
                        out[0] = in[a];
                        out[1] = in[b];
                }
                else                        /* Ok, swap the two elements. */
                {
                        out[0] = in[b];
                        out[1] = in[a];
                }
                compares++;
        }
        else
        {
                /* Must partition array of 3-or-more elements. */
                m = a + (b - a)/2;              /* Find the middle. */
                merge_sort(in,a,m,out1);       /* Sort first half. */
                merge_sort(in,m+1,b,out2);     /* Sort second half. */

                /* Now merge the sorted halves together. */
                merge_array(out1,out2,1+m-a,b-m,out);
        }
}

void merge_array(int in1[], int in2[], int n1, int n2, int out[])
{
        int i = 0,j = 0,k = 0;

        while((i < n1) && (j < n2))
        {
                /* Is first array element the smallest? */
                if(in1[i] <= in2[j])
```

```
        {
                out[k] = in1[i];        /* Write to output. */
                i++;                    /* Adjust in1 pointer. */
        }
        else                  /* Second array element is smaller. */
        {
                out[k] = in2[j];        /* Write to output. */
                j++;                    /* Adjust in2 pointer. */
        }
        k++;                /* Adjust output pointer. */
        compares++;
}


/* Are any elements left in first array? */
if(i != n1)
{
        do      /* Write remaining in1 elements to output. */
        {
                out[k] = in1[i];
                i++;
                k++;
        } while(i < n1);
}
else                /* Write remaining elements from in2 to output. */
{
        do
        {
                out[k] = in2[j];
                j++;
                k++;
        } while(j < n2);
}
}
```

The execution of Program 3.16 gives the following result:

```
Unsorted array =>   6   7   5   8   4   9   3   0   2
Sorted array   =>   0   2   3   4   5   6   7   8   9

The number of comparisons is 19
```

The number of comparisons is composed of two portions: the comparisons made when the arrays are subdivided, and the comparisons made when they are merged. The 19 comparisons made here are significantly smaller than the 72 of the bubble sort.

Where are all the subarrays stored? This is a good question. The merge sort shown in Program 3.16 relies on *recursion* to keep track of the subarrays. When merge_sort is initially called, we have

```
merge_sort(inarray, 0, 8, outarray)
```

This causes the program to create a memory image (containing code and data) to execute `merge_sort`, which computes the middle of the input array and splits it into two parts. Each part is passed to its *own* copy of `merge_sort()`, as in

```
merge_sort(in,0,4,out1)
merge_sort(in,5,8,out2)
```

There are now *three* copies of `merge_sort()` stored in memory. Copy 2 splits its input array into the two parts

```
merge_sort(in,0,2,out1)
merge_sort(in,3,4,out2)
```

and copy 3 splits its input into the two parts

```
merge_sort(in,5,6,out1)
merge_sort(in,7,8,out2)
```

There are now *seven* copies of `merge_sort()` in memory.

Finally, copy 4 splits its input into

```
merge_sort(in,0,1,out1)
merge_sort(in,2,2,out2)
```

Thus there are a total of *nine* copies of `merge_sort()` in memory simultaneously. This is the one disadvantage of `merge_sort()`. It requires a substantial amount of memory to perform its job. This indicates that there is a need to balance efficiency (the number of comparisons) against the amount of storage required. Small arrays are not a problem. But consider an array containing 10,000 elements. There could easily be over 8,000 separate copies of `merge_sort()` running (two with 5,000 numbers, four with 2,500, eight with 1,250, 16 with 625, etc.). An array this large would surely eat up all available memory before sorting could be completed.

However, for small arrays without numeric restrictions on the elements, merge sort is a good solution.

Quick Sort

The **quick sort** technique—the last of our sorting techniques—is generally regarded as the most efficient when used in its ideal form. The form used here is not ideal, as you will see, but works very well and is comparable to the efficiency of merge sort.

Figure 3.12 shows an array of numbers that will be sorted using quick sort. The idea behind quick sort is to choose an array *partitioning* element, which is called a **pivot.** The array is then divided into two parts. One part contains elements that are less than or equal to the pivot. The other part contains elements that are greater than the pivot. As Figure 3.12 shows, the first element in the initial array (3) is chosen as the pivot. The pivot is then compared with the other elements, resulting in the new arrays shown in step 2. Notice that the pivot element is in the correct position between the two sets of elements. The pivot has already been sorted into its correct position.

In step 2, new pivot values are chosen for both arrays and the arrays are partitioned again, resulting in the arrays shown in step 3. When an array contains a single element, we

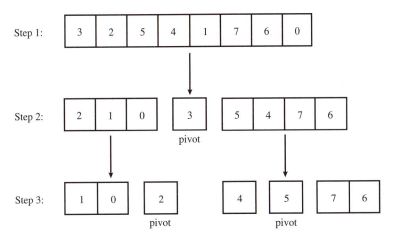

Figure 3.12   Partitioning an Array During Quick Sort

are done partitioning. When an array contains two elements, we need to perform one comparison to get the two elements into their correct order. For example, single comparisons are needed in step 3 on the 1,0 and 7,6 arrays.

At the completion of step 3 (in this example), all numbers are in their correct positions. The individual arrays need to be combined back into a single result array. This does not require any additional comparisons (as merge sort does), because the elements are already completely sorted.

Program 3.17 shows how quick sort is implemented. Once again you will see that *recursion* is used to partition subarrays at each step. The original input array is partitioned into two subarrays with each new call to quick_sort(). Thus we are required to provide storage space for the subarrays (in1 and in2) within quick_sort().

Program 3.17

```c
#include <stdio.h>

void quick_sort(int in[], int a, int b, int out[]);
void showarray(int in[], int k);
int compares = 0;

main()
{
        int inarray[20] = {6, 7, 5, 8, 4, 9, 3, 0, 2};
        int n = 9;
        int outarray[20];

        printf("Unsorted array => ");
        showarray(inarray,n);
        quick_sort(inarray,0,n-1,outarray);
        printf("Sorted array   => ");
        showarray(outarray,n);
```

```
            printf("\nThe number of comparisons is %d",compares);
}

void showarray(int in[], int k)
{
        int i;

        for(i = 0; i < k; i++)
                printf("%4d",in[i]);
        printf("\n");
}


void quick_sort(int in[], int a, int b, int out[])
{
        int pivot, i = 0, j = 0, k = 1, z = 0;
        int in1[20], in2[20];
        int out1[20], out2[20];

        if(b != -1)              /* Just one element? */
                if(a == b)
                        out[0] = in[a];
                else

                /* Only two elements? */
                if(1 == (b - a))
                {
                        if(in[a] <= in[b])              /* Do not swap. */
                        {
                                out[0] = in[a];
                                out[1] = in[b];
                        }
                        else                            /* Swap them. */
                        {
                                out[0] = in[b];
                                out[1] = in[a];
                        }
                        compares++;
                }
                else             /* Handle 3-or-more elements */
                {
                        pivot = in[0];                  /* Pick pivot. */
                        while(k <= b)
                        {
                                /* Choose an output array to write to. */
                                if(pivot > in[k])        /* Compare pivot. */
                                {
                                        /* Write smaller output array. */
                                        in1[i] = in[k];
                                        i++;
                                }
```

```
             else      /* Pivot is smaller. */
             {
                      /* Write larger output array. */
                      in2[j] = in[k];
                      j++;
             }
             k++;                  /* Adjust input pointer. */
             compares++;
     }

     /* Sort smaller partition. */
     quick_sort(in1,0,i-1,out1);

     /* Sort larger partition. */
     quick_sort(in2,0,j-1,out2);

     /* Write smaller array to output. */
     for(k = 0; k < i; k++)
     {
             out[z] = out1[k];
             z++;
     }
     out[z] = pivot;            /* Write pivot to output. */
     z++;

     /* Write larger array to output. */
     for(k = 0; k < j; k++)
     {
             out[z] = out2[k];
             z++;
     }
   }
}
```

Executing `quick_sort()` on our sample array gives the following result:

```
Unsorted array =>   6   7   5   8   4   9   3   0   2
Sorted array   =>   0   2   3   4   5   6   7   8   9
```

```
The number of comparisons is 21
```

This is only slightly less efficient than merge sort (which required only 19 comparisons). What is interesting is this: if the ordering of the original data is changed, we get a different result. Consider this second execution of quick sort with element values 5 and 3 interchanged:

```
Unsorted array =>   6   7   3   8   4   9   5   0   2
Sorted array   =>   0   2   3   4   5   6   7   8   9
```

```
The number of comparisons is 17
```

We have saved four comparisons by changing the original order of the input array. If this is done with merge sort, 19 comparisons are still needed. So, in quick sort, the order of the array elements has an effect on the efficiency. Thus, in an ideal quick sort application, the pivot element is not simply chosen as the first element in each subarray. Instead, the *median* element is chosen. For instance, given the numbers

6 7 5 8 4 9 3 0 2

the first pivot element would be 5, because there are as many element values below 5 as there are above it. Using the median element value as the pivot helps keep the size of the partitioned arrays equal, resulting in fewer levels of recursion (and fewer comparisons).

qsort()

C/C++ provides a built-in quick sort function in <stdlib.h>. The function name is qsort() and works with *any* numeric data type. The qsort() function requires four parameters: (1) a pointer to the array to be sorted, (2) the size of the array, (3) the size of elements in the array, and (4) a compare function.

The size of each element is specified because qsort() is able to sort int-, float-, and double-valued elements. The compare function is written for a specific data type and is used by qsort() to perform element comparisons. The compare function must return the following when comparing elements a and b:

- a negative integer if a < b
- 0 if a = b
- a positive integer if a > b

Program 3.18 shows how to use the built-in qsort() function.

Program 3.18

```
#include <stdio.h>
#include <stdlib.h>

void showarray(int in[],int k);
int cmp(const void *a, const void *b);
int compares = 0;

main()
{
        int inarray[20] = {6, 7, 5, 8, 4, 9, 3, 0, 2};
        int n = 9;

        printf("Unsorted array => ");
        showarray(inarray,n);
        qsort(inarray,n,sizeof(inarray[0]),cmp);
        printf("Sorted array   => ");
        showarray(inarray,n);
        printf("\nThe number of comparisons is %d",compares);
}
```

```
int cmp(const void *a, const void *b)
{
        compares++;
        return(*((int *) a) - *((int *) b));
}

void showarray(int in[], int k)
{
        int i;

        for(i = 0; i < k; i++)
                printf("%4d",in[i]);
        printf("\n");
}
```

Program 3.18 shows how the qsort() function is used to sort our sample array. The compare function, called cmp(), has a rather cryptic definition:

```
int cmp(const void *a, const void *b);
```

which indicates that pointers are passed to the cmp() function, but the data type of the pointer is unspecified. Within the actual function, we have

```
return(*((int *) a) - *((int *) b));
```

which uses a technique called *type casting* to force the pointers to access integer values. Thus,

```
*((int *) a)
```

actually represents an integer value stored at location a. So, the return() statement is actually subtracting two integers in this case.

If you need to sort floating-point numbers with qsort(), the cmp() function must be changed to

```
return(*((float *) a) - *((float *) b));
```

In addition, you will notice that the call to qsort() in Program 3.18 contains the sizeof() function:

```
qsort(inarray,n,sizeof(inarray[0]),cmp);
```

The sizeof() function returns a value to qsort() indicating what type of elements are being sorted.

Execution of Program 3.18 produces the output

```
Unsorted array =>   6   7   5   8   4   9   3   0   2
Sorted array   =>   0   2   3   4   5   6   7   8   9

The number of comparisons is 23
```

As you can see, the qsort() routine is comparable in efficiency to the quick sort and merge sort routines covered in this section.

Conclusion

This section showed several powerful techniques for sorting numbers. It is important to remember that the most efficient sorting algorithms require the fewest comparisons. Test your knowledge of the ideas presented in this section by trying the following section review.

3.4 Section Review

1. Why does merge sort require fewer comparisons than bubble sort?
2. For any list of data, what is the minimum number of times a sorting program must go through all the numbers before the sort is considered complete? Under what circumstances would this happen?
3. What determines if a list will be sorted in ascending or descending order?
4. In order to sort into ascending order the list

$$8 \quad 7 \quad 3 \quad 1$$

   how many passes through the list are required by:
   (a) bubble sort?
   (b) bucket sort?
   (c) merge sort?
5. What makes the bucket sort so efficient? Are there any limitations to a bucket sort?
6. How many levels of recursion are needed by merge sort to decompose the following list of numbers?

$$0 \quad 3 \quad 8 \quad 1 \quad 9 \quad 2 \quad 6 \quad 4 \quad 7 \quad 5$$

7. What are the differences between merge sort and quick sort?
8. Is there a difference between sorting numbers and sorting character strings?

3.5   Multidimensional Numeric Arrays

Discussion

In the last few sections, you worked with arrays that had a single dimension. This means that there was only one index. In many applications, it is common to find arrays with more than one dimension. These are called **multidimensional arrays**. This section introduces two-dimensional arrays and shows several applications with them.

Basic Idea

The only kinds of arrays you can initialize are static and external. In working with strings, you could initialize a string array as shown in Program 3.19.

Program 3.19

```c
#include <stdio.h>

main()
{
        static char array[7] = {'H', 'e', 'l', 'l', 'o'};

        printf("%s",array);
}
```

Execution of Program 3.19 will produce

```
Hello
```

The array initialization is performed using the { }. Inside these, separated by commas, are the individual characters to be used in the array. All arrays may be initialized this way. This is not the most efficient method for strings, but it is quite easy for numbers. Consider the one-dimensional array in Program 3.20.

Program 3.20

```
#include <stdio.h>

main()
{
        int array[3] = {10,20,30};
        int index;

        for(index = 0; index < 3; index++)
        {
                printf("array[%d] = %d\n",index,array[index]);
        }
}
```

Execution of Program 3.20 produces

```
array[0] = 10
array[1] = 20
array[2] = 30
```

To initialize this array, the { } are again used. Values assigned to each element of the array are again separated by commas: {10,20,30}.

Arrays of more than one dimension may be initialized as shown in the next program. This program has a two-dimensional array. You can visualize a two-dimensional array as a checkerboard pattern where each square is identified by a unique row and column number. Each square contains data. This concept is shown in Figure 3.13. Such an arrangement is usually referred to as a **matrix.**

Program 3.21 shows how a two-dimensional array can be utilized.

Program 3.21

```
#include <stdio.h>

main()
{
        int array[2][3] = {
                                {10,20,30},
                                {11,21,31}
                            };
        int row;
        int column;

        for(row = 0; row < 2; row++)
```

(Column)

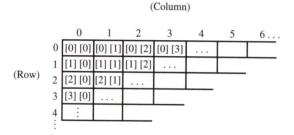

Figure 3.13   Concept of a Matrix

```
        {
                for(column = 0; column < 3; column++)
                        printf("%5d",array[row][column]);
                printf("\n\n");
        }
}
```

Execution of Program 3.21 produces

```
10    20    30

11    21    31
```

Program Analysis

First a two-dimensional array is declared and initialized by

```
static int array[2][3] = {
                            {10,20,30},
                            {11,21,31}
                         };
```

The indexes `[2][3]` indicate that the array is a two-dimensional array containing two **rows** (numbered 0 and 1) and three **columns** (numbered 0 through 2). Note that each dimension of the array uses a new set of `[]`. The way in which the compiler lays out memory is to lay out one row at a time with a given number of columns. This arrangement in memory is illustrated in Figure 3.14, and is called **row-major order.**

The method of initializing each element is done by specifying each element in the first row, then each element in the second row. This could have been done in the declaration above by

```
{{10,20,30},{11,21,31}}
```

However, it is more descriptive of an actual two-dimensional matrix to lay it out as shown.

Next, two variables are declared:

```
int row;
int column;
```

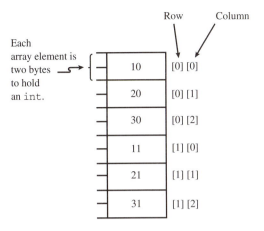

Figure 3.14 Memory Allocation with Rows and Columns for a Two-Dimensional Array

These two variables will be used to step through each element of the array so its value can be displayed. This is accomplished by the nested C `for()` loops:

```
for(row = 0; row < 2; row++)
{
    for(column = 0; column < 3; column++)
        printf("%5d",array[row][column]);
    printf("\n\n");
}
```

Remembering that the index of `row` starts with 0 and ends with 1, whereas the index of `column` starts with 0 and ends with 2, the two loops cause each element value in the array to be displayed through the variable reference

```
array[row][column]
```

To see how this is done, note in Figure 3.14 that, the first time through the loop, `row` = 0 and `column` = 0; thus, the first element to be displayed by the `printf()` function is `array[0][0]`, which has the value of 10. The next element to be displayed is `array[0][1]`, which has a value of 20. This process continues until the nested `for()` loop reaches the count of 3, and then the `printf("\n\n");` function causes two blank lines, and the outer loop increments and the process begins again, this time displaying the values of each column in the second row.

There is a **field width specifier** used with the format specifier in the `printf()` function of this program:

```
printf("%5d",array[row][column]);
```

Note the `%5d`. The 5 means to use five characters when printing the output.

Array Applications

Arrays have many applications in the solution of technical problems. Many times, the use of arrays requires manipulation of the array elements. Hence it's important to develop programming skills that allow calculations with arrays.

One of the simplest processes to perform with array arithmetic is to determine the sum of any column or any row. Program 3.22 determines the sum of the first column of the two-dimensional array of Program 3.21.

Program 3.22

```c
#include <stdio.h>

int add_column(int arrayin[][3]);

main()
{
        int array[2][3] = {
                             {10,20,30},
                             {11,21,31}
                      };

        int row;
        int column;
        int first_column_sum;

        for(row = 0; row < 2; row++)
        {
                for(column = 0; column < 3; column++)
                        printf("%5d", array[row][column]);
                printf("\n\n");
        }

        first_column_sum = add_column(array);
        printf("The sum of the first column is %d",first_column_sum);
}

int add_column(int arrayin[][3])
{
        int row;
        int column_sum;

        column_sum = 0;

        for(row = 0; row < 2; row++)
                column_sum += arrayin[row][0];

        return(column_sum);
}
```

Execution of Program 3.22 produces

```
10    20    30

11    21    31
The sum of the first column is 21
```

This seems like a lot of work just to add two numbers. However, this is just a simple example to demonstrate a powerful concept—arithmetic operations using arrays.

Program Analysis

The program starts by first declaring a function prototype:

```
int add_column(int arrayin[][3]);
```

Because an array of more than one dimension will be used, C/C++ requires that the limits of other dimensions be specified within the formal parameter list. The reason for this is the way arrays are stored. In this case, for the two-dimensional array, the compiler needs to know how many columns will be required for each of the rows. In this manner it can properly set its array pointer.

The array elements are declared as in Program 3.21:

```
int array[2][3] = {
                    {10,20,30},
                    {11,21,31}
                  };
```

And the variables for `main()` are declared:

```
int row;
int column;
int first_column_sum;
```

Note the addition of the new variable `first_column_sum`, which will be used to store the value of the sum for the first column.

Next, the array is displayed as in Program 3.21:

```
for(row = 0; row < 2; row++)
{
    for(column = 0; column < 3; column++)
        printf("%5d",array[row][column]);
    printf("\n\n");
}
```

Next, the function that will take the sum of the first column and return the value is called:

```
first_column_sum = add_column(array);
```

Note, as before, that when passing the address of the array to the called function it is only necessary to pass the identifier for the array variable. This, of course, is the starting address of the array.

This is a good time to present the details of the called function. The function is of type `int` and defines two variables:

```
int add_column(int arrayin[][3])
{
    int row;
    int column_sum;
```

The variable `column_sum` will be used to store the value of the required sum. It is first initialized to 0.

```
column_sum = 0;
```

Then it is used in a `for()` loop that uses the `+=` to generate the sum of `arrayin[0][0] + arrayin[1][0]`. This is accomplished by the following loop:

```
for(row = 0; row < 2; row++)
    column_sum += arrayin[row][0];
```

The final value is returned to the calling function:

```
return(column_sum);
```

After this, the final answer is displayed:

```
printf("The sum of the first column is %d",first_column_sum);
```

The next program illustrates a method of adding both columns of the matrix.

Adding More Columns

Consider Program 3.23. It expands on Program 3.22 and adds all columns of the given matrix.

Program 3.23

```
#include <stdio.h>

void add_columns(int arrayin[][3], int column_value[]);

main()
{
        int array[2][3] = {
                            {10,20,30},
                            {11,21,31}
                          };
        int row;
        int column;
        int column_value[3];

        for(row = 0; row < 2; row++)
        {
                for(column = 0; column < 3; column++)
                        printf("%5d",array[row][column]);
                printf("\n\n");
        }

        add_columns(array, column_value);

        for(column = 0; column < 3; column++)
```

```
        printf("The sum of column %d is %d\n",column,
                column_value[column]);
}

void add_columns(int arrayin[][3], int column_value[])
{
        int row;
        int column;

        for(column = 0; column < 3; column++)
        {
                column_value[column] = 0;
                for(row = 0; row < 2; row++)
                        column_value[column] += arrayin[row][column];
        }
}
```

When Program 3.23 is executed, the output will be

```
        10    20    30

        11    21    31
The sum of column 0 is 21
The sum of column 1 is 41
The sum of column 2 is 61
```

Note now that each column in the matrix is totaled.

Program Analysis

Program 3.23 incorporates a few additions to Program 3.22. First, the function prototype is changed to a type void, and its argument is expanded to include an array that will contain the sum of each column:

```
void add_columns(int arrayin[][3], int column_value[]);
```

The function definition is also expanded:

```
void add_columns(int arrayin[][3], int column_value[])
{
    int row;
    int column;

    for(column = 0; column < 3; column++)
    {
        column_value[column] = 0;
        for(row = 0; row < 2; row++)
                column_value[column] = arrayin[row][column];
    }
}
```

Note now that there is a `for()` loop that sums each column of the array using the `+=` operator. Also note that within the loop, the array variable `column_value[column]` is initialized to zero each time. This is to ensure that the `+=` operation starts with a zero value in this variable. The answers for the sum of each column are stored in the arrayed variable `column_value[column]`. It is this array that is returned to the calling function (`main()`):

```
add_columns(array, column_value);
```

Observe that `main()` has defined a new array variable:

```
int column_value[3];
```

This is used as the actual parameter of the called function.

What is important to realize is that two things are happening when this function is being called. First, the starting address of the arrayed variable `array` that contains the values of the array is being passed to the called function. Second, the arrayed variable `column_value` is being used to return the starting address of a second array that contains the values of the required column sums.

When `add_columns()` returns, the output values are displayed as follows:

```
for(column = 0; column < 3; column++)
   printf("The sum of column %d is %d\n",column,column_value[column]);
```

The last program in this section computes the sum of each column and each row of the matrix. Program 3.24 uses two separate functions to do this. One function calculates the column sum; the other calculates the row sum.

Program 3.24

```
#include <stdio.h>

int add_columns(int arrayin[][3], int column_value[]);
int add_rows(int arrayin[][3], int row_value[]);

main()
{
        int array[2][3] = {
                                {10,20,30},
                                {11,21,31}
                           };

        int row;
        int column;
        int column_value[3];
        int row_value[2];

        for(row = 0; row < 2; row++)
        {
                for(column = 0; column < 3; column++)
                        printf("%5d",array[row][column]);
```

```
                printf("\n\n");
        }

        add_columns(array,column_value);

        for(column = 0; column < 3; column++)
                printf("The sum of column %d is %d\n",
                        column,column_value[column]);

        add_rows(array, row_value);

        for(row = 0; row < 2; row++)
                printf("The sum of row %d is %d\n",row,row_value[row]);
}

int add_columns(int arrayin[][3], int column_value[])
{
        int row;
        int column;

        for(column = 0; column < 3; column++)
        {
                column_value[column] = 0;

                for(row = 0; row < 2; row++)
                        column_value[column] += arrayin[row][column];
        }
}

int add_rows(int arrayin[][3], int row_value[])
{
        int row;
        int column;

        for(row = 0; row < 2; row++)
        {
                row_value[row] = 0;

                for(column = 0; column < 3; column++)
                        row_value[row] += arrayin[row][column];
        }
}
```

Execution of Program 3.24 produces

```
        10    20    30

        11    21    31
The sum of column 0 is 21
The sum of column 1 is 41
```

```
The sum of column 2 is 61
The sum of row 0 is 60
The sum of row 1 is 63
```

Matrix multiplication is another useful matrix operation, because we are often required to multiply matrices together to get a desired result. The general rule for multiplying two matrices together requires that the number of columns in the first matrix equal the number of rows in the second matrix. For example, any *square* matrix (a matrix having the same number of rows and columns) may be multiplied by itself, because it has an equal number of rows and columns. Matrices with different dimensions must conform to the general rule or they cannot be multiplied. Consider the following list of matrices:

- A[2][3]*B[3][4]
- C[1][4]*D[4][2]
- E[2][3]*F[4][3]

Only the A*B and C*D matrix products are allowed, because they conform to the general rule. Product E*F is not possible, because E's three columns do not equal F's four rows.

Figure 3.15 shows why the general rule is required. Two matrices (MATA and MATB) are being multiplied. To get any new element in the result matrix (MATC), each individual row element in the first matrix (MATA) is multiplied by a corresponding column element in the second matrix (MATB). The individual products are added together to create the result element (in MATC). The general rule guarantees that there are matched pairs of numbers in each row and column.

To multiply the entire pair of matrices, each row in the first matrix is multiplied by each column in the second matrix. The result of this process is shown in Figure 3.16. Study the figure and make sure you see how each element of the result matrix (MATC) is found.

Program 3.25 implements this process and multiplies a [2][3] matrix by a [3][2] matrix, which results in a [2][2] matrix. A set of nested `for` loops is used to generate the row and column indices in computing the individual elements of the result matrix. The dimensions

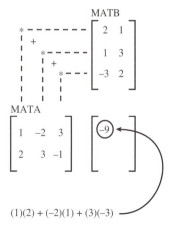

Figure 3.15   Finding One Element of a Matrix Product

MATB
$$\begin{bmatrix} 2 & 1 \\ 1 & 3 \\ -3 & 2 \end{bmatrix}$$

MATA
$$\begin{bmatrix} 1 & -2 & 3 \\ 2 & 3 & -1 \end{bmatrix}$$

MATC
$$\begin{bmatrix} -9 & 1 \\ 10 & 9 \end{bmatrix}$$

Figure 3.16   Product of Two Matrices

of the result matrix are based on the dimensions of the two matrices being multiplied. The number of rows of the first matrix and the number of columns of the second matrix are the dimensions of the result matrix.

Program 3.25

```c
#include <stdio.h>

main()
{
        int mata[2][3] = {{1, -2,  3},
                          {2,  3, -1}};
        int matb[3][2] = {{ 2, 1},
                          { 1, 3},
                          {-3, 2}};
        int matc[2][2];
        int r,c,v,psum;

        for(r = 0; r < 2; r++)
                for(c = 0; c < 2; c++)
                {
                        psum = 0;
                        for(v = 0; v < 3; v++)
                                psum += mata[r][v] * matb[v][c];
                        matc[r][c] = psum;
                }
        printf("The array product is:\n");
        for(r = 0; r < 2; r++)
        {
                for(c = 0; c < 2; c++)
                        printf("%5d",matc[r][c]);
                printf("\n");
        }
}
```

Dynamic Linking

Dynamic linking is a technique used for efficient storage and retrieval of disk files. It is used in conjunction with a special area on the disk called the *file allocation table (FAT)*. The FAT is a block of numbers describing how sectors (or allocation units) on the disk have been allocated. Each entry in the FAT is interpreted as one of the following:

- Free sector
- Allocated sector
- Bad sector
- Final sector in a file

One of the most interesting benefits of using a FAT is that files need not be stored in consecutive sectors (as many people imagine they are). For example, suppose that the entire disk does not contain a contiguous group of sectors numbering more than six. A disk operating system that does not use a FAT (together with dynamic linking) will not be able to store a file containing ten sectors of data. However, with dynamic linking, the ten sectors can reside *anywhere* on the disk.

Dynamic linking works as follows. A sector's entry in the FAT contains a number that indicates one of the following:

- this is the last sector in the file
- the next sector is sector___

Thus, to string a bunch of sectors together, we need only place the next sector number in the previous FAT entry. To illustrate this concept, consider this simple 16-sector FAT:

```
0    0   5   4    2   13   12   9
0   99   0   0   99    6    0   0
```

Each nonzero element in the FAT indicates a used sector, except for element value 99, which indicates the last sector in a file. Each zero element indicates a free sector. Sector 0 may not be assigned, because it is where we are storing the FAT.

The following directory information associated with this FAT indicates that two files are stored:

File	Starting Sector
ABC	3
DEF	7

What sectors are assigned to each file? File ABC begins at sector 3. Sector 3's entry in the FAT contains 4. This indicates that the next sector in file ABC is sector 4. Sector 4's entry is 2. This is the third sector in file ABC. Continuing with this process we get the *chain* of sector numbers for file ABC:

$$3 \ 4 \ 2 \ 5 \ 13 \ 6 \ 12 \ 99$$

A similar method gives the following sector numbers for file DEF:

$$7 \ 9 \ 99$$

which is a smaller file.

The chain of sector numbers associated with each file is the dynamic chain for that file.

Program 3.26 uses this technique to access a FAT capable of holding 64 sectors (of which only 63 are usable, because one sector is reserved for the FAT). A function called dylink() is used to search through the FAT until the 99 is found. A second function, free_sectors(), is used to determine how many sectors are available for use.

Program 3.26

```
#include <stdio.h>

void dylink(int cp);
void free_sectors(void);

        int fat[64] = {0,   0,   99, 54, 5,   6,   38, 24,
                       0,   10,  49, 15, 59, 0,   12, 0,
                       0,   99,  0,  0,  2,   0,   44, 0,
                       29,  0,   11, 0,  0,   3,   0,  0,
                       4,   17,  0,  99, 0,   0,   39, 9,
                       0,   0,   6,  0,  45, 46, 26, 0,
                       0,   33,  0,  0,  0,   0,   55, 56,
                       57,  99,  0,  0,  61, 20, 0,  0};

main()
{
        int chains[] = {7, 32, 60, 14};
        int i;

        for(i = 0; i < 4; i++)
        {
                printf("File #%d dynamic chain: ",i+1);
                dylink(chains[i]);
        }
        printf("\n");
        free_sectors();
}

void dylink(int cp)
{
        do
        {
                printf("%d\t",cp);
                if((cp != 0) && (cp != 99))
                        cp = fat[cp];
        } while ((cp != 0) && (cp != 99));
        if(cp == 0)
                printf("?\nError! Lost chain!");
        printf("\n");
}

void free_sectors()
{
        int j,free = 0;
```

```
        for(j = 1; j < 64; j++)
                if(fat[j] == 0)
                        free++;
        printf("There are %d free allocation units.",free);
}
```

Execution of Program 3.26 yields

```
File #1 dynamic chain: 7        24      29      3       54
55      56      57
File #2 dynamic chain: 32        4       5      6       38
39       9      10      49      33      17
File #3 dynamic chain: 60       61      20      2
File #4 dynamic chain: 14       12      59      ?
Error! Lost chain!
```

```
There are 30 free allocation units.
```

Notice that there is a problem with file #4. The fourth sector in the file does not exist. This is one of the problems inherent with the use of dynamic file allocation. Sometimes, owing to incorrect use of the file system, a file's dynamic chain is corrupted. In the case of file #4, sector 59's slot contains a zero, which indicates that the chain for file #4 was broken. There is another lost chain beginning at sector 44.

The FAT in Program 3.26 contains other problems as well. For instance, the slot for sector 12 contains the value 59, but no other entries in the FAT contain 12. Thus, there is no way to get to sector 12's information. This type of problem is referred to as a *lost allocation unit*. Try to find the other lost allocation units. Lost allocation units reduce the usable storage space on the disk. It is possible to identify lost allocation units and reclaim them. You should figure out a way to do this yourself.

A Histogram Generator

When large amounts of data are examined, one useful technique for evaluation of the entire block of data is the histogram. A histogram contains the frequency of occurrence for each different data value in the block of data. For example, consider this short list of numbers:

$$3 \quad 7 \quad 4 \quad 2 \quad 3 \quad 6 \quad 7 \quad 8 \quad 2 \quad 3 \quad 9$$

This list contains two 2s, three 3s, one 4, one 6, two 7s, one 8, and one 9. Thus, the histogram might look like this:

```
0: 0
1: 0
2: 2
3: 3
4: 1
5: 0
6: 1
7: 2
8: 1
9: 1
```

The purpose of Program 3.27 is to generate a histogram for a block of 100 data values. The range of the data values is from 1 to 10.

Program 3.27

```
#include <stdio.h>
#include <stdlib.h>

main()
{
        int values[100];
        static int hist[10];
        int i;

        for(i = 0; i < 100; i++)
                values[i] = 1 + rand() % 10;
        printf("The initial set of numbers is:\n");
        for(i = 0; i < 100; i++)
        {
                if(0 == i % 10)
                        printf("\n");
                printf("%4d",values[i]);
        }
        for(i = 0; i < 100; i++)
                hist[values[i] - 1]++;
        printf("\n\nThe histogram for the given set of numbers is:\n\n");
        for(i = 0; i < 10; i++)
                printf("%4d:\t%d\n",i + 1,hist[i]);
}
```

The data values are generated by the rand() function found in <stdlib.h>. The rand() function returns an integer in the range 0 to RAND_MAX (the value of which is pre-defined in <stdlib.h>). The 1 to 10 data value is determined by the following formula:

```
values[i] = 1 + rand() % 10;
```

The % operator calculates the integer *remainder* of the rand() value divided by 10. The remainder must be between 0 and 9. Thus, values[i] will be between 1 and 10.

Execution of Program 3.27 produces

```
The initial set of numbers is:
```

2	8	5	1	10	5	9	9	3	5
6	6	2	8	2	2	6	3	8	7
2	5	3	4	3	3	2	7	9	6
8	7	2	9	10	3	8	10	6	5
4	2	3	4	4	5	2	2	4	9
8	5	3	8	8	10	4	2	10	9
7	6	1	3	9	7	1	3	5	9
7	6	1	10	1	1	7	2	4	9
10	4	5	5	7	1	7	7	2	9
5	10	7	4	8	9	9	3	10	2

The histogram for the given set of numbers is:

```
 1:     7
 2:    14
 3:    11
 4:     9
 5:    11
 6:     7
 7:    11
 8:     9
 9:    12
10:     9
```

Verify for yourself that the histogram is correct.

Finding Standard Deviation

Economists and statisticians love finding the standard deviations of groups of numbers. For the student, standard deviation has always been simply a tough programming assignment. Program 3.28 uses the formula shown in Figure 3.17 to determine the standard deviation of a set of numbers. In the formula, N equals the number of data values, A equals the average of the data values, and X_i indicates data value i. So, to find the standard deviation of a group of numbers, we must first find the average A. This average is then subtracted from each data value. The difference is squared and added to a running total. This total is then divided by $N-1$ (for theoretical reasons that make the deviation more accurate). Then the square root is taken to find the standard deviation.

Program 3.28

```c
#include <stdio.h>
#include <stdlib.h>
#include <math.h>

main()
{
        int values[24];
        int i, sum = 0;
        float ave, temp, squares = 0.0, stdev;

        for(i = 0; i < 24; i++)
                values[i] = 50 + rand() % 45;
        printf("The set of test scores is:\n");
        for(i = 0; i < 24; i++)
        {
                if(0 == i % 8)
```

$$S.D. = \sqrt{\frac{1}{N-1} [\sum_{i=1}^{N} (X_i - A)^2]}$$

Figure 3.17   Standard Deviation Formula

```
                              printf("\n");
                     printf("%4d",values[i]);
          }
          for (i = 0; i < 24; i++)
                sum += values[i];
          ave = sum / 24.0;
          printf("\n\nThe average is %6.2f\n",ave);
          for(i = 0; i < 24; i++)
          {
                temp = values[i] - ave;
                squares += temp * temp;
          }
          stdev = sqrt(squares/23.0);
          printf("The standard deviation is %6.2f",stdev);
}
```

Sample execution of Program 3.28 produces

```
The set of test scores is:

   91  67  84  90  94  69  53  68
   57  79  85  70  66  92  66  91
   75  67  62  86  86  74  82  68

The average is  75.92
The standard deviation is  11.95
```

Here we see the standard deviation computed for a typical set of test scores. Note that the square-root function used to compute the standard deviation is called sqrt() and is found in <math.h>.

Magic Squares

We finish this section with an interesting matrix application. A *magic square* is a square matrix having an odd number of rows and columns, whose rows and columns (and even both diagonals) add up to the same value. For example, examine this 3-by-3 magic square:

$$6 \quad 1 \quad 8$$
$$7 \quad 5 \quad 3$$
$$2 \quad 9 \quad 4$$

The numbers in each row and column add up to 15. Even both diagonals add up to 15.

The technique used to generate a magic square is very simple. Begin with the value 1 in the middle element of the first row in the matrix. Then always move up and to the left one position when writing the next element value. The rows wrap around in such a way that the top row and bottom row are *next to* each other. The same is true for the left and right columns. If the new position is already occupied, return to the previous position and go down one row and resume.

Program 3.29 shows how this technique is implemented. Because even-sized matrices are not allowed, the program tests the input size to guarantee it is odd.

Program 3.29

```c
#include <stdio.h>

main()
{
        static int magic[9][9];
        int row,col,k,n,x,y;

        printf("Enter size of magic square => ");
        scanf("%d",&n);
        if(0 == n % 2)
        {
                printf("Sorry, you must enter an odd number.");
                exit(0);
        }
        k = 2;
        row = 0;
        col = (n - 1)/2;
        magic[row][col] = 1;
        while(k <= n*n)
        {
                x = (row - 1 < 0) ? n - 1 : row - 1;
                y = (col - 1 < 0) ? n - 1 : col - 1;
                if(magic[x][y] != 0)
                {
                        x = (row + 1 < n) ? row + 1 : 0;
                        y = col;
                }
                magic[x][y] = k;
                row = x;
                col = y;
                k++;
        }
        for(row = 0; row < n; row++)
        {
                for(col = 0; col < n; col++)
                        printf("\t%d", magic[row][col]);
                printf("\n");
        }
}
```

A few sample executions of Program 3.29 follow:

```
Enter size of magic square => 3
        6       1       8
        7       5       3
        2       9       4

Enter size of magic square => 4
Sorry, you must enter an odd number.
```

```
Enter size of magic square => 5
        15       8       1      24      17
        16      14       7       5      23
        22      20      13       6       4
         3      21      19      12      10
         9       2      25      18      11
```

Can you determine a formula that predicts the sum of any row/column for a given size *N*?

Conclusion

This section presented the concept of arrays with more than one dimension. We specifically looked at a structure called a two-dimensional array. We learned that a two-dimensional array is often called a matrix and consists of rows and columns. We also looked at several applications that use a two-dimensional array structure. Test your understanding of the material presented by trying the following section review.

3.5 Section Review

1. What is row-major order?
2. How do you tell C/C++ that you want to create a multidimensional array?
3. State a way to initialize a multidimensional array.
4. Why is it useful to use field width specifier when formatting the output of a two-dimensional array?
5. What must you do before using the += operator with an uninitialized array?

3.6   Eight-Queens Puzzle

Discussion

This application solves an interesting chess puzzle. Two-dimensional arrays are used to represent the chessboard and generate index values. Bounds checking is performed to restrict array access.

The Problem

The problem being solved is called the *Eight-Queens puzzle,* which asks "Is it possible to place eight Queens on a chessboard, so that none of the Queens occupy the same row, column, or diagonal?"

One complication of this problem is that there are so many different ways to place the eight Queens. There are, in fact, 8^8 different Queen patterns, which is just over 16.7 *million.* Only a fraction of these 16 million patterns are legal solutions to the Eight-Queens puzzle. Is it possible to find a solution without having to check all 16 million patterns?

The Search Algorithm

The **search algorithm** used to solve the Eight-Queens puzzle employs recursion to implement a search technique called **backtracking.** The recursive search function finds a legal

Queen position on a specific row on the chessboard. Backtracking refers to taking a step backwards when you make a wrong turn. When the algorithm discovers an illegal Queen position, it backtracks to a position where it can make a different choice. This may involve backing up to a previous row, and not just to a different position on the current row. The basic algorithm is as follows:

1. Pick a position for the Queen.
2. If legal, go to next row.
3. If illegal, pick the next position.
4. If no legal position is found, back up one row.

If legal positions are found for all eight rows, the problem is solved.

The statements that make up the `main()` function for the Eight-Queens puzzle look like this:

```
main()
{
    if (solve_row(0))          /* If puzzle has a solution */
        show_board();          /* display the chessboard. */
    else
        printf("No solution!\n");
}
```

The `solve_row()` function is called to start the solution at row 0. If `solve_row()` is able to recursively find a solution, it returns TRUE. This in turn allows the `if()` statement to display the results by calling `show_board()`.

If no solution is possible, `solve_row()` returns FALSE. This can happen at any level of the solution process, and is the means of implementing backtracking by returning to a previous recursive level in the solution process.

The recursive `solve_row()` function uses a `while()` loop to check all possible Queen positions in row `r`:

```
int solve_row(int r)
{

    int c;                 /* Column counter. */
    int done;              /* TRUE when a legal position is found. */

    if (r == 8)            /* Break recursive loop? */
        return(TRUE);
    c = 0;                 /* Initial Queen position within row. */
    done = FALSE;
    while((c < 8) && !done)                /* Try all 8 positions if necessary. */
    {
        if (legal(r,c))              /* Is the Queen safe? */
        {
            board[r][c] = TRUE;           /* Mark position. */
            done = solve_row(r+1);        /* Solve next row based */
                                          /* on this position. */
```

```
            if (!done)          /* Was a solution possible? */
                board[r][c] = FALSE;      /* No, try again. */
        }
        c++;                /* Next Queen position. */
    }
    return(done)          /* Return FALSE if no positions */
                          /* were legal. */
}
```

The `legal()` function pretends that a new Queen is placed at location `[r][c]`. All rows, columns, and diagonals from this position are scanned for previously placed Queens. Figure 3.18 shows the eight search directions. If any Queens are found, `legal()` returns FALSE.

The code for `legal()` is as follows:

```
int legal(int r, int c)
{
    /* This array contains the row and column deltas */
    /* used to adjust the row and column counters. */
    int dirs[8][2] = { {-1,0}, {-1,1}, {0,1}, {1,1},
                {1,0}, {1,-1}, {0,-1}, {-1,-1}};
    int i;            /* Direction counter. */
    int cr,cc;        /* Check row and column. */

    for(i = 0; i < 8; i++)           /* Check all 8 directions. */
    {
        cr = r + dirs[i][0];        /* Get first position to check. */
        cc = c + dirs[i][1];
        while(inbounds(cr) && inbounds(cc))
            if (board[cr][cc])         /* TRUE if occupied. */
                return(FALSE);        /* Move is illegal. */
            else
            {
                cr += dirs[i][0];    /* Get next position. */
                cc += dirs[i][1];
            }
    }
    return(TRUE);             /* Never saw a Queen, move is legal. */
}
```

The `cr` and `cc` variables contain the position of the next `board` element to check. `cr` and `cc` are updated by adding the corresponding delta from the `dirs` array. Positions are scanned until a Queen is found or the edge of the board is encountered.

The Complete Program

Program 3.30 shows the complete Eight-Queens puzzle solution. The `show_board()` function uses the contents of the global `board` array to display the Eight-Queens pattern if a solution exists.

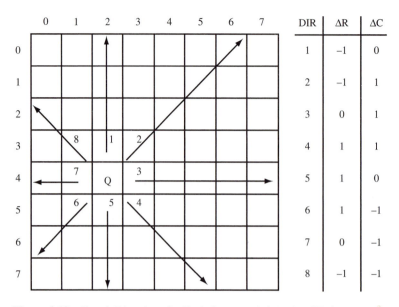

Figure 3.18 Search Directions for Each Queen and Associated Deltas

Program 3.30

```c
#include <stdio.h>

#define FALSE 0
#define TRUE  1
#define inbounds(x) ((x >= 0) && (x < 8))

/*********************************************************************/
/*                   Eight - Queens Puzzle                          */
/*********************************************************************/
/*                   Developed by A. King                           */
/*                                                                  */
/*********************************************************************/
/*      This program uses recursion to find the positions where    */
/*      eight Queens may be placed on a chessboard so that:         */
/*          * No two Queens are on the same row.                    */
/*          * No two Queens are in the same column.                 */
/*          * No two Queens are on the same diagonal.               */
/*********************************************************************/
/*                   Function Prototypes                            */
/*------------------------------------------------------------------*/

/* This function displays an 8 by 8 chess board with Queens on it.  */
/*------------------------------------------------------------------*/

void show_board(void);

/* This function recursively solves the puzzle beginning at row r.  */
```

```c
/* Returns TRUE if a solution exists beginning at row r.            */
/*----------------------------------------------------------------*/

int solve_row(int r);

/* This function returns TRUE if a Queen can be placed at position  */
/* (r,c) on the board.                                              */
/*----------------------------------------------------------------*/

int legal(int r, int c);

/******************************************************************/
/*                    Global Variables                            */
/*----------------------------------------------------------------*/

        int board[8][8];              /* 8 by 8 chessboard. */

/*----------------------------------------------------------------*/

main()
{
        if (solve_row(0))             /* If puzzle has a solution */
                show_board();         /* display the chessboard. */
        else
                printf("No solution!\n");
}

/*----------------------------------------------------------------*/

void show_board()
{
        int r,c;

        printf("The position of each Queen is:\n  ");
        for(c = 0; c < 8; c++)
                printf(" %1d",c);
        printf("\n");
        for(r = 0; r < 8; r++)
        {
                printf("%1d ",r);
                for(c = 0; c < 8; c++)
                        if (board[r][c])
                                printf(" Q");
                        else
                                printf("  ");
                printf("\n");
        }
}

/*----------------------------------------------------------------*/

int solve_row(int r)
```

```
{
        int c;                    /* Column counter. */
        int done;                 /* TRUE when a legal position is found. */

        if (r == 8)               /* Break recursive loop? */
                return(TRUE);
        c = 0;                    /* Initial Queen position within row. */
        done = FALSE;
        while((c < 8) && !done)          /* Try all 8 positions if necessary. */
        {
                if (legal(r,c))                /* Is the Queen safe? */
                {
                        board[r][c] = TRUE;    /* Mark position. */
                        done = solve_row(r+1);  /* Solve next row based */
                                                /* on this position. */
                        if (!done)              /* Was a solution possible? */
                                board[r][c] = FALSE;    /* No, try again. */
                }
                c++;                            /* Next Queen position. */
        }
        return(done);                          /* Return FALSE if no positions */
                                               /* were legal. */
}

/*----------------------------------------------------------------*/

int legal(int r, int c)
{
        /* This array contains the row and column deltas */
        /* used to adjust the row and column counters. */
        int dirs[8][2] = { {-1,0}, {-1,1}, {0,1}, {1,1},
                           {1,0}, {1,-1}, {0,-1}, {-1,-1}};
        int i;          /* Direction counter. */
        int cr,cc;      /* Check row and column. */

        for(i = 0; i < 8; i++)            /* Check all 8 directions. */
        {
                cr = r + dirs[i][0];    /* Get first position to check. */
                cc = c + dirs[i][1];
                while(inbounds(cr) && inbounds(cc))
                        if (board[cr][cc])              /* TRUE if occupied. */
                                return(FALSE);          /* Move is illegal. */
                        else
                        {
                                cr += dirs[i][0];       /* Get next position. */
                                cc += dirs[i][1];
                        }
        }
        return(TRUE);              /* Never saw a Queen, move is legal. */
}
```

```
     0   1   2   3   4   5   6   7
   +---+---+---+---+---+---+---+---+
 0 | Q |   |   |   |   |   |   |   |
   +---+---+---+---+---+---+---+---+
 1 |   |   |   |   | Q |   |   |   |
   +---+---+---+---+---+---+---+---+
 2 |   |   |   |   |   |   |   | Q |
   +---+---+---+---+---+---+---+---+
 3 |   |   |   |   |   | Q |   |   |
   +---+---+---+---+---+---+---+---+
 4 |   |   | Q |   |   |   |   |   |
   +---+---+---+---+---+---+---+---+
 5 |   |   |   |   |   |   | Q |   |
   +---+---+---+---+---+---+---+---+
 6 |   | Q |   |   |   |   |   |   |
   +---+---+---+---+---+---+---+---+
 7 |   |   |   | Q |   |   |   |   |
   +---+---+---+---+---+---+---+---+
```

Figure 3.19   Eight-Queens Solution

The execution of Program 3.30 results in the following output:

```
The position of each Queen is:
   0 1 2 3 4 5 6 7
0  Q
1          Q
2              Q
3            Q
4      Q
5            Q
6      Q
7          Q
```

Note that no two Queens occupy the same row, column, or diagonal.

Figure 3.19 represents the same solution in an 8-by-8 grid that allows the diagonals to be examined more easily.

It would be very interesting to count the number of times the legal() function is called. This number will surely be significantly smaller than the 16 million different Queen patterns required when not using backtracking.

Conclusion

In this section we examined how arrays can be combined with recursion to provide a very powerful solution-space search technique called backtracking. Test your understanding of this material with the following section review.

3.6 Section Review

1. How are all 64 board locations initialized to empty (FALSE)?
2. How is recursion stopped in solve_row()?

3. What is backtracking?
4. What does `inbounds()` do?
5. What board positions are examined when `legal(3,5)` is called?

Study Questions

General Concepts

Section 3.1

1. What is meant by the term *numeric array?*
2. State how you would declare a numeric array of ten elements.
3. What is the index of the first element of the array in Question 2? What is the index of the last element?
4. What is the difference between a local array and a global array?
5. What is accomplished when a static array is declared?

Section 3.2

6. When we pass an array to a function, how many elements of the array are passed?
7. Describe the process used to pass an array between functions.
8. Is it necessary to pass a global array?
9. When a local array is passed to a function, is it necessary to use the address operator? Why or why not?

Section 3.3

10. Explain the basic idea behind applications of arrays.
11. Explain how a program could be developed to find the largest element in an array.
12. What is an easy method of getting user input values into an array?
13. How can the values of an array index be manipulated?
14. When might we wish to swap elements in an array?

Section 3.4

15. Explain the basic differences among bubble sort, bucket sort, merge sort, and quick sort.
16. How does element order affect sorting efficiency?
17. Explain how to merge two ordered arrays.
18. How does recursion assist the sorting process?
19. Why is the choice of a pivot so important in quick sort?

Section 3.5

20. What is meant by row-major order in regard to the storage of matrix elements?
21. How is a matrix passed between functions?
22. How many math operations (+ and *) are required to multiply a 3-by-4 matrix by a 4-by-2 matrix?
23. What is the technique behind dynamic linking?
24. How is the `hist` array indexed in Program 3.27?
25. Why is an array needed to store the numbers in Program 3.28?

Section 3.6

26. How can a counter variable be added to `legal()` to keep track of how many times `legal()` is called?
27. Describe the actions of `solve_row(7)` when Program 3.30 executes.

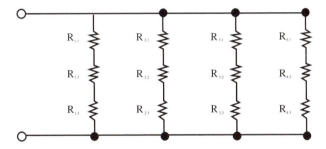

Figure 3.20   Circuit for Questions 28, 29, and 30

Program Design

Each of the following programs will require the use of a one- or two-dimensional array. In order to test each program, you will have to make up your own set of test data and properly initialize any arrays that require data from the user.

28. The circuit in Figure 3.20 is a series parallel circuit. Develop a program that will compute the total resistance of any branch selected by the program user. The total resistance of any one branch is:

$$R_T = R_1 + R_2 + R_3$$

Where

$$R_T = \text{Total branch resistance in ohms.}$$
$$R_1, R_2, R_3 = \text{Value of each resistor in ohms.}$$

29. Modify the program you developed in Question 28 so that the total resistance of any combination of branches may be found by the program user. The total resistance of any parallel branch is found by first determining the total resistance of that branch, and then using the parallel resistance formula for finding the total resistance. The parallel resistance formula is

$$R_T = 1/(1/R_{T1} + 1/R_{T2} \ldots + 1/R_{TN})$$

Where

$$R_T = \text{Total resistance in ohms.}$$
$$R_{T1}, R_{T2}, \ldots R_{TN} = \text{Total branch resistance in ohms.}$$

30. Expand the modified program from Question 29 so that the program user can enter the value of each resistor and the resistors will be displayed in numerical order.

31. Develop a C program that computes the power dissipation of each resistor in a series circuit. The program user may select how many resistors there will be in the circuit. The program will sort the resistors by their power dissipation and display their values and subscript numbers (the subscript numbers represent the order in which they appear in the circuit). The program user enters the value of the voltage source in volts. Power dissipation in a resistor may be determined by

$$P = I^2 R$$

Where

$$P = \text{Power dissipation in watts.}$$
$$I = \text{Current in the resistor in amps.}$$
$$R = \text{Value of resistor in ohms.}$$

The current in each resistor in a series circuit is the same. It may be determined from

$$I = V_S/R_T$$

Where

I = Circuit current in amps.
V_S = Source voltage in volts.
R_T = Total circuit resistance in ohms.

32. Write a program that will normalize the 20 floating point numbers saved in the array STATS. To normalize an array of numbers, first find the largest number in the array, then divide each number in the array by the largest number. Each resulting value will then be between 0 and 1.

33. Figure 3.21 shows the schematic of a low-pass filter. The corner frequency of the filter is found by the formula $F_c = 1/(2\pi RC)$. The operation of the low-pass filter is as follows: Input signals whose frequencies are lower than F_c pass through the filter with a small loss in amplitude. Signals whose frequencies are larger than F_c pass through with a large loss in amplitude. The output voltage of the low-pass filter is found by the formula:

$$V_o = V_i / (\text{sqrt}(1 + (F/F_c)^2))$$

where F is the applied frequency. Write a program that will display the frequency and output voltage for a low-pass filter at the following frequencies:

$0.1*F_c$ $0.25*F_c$ $0.5*F_c$ $0.75*F_c$ $0.9*F_c$
F_c $2*F_c$ $5*F_c$ $7.5*F_c$ $10*F_c$

Let V_i = 100 volts, R = 1000 ohms, and C = 0.1 microfarads. Save each frequency/voltage pair in an array and scan the array for the frequency at which V_o is closest to 70.7 volts. Display the resulting frequency value also.

34. Write a program that will match each resistor from list A with each resistor from list B (totaling 20 pairs), and compute the total resistance, the current supplied by a 50-volt battery to the total resistance, and the voltage across each resistor. For example, the first pair of resistors is 100 ohms, 270 ohms. The resulting display should be:

R1	R2	Rt	I	V1	V2
100	270	370	0.135	13.5	36.5

The lists of resistor values are as follows:

List A	List B
100	270
150	330
220	470
270	560
330	

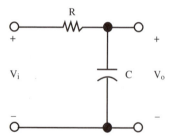

Figure 3.21   Circuit for Question 33

35. Develop a program that will display the amount of money in any safety deposit box that is contained in a wall that has ten rows and eight columns of these boxes.

36. Write a program that will generate and display a random 10-by-10 array of numbers between 50 and 200.

37. A five-card poker hand is represented by the two-dimensional integer array CARDS[2][5]. The first row in CARDS contains the card numbers, which are:

2 through 10	: 2 through 10
Jack	: 11
Queen	: 12
King	: 13
Ace	: 14

The second row contains the suit number for each card. The suit numbers are defined as:

Clubs	: 1
Diamonds	: 2
Hearts	: 3
Spades	: 4

Write a C function that will analyze the poker hand and determine if any of the following are present:

> Royal flush (10, J, Q, K, A of same suit)
> Straight flush (any consecutive group of five cards in same suit)
> Four of a kind
> Full house (three of a kind and two of a kind)
> Flush (all five cards in same suit)
> Straight (any consecutive group of five cards from any suit)
> Three of a kind
> Two pair
> One pair

Assign any values you wish to the poker hands shown.

38. The Knight on a chess board may move from its current position to any of the positions shown in Figure 3.22. Assuming row and column numbers are from 1 to 8, write a function that determines if a Knight is being legally moved from OldRow, OldColumn to NewRow, NewColumn. Return 1 if the move is valid and 0 otherwise.

39. Write a program that computes all factors of a user-supplied integer. Store the factors in an array called FACTORS.

40. Modify the program in Question 39 to determine if the input number is a *perfect* number. A perfect number is a number whose factors add up to itself. For example, 6 is a perfect number, because its factors (1, 2, and 3) add up to 6. The number itself is not considered a factor in this case.

41. Another technique used to sort numbers is called *insertion* sort. In this technique, each new number is inserted into the correct position of an in-order array. For example, given the array

$$5 \quad 6 \quad 9 \quad 12 \quad 24 \quad 39 \quad 52$$

the new value 18 will be inserted between the 12 and the 24 by moving elements 24, 39, and 52 up one position in the array. Write a program that performs an insertion sort. Use the example array as the initial array. Allow the user to enter three numbers, one at a time. Show the resulting array after each insertion.

42. Write a function that determines the minimum value and maximum value of an array of K integers using only one pass through the numbers.

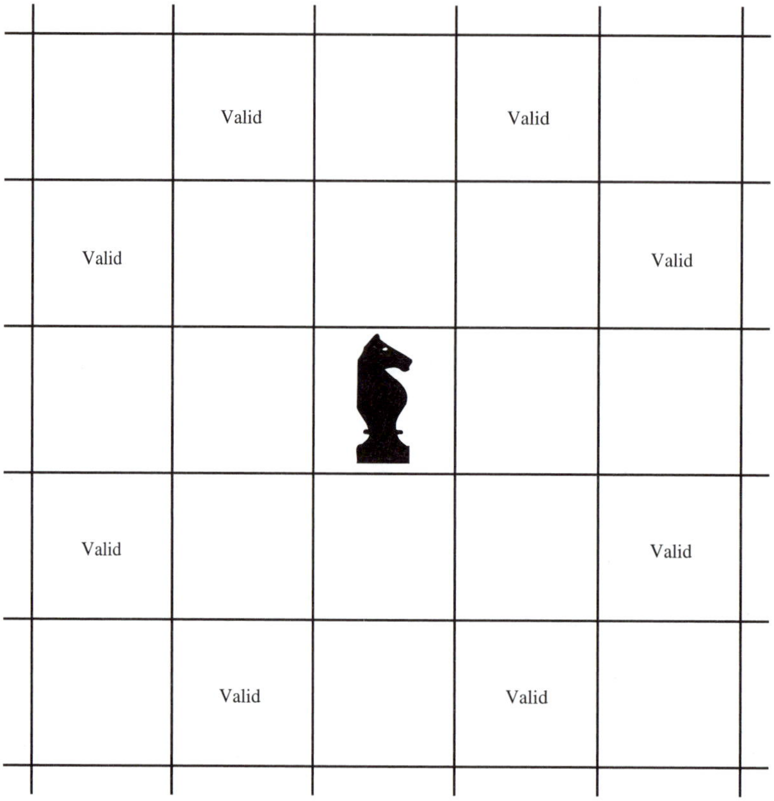

Figure 3.22   Diagram for Question 38

43.   A two-dimensional array LINES[3][4] contains a set of three endpoint coordinates. For example, if the first row of LINES contains the numbers 10, 20, 100, and 20, the endpoints of the first line are (10,20) and (100,20). Write a function that determines if the three lines form a triangle. Return 1 if a valid triangle exists and 0 otherwise.

44.   Write a function that transposes a square matrix. For example, given this matrix:

$$1 \quad 2 \quad 3$$
$$4 \quad 5 \quad 6$$
$$7 \quad 8 \quad 9$$

your function should create the following transposed matrix:

$$1 \quad 4 \quad 7$$
$$2 \quad 5 \quad 8$$
$$3 \quad 6 \quad 9$$

45.   Add a function to Program 3.26 that identifies lost allocation units.

46.   Write a program that finds the histogram of a two-dimensional matrix of integers DATA[8][8]. Then find the histogram element that has the highest frequency count and use this value to do the following: if a DATA element is smaller than the histogram element, replace the DATA element with 0, otherwise replace it with 1.

47.   Determine a formula to predict the sum of any row or column in a magic square of size N.

4   User-Defined Data Structures

Objectives

This chapter provides you the opportunity to learn:

1. The meaning of enumerated data types in C/C++.
2. How to define your own data types.
3. The meaning of data structures.
4. Why data structures are useful.
5. Arranging data structures as arrays.
6. How to develop complex data structures.
7. How to use the C/C++ `union`.

Key Terms

Enumerated   Template
Type Definition   Structure Tag
Structure Members   Member Declaration List
Structure   `union`
Member-of Operator   Emulators

Outline

Introduction

Up to this point, you have been concerned primarily with working with only one data type at a time. For example, when you worked with arrays, the array was of a single type (such as `int` or `char`). A single data type has a simple data structure. In complex applications, you may use more than one data type at a time. This chapter will show you how to do this.

This is a very useful chapter. Essentially this chapter will show you how to develop programs that will handle more complex technology problems.

4.1   Enumerating Types

Discussion

This section presents another way of expressing data. Up to this point you have had the `#define` statement. Now you will have the opportunity to learn another method for expressing data that will give your programs even greater readability. The material you learn here will help set the stage for the remaining sections of this chapter.

Expressing Data

There is another way of expressing data. It is called the `enum` (for **enumerated**). What this does is to hold one integer value from a fixed set of identified integer constants.

The form of `enum` is as follows:

```
enum tag { enumeration-list }
```

The enumeration declaration presents the name of an enumeration variable and then defines the names within the enumeration list. The declaration begins with the keyword `enum`. The resulting `enum` variable can then be used anywhere an `int` type is used. An example is illustrated in Program 4.1.

Program 4.1

```
#include <stdio.h>

enum color_code {black, brown, red, orange, yellow};

main()
{
        enum color_code color;
        char value;
```

```
        printf("Input an integer from 0 to 4 => ");
        value = getchar();

        switch(value)
        {
                case '0' : color = black;
                           break;
                case '1' : color = brown;
                           break;
                case '2' : color = red;
                           break;
                case '3' : color = orange;
                           break;
                case '4' : color = yellow;
                           break;
        }

        switch(color)
        {
                case black  : printf("Color is black.");
                              break;
                case brown  : printf("Color is brown.");
                              break;
                case red    : printf("Color is red.");
                              break;
                case orange : printf("Color is orange.");
                              break;
                case yellow : printf("Color is yellow.");
                              break;
        }
}
```

Program 4.1 asks the program user to input an integer from 0 to 4. The program will then give the program user the equivalent resistor color code for that number. As an example

```
Input an integer from 0 to 4 => 3
Color is orange.
```

The important point of this program is that it uses the enum data type to make the source code more readable.

Program Analysis

First, an enumerated data type is declared outside of main():

```
enum color_code {black, brown, red, orange, yellow};
```

What this does is declare color_code to be an enumerated type. The list within the braces shows the constant names that are valid values of the enum color_code variable.

Next, inside `main()`, is the declaration of an enumerated variable of type `color_code`:

```
main()
{
        enum color_code color;
```

This means that the variable `color` may have any of these values: black, brown, red, orange, or yellow.

Look at what the first `switch()` does.

```
switch (value)
{
        case '0'  :  color = black;
                      break;
        case '1'  :  color = brown;
                      break;
        case '2'  :  color = red;
                      break;
        case '3'  :  color = orange;
                      break;
        case '4'  :  color = yellow;
                      break;
}
```

From the user input it assigns color value to the variable `color`. Hence, if the user selects 3 for an input, the variable `color` will be assigned the value of `orange`. This data is then used in the next `switch()`:

```
switch (color)
{
        case black   :  printf("Color is black.");
                          break;
        case brown   :  printf("Color is brown.");
                          break;
        case red     :  printf("Color is red.");
                          break;
        case orange  :  printf("Color is orange.");
                          break;
        case yellow  :  printf("Color is yellow.");
                          break;
}
```

This results in a very descriptive `case`. You should note that `enum` does not introduce a new basic data type. Variables of the `enum` type are treated as if they were of type `int`. What `enum` does is improve the readability of your programs.

Another Form

Another method of displaying an `enum` declaration is in the vertical form, as follows:

```
enum color_code
{
     black,
```

```
            brown,
            red,
            orange,
            yellow
    }
```

Enumeration Example

To demonstrate exactly what is going on in an enum data type, look at Program 4.2.

Program 4.2

```
#include <stdio.h>

enum color_code {black, brown, red, orange, yellow};

main()
{
        enum color_code color;

        for(color = black; color <= yellow; color++)
                printf("Digital value of enum type color => %d\n", color);
}
```

Execution of Program 4.2 yields

```
Digital value of enum type color => 0
Digital value of enum type color => 1
Digital value of enum type color => 2
Digital value of enum type color => 3
Digital value of enum type color => 4
```

Note that the enum type is used in the for() loop just as if it were of type int.

Assigning enum Values

The enum type may also be assigned values—as long as they are integer values. This is demonstrated in Program 4.3. This program solves for the total current for a given voltage source when the Thevenin* equivalent voltage and resistance are known. In this program, the Thevenin equivalent voltage is 12 volts and the Thevenin equivalent resistance is 150 ohms. Note how these values are set by the enum type.

Program 4.3

```
#include <stdio.h>

        enum thevenin {source = 12, resistance = 150};

main()
```

---

*The Thevenin equivalent form of any resistive circuit consists of an equivalent voltage source and an equivalent resistance. These values depend on the values of the original circuit. This method is used to simplify resistive circuits to a single voltage source and single resistor connected in series.

```
{
        float load;
        float current;

        printf("Input value of load resistor => ");
        scanf("%f",&load);

        current = source/(resistance + load);

        printf("The circuit current is %f amps.", current);
}
```

In Program 4.3, the enum data type thevenin is assigned values of source (which is set equal to 12) and resistance (set equal to 150). These constant names are then used inside the program to do the necessary calculations. Again, the purpose here is to make the program more readable and allow easy changes in the constant assignments used in the program.

Conclusion

This section introduced the enum. Here you discovered another method of using data in your program to improve its readability. You also saw that the use of the enum is compatible with the int. Check your understanding of this section by trying the following section review.

4.1 Section Review

1. In C, what does the keyword enum mean?
2. State what an enum data type does.
3. For the following code, what is the integer value of first?

   ```
   enum numbers {first, second, third}
   ```

4. What is the main purpose of using an enum?
5. Can an enum constant be set to a given integer value? Give an example.

4.2 Naming Your Own Data Types

Discussion

In Section 4.1, you were introduced to a method of making your program easier to read. This section elaborates on that theme. However, unlike the previous section, this section will show you how to name your own data types.

Introducing typedef

The use of the typedef (**type definition**) allows you to define names for a data type. A typedef declaration is similar to a variable declaration except that the keyword typedef is used. The form is

```
typedef type-specifier declarator
```

For example, you could have:

```
typedef char LETTER;
```

This now declares LETTER as a synonym for char. This means that LETTER can now be used as a variable declaration such as

```
LETTER character;
```

instead of

```
char character;
```

As an example, suppose you have a program that is part of an automated testing system. In this program the user inputs the status of an indicator light and the program gives a response depending on the given status. The program could be written as shown in Program 4.4.

Program 4.4

```
#include <stdio.h>

void test_it(void);
int check_lights(char condition);

main()
{
        test_it();
}


void test_it()
{
        char input;

        printf("\n\n1] Red  2] Green  3] Off \n\n");
        printf("Select light condition by number => ");
        input = getchar();

        check_lights(input);
}

int check_lights(char condition)
{
        switch(condition)
        {
                case '1': printf("Check system pressure.");
                        break;

                case '2': printf("System OK.");
                        break;

                case '3': printf("Check system fuse.");
                        break;
        }
}
```

Execution of Program 4.4 produces

```
1] Red  2] Green  3] Off
Select light condition by number => 2
System OK.
```

However, the program could be made more descriptive by defining a data type called light_status. The same program using this new type definition is illustrated by Program 4.5.

Program 4.5

```
#include <stdio.h>

        typedef enum light_status {Red, Green, Off};
void test_it(void);
int check_lights(enum light_status condition);

main()
{
        test_it();
}


void test_it()
{
        char input;
        enum light_status reading;

        printf("\n\n1] Red  2] Green  3] Off \n\n");
        printf("Select light condition by number => ");
        input = getchar();

        switch (input)
        {
                case '1' : reading = Red;
                           break;
                case '2' : reading = Green;
                           break;
                case '3' : reading = Off;
                           break;
        }

        check_lights(reading);
}

int check_lights(enum light_status condition)
{
        switch(condition)
        {
                case Red  : printf("Check system pressure.");
                            break;
```

```
            case Green: printf("System OK.");
                        break;

            case Off  : printf("Check system fuse.");
                        break;
      }
}
```

The output of Program 4.5 is the same as that of Program 4.4. The difference is that a new type name is created for an existing data type. This allows new identifiers to be defined as this data type. This can be done in the bodies of functions as well as in the function parameters. It's important to note that the `typedef` declaration does not create types. It simply creates synonyms for existing types.

Program Analysis

The keyword `typedef` is used to indicate that a new definition is to be used for a data type.

```
typedef enum light_status {Red, Green, Off};
```

In this case, the data type is an `enum` type called `light_status`. It consists of the enumerated constants `Red`, `Green`, and `Off`. Now other variables may be defined in terms of this new data type. Look at the formal parameter of the function prototype:

```
int check_lights(enum light_status condition);
```

It declares a new variable `condition` as a type `light_status`. It is used again in the definition of function `test_it()`.

```
void test_it()
{
      char input;
      enum light_status reading;
```

This means that the variable `reading` is the enumerated data type `light_status` and can assume the values `Red`, `Green`, and `Off`.

After the variable `reading` is assigned one of these three values by the `switch()`, it is then passed to the called function `check_lights()`.

```
switch (input)
{
      case '1' : reading = Red;
                 break;
      case '2' : reading = Green;
                 break;
      case '3' : reading = Off;
                 break;
}

check_lights(reading);
```

Next it is used in the called function as part of the `switch()` to make the code more readable:

```
int check_lights(enum light_status condition)
{

        switch (condition)
        {
                case Red    : printf("Check system pressure.");
                              break;
                case Green  : printf("System OK.");
                              break;
                case Off    : printf("Check system fuse.");
                              break;

        }

}
```

Other Applications

Another application of the `typedef` is:

```
typedef char *STRING;
```

This allows you to use the new word `STRING` as a pointer to `char`:

```
STRING inputname;
```

Here, `inputname` is defined as a type `STRING` which is really a pointer to `char` (`char *`).

You will see even more powerful applications of the `typedef` in the sections that follow.

Conclusion

This section introduced you to a method for naming data types. Here you saw how to implement this in a program where you could create new identifiers in terms of this new data type. Check your understanding of this section by trying the following section review.

4.2 Section Review

1. State what the `typedef` does.
2. For the following code, what is the resulting new name of the data type?

   ```
   typedef char name[20];
   ```

3. What is the main purpose of using the `typedef`?

4.3   Using `struct` to Create a Data Structure

Discussion

Up to now, you have been using arrays and pointers to create items of the same data type. You have never mixed a type `char` and a type `int` within a single data type. Understandably, you may not have even considered the possibility. However, most of the everyday

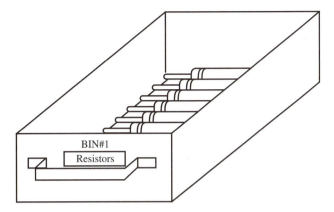

Figure 4.1   Box of Resistors

"keeping track of things" requires the use of more than one data type. Consider your checking account. Each check you write must have your name on it (a type char), the amount of the check (a type float), and the check number (a type int). All of this information (plus a lot more) is contained on this one item called a check. Because this is a very natural way of arranging information, C/C++ provides a method for you to accomplish the same thing. Doing this makes your program more readable and makes it easier to handle complex data consisting of many different types that are logically related.

The Structure

A structure declaration names a structure variable and then states a sequence of variable names—called **structure members**—which may have different types. The basic form is

```
struct
{
        type    identifier_1;
        type    identifier_2;
          .
          .
          .
        type     identifier_N;
}   structure_identifier;
```

Note that structure declarations begin with the keyword struct.

As an example of the use of a structure, consider a box of parts, as shown in Figure 4.1.

Assume that this box of parts consists of one type of resistor. Assume for the moment that there are three things you wish to keep track of concerning these resistors: the name of the manufacturer, the quantity of resistors in the box, and the price of each resistor. You could develop a program that would easily do this without using the concept of a structure, but to keep things simple for now, the **structure** will be used to keep this inventory. Program 4.6 illustrates the construction of a structure.

Program 4.6

```
#include <stdio.h>

main()
{
        struct
        {
                char    manufacturer[20]; /* Resistor manufacturer.   */
                int     quantity;          /* Number of resistors left. */
                float price_each;          /* Cost of each resistor.    */
        } resistors;
}
```

Figure 4.2 illustrates the key points for the format of a structure.

Note that the structure in Program 4.6 consists of a collection of data elements, called members, which may consist of the same type or different types that are logically related. The data types are char for the variable manufacturer, int for the variable quantity, and float for the variable price_each. The general form is

```
struct
{
        type      identifier_1;
        type      identifier_2;
        .
        .
        .
        type      identifier_N;
}   structure_identifier;
```

Where

struct	=	Keyword indicating that a structure follows.
{	=	Necessary opening brace to indicate that a list of structure elements is to follow.
type	=	The type for each element.
identifier	=	The variable identifier for the structure member.
}	=	Necessary closing brace.
structure_identifier		Defines the structure variable.

Putting Data into a Structure

Now that you've seen what a structure looks like, you need to know how to get values into the structure members. Program 4.7 shows you how this is done. The program gets information from the program user concerning the manufacturer of the resistors, the quantity of resistors in the bin, and the unit price of the resistors. It then calculates the total value of all the resistors, displaying this along with the information put in by the program user.

The method of getting data into and out of a structure member is by using the **member-of operator.** The member-of operator specifies the name of the structure member and the structure of which it is a member. For example, in Program 4.7,

```
resistors.manufacturer
```

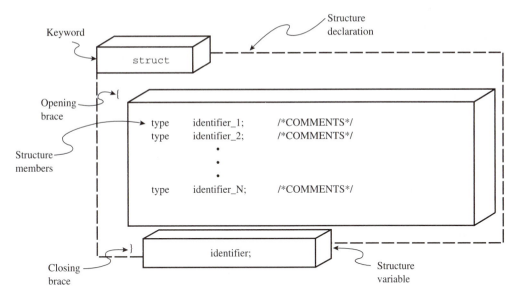

Figure 4.2   Key Parts of a Structure

represents the variable `manufacturer`, which is a member of the structure `resistors`. Note that the member-of operator is represented by the period (.).

Program 4.7

```c
#include <stdio.h>

main()
{
        struct
        {
                char  manufacturer[20];   /* Resistor manufacturer.     */
                int   quantity;           /* Number of resistors left.  */
                float price_each;         /* Cost of each resistor.     */
        } resistors;

        float total_value;                /* Total value of parts.      */

        /* Display variables:*/

        /* Get name of manufacturer:*/

        printf("Name of manufacturer => ");
        gets(resistors.manufacturer);

        /* Get number of parts left:*/

        printf("Number of parts left => ");
        scanf("%d",&resistors.quantity);
```

```
/* Get cost of each part:*/

printf("Cost of each part => ");
scanf("%f",&resistors.price_each);

/* Calculate total value:*/

total_value = resistors.quantity * resistors.price_each;

/* Display variables:*/

printf("\n\n");
printf("Item:            Resistors\n\n");
printf("Manufacturer:    %s\n",resistors.manufacturer);
printf("Cost each:       $%f\n",resistors.price_each);
printf("Quantity:        %d\n",resistors.quantity);
printf("Total value:     $%f\n",total_value);
}
```

Assuming the user inputs the following, execution of Program 4.7 results in

```
Name of manufacturer => Ohmite
Number of parts left => 10
Cost of each part => 0.05

Item:            Resistors
Manufacturer:    Ohmite
Cost each:       $0.050000
Quantity:        10.000000
Total value:     $0.500000
```

Program Analysis

Program 4.7 starts with the same structure as before and also declares another variable, `total_value`.

```
main()
{

    struct
    {
        char    manufacturer[20];   /* Resistor manufacturer.     */
        int     quantity;           /* Number of resistors left. */
        float   price_each;         /* Cost of each resistor.     */
    } resistors;

    float total_value;              /* Total value of parts.      */
```

The variable `total_value` will be used to hold the value that represents the total value of all the resistors in the parts bin.

Next the program gets the name of the resistor manufacturer from the program user.

```
/* Get name of manufacturer:*/

printf("Name of manufacturer => ");
gets(resistors.manufacturer);
```

Note how this is done. The name of the resistor manufacturer must be placed in the member `char manufacturer[20];`. Because the variable `manufacturer[20]` is contained in the structure referred to by the variable `resistors`, this must somehow be shown in the program. This is done by the member-of operator ".".

```
resistors.manufacturer
```

The member-of operator specifies the name of the structure member and the structure of which it is a member. This member-of operator is used again to get the data for the remaining two structure member variables:

```
/* Get number of parts left:*/

printf("Number of parts left => ");
scanf("%d",&resistors.quantity);

/* Get cost of each part:*/

printf("Cost of each part => ");
scanf("%f",&resistors.price_each);
```

Note that this time the address-of `&` operator is needed because of the use of the `scanf()` function. But the member-of operator is still the same:

```
structure_name.member_name
```

Next, a calculation is performed using the member-of operator:

```
/* Calculate total value:*/

total_value = resistors.quantity * resistors.price_each;
```

Again, the name of the structure and the name of the member are used to identify the structure variables. The results are then displayed. Note that the variable `total_value` does not require a member-of operator because it is not a member of any structure.

```
/* Display variables:*/

printf("\n\n");
printf("Item:          Resistors\n\n");
printf("Manufacturer:  %s\n",resistors.manufacturer);
printf("Cost each:     $%f\n",resistors.price_each);
printf("Quantity:      %d\n",resistors.quantity);
printf("Total value:   $%f\n",total_value);
```

Conclusion

This section introduced you to the concept of a structure. In the next section you will see other, more powerful ways of applying a structure. For now, test your understanding of this section by trying the following section review.

4.3 Section Review

1. State why the information on a check from a checking account can be treated as a structure.
2. What is a structure?
3. Describe the format of a structure presented in this section.
4. State how a structure member variable is programmed for getting data and displaying data.
5. Give an example of the structure from Question 4.

4.4   Accessing Structure Elements

Discussion

In the previous section, you were introduced to the concept and form of a structure. In this section, you will see different ways of letting your program know that you are creating a structure. You will also discover how to name function types, declare functions as structures, and pass structures between functions.

The Structure Tag

In the previous section, the structure for an inventory of resistors of the same type contained in a storage box was demonstrated. Take a closer look at where the structure was defined:

```
main()
{

      struct
      {
              char    manufacturer[20];    /* Resistor manufacturer.    */
              int     quantity;            /* Number of resistors left. */
              float   price_each;          /* Cost of each resistor.    */
      } resistors;
```

It was defined inside `main()`, and as a consequence will be known only to `main()`. Another method of developing a structure is to define the structure before `main()`. This method creates a global variable.

C/C++ has a method of announcing the format of a structure that will serve as a **template** that can then be used by any function within the program. This is illustrated in Program 4.8. The output of this program is exactly the same as that of Program 4.7. The difference is the way the structure is placed in the program.

Program 4.8

```
#include <stdio.h>

struct parts_record
{
```

```
        char  manufacturer[20];        /* Resistor manufacturer.    */
        int   quantity;                /* Number of resistors left.  */
        float price_each;              /* Cost of each resistor.     */
};

main()
{
        struct parts_record resistors;  /* Structure variable.       */
        float total_value;              /* Total value of parts.      */

        /* Get name of manufacturer:*/

        /* Get number of parts left:*/

        /* Get cost of each part:*/

        /* Calculate total value:*/

        /* Display variables:*/
}
```

Program Analysis

Program 4.8 declares a structure type called `parts_record`. There is no variable identifier; `parts_record` is called a **structure tag.** The structure tag is an identifier that names the structure type defined in the **member declaration list.** Note that this was done after the keyword `struct`.

```
struct parts_record
{
        char   manufacturer[20];    /* Resistor manufacturer.     */
        int    quantity;            /* Number of resistors left. */
        float  price_each;          /* Cost of each resistor.     */
};
```

Now any function within the program can use this structure by making reference to the structure tag. This was done in `main()`.

```
main()
{
        struct parts_record resistors; /* Structure variable. */
```

Note the format of the declaration. It uses the keyword `struct` and the tag identifier `parts_record`, which defines the variable `resistors` as the structure tagged `parts_ record`. The general form of the declaration when a structure tag is used is

```
struct tag variable_identifier;
```

The same method is used to access the individual members of the structure as before, using the member-of operator ".". For example, `resistors.quantity` identifies the structure member `quantity`. Using the tag method and declaring the structure outside of `main()` sets a template that may now be used by any function within the program.

Naming a Structure

Another method of identifying a structure is to use the `typedef`. This can be accomplished as shown in Program 4.9.

Program 4.9

```c
#include <stdio.h>

typedef struct
{
        char   manufacturer[20];        /* Resistor manufacturer.    */
        int    quantity;                /* Number of resistors left.  */
        float price_each;               /* Cost of each resistor.     */
} parts_record;                         /* Name for this structure.   */

main()
{
        parts_record resistors;         /* Structure variable.        */
        float total_value;              /* Total value of parts.      */

        /* Get name of manufacturer:*/

        /* Get number of parts left:*/

        /* Get cost of each part:*/

        /* Calculate total value:*/

        /* Display variables:*/
}
```

Program 4.9 does exactly the same thing as Program 4.8. The difference is in how the structure is declared. This time, the `typedef` is used to name the structure type `parts_record`.

```c
typedef struct
{
        char   manufacturer[20];        /* Resistor manufacturer.    */
        int    quantity;                /* Number of resistors left.  */
        float  price_each;              /* Cost of each resistor.     */
} parts_record;                         /* Name for this structure.   */
```

Note that a structure tag is not used. Instead, the structure variable `parts_record` is now being named as a data type by the keyword `typedef`. The advantage of doing this is that (as before) you can use the defined structure in any function. However, you only need to declare local structure variables in terms of this new type definition. This is done inside `main()` to keep the record variable `resistors` local.

```c
main()
{
        parts_record resistors;     /* Structure variable.        */
```

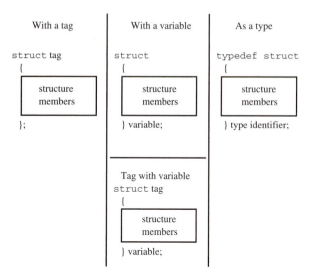

Figure 4.3 Methods of Declaring Structures

Note that the structure variable `resistors` is used as its data type `parts_record`. Again, you still access each member of the structure by the member of operator; for example, `resistors.quantity` identifies the structure member `quantity`.

The various ways of declaring structures are illustrated in Figure 4.3.

Structure Pointers

You can declare a structure variable to be of type pointer. This is illustrated in Program 4.10. Notice that the `typedef` is used to define the structure type. The program does exactly the same thing as before; however, it is now doing it by using a structure pointer.

Program 4.10

```
#include <stdio.h>

typedef struct
{
        char   manufacturer[20];        /* Resistor manufacturer.    */
        int    quantity;                /* Number of resistors left. */
        float price_each;               /* Cost of each resistor.    */
} parts_record;

main()
{
        part_record newpart;            /* Structure variable.       */
        parts_record *rcd_ptr;          /* Structure pointer.        */
        float total_value;              /* Total value of parts.     */

        /* Initialize pointer to structure.*/
        red_ptr = &newpart;
```

```
/* Get name of manufacturer:*/
printf("Name of manufacturer => ");
gets(rcd_ptr -> manufacturer);

/* Get number of parts left:*/

printf("Number of parts left => ");
scanf("%d",&rcd_ptr -> quantity);

/* Get cost of each part:*/

printf("Cost of each part => ");
scanf("%f",&rcd_ptr -> price_each);

/* Calculate total value:*/

total_value = rcd_ptr -> quantity * rcd_ptr -> price_each;

/* Display variables:*/

printf("\n\n");
printf("Item:          Resistors\n\n");
printf("Manufacturer:  %s\n",rcd_ptr -> manufacturer);
printf("Cost each:     $%f\n",rcd_ptr -> price_each);
printf("Quantity:      %d\n",rcd_ptr -> quantity);
printf("Total value:   $%f\n",total_value);
```

}

Note that the structure pointer is declared the same way a pointer is normally declared:

```
main()
{
        parts_record *rcd_ptr; /* Structure pointer. */
```

However, `rcd_ptr` is now a pointer to a structure, and as a result, when an individual member of the structure is to be accessed, a special symbol `->` must be used:

```
/* Get name of manufacturer: */

printf("Name of manufacturer => ");
gets(rcd_ptr -> manufacturer);
```

The symbol `->` refers to the member of a structure pointed to by a pointer. Effectively, this replaces the member of operator "." used in previous examples.

Because a structure may be defined as a pointer, it may also use the address-of `&` operator as with any other variable. This means that the address of a structure may be assigned to a structure pointer.

A Function as a Structure

You may declare a function to be of a structure type. This is demonstrated in Program 4.11. Again, the program does exactly the same thing as previous ones; the difference is that now `main()` is serving as the function that simply calls other functions. It is the other functions that do all the work. Note in the program that the function `get_input()` is declared as a type defined by `parts_record`. Thus, this function itself now has a record structure. Note also that a structure variable is used as a function argument to pass the structure data to the function `display_output()`.

Program 4.11

```
#include <stdio.h>

typedef struct
{
        char   manufacturer[20];          /* Resistor manufacturer.          */
        int    quantity;                  /* Number of resistors left.       */
        float price_each;                 /* Cost of each resistor.          */
} parts_record;

parts_record get_input(void);                            /* Get user input.*/
void display_output(parts_record resistor_record);       /* Display output.*/

main()
{
        parts_record resistor_box;        /* Declares a structure variable. */

        resistor_box = get_input();       /* Get user input. */
        display_output(resistor_box);     /* Display output. */
}

parts_record get_input()                  /* Get user input. */
{
        parts_record resistor_information;

        /* Get name of manufacturer:*/

        printf("Name of manufacturer => ");
        gets(resistor_information.manufacturer);

        /* Get number of parts left:*/

        printf("Number of parts left => ");
        scanf("%d",&resistor_information.quantity);

        /* Get cost of each part:*/

        printf("Cost of each part => ");
        scanf("%f",&resistor_information.price_each);

        return(resistor_information);
}

void display_output(parts_record resistor_information)
```

```
{
        /* Display variables:*/

        printf("\n\n");
        printf("Item:          Resistors\n\n");
        printf("Manufacturer:  %s\n",resistor_information.manufacturer);
        printf("Cost each:     $%f\n",resistor_information.price_each);
        printf("Quantity:      %d\n",resistor_information.quantity);
}
```

Program Analysis

The first new material in Program 4.11 is in the function prototypes:

```
parts_record get_input(void);   /* Get user input. */
```

The typedef has been used to give the name parts_record to the structure. Now, the function get_input() is being defined as a type parts_record.

The next item is the use of a structure type as a formal parameter:

```
void display_output(parts_record resistor_record); /* Display output. */
```

Here, the formal parameter resistor_record is of type parts_record (which is the name for the previously defined structure type). This means that the argument passed to this function must be of the same type. This is what happens in the body of main().

```
main()
{
        parts_record resistor_box;    /* Declares a structure variable. */

        resistor_box = get_input();   /* Get user input. */
        display_output(resistor_box); /* Display output. */
}
```

The variable resistor_box is defined as the type parts_record (as were the other structure variables). Now, because resistor_box and get_input() are both of the same type of structure, one may be assigned to the other.

Next, in the definition of the get_input() function, the whole structure is returned back using the defined variable resistor_information, which is again of type parts_record.

The last function, display_output(), simply takes the actual parameter from main() (which now contains the structure data) and uses it to display the output data.

Conclusion

This section demonstrated various forms of the structure. Here you saw different ways of letting your program know that you are creating a structure. You also saw how to name function types, declare functions as structures, and pass structures between functions. Check your understanding of this section by trying the following section review.

4.4 Section Review

1. Describe what is meant by a structure tag.
2. Give an example of a structure tag.
3. Can a structure be a variable type? Explain.
4. How is a structure member pointed to when a structure pointer is used?
5. What are the three operations that are allowed with structures?

4.5   The union

Discussion

This section presents the **union,** which you will see is similar to a structure in many ways but with an important difference. This section brings together much of the material that has been presented up to this point.

The union

The union is similar to a structure. The difference is that a union is used to store different data types in the same memory location.

The format of a union is

```
union tag
{

        type    member_identifier₁
        type    member_identifier₂
              .
              .
              .
        type    member_identifierₙ
}
```

As you can see, a union declaration has the same form as the structure declaration. The difference is the keyword union. A union declaration names a union variable and states the set of variable values (members) of the union. These members can have different types. What happens in a union is that a union type variable will store one of the values defined by that type. Program 4.12 demonstrates the action of a union.

Program 4.12

```
#include <stdio.h>

main()
{
        union    /* Define union. */
        {
                int    integer_value;
                float value;
```

```
} integer_or_float;

printf("Size of the union => %d bytes.\n", sizeof(integer_or_float));

/* Enter an integer and display it: */

integer_or_float.integer_value = 123;
printf("The integer value is %d\n", integer_or_float.integer_value);
printf("Starting address is => %d\n", &integer_or_float.integer_value);

/* Enter a float and display it: */

integer_or_float.value = 123.45;
printf("The float value is %f\n", integer_or_float.value);
printf("Starting address is => %d\n", &integer_or_float.value);
}
```

Execution of Program 4.12 produces

```
Size of the union => 4
The integer value is 123
Starting address is => 7042
The float value is 123.45
Starting address is => 7042
```

What you see from the output above is that the size of the union is 4 bytes. This is because it takes 4 bytes to store a type `float`. First, an integer value is stored and then retrieved from this memory location (shown with a starting address of 7042). Then a float value is stored and retrieved from the same memory space.

As shown in Program 4.12, the union declarations have the same form as structure declarations. The difference is that the keyword `union` is used in place of the keyword `struct`. The rules covered up to this point for structures also apply to unions. The amount of storage required for a union variable is the amount of storage required for the largest member of the union. All members are stored in the same memory space (but not at the same time) with the same starting address.

Conclusion

This section presented the `union`. This is a powerful new tool for handling complex data structures. In the next section, you will see how structures and arrays may be mixed to handle even more complex data structures. Check your understanding of this section by trying the following section review.

4.5 Section Review

1. Describe the purpose of a `union`.
2. How is a `union` declared?
3. How much storage space is required for a `union`?

4.6   Structures Within Structures

Discussion

Structures are rich in the variety of ways they may be used. This section will demonstrate some of them. You will find many potential technical applications for this powerful feature.

Structures Within Structures

You can have a structure within another structure. Consider Program 4.13.

Program 4.13

```
#include <stdio.h>

typedef struct
{
        int member_1;
        char member_2;
        float member_3;
} first_structure;

struct second_structure
{
        first_structure  second_member_1;
        int              second_member_2;
        char             second_member_3;
}

main()
{
}
```

As you can see from Program 4.13, the structure `second_structure` contains the structure `first_structure` in the member called `second_member_1`. This is a case of a structure containing another structure. The parts inventory program could use a structure within a structure such as this. For example, the manufacturer of the part could in itself be a structure that would contain the address and telephone number as members.

Arrays Within Structures

You can also have arrays within structures. For example, consider Program 4.14. Here, one member of the structure is a two-dimensional array. Recall that you used character arrays to represent strings in previous structures. This is no different.

Program 4.14

```
#include <stdio.h>

struct structure_tag
{
```

```
        float array_variable[5][6];
        int   second_member_2;
        char  second_member_3;
}

main()
{
}
```

As you can see from Program 4.14, the member `array_variable[5][6]` is a two-dimensional array contained within the structure.

Multidimensional Structure Arrays

You may also have multidimensional arrays that are structures. Consider Program 4.15. Here you have a two-dimensional array that is a structure that contains three members, one of which is itself a two-dimensional array.

Program 4.15

```
#include <stdio.h>

typedef struct
{
        float array_variable[5][6];
        int   second_member_2;
        char  second_member_3;
} record_1;

typedef my_record complex_array[3][2];

main()
{
}
```

As shown in Program 4.15, `complex_array[3][2]` is a two-dimensional array of type `my_record`. Thus you have a data structure where there are actually $3 \times 2 = 6$ structures, each of which contains three members, one of which is an array itself.

Conclusion

A rich variety of structures and arrays is available. In this section you saw a few examples of the possibilities. Check your knowledge of this section by trying the following section review.

4.6 Section Review

1. Can a structure be an array? Explain.
2. Can a structure contain another structure? Explain.
3. Is it possible for an array to be a structure type that contains an array as one of its members? Explain.

4.7   Application Program: MiniMicro

Discussion

In this section we will develop and examine the operation of a simple microprocessing system called MiniMicro. The instruction set of the machine is shown in Table 4.1. The types of instructions included in MiniMicro are typical of those found on most microprocessors. The power of the `enum` data type allows us to define the LOAD, ADD, and other instructions shown in Table 4.1 without having to assign any meanings or values to them. However, we can write a program for MiniMicro using combinations of instructions, and actually come up with a working machine.

The Problem

MiniMicro operates like any microprocessor, running the same sequence of operations over and over:

- Fetch instruction
- Decode instruction
- Execute instruction

Because the machine must read memory to fetch an instruction, we must provide memory for the program and data and also a pointer that allows MiniMicro to access memory. Some instructions use the pointer to read data during their execution phase (LOAD, ADD, SUB, MUL, and DIV), and other instructions load the pointer with a new value (JNZ, JMP, JSR, and RET).

Developing the Algorithm

The steps required in the MiniMicro application are as follows:

1. Fetch instruction.
2. Read instruction operand from next location.
3. Decode instruction.
4. Execute instruction.

Table 4.1   MiniMicro Instruction Set

Instruction Syntax	Operation
LOAD value	Load accumulator with value
ADD value	Add value to accumulator
SUB value	Subtract value from accumulator
MUL value	Multiply accumulator by value
DIV value	Divide accumulator by value
PRINT	Display accumulator contents
JNZ address	Jump to address if accumulator is not zero
JMP address	Jump to address
JSR address	Jump to subroutine beginning at address
RET	Return from subroutine
STOP	Stop execution

Each step requires knowledge about the machine's instruction pointer. The execute step utilizes the machine's accumulator. Recursion will be used to execute the JSR and RET instructions, because they both change and restore the instruction pointer during execution. In order to make the accumulator available to all levels of recursion (in case nested subroutines are used), the accumulator is defined as a *global* variable.

The Overall Process

Examine Program 4.16. The program contains a do() loop that performs all actions necessary to execute a single instruction. A switch() statement is used to decode the fetched instruction. Each line of the switch() statement represents one of MiniMicro's enumerated instructions.

Program 4.16

```
#include <stdio.h>

        /* Define instruction set. */
        enum iset {LOAD, ADD, SUB, MUL, DIV, PRINT,
                   JNZ, JMP, JSR, RET, STOP};

        /* Load program into memory. */
        int mem[256] = {LOAD, 100, JSR, 6, PRINT, STOP,
                        MUL, 9, DIV, 5, ADD, 32, RET};

        int acc;          /* Accumulator. */

void exec(int pc);

main()
{
        exec(0);          /* Begin execution at address 0. */
}

void exec(int pc)
{
        int ip;           /* Instruction pointer. */
        int inst;         /* Instruction. */
        int iop;          /* Instruction operand. */

        ip = pc;          /* Load instruction pointer. */
        do
        {
                inst = mem[ip++];       /* Fetch instruction. */
                iop = mem[ip++];        /* Read operand too. */
                switch(inst)
                {
                        case LOAD : acc = iop; break;
                        case ADD  : acc += iop; break;
                        case SUB  : acc -= iop; break;
```

```
                        case MUL   : acc *= iop; break;
                        case DIV   : acc /= iop; break;
                        case PRINT :
                        {
                                printf("ACC = %5d\n",acc);
                                ip--;   /* Fix ip. */
                                break;
                        }
                        case JNZ   : ip = (acc != 0) ? iop : ip; break;
                        case JMP   : ip = iop; break;
                        case JSR   : exec(iop); break;
                        case RET   : return; break;
                        case STOP  : break;
                }
        } while (inst != STOP);
}
```

Notice how the JSR instruction is implemented:

```
case JSR : exec(iop); break;
```

A recursive call to exec() is used to handle subroutines. The address of the subroutine is passed to exec() via iop. This allows multiple instruction pointers to exist simultaneously.

When the RET instruction executes, its switch() statement:

```
case RET : return; break;
```

simply causes the current level of recursion to terminate and pass control back to the previous level, where the original value of the instruction pointer is restored.

The do() loop is repeated until the STOP instruction is encountered.

Table 4.2 shows an example of a MiniMicro program that converts 100 degrees Celsius into Fahrenheit. Note that the actual conversion is performed in a subroutine.

A sample execution of Program 4.16 is as follows:

```
ACC =  212
```

which is the correct Fahrenheit temperature.

Table 4.2 Example MiniMicro Program

Address	Instruction	Comment
0	LOAD 100	Load accumulator with 100
2	JSR 6	Jump to subroutine at address 6
4	PRINT	Display accumulator
5	STOP	Halt
6	MUL 9	Multiply accumulator by 9
8	DIV 5	Divide accumulator by 5
10	ADD 32	Add 32 to accumulator
12	RET`	Return from subroutine

Conclusion

The MiniMicro machine is a good example of where enumeration is used in the real world. Even though our machine has a limited instruction set, adding more instructions is as simple as adding new enumerated types to our list, with the appropriate `case` statements within the `switch()`. Programs such as Program 4.16 are often called **emulators,** because they emulate (mimic) the operation of an actual machine, without the need for the actual machine to exist.

Test your understanding of the material in this section with the following section review.

4.7 Section Review

1. Why is `enum` used to define MiniMicro's instruction set?
2. Explain how `JSR` works.
3. What is the maximum number of instructions possible?
4. How can a new instruction be added to MiniMicro?
5. What is an emulator?

Study Questions

General Concepts

Section 4.1

1. What data type is used to describe a discrete set of integer values?
2. Give the integer value of the first declared enumerated data type.
3. Does the `enum` create a new data type? Explain.
4. Demonstrate how the `enum` data type can be assigned an integer value.

Section 4.2

5. Does the `typedef` create a new data type? Explain.
6. State the purpose of the `typedef`.
7. Give the resulting new name of the data type for the following code:

```
typedef struct {
               int value1;
               } structure;
```

Section 4.3

8. Define a structure.
9. Give an example of a common everyday system that utilizes the concept of a structure.
10. Illustrate the syntax of a structure as presented in this section.
11. Explain what the member-of operator does. What symbol is used for this operator for a simple structure?

Section 4.4

12. What is the identifier that names the structure type defined in the member declaration list of the structure called?
13. Give an example of the use of a structure tag.
14. What is the purpose of the –> symbol as applied to structures?
15. State the three operations that are allowed with structures.

Section 4.5
16. State how one or more different data types may be stored in the same memory location.
17. State the difference between declaring a structure and a union.

Section 4.6
18. Can a structure have a member that is another structure? Explain.
19. Can array of structures contain an array as one of its members? Explain.
20. Can array of structures be a member of another array of structures? Explain.

Section 4.7
21. What happens if RET is the first instruction in a MiniMicro program?
22. Why is it necessary to fix the ip variable in the PRINT instruction?

Program Design
When writing the following programs, utilize the new data structures discussed in this chapter. The use of pointers and recursion is also suggested for those applications that make best use of them.

23. Write a program that uses a structure to store four different resistor values for a series circuit. Compute the total resistance of the circuit by adding the individual resistor values together.
24. Repeat Question 23 for a parallel circuit structure.
25. Write a program that allows the user to enter the following commands: HEAT, COOL, and SET. The program must maintain a temperature variable whose initial value is 60 degrees. HEAT adds 5 degrees and COOL subtracts 5 degrees from the temperature. SET allows the user to change the temperature instantly.
26. Write a program that displays all combinations of the enum types RED, GREEN, and BLUE.
27. Develop a program that uses a structure that will allow the program user to input the following data concerning a business client: name, address, phone number, and credit rating (good or bad).
28. Create a program that demonstrates an arrayed structure that contains an arrayed structure element.
29. Design a program that uses a structure to keep the following information on the status of a design project: ID number, project name, client name, due date, and project completed (yes or no).
30. Develop a program that uses a structure for the following information about different patients for a private practice: name, address, date of birth, gender, dates of visitation, amount owed, and medical problem.
31. Create a program using a structure that will keep track of three different production schedules, each of which contains the following information: production ID number, manufactured item, and customer name. The program is also to contain a structure on up to five employees within the production schedule structure. This should contain the following information: employee ID number, name, title, and hourly wage.

5 Linked-Lists

Objectives

This chapter gives you the opportunity to learn:

1. What a node is and how it is used.
2. The difference between static and dynamic memory allocation.
3. How to create and use linked-lists.
4. When to use a linked-list.
5. About data structures that utilize multiply linked-lists.
6. How a linked-list works in C/C++.

Key Terms

Data Field

NULL

Head

Tail

Garbage

Doubly Linked-List

Ring

Multiply Linked-Lists

Outline

Introduction

There are many times when we do not know how much data a program may be required to work with during a particular execution. For example, a program designed to play chess may use different amounts of storage depending on how the game pieces are positioned. Whenever we use an array in an application, its length must be specified *in advance* to allow the compiler to set aside the required storage space. The chess program may have trouble with this approach, since there is no way to know what the moves will be in advance.

The solution to this problem, and others, is a data structure called the linked-list. This chapter is designed to show you how to create and modify linked-lists, and use them efficiently.

5.1   The Concept of a Node

Linked-lists are based on the utilization of *nodes* of data. A node, in its most basic form, consists of two parts: a data area and a pointer. Anything may be stored in the data area (integers, floats, characters, strings, arrays, etc.). The pointer area contains at least one pointer (address) and *points* to another node of information. Figure 5.1 gives a structural representation of a node. The two portions of the node have been given the names *data* and *link* and are commonly referred to as the **data field** and the *link field*. The data field of the node contains the code for the letter 'x'. Usually, a group of nodes is associated with a data structure. The data structures that commonly make use of nodes are *linked-lists, stacks, queues,* and *binary trees*.

As previously mentioned, a data structure usually consists of a group of nodes. In an array, each data element occupies a consecutive memory location. Nodes, on the other hand, may be spread out over many different locations within memory. This is where the link field of the node becomes necessary. The link field contains a pointer (indicated by the arrow coming out of the link field) that shows to which other node (if any) the current node is connected. Figure 5.2 shows how three nodes are connected through their various link fields.

This collection of nodes is called a linked-list. Notice that the link field of the first node points to the second node, and that the link field of the second node points to the third node. The link field of the third node contains NULL. This indicates that the third node is the *end* of the linked-list. The entire linked-list is pointed to by the variable list.

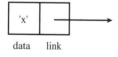

data   link

Figure 5.1   A Node Containing the Letter 'x'

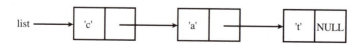

Figure 5.2   A Three-Node Linked-List

To define a node for the linked-list, we use the following structure:

```
typedef struct node
{
        char data;              /* Data field. */
        struct node *link;      /* Link field. */
} LNODE;
```

The data field in the LNODE structure reserves room for a single character. This part of the structure must be changed if the linked-list will be used to store integers, floats, arrays, or some other kind of data. The link field is written in such a way that the structure contains a pointer to a similar LNODE structure.

How are nodes created? To answer this question, let us review how a string of characters is created. The statement

```
char string[20] = "Press Return!";
```

reserves 20 consecutive memory locations (plus a 21st for the '\0' terminator) for the string characters. This type of memory allocation is performed when the program is compiled. During execution, only the 20 reserved memory locations can be used for the string. If the program attempts to use more than 20 locations (during a strcat() operation) it is very possible that other reserved memory locations (or even the actual code of the program) will be overwritten. For this reason, nodes are created *dynamically* (whenever they are needed) and assigned unused memory locations during run time. This way, new nodes may be created and utilized as long as there is available free memory. Do you see the difference between compile time memory allocation and run-time memory allocation?

The <stdlib.h> library contains a function called malloc(), which is used to perform dynamic storage allocation during run time. The number of new bytes required is passed to malloc(), which returns a pointer (an address) to the block of new bytes if they are available. If the requested memory is not available, malloc() returns a NULL pointer. So, to request memory space for a new node, we use the following statement:

```
ptr = malloc(sizeof(LNODE));
```

The sizeof() function determines the size, in bytes, of the LNODE structure. The address of the memory allocated by malloc() is saved in the pointer variable ptr, which must be defined as follows:

```
LNODE *ptr;
```

Allocating memory in this fashion allows the size of the data structure to be determined while the program is *executing,* instead of when it is compiled. The advantage is clear: we do not have to reserve memory in advance for our data structure. For example, a sorting program may not know in advance how many data items there will be. So, how many should be reserved? Ten? Twenty? One thousand? Even so, what if there is one more number inputted to the program than the programmer has reserved space for? Who knows what will happen then?

Conclusion

In this section you were introduced to the concept of a node. Test your understanding with the following section review.

5.1 Section Review

1. What is a node?
2. What is the link field used for?
3. What is a linked-list?
4. What are the differences between static allocation and dynamic allocation?

5.2   Initializing a Linked-List

A linked-list is created by dynamically allocating chunks of memory large enough to contain the size of one node. The nodes are usually created one at a time and can be added to the list in many different ways. No matter what method is used when nodes are added to the list, the link fields must be initialized so that they point to the next node in the list or to NULL (the end of the list).

Program 5.1 shows how a three-element linked-list is created.

Program 5.1

```
#include <stdio.h>
#include <stdlib.h>

        typedef struct node
        {
                char data;
                struct node *link;
        } LNODE;

void show_list(LNODE *ptr);

main()
{
        LNODE *n1, *n2, *n3;

        n1 = malloc(sizeof(LNODE));
        n2 = malloc(sizeof(LNODE));
        n3 = malloc(sizeof(LNODE));

        n1->data = 'c';
        n1->link = n2;
        n2->data = 'a';
        n2->link = n3;
        n3->data = 't';
        n3->link = NULL;

        printf("The linked-list is as follows: ");
        show_list(n1);
}

void show_list(LNODE *ptr)
{
        while(ptr != NULL)
```

```
          {
                  printf("%c",ptr->data);
                  ptr = ptr->link;
          }
          printf("\n");
  }
```

Note how the nodes are allocated with `malloc()`, and then assigned their respective data field and link field values. For example, the first node is loaded with information as follows:

```
n1->data = 'c';
n1->link = n2;
```

Thus, the link field of the first node points to the second node in the list. The second node is initialized in a similar fashion. The third node has NULL loaded into its link field to indicate the end of the linked-list.

The function `show_list()` traverses the linked-list, beginning with the first node, printing the character stored in each data field, until the NULL pointer is encountered. `show_list()` is passed the address of the first node (n1) via the pointer parameter `*ptr`. Execution of Program 5.1 is as follows:

```
The linked-list is as follows: cat
```

Remember that *any* type of data can be stored in a node. The programs that follow will all use single-character data fields to demonstrate various operations on linked-lists.

Conclusion

A simple method of initializing a linked-list was demonstrated in this section. Test your understanding with the following section review.

5.2 Section Review

1. What is done with the addresses returned by `malloc()`?
2. Does it matter what order the `n1.link`, `n2.link`, and `n3.link` fields are initialized before calling `show_list()`?
3. How does `show_list()` know when it has reached node n3?

5.3   Adding a Node to a Linked-List

Since linked-lists are created dynamically, during run time, there are several cases to consider when adding a node. These cases are as follows:

- The linked-list may be empty.
- The node is added to the beginning of the list.
- The node is added to the end of the list.
- The node is added somewhere in the middle of the list.
- The node is not created because system memory is exhausted.

The method used to add a node to a linked-list is chosen by the programmer for one reason or another. For example, it is very efficient to add a node to the beginning of a linked-list, but possibly inefficient to add one to the end, especially for long lists. We will see why shortly.

Program 5.2 adds nodes to the end of a linked-list as it is created by a user. Three of the conditions listed can apply to this program: the linked-list is empty, the node is added at the end of the list, or the node is not created. Let us assume this last condition will not occur since Program 5.2 does not require a lot of memory. The user simply enters characters one by one, which are placed into newly allocated nodes. The list is complete when the user presses the return key.

Program 5.2

```
#include <stdio.h>
#include <stdlib.h>

        typedef struct node
        {
                char data;
                struct node *link;
        } LNODE;

void show_list(LNODE *ptr);
void add_node(LNODE **ptr, char item);

main()
{
        LNODE *n1 = NULL;
        char item;

        do
        {
                printf("\nEnter item: ");
                item = getche();
                if(item != '\r')
                        add_node(&n1,item);
        } while(item != '\r');
        printf("\nThe new linked-list is: ");
        show_list(n1);
}

void show_list(LNODE *ptr)
{
        while(ptr != NULL)
        {
                printf("%c",ptr->data);
                ptr = ptr->link;
        }
        printf("\n");
}

void add_node(LNODE **ptr, char item)
```

```
{
        LNODE *p1, *p2;

        p1 = *ptr;
        if(p1 == NULL)
        {
                p1 = malloc(sizeof(LNODE));
                if(p1 != NULL)
                {
                        p1->data = item;
                        p1->link = NULL;
                        *ptr = p1;

                }
        }
        else
        {
                while(p1->link != NULL)
                        p1 = p1->link;
                p2 = malloc(sizeof(LNODE));
                if(p2 != NULL)
                {
                        p2->data = item;
                        p2->link = NULL;
                        p1->link = p2;

                }

        }

}
```

Figure 5.3 shows the three-step process required to add a new node to an existing linked-list. Notice that the new node is added to the end of the list. If the list was originally empty, the process requires a different step 3, in which the list variable is assigned the address of the new node.

A sample execution of Program 5.2 is as follows:

```
Enter item: c
Enter item: p
Enter item: u
Enter item:
The new linked-list is: cpu
```

Notice that the add_node() function uses a while() loop to search for the last node in the linked-list before the new node is allocated and attached to the list. This search for the NULL link could take a significant amount of time when the list is long. If efficiency is important, a second pointer can be used that always points to the *last* node in the list. This pointer must be updated every time a node is added.

Adding a new node to the beginning of a linked-list is a simpler matter.

Program 5.3 shows how the letter 's' is inserted into the beginning of a three-element linked-list 'cat' to make the new linked-list 'scat'. Care must be taken to update the pointer to the list correctly.

1. Get new node:

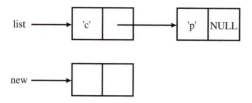

2. Assign data and link fields:

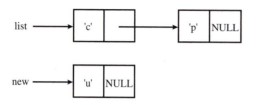

3. Establish link to existing list:

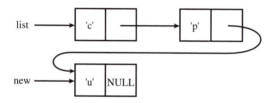

Figure 5.3   Adding a Node to a Linked-List

Program 5.3

```
#include <stdio.h>
#include <stdlib.h>

        typedef struct node
        {
                char data;
                struct node *link;
        } LNODE;

void show_list(LNODE *ptr);
void insert_at_head(LNODE **ptr, char item);

main()
{
        LNODE *n1, *n2, *n3;

        n1 = malloc(sizeof(LNODE));
        n2 = malloc(sizeof(LNODE));
        n3 = malloc(sizeof(LNODE));
```

```
                n1->data = 'c';
                n1->link = n2;
                n2->data = 'a';
                n2->link = n3;
                n3->data = 't';
                n3->link = NULL;

                printf("The linked-list is as follows: ");
                show_list(n1);
                insert_at_head(&n1,'s');
                printf("The new linked-list is: ");
                show_list(n1);
        }

        void show_list(LNODE *ptr)
        {
                while(ptr != NULL)
                {
                        printf("%c",ptr->data);
                        ptr = ptr->link;
                }
                printf("\n");
        }

        void insert_at_head(LNODE **ptr, char item)
        {
                LNODE *new;

                new = malloc(sizeof(LNODE));
                if(new != NULL)
                {
                        new->data = item;
                        new->link = *ptr;
                        *ptr = new;
                }
        }
```

Program 5.3 produces the following result during execution:

```
The linked-list is as follows: cat
The new linked-list is: scat
```

Program 5.4 also inserts a new node containing 's' into an existing list, but inserts it at the end of the list. This requires a search through the list to find the last node.

Program 5.4

```
#include <stdio.h>
#include <stdlib.h>

        typedef struct node
        {
                char data;
```

```
                struct node *link;
          } LNODE;

void show_list(LNODE *ptr);
void insert_at_tail(LNODE *ptr, char item);

main()
{
        LNODE *n1, *n2, *n3;

        n1 = malloc(sizeof(LNODE));
        n2 = malloc(sizeof(LNODE));
        n3 = malloc(sizeof(LNODE));

        n1->data = 'c';
        n1->link = n2;
        n2->data = 'a';
        n2->link = n3;
        n3->data = 't';
        n3->link = NULL;

        printf("The linked-list is as follows: ");
        show_list(n1);
        insert_at_tail(n1,'s');
        printf("The new linked-list is: ");
        show_list(n1);
}

void show_list(LNODE *ptr)
{
        while(ptr != NULL)
        {
                printf("%c",ptr->data);
                ptr = ptr->link;
        }
        printf("\n");
}

void insert_at_tail(LNODE *ptr, char item)
{
        LNODE *new;

        while(ptr->link != NULL)
                ptr = ptr->link;
        new = malloc(sizeof(LNODE));
        if(new != NULL)
        {
                ptr->link = new;
                new->data = item;
                new->link = NULL;
        }
}
```

This causes the original list `'cat'` to become `'cats'`, as shown in the following execution:

```
The linked-list is as follows: cat
The new linked-list is: cats
```

You may have noticed that the first node in the linked-list is referred to as the **head** and the last node as the **tail.** This is a common practice. It is also common practice for the programmer to keep track of each pointer, and use both of them accordingly. This allows quick insertion at each end of the list. You are encouraged to figure out how to use both pointers yourself.

Finally, inserting a node somewhere in the middle of a linked-list is useful for specific applications such as the *Insertion Sort,* which sorts a group of numbers by inserting them one at a time into their proper position in the sorted list. This technique is left as a programming exercise.

Conclusion

In this section you saw several methods used to add nodes to a linked-list. Check your understanding with the following section review.

5.3 Section Review

1. How many ways are there to add a node to a linked-list?
2. What types of conditions must be dealt with when adding a node to a linked-list?
3. How can a node be efficiently added to the end of a linked-list?
4. What is meant by head and tail?

5.4   Deleting a Node from a Linked-List

There are times when it is necessary to delete a node from a linked-list. Consider a function that builds a linked-list as it generates a set of graphical coordinates for an object. When the function is done using the linked-list, it must free the allocated node memory *before* returning to its caller. This can be accomplished by deleting nodes one at a time until the list is empty.

Just as there were three ways to add a node to a linked-list, there are three ways to delete a node. These cases are as follows:

- The node is deleted from the beginning of the list.
- The node is deleted from the end of the list.
- The node is deleted from somewhere in the middle of the list.

As always, care must be taken to correctly update the pointer fields during the operation.

Figure 5.4 shows how a node is removed from the head of a linked-list. The address in the link field of the first node replaces the address in the list variable (which causes the list variable to now point to the second node). The first node is then returned to the storage pool. This is accomplished through the use of the `<stdlib.h>` function `free()`. If the first node is not returned, it stays allocated. But because the list variable has been changed, there is no way to access the first node anymore (without guessing its address). In this case

1. Original list:

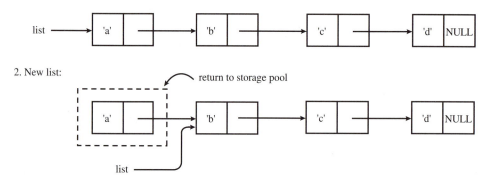

2. New list:

Figure 5.4   Removing a Node from the Head of a Linked-List

the first node has become **garbage.** When many nodes are discarded in this fashion it is possible to run out of memory for new nodes. A cleverly written *garbage collection* routine must then be used to retrieve all lost nodes.

Program 5.5 shows how a node is deleted from the beginning of a linked-list.

Program 5.5

```
#include <stdio.h>
#include <stdlib.h>

        typedef struct node
        {
                char data;
                struct node *link;
        } LNODE;

void show_list(LNODE *ptr);
void delete_head(LNODE **ptr);

main()
{
        LNODE *n1, *n2, *n3, *n4;

        n1 = malloc(sizeof(LNODE));
        n2 = malloc(sizeof(LNODE));
        n3 = malloc(sizeof(LNODE));
        n4 = malloc(sizeof(LNODE));

        n1->data = 'a';
        n1->link = n2;
        n2->data = 'b';
        n2->link = n3;
        n3->data = 'c';
        n3->link = n4;
        n4->data = 'd';
        n4->link = NULL;
```

```
        printf("The linked-list is as follows: ");
        show_list(n1);
        delete_head(&n1);
        printf("The new linked-list is: ");
        show_list(n1);
}

void show_list(LNODE *ptr)
{
        while(ptr != NULL)
        {
                printf("%c",ptr->data);
                ptr = ptr->link;
        }
        printf("\n");
}

void delete_head(LNODE **ptr)
{
        LNODE *p;

        p = *ptr;
        if(p != NULL)
        {
                p = p->link;
                free(*ptr);
        }
        *ptr = p;
}
```

The original linked-list is 'abcd'. Deleting the first node produces the new list, 'bcd'. This is supported by the result of executing Program 5.5:

```
The linked-list is as follows: abcd
The new linked-list is: bcd
```

Deleting a node from the end of a linked-list requires a search to find the last node in the list. Figure 5.5 shows the necessary steps. It is important to maintain two pointers during the deletion process. One pointer to the last node is insufficient, because the link field of the second-to-last node must be changed to NULL. Program 5.6 shows how this process is accomplished.

Program 5.6

```
#include <stdio.h>
#include <stdlib.h>

        typedef struct node
        {
                char data;
                struct node *link;
        } LNODE;
```

1. Original list:

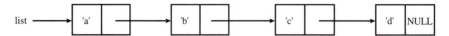

2. Find last node:

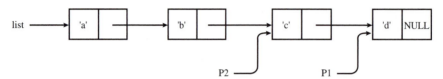

3. Reassign link field:

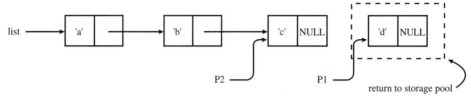

Figure 5.5 Removing a Node from the End of a Linked-List

```
void show_list(LNODE *ptr);
void delete_tail(LNODE **ptr);

main()
{
        LNODE *n1, *n2, *n3, *n4;

        n1 = malloc(sizeof(LNODE));
        n2 = malloc(sizeof(LNODE));
        n3 = malloc(sizeof(LNODE));
        n4 = malloc(sizeof(LNODE));

        n1->data = 'a';
        n1->link = n2;
        n2->data = 'b';
        n2->link = n3;
        n3->data = 'c';
        n3->link = n4;
        n4->data = 'd';
        n4->link = NULL;

        printf("The linked-list is as follows: ");
        show_list(n1);
        delete_tail(&n1);
        printf("The new linked-list is: ");
        show_list(n1);
}
```

```
void show_list(LNODE *ptr)
{
        while(ptr != NULL)
        {
                printf("%c",ptr->data);
                ptr = ptr->link;
        }
        printf("\n");
}

void delete_tail(LNODE **ptr)
{
        LNODE *p1, *p2;

        p1 = *ptr;
        if(p1 != NULL)
        {
                if(p1->link == NULL)
                {
                        free(*ptr);
                        *ptr = NULL;
                }
                else
                {
                        while(p1->link != NULL)
                        {
                                p2 = p1;
                                p1 = p1->link;
                        }
                        p2->link = NULL;
                        free(p1);
                }
        }
}
```

A sample execution of Program 5.6 is as follows:

```
The linked-list is as follows: abcd
The new linked-list is: abc
```

Note that in each of the previous four programs the complexity of the insert and delete functions was a result of the fact that the linked-list may contain 0, 1, or more elements. Different steps are required in each case.

Deleting a node from somewhere in the middle of a linked-list means we are looking for a specific node to delete. This requires a search to find the correct node to delete, and is accomplished by examining the data field of each node. The delete_tail() function in Program 5.6 requires a few simple modifications to allow deletions from the middle of the linked- list. You may want to hold off on these modifications until you have completed Section 5.5.

Conclusion

In this section you were introduced to the methods used to delete nodes from a linked-list. Check your understanding of this material with the following section review.

5.4 Section Review

1. How many ways can a node be deleted from a linked-list?
2. Why are two pointers necessary when deleting a node from the end of a linked-list?
3. How is a node deleted from the beginning of a linked-list?
4. What is garbage?
5. Why is the `free()` function used when deleting a node?

5.5   Searching a Linked-List

The last operation on linked-lists we will examine is that of searching a list for a particular item. Program 5.7 allows the user to enter the character to search for in a given linked-list.

Program 5.7

```
#include <stdio.h>
#include <stdlib.h>

        typedef struct node
        {
                char data;
                struct node *link;
        } LNODE;

void show_list(LNODE *ptr);
int search_list(LNODE *ptr, char item);

main()
{
        LNODE *n1, *n2, *n3, *n4;
        char item;
        int found;

        n1 = malloc(sizeof(LNODE));
        n2 = malloc(sizeof(LNODE));
        n3 = malloc(sizeof(LNODE));
        n4 = malloc(sizeof(LNODE));

        n1->data = 'a';
        n1->link = n2;
        n2->data = 'b';
        n2->link = n3;
        n3->data = 'c';
        n3->link = n4;
        n4->data = 'd';
        n4->link = NULL;
```

```
        printf("The linked-list is as follows: ");
        show_list(n1);
        printf("Enter character to search for: ");
        item = getche();
        found = search_list(n1,item);
        printf("\nThe character %c was",item);
        found ? printf(" ") : printf(" not ");
        printf("found in the list: ");
        show_list(n1);
}

void show_list(LNODE *ptr)
{
        while(ptr != NULL)
        {
                printf("%c",ptr->data);
                ptr = ptr->link;
        }
        printf("\n");
}

int search_list(LNODE *ptr, char item)
{
        if(ptr == NULL)
                return(0);
        else
        {
                do
                {
                        if(ptr->data == item)
                                return(1);
                        ptr = ptr->link;
                } while(ptr != NULL);
                return(0);
        }
}
```

Two executions of Program 5.7 follow:

```
The linked-list is as follows: abcd
Enter character to search for: e
The character e was not found in the list: abcd

The linked-list is as follows: abcd
Enter character to search for: c
The character c was found in the list: abcd
```

The results shown in these two executions demonstrate that there are two possible outcomes to the search:

• The node *is not* found in the linked-list.
• The node *is* found in the linked-list.

If the node is not in the list, the search must be stopped when the NULL pointer is encountered.

Note that the search time for a character that is not in the list increases when the number of nodes in the list increases. This may be a consideration in time-critical applications. For this reason, efficient searches are accomplished by using a different data structure called a hash table (covered in Chapter 9).

Conclusion

The last linked-list operation, searching, was presented in this section. Check your understanding of this material with the following section review.

5.5 Section Review

1. Why must the data field *and* the link field be examined during a search?
2. What are the two values returned by search_list()?
3. What does search_list() do when the linked-list being searched is empty?
4. In general, why is it inefficient to search a large linked-list?

5.6   Multiply Linked-Lists

It is possible to have two, three, or even more link fields in each node of a linked-list. Using only two link fields allows us to do the following:

- Make a **doubly linked-list** that has links running forwards *and backwards* in a list.
- Represent data structures such as two-dimensional matrices, ragged arrays, and binary trees (covered in Chapter 7). Simple examples of these structures are shown in Figure 5.6.

Other application-specific data structures can also be represented using multiple link fields. In this section we will examine the operation of a bidirectional **ring.** Figure 5.7 illustrates the use of a bidirectional ring to create a simple two-bit, or four-state, counter containing the values '0,' '1,' '2,' and '3.' The link fields are connected to allow for the counter to either increase or decrease with a wraparound from '0' to '3' and '3' to '0.'

By using either the up-link or down-link pointer fields, the various values, or states, of the counter can be cycled through. The data can be used for display purposes or used by some other process to control some piece of hardware. The state pointer is used to identify the current state. A more complex system will have additional states and many different interconnections between the states. Consider a graphics application where individual images are drawn to the screen in a certain order to simulate motion (walking, running, jumping). The sequence of images could be stored in a ring as a set of pointers (one pointer to a node). Stepping through the ring one node at a time selects the images in sequence. Adding or deleting nodes from the ring causes an instant change in the behavior of the object in the animation. Using a bidirectional ring allows the animation to be played backwards easily.

Conclusion

In Chapters 6 through 8 you will see other examples of **multiply linked-lists.** For now, check your understanding of the material with the following section review.

Matrix
pointer

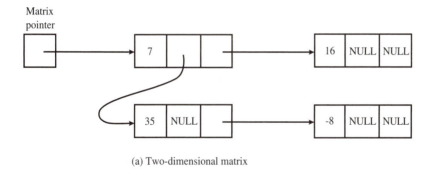

(a) Two-dimensional matrix

Array
pointer

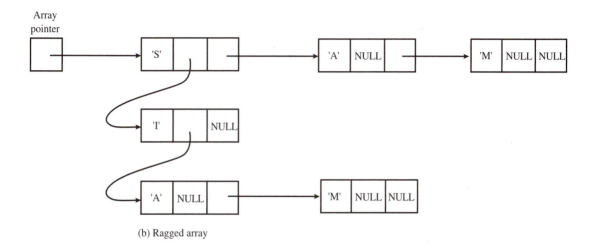

(b) Ragged array

Tree
pointer

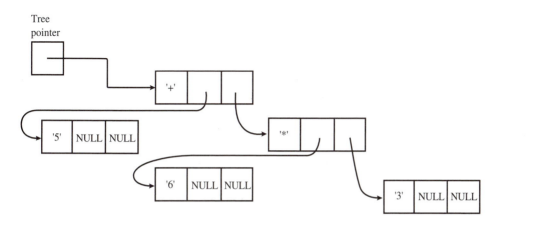

(c) Binary tree storing post-order expression 5 6 3 * +

Figure 5.6 Simple Dual-Link Data Structures

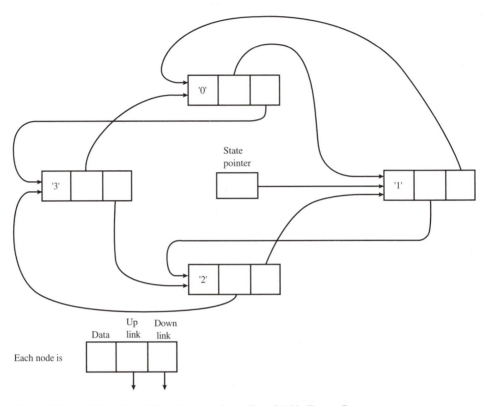

Figure 5.7   A Bidirectional Ring Representing a Two-Bit Up/Down Counter

---

5.6 Section Review

1. Why use more than one link in a linked-list?
2. Explain why there are so many NULL links in Figure 5.6.
3. What is the maximum number of links required to find any element in each of the data structures in Figure 5.6?
4. Are additional link fields needed to add four more states to the up/down counter of Figure 5.7?

5.7   A C++ Linked-List Object

When we use C++ to create linked-list objects, we automatically get the ability to maintain several linked-list objects simultaneously without the messy coding that would be necessary if we were using C. Because of this, linked-list objects add a new level of sophistication to C++ programs. Most of the following chapters provide C++ example programs to reinforce many of the data structures inside of an object oriented environment.

Let's begin by creating a class to describe the linked-list object. Remember, a C++ class definition is similar to a blueprint used to build a house. The C++ class definition is the blueprint for building the object. The class definition for a linked-list using our previous LNODE definition looks like this:

```
        typedef struct node
        {
              int data;
              struct node *link;
        } LNODE;

class LINKEDLIST {
public:
      LNODE *list_ptr;

      LINKEDLIST(void);
      void show_list(void);
      void insert_sort(int item);
};
```

The class LINKEDLIST uses the LNODE data structure to maintain the data and the pointer to the next element in the list. Three functions are defined in the class. The class uses a constructor, called LINKEDLIST(), when the linked-list is instantiated. The other two functions, show_list() and insert_sort(), are used to display the sorted list and add elements to the sorted list, respectively.

Program 5.8 uses this class definition to instantiate a linked-list object. The insert_sort() function is designed to add a new node into the linked-list object at the correct location. It requires two pointers to add a new node to the list. show_list() simply displays the contents of the linked-list object mylist.

Program 5.8

```
#include <iostream.h>
#include <stdlib.h>

#define FALSE 0
#define TRUE  1

        typedef struct node
        {
              int data;
              struct node *link;
        } LNODE;

class LINKEDLIST {
public:
      LNODE *list_ptr;

      LINKEDLIST(void);
      void show_list(void);
      void insert_sort(int item);
};
```

```
main()
{
        int i;
        int value;

        LINKEDLIST mylist;

        cout << "Input:   ";
        for(i = 0; i < 8; i++)
        {
                value = rand() % 256;
                cout << value << "\t";
                mylist.insert_sort(value);
        }
        cout << "\nOutput: ";
        mylist.show_list();
}


LINKEDLIST::LINKEDLIST()
{
        list_ptr = NULL;
}

void LINKEDLIST::insert_sort(int item)
{
        LNODE *p, *p1, *p2;
        int found;

        p = new LNODE;
        if (p == NULL)
                cout << "Error! Cannot allocate node.\n";
        else
        {
                p->data = item;
                if (list_ptr == NULL)
                {
                        p->link = NULL;
                        list_ptr = p;
                }
                else
                {
                        found = FALSE;
                        p1 = list_ptr;
                        p2 = p1;
                        do
                        {
                                if (item < p2->data)
                                        found = TRUE;
                                else
                                {
```

```
                                        p1 = p2;
                                        p2 = p2->link;
                                }
                        } while ((p2 != NULL) && !found);
                        if ((p1 == p2) && (p1 == list_ptr))
                        {
                                p->link = p1;
                                list_ptr = p;
                        }
                        else
                        {
                                p1->link = p;
                                p->link = p2;
                        }
                }
        }
}


void LINKEDLIST::show_list()
{
        LNODE *p;

        p = list_ptr;
        while(p != NULL)
        {
                cout << p->data << "\t";
                p = p->link;
        }
        cout << "\n";
}
```

A sample execution of Program 5.8 looks like this:

```
Input:  90     130  230  66   136  205  187  15
Output: 15     66   90   130  136  187  205  230
```

The numbers in the output list have been sorted into ascending order, just as insert_sort() was designed to do.

Conclusion

In this section we saw our first C++ class. Check your understanding of the material with the following section review.

5.7 Section Review

1. What advantage is there to using C++ to implement a linked-list?
2. What are the possible conditions that may occur when inserting a node into mylist?
3. What is the constructor LINKEDLIST() used for?

Study Questions

General Concepts

Section 5.1

1. What determines the size of a node?
2. Which is more convenient, static allocation or dynamic allocation?
3. Why does a linked-list require more memory space than an array when storing the same set of numbers?

Section 5.2

4. What is needed to access a linked-list?
5. How does `show_list()` know when it has reached the end of the linked-list?

Section 5.3

6. Is it easier to add a node to the beginning or the end of a linked-list?
7. What happens if the link field of the new node added to a list is unassigned?
8. When is it not possible to add a node to a linked-list?

Section 5.4

9. Is it possible to delete a node at the end of a linked-list using a single pointer?
10. How is a node deleted from the end of a linked-list?
11. What happens if we do not free allocated memory when deleting a node?

Section 5.5

12. What happens to the search time as the number of nodes increases?
13. How does the search algorithm know an item is not in the linked-list?
14. What conditions cause the search process to stop?

Section 5.6

15. Show how a set of five cities is connected using multiply linked-lists. Each city can have up to three connections.
16. Is there a limit to the number of links a node might have?

Section 5.7

17. What happens if a new node cannot be allocated in the `insert_sort()` function?
18. How is the list pointer initialized in Program 5.8?
19. How does `insert_sort()` determine if there is only one node in the list prior to insertion?

Program Design

When writing the following programs, use the new data structures discussed in this chapter. The use of pointers and recursion is also suggested for programs that can use them.

20. Write a program that accepts ten floats from the user, stores them in a linked-list, and then searches the list for the largest number and displays it.
21. Write a program that inserts a new integer into its correct position in an ordered linked-list. Use the following list in your program:

    6   13   29   32   45

    Test your program by inserting the following numbers: 3, 17, 40, and 50, one at a time.
22. Write a program that deletes a node from the middle of a linked-list.
23. Design a program to sort the items stored in a linked-list.
24. Write a program that stores a `char` in one node, a `string` in the next node, an `int` in the third node, a `float` in the fourth node, and a pointer to the two-dimensional array `stuff[][]` in the last node. Use the same node structure for all five nodes.

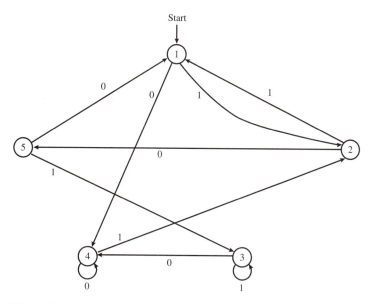

Figure 5.8   State Diagram for Questions 25 and 26

25. Design a program to implement the state diagram shown in Figure 5.8. The user enters a series of 1s and 0s and the program displays the state that is reached. For example, 110 takes you to state 4.
26. Write a program that determines all four-character strings that end up in state 3 using Figure 5.8.
27. Write a program that uses a bidirectional ring to store all of the uppercase letters in the alphabet. The data field should store two characters, one for the uppercase letter associated with the node and a second containing the encrypted character for the uppercase letter. Have the program encrypt and decrypt user input strings.
28. Figure 5.9 shows the definition of a node containing several link fields. Design a program that uses the node to speed up access to a linked-list containing sixteen or fewer nodes.

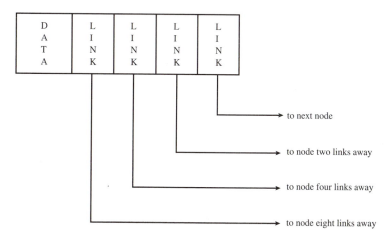

Figure 5.9   Node for Question 28

29. Write a program that reverses a linked-list so that the node that used to be the tail becomes the head.
30. Write a recursive function that displays the contents of a linked-list.
31. Design a C++ member function for the LINKEDLIST class called `delete_highest()` that finds and deletes the node containing the highest integer value in its data field.

6 Stacks and Queues

Objectives

This chapter gives you the opportunity to learn:

1. The differences between FIFO and LIFO data structures.
2. The difference between static and dynamic allocation methods.
3. The operation of stacks and queues.
4. How an executing C/C++ program uses the run-time stack.
5. How a queue can perform job scheduling.
6. How a prioritized queue works.

Key Terms

Push

En-queue

Pop

De-queue

Empty

Run-Time Stack

Calling Convention

Priority Queue

Priority

Outline

Introduction

In this chapter we will explore the operation of two similar data structures: the stack and the queue. Both structures have wide-ranging applications, including operating system control, natural language processing, telephone and network switches, expression evaluation, and simulation. Let us begin by examining the differences between stacks and queues.

6.1   FIFO Versus LIFO

FIFO and LIFO are acronyms that stand for, respectively, First-In-First-Out and Last-In-First-Out data structures. The FIFO is also commonly called a queue, and the LIFO a stack. The name of the operation to *add* an element to a stack is called **push.** The name of the operation to add an element to a queue is called **en-queue.** The name of the operation to *remove* elements from the stack and queue are called **pop** and **de-queue,** respectively. Table 6.1 summarizes the stack and queue operations. Figure 6.1 illustrates the differences between these two data structures.

First, notice that data enters *and exits* from the same end of the stack, whereas the queue has data entering at one end and leaving at the other end. This means that a single pointer will be sufficient for maintaining the stack, and two pointers must be used for queue operations.

Another difference between stacks and queues can be seen by examining the relationship between the input data and the output data. For example, in Figure 6.1 the four input characters 'L,' 'I,' 'F,' and 'O' come off the stack in *reverse* order. Compare this result with that of the queue, in which the four input characters 'F,' 'I,' 'F,' and 'O' come out of the queue in the *same order* that they went in.

Both stacks and queues have specific applications well suited to their characteristic operation. We will examine some of these applications in the remaining sections.

Conclusion

In this section you were introduced to the stack and queue data structures. Check your understanding of the material with the following section review.

6.1 Section Review

1. What does FIFO stand for?
2. What does LIFO stand for?
3. What are the differences between the FIFO and LIFO data structures?

Table 6.1   Stack and Queue Operations

Operation	Stack	Queue
Add an Item	PUSH	En-queue
Remove an Item	POP	De-queue

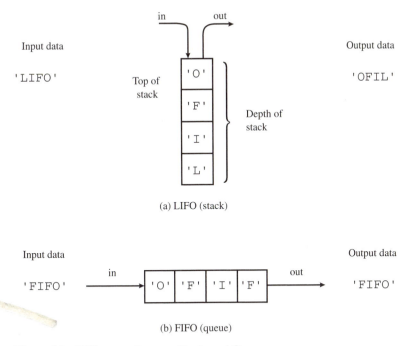

(a) LIFO (stack)

(b) FIFO (queue)

Figure 6.1   Differences Between Stacks and Queues

6.2   Static and Dynamic Considerations

The more items pushed onto a stack or entered into a queue, the more memory is required. This leads to an interesting question: How do we know if there is enough memory available to store all the items?

There are two ways to allocate memory for a stack or queue: statically or dynamically. In a static allocation, a fixed size block of memory is allocated for the stack or queue. A stack capable of storing 25 integers might be allocated a 50-byte block of memory (2 bytes per integer). If the programmer knows for certain that no more than 25 integers will ever be pushed onto the stack, the fixed size memory block will work fine.

If, however, the number of pushes is not known in advance, then it is possible that the statically allocated stack could fill up with data, and then overrun into some other data area when additional pushes are encountered. This situation generally leads to unpredictable program execution. Trying to fix the problem by allocating large memory blocks is not a very good solution either, because you may end up wasting much of the allocated memory when there is little stack activity. The same problems show up in statically allocated queues.

Dynamic memory allocation solves the static memory-size problem. Memory space to store a new stack or queue item is allocated only when needed. The number of items that can be stored depends only on the amount of free memory space in the system. The stack or queue can be as large or small as necessary, with no wasted space, since anything removed by a pop or de-queue operation will also free up its associated memory space.

One way to implement a dynamically allocated stack or queue is to use a linked-list. For a stack, the push and pop operations will both access the head of the list. Two pointers will be used to access a queue, one for the head and the second for the tail. Furthermore, the queue will require each node to have two links, one for the previous node and the second for the next node. All examples in the remaining sections will be based on linked-list representations of the stack and the queue.

Conclusion

In this section you were exposed to the limitations of static allocation in stack and queue structures. The more efficient dynamic allocation method was also covered. Check your understanding of this material with the following section review.

6.2 Section Review

1. What are the limitations of static allocation?
2. What happens if data is pushed too many times onto a statically allocated stack?
3. When is memory allocated in a dynamic-allocation scheme?
4. What limits the size of a stack or queue in a dynamic-allocation scheme?

6.3   Stack Operations

The operations that can be performed on a stack are push, pop, and **empty.** These three functions are all that is necessary to exploit the powerful features of the stack. Several push and pop operations are performed in Figure 6.2. The last item pushed is referred to as the *top of the stack.*

Since we will be using a linked-list to store the stack information, we must declare a stack variable that will point to the node at the top of the stack. This can be done in the following way:

```
LNODE *stack;
```

where LNODE is the same custom type used in Chapter 5 to define a node for a linked-list. Recall how it was structured:

```
typedef struct node
{
    char data;
    struct node *link;
} LNODE;
```

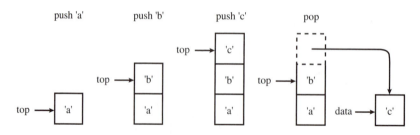

Figure 6.2   Stack Operation During Push and Pop

The first stack function we will look at is `empty()`. This function is necessary because we never want to try to pop an empty stack. The results would most likely be unpredictable. An empty stack is represented by storing a NULL pointer in the stack variable. The `empty()` function returns TRUE if the stack is empty. It returns FALSE if it is not empty.

The `empty()` function looks like this:

```
int empty(LNODE *ptr)
{
     if(ptr == NULL)
          return(TRUE);
     else
          return(FALSE);
}
```

If the stack variable contains NULL, there are no nodes in the stack's linked-list, so the stack is empty.

The `push()` function is used to add elements to the stack. `push()` adds elements to an empty stack or a stack that already contains data. The only difference between these two situations is found in the way the pointer is used to maintain the stack's linked-list of elements. If the stack is empty, the pointer field of the new node is initialized to NULL. If the stack is not empty, the pointer field of the new node is set to the address of the node that is currently the top of the stack. The stack variable is then updated to point to the address of the new node (the new top of the stack).

The `push()` function is implemented in the following fashion:

```
void push(LNODE **ptr, char item)
{
     LNODE *p;

     p = malloc(sizeof(LNODE));
     if (p == NULL)
               printf("Error! Cannot push new item.\n");
     else
     {
          p->data = item;
          if(empty(*ptr))
               p->link = NULL;
          else
               p->link = *ptr;
          *ptr = p;
     }
}
```

The `pop()` function does the opposite of the `push()` function. It returns the information located at the top of the stack and adjusts the stack pointer appropriately. Of course, we do not want to pop an empty stack.

```
void pop(LNODE **ptr, char *item)
{
     LNODE *p1;

     p1 = *ptr;
```

```
if(empty(p1))
{
    printf("Error! The stack is empty.\n");
    *item = '\0';
}
else
{
    *item = p1->data;
    *ptr = p1->link;
    free(p1);
}
}
```

Now that we have defined all of our functions, let us look at an application that uses a stack. Program 6.1 demonstrates the operation of a character stack by pushing and popping a sequence of characters.

Program 6.1

```
#include <stdio.h>
#include <stdlib.h>

#define FALSE 0
#define TRUE  1

        typedef struct node
        {
                char data;
                struct node *link;
        } LNODE;

void show_stack(LNODE *ptr);
int empty(LNODE *ptr);
void push(LNODE **ptr, char item);
void pop(LNODE **ptr, char *item);

main()
{
        LNODE *stacka = NULL;
        char item;

        push(&stacka,'a');
        push(&stacka,'b');
        push(&stacka,'c');
        printf("The stack is as follows: ");
        show_stack(stacka);
        pop(&stacka,&item);
        printf("\nThe first item popped is %c\n",item);
        pop(&stacka,&item);
        printf("The second item popped is %c\n",item);
        pop(&stacka,&item);
```

```
                printf("The third item popped is %c\n",item);
                pop(&stacka,&item);
}

void show_stack(LNODE *ptr)
{
        while(ptr != NULL)
        {
                printf("%c",ptr->data);
                ptr = ptr->link;
        }
        printf("\n");
}

int empty(LNODE *ptr)
{
        if(ptr == NULL)
                return(TRUE);
        else
                return(FALSE);
}

void push(LNODE **ptr, char item)
{
        LNODE *p;

        p = malloc(sizeof(LNODE));
        if (p == NULL)
                printf("Error! Cannot push new item.\n");
        else
        {
            p->data = item;
            if(empty(*ptr))
                p->link = NULL;
            else
                p->link = *ptr;
            *ptr = p;
        }
}

void pop(LNODE **ptr, char *item)
{
        LNODE *p1;

        p1 = *ptr;
        if(empty(p1))
        {
                printf("Error! The stack is empty.\n");
                *item = '\0';
```

```
        }
        else
        {
                *item = p1->data;
                *ptr = p1->link;
                free(p1);
        }
}
```

Program 6.1's execution looks like this:

```
The stack is as follows: cba

The first item popped is c
The second item popped is b
The third item popped is a
Error! The stack is empty.
```

Note that the first item pushed ('a') is the last item popped.

Another stack application involves reversing the characters of a string. Program 6.2 uses a stack to reverse the characters of a user-supplied string. Figure 6.3 shows the basic process. The string characters are pushed onto a stack one by one. When the entire string has been pushed onto the stack, the last character of the string is on top of the stack. As characters are now popped off the stack, they are written back into the string array beginning with the first position. Thus, the string is automatically reversed through the use of a single stack.

Program 6.2 makes use of the strlen() and push() functions to push all characters onto the stack, and then uses the pop() function to pop characters off the stack until it is empty. Note that the NULL character is never pushed, because it is not included in the length of the string determined by strlen().

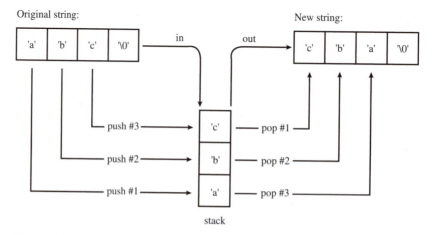

Figure 6.3   Reversing a String Using a Stack

Program 6.2

```c
#include <stdio.h>
#include <stdlib.h>

#define FALSE 0
#define TRUE  1

        typedef struct node
        {
                char data;
                struct node *link;
        } LNODE;

void show_stack(LNODE *ptr);
int empty(LNODE *ptr);
void push(LNODE **ptr, char item);
void pop(LNODE **ptr, char *item);

main()
{
        LNODE *stacka = NULL;
        char string[40], item;
        int i;

        printf("Enter a string: ");
        gets(string);
        for(i = 0; i < strlen(string); i++)
                push(&stacka,string[i]);
        printf("\nThe stack looks like this: ");
        show_stack(stacka);
        i = 0;
        while(!empty(stacka))
        {
                pop(&stacka,&string[i]);
                i++;
        }
        printf("\nThe new string is => %s",string);
}

void show_stack(LNODE *ptr)
{
        while(ptr != NULL)
        {
                printf("%c",ptr->data);
                ptr = ptr->link;
        }
        printf("\n");
}

int empty(LNODE *ptr)
{
```

```
                if(ptr == NULL)
                        return(TRUE);
                else
                        return(FALSE);
        }

void push(LNODE **ptr, char item)
{
        LNODE *p;

        p = malloc(sizeof(LNODE));
        if (p == NULL)
                printf("Error! Cannot push new item.\n");
        else
        {
            p->data = item;
            if(empty(*ptr))
                p->link = NULL;
            else
                p->link = *ptr;
            *ptr = p;
        }
}

void pop(LNODE **ptr, char *item)
{
        LNODE *p1;

        p1 = *ptr;
        if(empty(p1))
        {
                printf("Error! The stack is empty.\n");
                *item = '\0';
        }
        else
        {
                *item = p1->data;
                *ptr = p1->link;
                free(p1);
        }
}
```

Execution of Program 6.2 is as follows:

```
Enter a string: Microprocessors 123!

The stack looks like this: !321 srossecorporciM

The new string is => !321 srossecorporciM
```

Imagine what can be done if two or more stacks are used to process a string.

Conclusion

In this section we examined the implementation of a character stack. Test your under-standing of the material with the following section review.

6.3 Section Review

1. Why use a linked list instead of a character array?
2. Why is the `empty()` function necessary?
3. What happens when a push is made to an empty stack?
4. What is the last thing done by the `pop()` function?

6.4   Run-Time Stacks

The C/C++ run-time environment utilizes a **run-time stack** to keep track of various para-meters, pointers, and control information. The run-time stack is a dynamic data structure, changing size as functions start up and terminate. In this section we will examine how the run-time stack is organized and used with a program compiled for the 80x86 micro-processor family. Some knowledge of the 80x86 CPU architecture would be helpful, but is not necessary to understand the concepts being presented.

When a function uses memory, there are certain tasks that it must perform. Keep in mind that your program, when executed, is actually causing the microprocessor inside your system to perform specific tasks. It will cause bit patterns to be transferred between the microprocessor's internal registers and memory as well as many other details.

A function will use the stack to store key parts of the function. For this process, the stack pointer and base pointer are used. This process is illustrated in Figure 6.4.

The sequence shown in Figure 6.4 establishes a reference that will be used to access data located on the stack. The space just above the base pointer value contains the contents of the instruction pointer so that the program knows where to return to when the called function is completed. Note in the figure that the equivalent assembly language commands are given for each of these processes.

Saving Space for Data

A function will save memory space for any locally declared variables in the stack. This is done by decreasing the value of the stack pointer (called *going toward the top of the stack*). This is shown in Figure 6.5.

If, for example, the called function has two locally declared `int` type variables, four memory locations will be preserved for their values.

Saving Microprocessor Contents

There are times when may need the contents of some of the microprocessor registers to be preserved. This is usually because the values of these registers will be needed by the calling function, and the called function may modify them in some way in order to perform

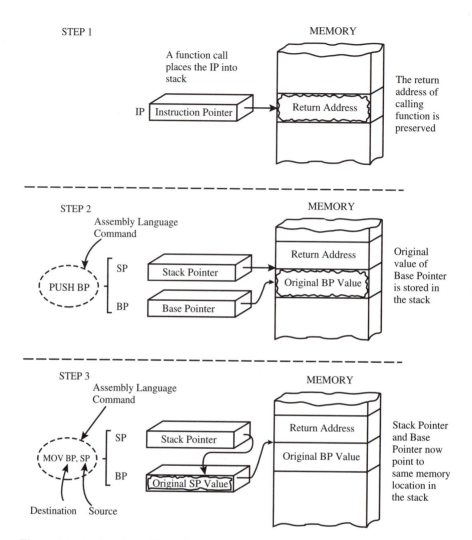

Figure 6.4 Setting Up the Frame Pointer

its required operation. Figure 6.6 shows how you would preserve the contents of the SI and DI registers onto the top of the stack.

Note that a PUSH command is used to store these contents. When returning from the called function, a POP command will be used to set these internal registers to their original values.

Arguments

So far, you have seen how a call to a function sets up the top of the stack. The bottom of the stack is also used for function arguments. Suppose, for example, that the prototype for the called function looks like this:

```
void function1(int val1, int val2);
```

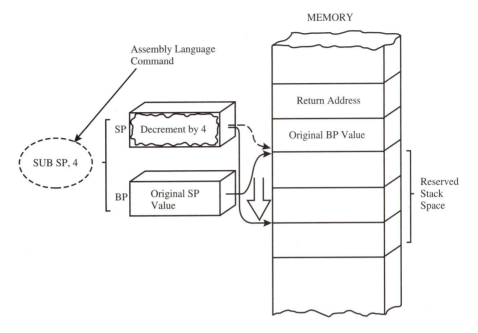

Figure 6.5   Saving Memory for Locally Declared Data

What is known as the C++ **calling convention** will cause the function parameters to be pushed onto the stack in a right-to-left order. This will immediately be followed by the address to which the program must return when the called function is completed. This process is illustrated in Figure 6.7.

The complete stack of a called function is shown in Figure 6.8. This entire portion of the run-time stack is called a stack *frame.*

When the called function has completed its execution, the original value of the IP will be returned to that register, and the data in the stack will no longer be used. This data is never erased, but it will be written over by the next called function. This is why data that is local to a function is available only when the function is active. This feature protects local data from being modified by another part of the program.

Storing Static Variables

Remember that a static variable has a lifetime that exceeds that of the function in which it is declared. Because of this, a variable of this type cannot be stored in the stack. Instead, variables that have a life longer than the function that called them are stored in the data segment of memory. In this manner, their values can be preserved.

Conclusion

In this section you got a basic idea of how a called function uses memory inside your computer. You will need this information in order to analyze assembly language programs

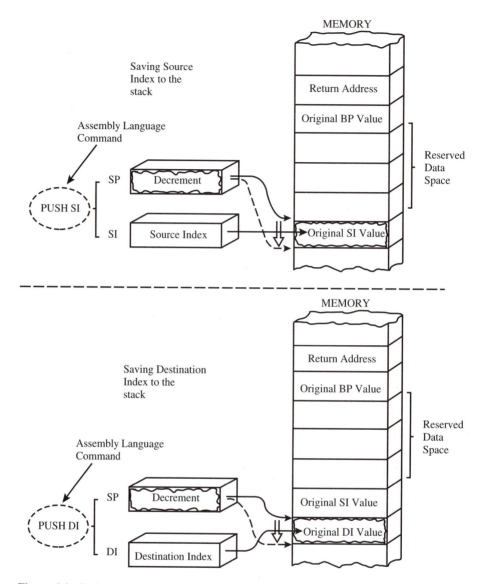

Figure 6.6   Saving the Contents of the Internal Registers

produced from your source code. Check your understanding of this section by trying the following section review.

6.4 Section Review

1.   When a function is called, what is the first internal register placed on the stack?
2.   Where on the stack are locally declared variables stored? Function parameters?
3.   What is a frame? How is it loaded?
4.   Why can't we store static data on the run-time stack?

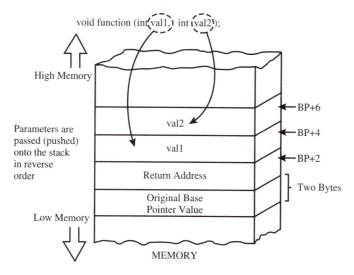

Figure 6.7 The Calling Convention

MEMORY

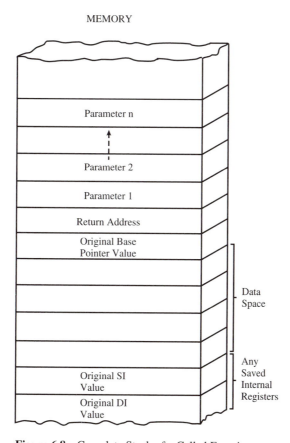

Figure 6.8 Complete Stack of a Called Function

6.5   Queue Operations

A data structure similar to a stack is the queue. The important difference between a stack and a queue is that the queue is a FIFO (First-In-First-Out) data structure. Figure 6.9 shows a sample queue after several *en-queue* (put data into the queue) and *de-queue* (take data from queue) operations.

As with the stack, we will see how a linked-list is used to implement the necessary operations. For a queue of characters, the structure of a node is defined as:

```
typedef struct node
{
    char data;
    struct node *link;
} LNODE;
```

which is the same node definition used in the stack example.

Since we are using a linked-list for implementation, it is easy to determine if the queue is empty:

```
int empty(LNODE *ptr)
{
    if(ptr == NULL)
        return(TRUE);
    else
        return(FALSE);
}
```

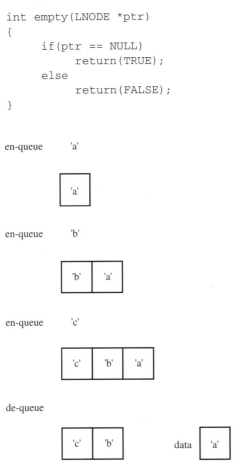

Figure 6.9 En-queue and De-queue Operations

To place data onto the queue, we only need to add the new data node to the head of the queue list.

```
void en_queue(LNODE **head, char item)
{
    LNODE *p;

    p = malloc(sizeof(LNODE));
    if(p != NULL)
    {
        p->data = item;
        p->link = *head;
        *head = p;
    }
}
```

To de-queue an item, we remove a node from the tail of the linked-list. If only one pointer to the list is maintained, it is necessary to search for the end of the list to get at the tail node. This can be done as follows:

```
void de_queue(LNODE **head, char *item)
{
    LNODE *p1, *p2;

    p1 = *head;
    if(empty(p1))
    {
        printf("Error! The queue is empty.\n");
        *item = '\0';
    }
    else
    {
        p2 = *head;
        while(p2->link != NULL)
        {
            p1 = p2;
            p2 = p2->link;
        }
        *item = p2->data;
        p1->link = NULL;
        free(p2);
        if(p1 == p2)
            *head = NULL;
    }
}
```

The code is complicated by the fact that we must maintain two pointers while searching for the last node.

If a *doubly linked-list* is used for queue implementation (as shown in Figure 6.10), it is an easy matter to de-queue an item, since a pointer to the tail is maintained along

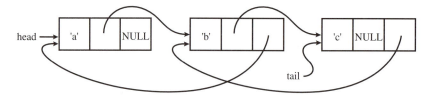

Figure 6.10   A Three-Element Queue Implemented with a Doubly Linked-List

with the head pointer. The `de_queue()` function for the doubly linked-list queue looks like this:

```
void de_queue(LNODE **head, LNODE **tail, char *item)
{
     LNODE *p;

     p = *tail;
     if(empty(p))
     {
          printf("Error! The queue is empty.\n");
          *item = '\0';
     }
     else
     {
          *item = p->data;
          *tail = p->blink;
          if (*tail == NULL)
               *head = NULL;
          else
               (*tail)->flink = NULL;
          free(p);
     }
}
```

Note that there is no need to search the list now to find the tail. Also, since backwards pointers are stored in each node, it is an easy matter to find the next-to-last node (to update its forward link). The new nodes required by the doubly linked-list are defined like this:

```
     typedef struct node
     {
          char data;
          struct node *flink;
          struct node *blink;
     } LNODE;
```

where `flink` and `blink` stand for forward-link and backward-link, respectively.

To display the current contents of the queue, we simply step through it node by node:

```
void show_queue(LNODE *ptr)
{
     while(ptr != NULL)
     {
```

```
                printf("%c",ptr->data);
                ptr = ptr->link;
        }
        printf("\n");
}
```

For the doubly linked-list, we use the `flink` pointer instead.

Program 6.3 shows how a queue is used to perform *Round-Robin job scheduling*. In round-robin scheduling, every job on the queue gets de-queued and en-queued in order of arrival, leaving for good when the execution time is complete. The structure of a queue node has been changed so that the time required for the job can be stored. Each time a job is removed from the queue, its time is decremented by one. When the job time gets to zero, the job is finished, otherwise it is placed back onto the queue.

Program 6.3

```
#include <stdio.h>
#include <stdlib.h>

#define FALSE 0
#define TRUE  1

        typedef struct node
        {
                char data;
                int num;
                struct node *link;
        } LNODE;

void show_queue(LNODE *ptr);
int empty(LNODE *ptr);
void en_queue(LNODE **head, char job, int time);
void de_queue(LNODE **head, char *job, int *time);

main()
{
        LNODE *qhead = NULL;
        char job;
        int time;

        printf("Starting job A with time of 5.\n");
        en_queue(&qhead,'A',5);
        printf("Starting job B with time of 2.\n");
        en_queue(&qhead,'B',2);
        printf("Starting job C with time of 3.\n");
        en_queue(&qhead,'C',3);
        printf("The queue is as follows: ");
        show_queue(qhead);
        printf("Running the jobs...\n");
        while (!empty(qhead))
        {
                de_queue(&qhead,&job,&time);
```

```
                        time--;
                        printf("Job: %c, %d\n",job,time);
                        if (time)
                                en_queue(&qhead,job,time);
                }
                printf("No jobs.\n");
        }

        void show_queue(LNODE *ptr)
        {
                while(ptr != NULL)
                {
                        printf("%c",ptr->data);
                        ptr = ptr->link;
                }
                printf("\n");
        }

        int empty(LNODE *ptr)
        {
                if(ptr == NULL)
                        return(TRUE);
                else
                        return(FALSE);
        }

        void en_queue(LNODE **head, char job, int time)
        {
                LNODE *p;

                p = malloc(sizeof(LNODE));
                if(p != NULL)
                {
                        p->data = job;
                        p->num = time;
                        p->link = *head;
                        *head = p;
                }
        }

        void de_queue(LNODE **head, char *job, int *time)
        {
                LNODE *p1, *p2;

                p1 = *head;
                if(empty(p1))
                {
                        printf("Error! The queue is empty.\n");
                        *job = '\0';
                        *time = 0;
                }
                else
```

```
                {
                        p2 = *head;
                        while(p2->link != NULL)
                        {
                                p1 = p2;
                                p2 = p2->link;
                        }
                        *job = p2->data;
                        *time = p2->num;
                        p1->link = NULL;
                        free(p2);
                        if(p1 == p2)
                                *head = NULL;
                }
}
```

The execution of Program 6.3 looks like this:

```
Starting job A with time of 5.
Starting job B with time of 2.
Starting job C with time of 3.
The queue is as follows: CBA
Running the jobs...
Job: A, 4
Job: B, 1
Job: C, 2
Job: A, 3
Job: B, 0
Job: C, 1
Job: A, 2
Job: C, 0
Job: A, 1
Job: A, 0
No jobs.
```

Since job A had the largest initial time, it stayed on the queue the longest. The opposite is true with job B, which only took two trips through the job queue.

Conclusion

In this section we examined the operations performed on a queue (FIFO) and saw how a queue could be used to schedule jobs. Check your understanding of this material with the following section review.

6.5 Section Review

1. Why is the de-queue operation so complicated when using a singly linked-list?
2. How does a FIFO data structure differ from a LIFO data structure?
3. How does a doubly linked-list improve de-queue time?
4. What is round-robin job scheduling?

6.6   Priority Queues

Unlike an ordinary queue, a **priority queue** de-queues items based on their **priority,** not simply their position in the queue. If all queue elements have the same priority, a priority queue operates like an ordinary queue. Otherwise, the element with the highest priority is de-queued first. If two or more elements have the same high priority, the element closest to the tail is de-queued. Figure 6.11 shows a sample priority queue and several operations performed on it.

Implementation could proceed in a number of ways. Items that are placed onto the priority queue could be put in their proper priority-based position by the en_queue() function (using an insertion sort technique). This allows a simple de-queue operation.

Another method would involve a simple en-queue operation (just place the new item at the head) and a complex de_queue() function to pick the highest priority item to de-queue. If a doubly linked-list is used to store the priority queue nodes, the de-queue operation could begin searching at the tail of the queue, keeping track of which node has the highest priority as it searches backwards. This guarantees that nodes with the same high priority will de-queue depending on which is closest to the tail. The priority_dequeue() function shown here uses this search method to find the node to remove and then calls

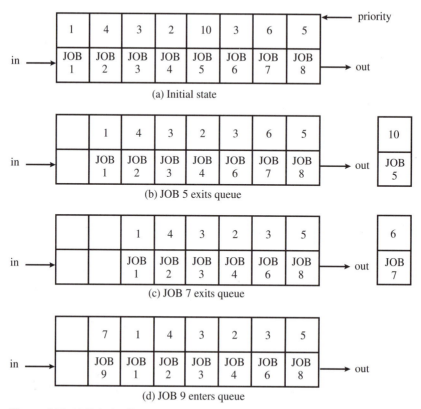

Figure 6.11   A Priority Queue

remove_node() to actually de-queue the item. The new LNODE structure includes an integer data type for the priority value.

```
typedef struct node
{
      char data;
      int priority;
      struct node *flink;
      struct node *blink;
} LNODE;

void priority_dequeue(LNODE **head, LNODE **tail, char *item)
{
      LNODE *p1, *p2;
      int priority;

      p1 = *tail;
      if(empty(p1))
      {
            printf("Error! The queue is empty.\n");
            *item = '\0';
      }
      else
      {
            priority = p1->priority;
            p2 = p1->blink;
            while (p2 != NULL)
            {
                  if (p2->priority > priority)
                  {
                        p1 = p2;
                        priority = p1->priority;
                  }
                  p2 = p2->blink;
            }
            *item = p1->data;
            remove_node(*head,*tail,p1);
      }
}
```

You are encouraged to write a program that demonstrates the use of priority_dequeue().

Conclusion

In this section we examined the operation of a priority queue. Check your understanding of the material with the following section review.

6.6 Section Review

1. What is the difference between an ordinary queue and a priority queue?
2. How is the highest-priority element selected to de-queue?

3.   What is the next job to come off the queue in Figure 6.11?
4.   Why are two pointers needed in `priority_dequeue()`?

6.7   Stack and Queue Objects

In this section we examine two C++ programs designed to show how to implement stack and queue objects. Program 6.4 defines the STACK class and uses it to evaluate arithmetic expressions.

Program 6.4

```
#include <iostream.h>
#include <stdio.h>
#include <stdlib.h>
#include <string.h>
#include <ctype.h>

#define FALSE 0
#define TRUE  1
#define equ(a,b,c) ((a == b) || (a == c))

        typedef struct node
        {
                char data;
                float num;
                struct node *link;
        } LNODE;

class STACK {
public:
        LNODE *stack_ptr;

        STACK(void);
        int empty(void);
        void push(char op,  float value);
        void pop(char *op,  float *value);
        char top(void);
};

void genval(void);
int highpri(char a,  char b);

        STACK opstack, float_stack;

main()
{
        char string[40],nop, top_op;
        float result;
        int i;

        cout << "Enter an expression: ";
```

```
        gets(string);
        for(i = 0; i < strlen(string); i++)
        {
                if (isdigit(string[i]))
                        float_stack.push('.', string[i] - '0');
                else
                if (opstack.empty())
                        opstack.push(string[i], 0);
                else
                {
                        top_op = opstack.top();
                        if (highpri(top_op,string[i]))
                                opstack.push(string[i], 0);
                        else
                        {
                                genval();
                                opstack.push(string[i], 0);
                        }
                }
        }
        while (!opstack.empty())
                genval();
        float_stack.pop(&nop,&result);
        cout << "\nThe result is " << result << "\n";
}

void genval()
{
        char nop,op;
        float v1,v2,result,nval;

        float_stack.pop(&nop,&v1);
        float_stack.pop(&nop,&v2);
        opstack.pop(&op,&nval);
        switch(op)
        {
                case '+': result = v2 + v1; break;
                case '-': result = v2 - v1; break;
                case '*': result = v2 * v1; break;
                case '/': result = v2 / v1; break;
        }
        float_stack.push('.',result);
}

int highpri(char a, char b)
{
        if (equ(a,'+','-') && equ(b,'*','/'))
                return TRUE;
        return FALSE;
}
```

```
STACK::STACK()
{
        stack_ptr = NULL;
}

int STACK::empty()
{
        if(stack_ptr == NULL)
                return(TRUE);
        else
                return(FALSE);
}

void STACK::push(char op, float value)
{
    LNODE *p;

    p = new LNODE;
    if (p == NULL)
                cout << "Error! Cannot push new item.\n";
    else
    {
        p->data = op;
        p->num = value;
        if(empty())
              p->link = NULL;
        else
              p->link = stack_ptr;
        stack_ptr = p;
    }
}

void STACK::pop(char *op, float *value)
{
        LNODE *p1;

        p1 = stack_ptr;
        if(empty())
        {
                cout << "Error! The stack is empty.\n";
                *op = '\0';
                *value = 0.0;
        }
        else
        {
                *op = p1->data;
                *value = p1->num;
                stack_ptr = p1->link;
                delete(p1);
        }
}
```

```
char STACK::top()
{
        if (stack_ptr != NULL)
                return stack_ptr->data;
        else
                return '\0';
}
```

Several sample executions of Program 6.4 demonstrate how both stack objects (`opstack` and `float_stack`) work together to generate the correct result.

```
Enter an expression: 1+2*3/4-5

The result is -2.5
```

When processing the input string, Program 6.4 pushes operations onto the `opstack` object depending on their priority compared with the top of stack operation. For example, Figure 6.12 shows the contents of `opstack` and `float_stack` after processing the input string up to the '`/`' operation.

When the '`/`' operation is processed, its priority (precedence) is compared with the operation on top of the `opstack` stack (which is '`*`'). Since '`/`' and '`*`' have the same priority, the '`*`' operation is performed by popping two numbers off of the `float_stack` stack, multiplying them, and pushing the result back onto `float_stack`. The '`*`' operation is popped off the `opstack` and then the '`/`' operation is pushed. The overall evaluation of the expression is as follows:

```
1 + 2 * 3 / 4 – 5
1 + 6 / 4 – 5
1 + 1.5 – 5
2.5 – 5
–2.5
```

See how you do on the rest of the sample executions:

```
Enter an expression: 1*3+5

The result is 8

Enter an expression: 1+3*5

The result is 16

Enter an expression: 9*9*9-8*8*8

The result is 217

Enter an expression: 4*3-6+8/2*5-3

The result is 23
```

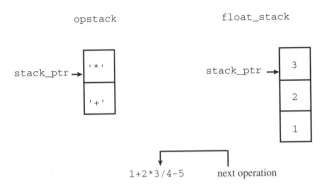

Figure 6.12   Contents of `opstack` and `float_stack`

It would be useful to add parenthesis processing to Program 6.4 to fully express any mathematical expression.

Program 6.5 demonstrates how a C++ QUEUE class is implemented. The queue is used as the control structure in a round-robin scheduler that has a small percentage of process time wasted due to I/O waits. A doubly linked-list is used to represent the queue, with each node capable of storing a character and an integer. The character indicates the job and the integer the remaining job time.

When a job is de-queued, there is a 25 percent chance that it will be suspended due to an I/O wait. The job time does not decrease in this case. The scheduler continues running jobs until the queue is empty.

Program 6.5

```
#include <iostream.h>
#include <stdio.h>
#include <stdlib.h>
#include <string.h>
#include <ctype.h>

#define FALSE 0
#define TRUE  1
#define MAXTIME 4
#define IOSLICE 25

        typedef struct node
        {
                char data;
                int num;
                struct node *flink;
                struct node *blink;
        } LNODE;

class QUEUE {
public:
        LNODE *queue_ptr;
```

```
            QUEUE(void);
            int empty(void);
            void en_queue(char job, int time);
            void de_queue(char *job, int *time);
    };

main()
{
            QUEUE myjobs;
            char job;
            int i, time;

            cout << "Generating 5 jobs...\n";
            for(i = 0; i < 5; i++)
            {
                    job = 'A' + i;
                    time = 1 + (rand() % (MAXTIME * 100))/100;
                    cout << "Job " << job << ", time " << time << "\n";
                    myjobs.en_queue(job,time);
            }
            cout << "Running...\n";
            while (!myjobs.empty())
            {
                    myjobs.de_queue(&job,&time);
                    if (IOSLICE > (rand() % 100))
                    {
                            cout << "Job " << job << ", I/O wait...\n";
                            myjobs.en_queue(job,time);
                    }
                    else
                    {
                            time--;
                            cout << "Job " << job << ", time " << time << "\n";
                            if (time)
                                    myjobs.en_queue(job,time);
                    }
            }
}

QUEUE::QUEUE()
{
            queue_ptr = NULL;
}

int QUEUE::empty()
{
            if(queue_ptr == NULL)
                    return(TRUE);
            else
```

```
                    return(FALSE);
}

void QUEUE::en_queue(char job, int time)
{
     LNODE *p;

     p = new LNODE;
     if (p == NULL)
                cout << "Error! Cannot en_queue new job.\n";
     else
     {
          p->data = job;
          p->num = time;
          if(empty())
          {
               p->flink = NULL;
               p->blink = NULL;
          }
          else
          {
               p->flink = queue_ptr;
               queue_ptr->blink = p;
          }
          queue_ptr = p;
     }
}

void QUEUE::de_queue(char *job, int *time)
{
         LNODE *p1, *p2;

         p1 = queue_ptr;
         if(empty())
         {
                 cout << "Error! The queue is empty.\n";
                 *job = '\0';
                 *time = 0;
         }
         else
         {
                 p2 = p1;
                 while (p1->flink != NULL)
                 {
                         p2 = p1;
                         p1 = p1->flink;
                 }
                 *job = p1->data;
                 *time = p1->num;
                 p2->flink = NULL;
                 if (p1 == p2)
```

```
                    queue_ptr = NULL;
            delete(p1);
        }
}
```

A sample execution of Program 6.5 clearly indicates the presence of I/O waiting time and the effect on job execution.

```
Generating 5 jobs...
Job A, time 4
Job B, time 2
Job C, time 2
Job D, time 3
Job E, time 1
Running...
Job A, I/O wait...
Job B, time 1
Job C, I/O wait...
Job D, time 2
Job E, time 0
Job A, I/O wait...
Job B, time 0
Job C, time 1
Job D, time 1
Job A, time 3
Job C, time 0
Job D, I/O wait...
Job A, I/O wait...
Job D, time 0
Job A, time 2
Job A, I/O wait...
Job A, time 1
Job A, time 0
```

In a typical operating system, system resources such as printers, hard drives, and I/O devices are each serviced by their own queues. The CPU has a queue also, the job queue used in previous examples. A simple diagram of a queued processing system is shown in Figure 6.13.

It would be challenging to add multiple queues to Program 6.5, to simulate the operation of many different system resource queues.

Conclusion

In this section we saw how C++ stack and queue objects were used for practical purposes. Check your understanding of this material with the following section review.

6.7 Section Review

1. How might a `union` type be useful in the `LNODE` definition?
2. How does Program 6.4 enforce operator precedence?
3. Are two pointers (`flink` and `blink`) really necessary in the `QUEUE` class?

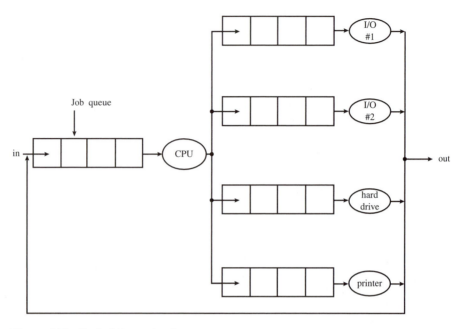

Figure 6.13   Typical Processing System

Study Questions

General Concepts

Section 6.1

1. What is the name of the operation to add an element to a stack?
2. What two operations can be performed on a queue?
3. What do stacks and queues have in common?

Section 6.2

4. When may a statically allocated stack or queue be used safely?
5. Why is a linked-list suitable for implementing stack and queue structures?
6. What is a disadvantage of a dynamically allocated stack or queue?

Section 6.3

7. How are push and pop operations performed using linked-lists?
8. What advantage does a linked-list stack have over an array-based stack?
9. How does a single stack reverse a character string?

Section 6.4

10. How does a C/C++ program use its run-time stack?
11. Why is the size of the run-time stack always changing?
12. What happens if the run-time stack runs out of stack space?

Section 6.5

13. What does FIFO stand for?
14. Is it necessary to use two pointers to maintain a queue?
15. How does a queue support round-robin scheduling?

Section 6.6

16. When does a priority queue act like an ordinary queue?
17. How is an element chosen when de-queueing from a priority queue?
18. Does it make any difference if elements in a priority queue are in their correct positions or in any random order?

Section 6.7

19. Why are the `opstack` and `float_stack` objects declared globally in Program 6.4?
20. If the top-of-stack operation is `'/'`, what happens if the new operation is `'+'`?
21. Is it possible, however unlikely, for a job to circulate on the queue forever, never completing execution, in Program 6.5?

Program Design

When writing the following programs, use the new data structures discussed in this chapter. The use of pointers and recursion is also suggested for the programs that can use them. Be sure to fully test the structures you design.

22. Another common job scheduling algorithm is known as Shortest Job First. Design a priority queue that chooses the job with the shortest execution time, runs it completely, and returns to the queue for the next shortest job.
23. Develop a C++ class that implements a linked-list stack of characters. Use the `stack` object to determine if an input string is a palindrome.
24. Modify the `STACK` class so that subclasses may instantiate character, string, integer, or floating-point stacks.
25. Write a driver program to test the `priority_dequeue()` function.
26. Add parenthesis processing to Program 6.4 to evaluate more complex mathematical expressions. Test your program by evaluating five different expressions of varying degrees of complexity (such as several levels of parentheses).
27. Develop a stack-based post-order expression evaluator. For example, inputting 5 4 3 + 7 * - results in a value of -44.
28. Create a C++ program that implements a complex en-queue function with a simple de-queue function.
29. Design a fixed-length queue of eight characters so that it en-queues keyboard characters until the word SECURITY has been entered.
30. Design a queue capable of recognizing the pattern "001011011110," a 12-character sequence of '1' and '0' codes.
31. Show how a stack can be used to convert an unsigned integer into its corresponding 5-digit ASCII numeric sequence, such as "00143" or "65535."
32. Show how a queue can be used as a "data delay line" where data values are fed into the queue with every pass through a loop, but exit four passes later. Display the input stream and output stream of characters as follows:

    Input: `12345678901234567890abcde`
    Output: `----12345678901234567890abcde`

33. Add the ability of accepting negative numbers to Program 6.4 through the use of the unary minus '–' operator, as in:

    –6+–2   or   5*–4

7 Trees

Objectives

This chapter gives you the opportunity to learn:

1. How a tree is structured.
2. Different methods used to build trees.
3. About two different types of trees.
4. Several different methods used to traverse a tree.
5. How to search a tree.
6. How a tree object is used in C++.

Key Terms

Root Node   Branches
Child Node   Hierarchy
Parent Node   Unbalanced Tree
Cycle   Balanced Tree
Traverse   Skewed
Pre-order Traversal   Generalized Tree
Post-order Traversal   In-Order Traversal
Binary Tree   Depth

Outline

Introduction

The tree data structure is useful when we want to access many items of data in an efficient way. Sometimes a tree is designed to contain predefined data in a certain order. When this order is fixed, a disk file can contain the data and read it in when necessary. Conversely, a tree can also be built on the fly, such as when evaluating mathematical expressions. As you will see, a tree can be used in many different types of situations.

7.1   Terminology

A *tree* is another data structure that is built using nodes. As its name indicates, the tree's nodes are arranged in a structured way, resembling an upside-down tree. A tree has a **root node** from which every node in the tree is reachable. The particular path taken to each node follows branches that proceed deeper into the tree with each step. As Figure 7.1(a) indicates, the six-node tree has one root node, two nodes one level below root, and three nodes at two levels below root. There are many different paths from the root node to the five other nodes.

It is common to refer to nodes in a tree as a **child node** or **parent node.** Any node can have zero or more children. In Figure 7.1(a), B and C are the children of A (the parent). D, E, and F are the children of parent node B. Node C has no children. Thus, the nodes in a tree have zero or more links coming out of them. The links always proceed to a deeper level in the tree. Compare this with Figure 7.1(b), which shows a six-node graph. It is difficult to pick a root node, is it not? The nodes in the graph are not arranged in any particular depth. Furthermore, notice that there are **cycles** in the graph as well. One cycle is D-C-E. Another

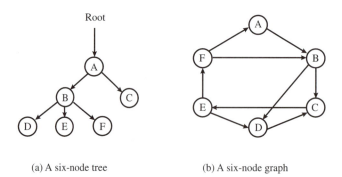

(a) A six-node tree   (b) A six-node graph

Figure 7.1 Comparing a Tree and a Graph

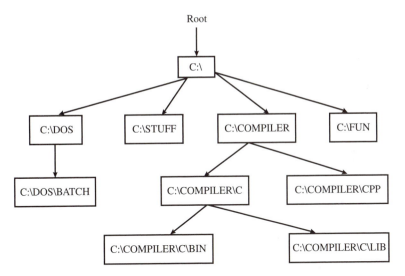

Figure 7.2   Storing a Directory Structure in a Tree

cycle is B-C-E-F. There are other cycles as well. Finding a path through the graph from one node to another is not as straightforward as it is for a tree (which does not allow cycles).

We typically **traverse** a tree to arrange or display its information in a particular order. There are several different ways to traverse a tree. One method is called **pre-order** traversal, which involves looking at the node information before looking at its links. Using Figure 7.1(a), a pre-order traversal gives A-B-D-E-F-C. Another method performs a **post-order traversal.** For the post-order traversal, the node information is accessed after the links. The post-order traversal of the tree in Figure 7.1(a) is D-E-F-B-C-A.

Figure 7.2 shows one application of a tree. The directory structure of a personal computer hard drive is organized as a tree. Each new level in the tree contains subdirectories for the level above it. The operating system has specific rules about how the directory structure may be navigated. Some DOS commands, such as DIR and XCOPY, can be instructed to traverse all subdirectory links from any directory.

We will look at algorithms to perform these traversals and also at a special type of tree called a **binary tree.** A binary tree is a tree that is written to adhere to some specific rules. These rules specify a parent node may contain either 0, 1, or 2 children. Any node can thus have at most two **branches** (links) to its children. The trees in Figures 7.1(a) and 7.2 are not binary trees.

Binary trees are especially useful for evaluating mathematical expressions with enforced rules of operator precedence. We will see example applications utilizing binary trees and the operations commonly performed on them.

Conclusion

In this section you were introduced to the basic structure of a tree. Check your understanding of the material with the following section review.

7.1 Section Review

1. Is there a restriction on the number of child nodes on a tree?
2. What is the difference between a child node and a parent node?
3. Show how your phone number can be stored as a tree of seven nodes.
4. What is a traversal?
5. Can any tree be a binary tree?

7.2 The Hierarchy of a Tree

Hierarchy refers to order, and there is an order associated with the way a tree is structured. The hierarchy can actually affect the efficiency of functions that use the tree. Consider the two trees shown in Figure 7.3. In Figure 7.3(a) seven nodes are used to store

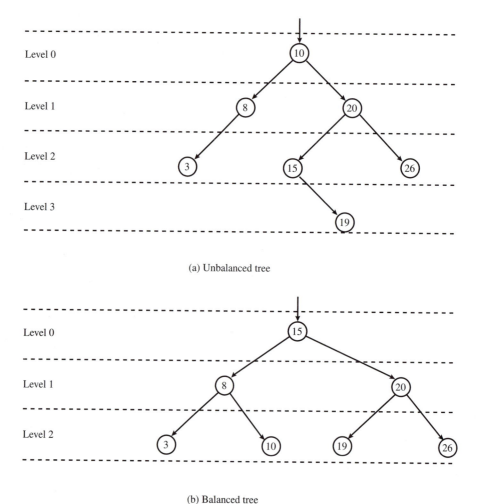

(a) Unbalanced tree

(b) Balanced tree

Figure 7.3   Two Trees Storing the Same Data

a sorted group of numbers. For any node in the tree, the values stored in nodes reachable from the left link are smaller than the current node. Node values accessed via the right link are larger. Note that the node containing 19 is the only node in level 3. Also note that there is a free spot for a node in level 2, off the unused right link of the node storing the value 8. This is an example of an **unbalanced tree.**

In Figure 7.3(b) the same values are stored in a **balanced tree.** In a balanced tree, an entire level of nodes must fill up before any nodes are placed at a lower level. Now the node storing 19 has been moved up into level 2 (and other nodes, particularly the root node, have been rearranged).

What is the difference between a balanced tree of data and an unbalanced tree of data? Look at Figure 7.4 for a clue. This binary tree is **skewed.** Since no right links are ever used, it is not possible to skip over any nodes when searching the tree, as we are able to do with the trees in Figure 7.3. This means that searches, in general, take longer on unbalanced (especially skewed) trees. It is worth the time and effort to develop a function that balances a binary tree, to ensure reasonably fast searches.

Another aspect of the hierarchy for a given tree is the type of nodes used. A tree may be composed of identical nodes or many different node types. This will have an impact on the techniques used to traverse or search the tree, as well as functions that modify the tree.

An interesting approach to representing any type of tree (variable number of children for each parent, different types of data stored in each node) is diagrammed in Figure 7.5. The **generalized tree** in Figure 7.5(a) contains a `float` in the root node (1.9), a `char` `'x'` and a string `"Floor"` as children of the root node, and three other child nodes, all `int`s, off the `"Floor"` node. Four different data types are stored, and both 2-link and 3-link nodes are used.

Figure 7.5(b) shows how the generalized tree can be implemented as a linked-list with three link fields. The first link field is a pointer to the appropriate data type. The second link field is used to connect to the next level's child list. If this link field is `NULL`, there are no children. The third link field is used to link the child nodes together.

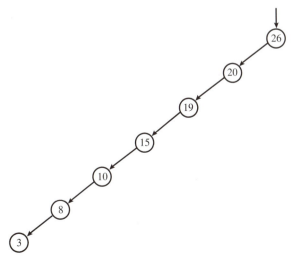

Figure 7.4   Skewed Binary Tree

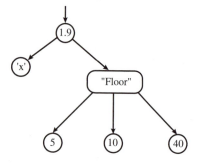

(a) Generalized tree

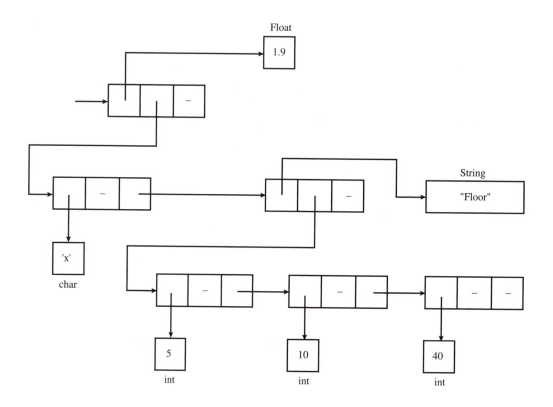

(b) Triple-link node structure

Figure 7.5   Representing a Generalized Tree

Using a node of pointers provides a great deal of flexibility. Traversing and searching is simplified, as there are a fixed number of links. Recursion can be used to keep track of your position in the list during a traversal or search. Adding or removing a node requires the typical pointer manipulation already developed for multiply linked-lists.

Conclusion

In this section you were exposed to the hierarchy of trees. We learned that a tree may be unbalanced, balanced, or skewed, and how to represent a generalized tree hierarchy. Check your understanding of this material with the following section review.

7.2 Section Review

1. How does the hierarchy of a tree affect search time?
2. How do the nodes in a tree control its hierarchy?
3. What is a binary tree?
4. How is a linked-list used to represent a tree?

7.3   Binary Trees

A binary tree is a specific data structure composed of nodes containing a data field and two link fields, as shown in Figure 7.6. The link fields are called *left child* and *right child*. The term "binary" comes from the fact that each node has the capability of pointing to exactly two other nodes. The first node in the tree is commonly called the *root* node, and is located at the top of the tree's diagram. Figure 7.7 shows a sample binary tree. The root node of the tree is the node containing the '*' sign. The binary tree in Figure 7.7 was constructed in such a way that each link field points to one of three places: to a node containing a math operation, to a node containing a variable name, or to NULL. It is important to be able to traverse the binary tree and access the information contained within it. During a traversal, the data stored at each node is displayed or accessed.

There are three common forms of traversal: *pre-order, in-order,* and *post-order.* In all traversal methods, we attempt to go down the tree to the left as far as possible before going to the right. Our trip down the tree continues until we encounter NULL in a link field. The results of each traversal method are different, because each method displays/accesses the node's data field at a different time.

For example, in a pre-order traversal, the following steps are performed at each node:

Access data field;
access left child;
access right child.

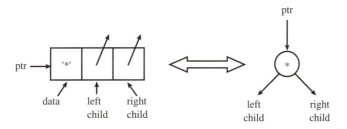

Figure 7.6   A Sample Node in a Binary Tree

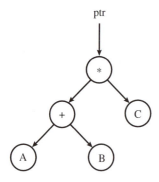

Figure 7.7   A Sample Binary Tree

An **in-order traversal** accesses the data field like this:

> Access left child;
> access data field;
> access right child.

A post-order traversal does the following:

> Access left child;
> access right child;
> access data field.

Figure 7.8 shows the order in which the nodes in our sample binary tree are accessed by all three techniques. The results of each traversal are as follows:

```
Pre-order:    *+ABC
In-order:     A+B*C
Post-order:   AB+C*
```

These traversal techniques are easily implemented through the use of recursive function calls, as Program 7.1 illustrates.

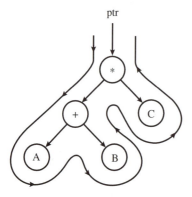

Figure 7.8   Binary Tree Traversal

Program 7.1

```c
#include <stdio.h>
#include <stdlib.h>

        typedef struct node
        {
                char data;
                struct node *lchild;
                struct node *rchild;
        } LNODE;

void build_tree(LNODE **ptr);
void pre_order(LNODE *ptr);
void in_order(LNODE *ptr);
void post_order(LNODE *ptr);

main()
{
        LNODE *tree;

        build_tree(&tree);
        printf("Pre-order traversal  => ");
        pre_order(tree);
        printf("\nIn-order traversal   => ");
        in_order(tree);
        printf("\nPost-order traversal => ");
        post_order(tree);
}

void build_tree(LNODE **ptr)
{
        LNODE *n1, *n2, *n3, *n4, *n5;

        n1 = malloc(sizeof(LNODE));
        n2 = malloc(sizeof(LNODE));
        n3 = malloc(sizeof(LNODE));
        n4 = malloc(sizeof(LNODE));
        n5 = malloc(sizeof(LNODE));
        n1->data = '*';
        n1->lchild = n2;
        n1->rchild = n3;
        n2->data = '+';
        n2->lchild = n4;
        n2->rchild = n5;
        n3->data = 'C';
        n3->lchild = NULL;
        n3->rchild = NULL;
        n4->data = 'A';
        n4->lchild = NULL;
        n4->rchild = NULL;
        n5->data = 'B';
```

```
                n5->lchild = NULL;
                n5->rchild = NULL;
                *ptr = n1;
}

void pre_order(LNODE *ptr)
{
        if(ptr != NULL)
        {
                printf("%c",ptr->data);
                pre_order(ptr->lchild);
                pre_order(ptr->rchild);
        }
}

void in_order(LNODE *ptr)
{
        if(ptr != NULL)
        {
                in_order(ptr->lchild);
                printf("%c",ptr->data);
                in_order(ptr->rchild);
        }
}

void post_order(LNODE *ptr)
{
        if(ptr != NULL)
        {
                post_order(ptr->lchild);
                post_order(ptr->rchild);
                printf("%c",ptr->data);
        }
}
```

Examine the method used to build the binary tree at the beginning of the program. The build_tree() function creates the five-node tree and returns the pointer to the root node (n1). The tree represents a mathematical expression whose original form was:

(A + B) * C

Usually, the binary tree for a mathematical expression is constructed by a function that follows some simple guidelines for operator precedence.
    Execution of Program 7.1 produces

```
Pre-order traversal  => *+ABC
In-order traversal   => A+B*C
Post-order traversal => AB+C*
```

You are encouraged to devise your own trees using Program 7.1 and perform the traversals yourself.

Node Counting

Program 7.2 contains the statements needed to count the nodes in the binary expression tree previously examined in Figure 7.7.

Program 7.2

```
#include <stdio.h>
#include <stdlib.h>

        typedef struct node
        {
                char data;
                struct node *lchild;
                struct node *rchild;
        } LNODE;

        int number_of_nodes;

void build_tree(LNODE **ptr);
void count_nodes(LNODE *ptr);

main()
{
        LNODE *tree;

        build_tree(&tree);
        printf("Number of nodes => ");
        count_nodes(tree);
        printf("%d", number_of_nodes);
}

void build_tree(LNODE **ptr)
{
        LNODE *n1, *n2, *n3, *n4, *n5;

        n1 = malloc(sizeof(LNODE));
        n2 = malloc(sizeof(LNODE));
        n3 = malloc(sizeof(LNODE));
        n4 = malloc(sizeof(LNODE));
        n5 = malloc(sizeof(LNODE));
        n1->data = '*';
        n1->lchild = n2;
        n1->rchild = n3;
        n2->data = '+';
        n2->lchild = n4;
        n2->rchild = n5;
        n3->data = 'C';
        n3->lchild = NULL;
        n3->rchild = NULL;
        n4->data = 'A';
        n4->lchild = NULL;
```

```
                n4->rchild = NULL;
                n5->data = 'B';
                n5->lchild = NULL;
                n5->rchild = NULL;
                *ptr = n1;
}

void count_nodes(LNODE *ptr)
{
        if(ptr != NULL)
        {
                number_of_nodes++;
                count_nodes(ptr->lchild);
                count_nodes(ptr->rchild);
        }
}
```

A pointer to the root node of the tree is passed to the count_nodes() function, which counts the number of nodes contained in the tree. From Figure 7.7 it is clear that the tree contains five nodes. Program 7.2 agrees, as shown by its sample execution:

```
Number of nodes => 5
```

The technique used to count the nodes is similar to that used to perform a traversal. As each new node is reached, a counter is incremented. Then the left child and right child nodes (if any) are examined recursively.

Finding the Depth of a Tree

The **depth** of a tree is the number of the level containing the last group of child nodes. The depth of the tree in Figure 7.8 is two, which indicates that there are three levels (0, 1, and 2). Counting nodes and finding the depth are useful operations to perform, especially if we are working towards a function that balances a binary tree. Program 7.3 shows how the depth of a binary tree can be determined.

Program 7.3

```
#include <stdio.h>
#include <stdlib.h>

        typedef struct node
        {
                char data;
                struct node *lchild;
                struct node *rchild;
        } LNODE;

        int depth;

void build_tree(LNODE **ptr);
void find_depth(LNODE *ptr, int level);
```

```
main()
{
        LNODE *tree;

        build_tree(&tree);
        find_depth(tree,0);
        printf("The depth of the tree is %d\n", depth);
}

void build_tree(LNODE **ptr)
{
        LNODE *n1, *n2, *n3, *n4, *n5;

        n1 = malloc(sizeof(LNODE));
        n2 = malloc(sizeof(LNODE));
        n3 = malloc(sizeof(LNODE));
        n4 = malloc(sizeof(LNODE));
        n5 = malloc(sizeof(LNODE));
        n1->data = '*';
        n1->lchild = n2;
        n1->rchild = n3;
        n2->data = '+';
        n2->lchild = n4;
        n2->rchild = n5;
        n3->data = 'C';
        n3->lchild = NULL;
        n3->rchild = NULL;
        n4->data = 'A';
        n4->lchild = NULL;
        n4->rchild = NULL;
        n5->data = 'B';
        n5->lchild = NULL;
        n5->rchild = NULL;
        *ptr = n1;
}

void find_depth(LNODE *ptr, int level)
{
        if(ptr != NULL)
        {
                if (level > depth)
                        depth++;
                find_depth(ptr->lchild, level+1);
                find_depth(ptr->rchild, level+1);
        }
}
```

The recursive function `find_depth()` compares the current value of `level` with the value stored in the global variable `depth`. If `depth` is smaller than `level`, it is incremented. The current level is maintained by passing `level+1` to recursive calls of `find_depth()`.

A sample execution of Program 7.3 is as follows:

```
The depth of the tree is 2
```

Try your own trees with the `find_depth()` function. Does it have any limitations?

Conclusion

In this section we examined a number of operations on a special type of tree called a binary tree. Test your understanding of the material with the following section review.

7.3 Section Review

1. What does the depth of a tree represent?
2. How is each node accessed during a pre-order traversal?
3. What condition occurs to stop the recursive function calls in `find_depth()`?

7.4   Traversing Generalized Trees

Take another look at Figure 7.2. The directory structure is stored in a generalized tree, since each node has a variable number of links. Recall that we can use doubly linked-lists to represent the tree, one link for the current level and the other for the next level. Program 7.4 shows how the tree of Figure 7.2 is constructed and traversed.

Program 7.4

```
#include <stdio.h>
#include <stdlib.h>
#include <string.h>

        typedef struct node
        {
                char data[12];
                struct node *next_level;
                struct node *next_child;
        } LNODE;

void build_tree(LNODE **ptr);
void show_directory(LNODE *ptr, char current_path[]);

main()
{
        LNODE *tree;

        build_tree(&tree);
        printf("The directory listing is:\n\n");
        show_directory(tree, "C:");
}

void build_tree(LNODE **ptr)
```

```
{
        LNODE *nodes[10];
        char *dirnames[] = {"", "DOS", "STUFF", "COMPILER", "FUN",
                           "BATCH", "C", "CPP", "BIN", "LIB"};
        int i;

        for(i = 0; i < 10; i++)
        {
                nodes[i] = malloc(sizeof(LNODE));
                strcpy(nodes[i]->data,dirnames[i]);
        }
        nodes[0]->next_child = NULL;
        nodes[0]->next_level = nodes[1];
        nodes[1]->next_child = nodes[2];
        nodes[1]->next_level = nodes[5];
        nodes[2]->next_child = nodes[3];
        nodes[2]->next_level = NULL;
        nodes[3]->next_child = nodes[4];
        nodes[3]->next_level = nodes[6];
        nodes[4]->next_child = NULL;
        nodes[4]->next_level = NULL;
        nodes[5]->next_child = NULL;
        nodes[5]->next_level = NULL;
        nodes[6]->next_child = nodes[7];
        nodes[6]->next_level = nodes[8];
        nodes[7]->next_child = NULL;
        nodes[7]->next_level = NULL;
        nodes[8]->next_child = nodes[9];
        nodes[8]->next_level = NULL;
        nodes[9]->next_child = NULL;
        nodes[9]->next_level = NULL;
        *ptr = nodes[0];
}

void show_directory(LNODE *ptr, char current_path[])
{
        char path[80];

        strcpy(path,current_path);
        if (strlen(path) != 3)
            strcat(path,"\\");
        if(ptr != NULL)
        {
                strcat(path,ptr->data);
                printf("%s\n",path);
                show_directory(ptr->next_level, path);
                show_directory(ptr->next_child, current_path);
        }
}
```

The `build_tree()` function allocates memory for ten nodes and stores their addresses in an array of pointers:

```
LNODE *nodes[10];
char *dirnames[] = {"", "DOS", "STUFF", "COMPILER", "FUN",
                    "BATCH", "C", "CPP", "BIN", "LIB"};
int i;

for(i = 0; i < 10; i++)
{
    nodes[i] = malloc(sizeof(LNODE));
    strcpy(nodes[i]->data,dirnames[i]);
}
```

At the same time, the data field of each node is assigned its associated directory name from Figure 7.2. The LNODE structure allocated by `malloc()` is defined like this:

```
typedef struct node
{
    char data[12];
    struct node *next_level;
    struct node *next_child;
} LNODE;
```

The tree built by `build_tree()` is traversed recursively by `show_directory()` in such a way that the results are similar to what the DOS command DIR /S would display. The `current_path` parameter passed into each new level of recursion keeps track of the sub-path leading to the current directory.

A sample execution of Program 7.4 is as follows:

```
The directory listing is:

C:\
C:\DOS
C:\DOS\BATCH
C:\STUFF
C:\COMPILER
C:\COMPILER\C
C:\COMPILER\C\BIN
C:\COMPILER\C\LIB
C:\COMPILER\CPP
C:\FUN
```

It is also useful to display the directory information so that each new level is indented to further illustrate subdirectories. This can be accomplished by keeping track of the current level while traversing the directory tree.

If a tree containing different node types must be traversed, some method must be used to determine how many link fields there are in a given node. This could easily be accomplished by storing an integer as part of the data field that indicates the number of links.

Then we store the desired number of links in an array of pointers. For example, examine the following node definition:

```
typedef struct node
{
    char model;
    float size;
    int link_count;
    struct node *links[3];
} LNODE;
```

The `link_count` variable tells us how many link fields there are in the node (three in this case). We can now select pointers from the `links` array and navigate the tree. So, no matter what type of node is used (uniform links or variable), there are ways to efficiently traverse trees constructed from them.

Conclusion

In this section we saw two methods for representing generalized trees and how to traverse them. Test your understanding of the material with the following section review.

7.4 Section Review

1. What are uniform and variable links?
2. What is the difference between a generalized tree and a binary tree?
3. Why might it be necessary to keep track of the level of recursion when traversing a directory tree?

7.5 Searching a Tree

Searching a tree is an operation well suited for the power of recursion. Let us first look at how a binary tree is searched. Then we will examine how a generalized tree is searched.

Binary Search

The binary search is a very efficient search technique commonly used with binary trees. Figure 7.9 shows a sample binary tree containing integer-based nodes. The tree is structured in such a way that the integers it contains have already been placed into their correct positions (for searching purposes). For example, notice that all nodes reachable from the left child of the root node have values (2, 3, 5, and 6) smaller than the root node value (7). All nodes reachable from the right child of the root node have values (12, 13, and 17) that are greater than the root node value. Searching the tree for a particular value—6, for example—involves the following tests:

1. Does the current node value equal the search value?

In this case the answer is no, because the current node value is 7.

2. Is the search value smaller than the current node value? If yes, make the current node the left child node.

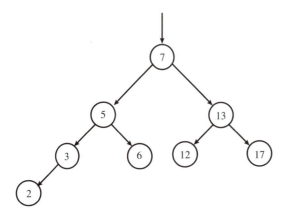

Figure 7.9   Binary Tree Containing Sorted Integers

In this case the answer is yes, because 6 is smaller than 7. So, the current node value becomes 5. Now step 1 is repeated again. Because 5 does not equal 6, we go on to step 2. The search value is not smaller than the current node value, which takes us to step 3.

3. Make the current node the right child node.

This causes the current node value to become 6. When step 1 is repeated again, we find our match. Thus, the procedure for a binary search involves taking left and right turns as we go down the tree looking for our search value.

In cases where the search value is not in the tree, steps 2 and 3 will eventually encounter NULL as the left or right pointer. If this happens, the search is terminated and we conclude that the search value does not exist within the tree.

Program 7.5 contains the function binary_search(), which implements the three-step search technique we just saw. Once again we use a recursive function call (binary_search() calls itself) to traverse the binary tree.

Program 7.5

```
#include <stdio.h>
#include <stdlib.h>

#define FALSE 0
#define TRUE  1

        typedef struct node
        {
                int data;
                struct node *lchild;
                struct node *rchild;
        } LNODE;

void build_tree(LNODE **ptr);
int binary_search(LNODE *ptr, int item);

main()
{
```

```
            LNODE *tree;
            int sval, found;

            build_tree(&tree);
            printf("Enter value to search for => ");
            scanf("%d",&sval);
            found = binary_search(tree,sval);
            printf("The value %d has",sval);
            found ? printf(" ") : printf(" not ");
            printf("been found in the binary tree.");
    }

void build_tree(LNODE **ptr)
{

            LNODE *nodes[8];
            int i,numbers[] = {7, 5, 13, 3, 6, 12, 17, 2};

            for(i = 0; i < 8; i++)
            {
                    nodes[i] = malloc(sizeof(LNODE));
                    nodes[i]->data = numbers[i];
            }
            nodes[0]->lchild = nodes[1];
            nodes[0]->rchild = nodes[2];
            nodes[1]->lchild = nodes[3];
            nodes[1]->rchild = nodes[4];
            nodes[2]->lchild = nodes[5];
            nodes[2]->rchild = nodes[6];
            nodes[3]->lchild = nodes[7];
            nodes[3]->rchild = NULL;
            for(i = 4; i < 8; i++)
            {
                    nodes[i]->lchild = NULL;
                    nodes[i]->rchild = NULL;
            }
            *ptr = nodes[0];
    }

int binary_search(LNODE *ptr, int item)
{
            if(ptr == NULL)
                    return(FALSE);
            else
            if(ptr->data == item)
                    return(TRUE);
            else
            if(item < ptr->data)
                    binary_search(ptr->lchild, item);
            else
                    binary_search(ptr->rchild, item);
    }
```

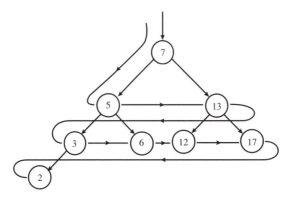

Figure 7.10   Breadth-First Search of a Binary Tree

Two executions of Program 7.5 follow, one successful and the other unsuccessful.

```
Enter value to search for => 6
The value 6 has been found in the binary tree.

Enter value to search for => 22
The value 22 has not been found in the binary tree.
```

A balanced tree of 1,024 nodes can be searched with 10 for fewer comparisons using `binary_search()`. Try to determine why this is so.

Depth-First and Breadth-First Searching

The depth-first and breadth-first search techniques are fundamentally different. The depth-first search is already familiar to us, because it is the search technique used to traverse the binary tree in Program 7.2 (and previously to accomplish pre-, in-, and post-order traversals in Program 7.1). A depth-first search goes as far down the left side of the binary tree as it can. When NULL is encountered, the search switches to the bottommost right child and resumes.

A breadth-first search accesses the nodes of the tree in a different order. As Figure 7.10 shows, nodes are accessed one level at a time, beginning with the first level (the root node). The child nodes of the root node (which occupy level 2) are accessed next. Then their child nodes are all accessed (the four nodes at level 3), and so on. This search technique is easily accomplished with the use of a queue. Only two steps are needed to control the queue:

1. Remove a node from the queue. This becomes the current node.
2. Place all child nodes of the current node onto the queue.

The queue is initially loaded with the root node of the tree. Steps 1 and 2 are repeated until the queue is empty. For the tree shown in Figure 7.10, the queue takes on the following values during a breadth-first search:

```
7                        -- initial node
13    5                  -- 7's children added
6     3    13            -- 5's children added
```

```
17    12    6    3    -- 13's children added
2     17    12   6    -- 3's children added
2     17    12
2     17
2
```

Program 7.6 uses a queue of tree node pointers to implement a breadth-first search.

Program 7.6

```
#include <stdio.h>
#include <stdlib.h>

#define FALSE 0
#define TRUE  1

        typedef struct tnode
        {
                int data;
                struct tnode *lchild;
                struct tnode *rchild;
        } TNODE;

        typedef struct qnode
        {
                struct tnode *tptr;
                struct qnode *link;
        } QNODE;

void build_tree(TNODE **ptr);
void bfs(TNODE *ptr);
void dfs(TNODE *ptr);
void show_queue(QNODE *ptr);
int empty(QNODE *ptr);
void en_queue(QNODE **head, TNODE *ptr);
void de_queue(QNODE **head, TNODE **ptr);


main()
{
        TNODE *tree;

        build_tree(&tree);
        printf("Depth-First Search   => ");
        dfs(tree);
        printf("\nBreadth-First Search => ");
        bfs(tree);
}

void build_tree(TNODE **ptr)
{
```

```
        TNODE *nodes[8];
        int i,numbers[] = {7, 5, 13, 3, 6, 12, 17, 2};

        for(i = 0; i < 8; i++)
        {
                nodes[i] = malloc(sizeof(TNODE));
                nodes[i]->data = numbers[i];
        }
        nodes[0]->lchild = nodes[1];
        nodes[0]->rchild = nodes[2];
        nodes[1]->lchild = nodes[3];
        nodes[1]->rchild = nodes[4];
        nodes[2]->lchild = nodes[5];
        nodes[2]->rchild = nodes[6];
        nodes[3]->lchild = nodes[7];
        nodes[3]->rchild = NULL;
        for(i = 4; i < 8; i++)
        {
                nodes[i]->lchild = NULL;
                nodes[i]->rchild = NULL;
        }
        *ptr = nodes[0];
}

void dfs(TNODE *ptr)
{
        if(ptr != NULL)
        {
                printf("%4d",ptr->data);
                dfs(ptr->lchild);
                dfs(ptr->rchild);
        }
}

void bfs(TNODE *ptr)
{
        QNODE *qhead = NULL;
        TNODE *p;

        en_queue(&qhead, ptr);
        while(!empty(qhead))
        {
                de_queue(&qhead, &p);
                printf("%4d",p->data);
                if(p->lchild != NULL)
                        en_queue(&qhead, p->lchild);
                if(p->rchild != NULL)
                        en_queue(&qhead, p->rchild);
        }
}
```

```
int empty(QNODE *ptr)
{
        if(ptr == NULL)
                return(TRUE);
        else
                return(FALSE);
}


void en_queue(QNODE **head, TNODE *ptr)
{
        QNODE *p;

        p = malloc(sizeof(QNODE));
        if(p != NULL)
        {
                p->tptr = ptr;
                p->link = *head;
                *head = p;
        }
}


void de_queue(QNODE **head, TNODE **ptr)
{
        QNODE *p1, *p2;

        p1 = *head;
        if(empty(p1))
        {
                printf("Error! The queue is empty.\n");
                *ptr = NULL;
        }
        else
        {
                p2 = *head;
                while(p2->link != NULL)
                {
                        p1 = p2;
                        p2 = p2->link;
                }
                *ptr = p2->tptr;
                p1->link = NULL;
                free(p2);
                if(p1 == p2)
                        *head = NULL;
        }
}
```

Note that two different structures are used in Program 7.6.

These structures are the TNODE (tree node) and QNODE (queue node) structures. Both structures are utilized by the queuing functions. The depth-first and breadth-first searches are implemented via the `dfs()` and `bfs()` functions. A sample execution shows how the results of the two searches differ:

```
Depth-First Search   =>   7   5   3   2   6   13  12  17
Breadth-First Search =>   7   5   13  3   6   12  17  2
```

Each search technique has its own advantages and disadvantages. To illustrate, consider a chess-playing program. After only a few moves, the program will already be using a large decision tree to evaluate what move to make next. A depth-first search may spend a great deal of time looking at nodes on the left side of the search tree before getting to a more desirable choice node on the right side. A breadth-first search will usually get to the same node more quickly.

On the other hand, a program designed to pack items into a box might arrive at a solution right away via a depth-first search down the left side of a decision tree, whereas a breadth-first search might waste time considering many different partial solutions. Knowing when to use a particular search technique comes with practice.

Generalized Tree Searches

As we saw in the previous section, nodes in a generalized tree should contain enough information to indicate how many link fields there are, and room for storing each link. A search algorithm can access the links as necessary to find the target node. If different data types are used as well, it would be good to have several search functions (one for `char`, `int`, `float`, etc.), unless a `union` is used in the data field. The `find_int()` function shown here is used to find an integer in a generalized tree built from nodes defined like this:

```c
typedef struct node
{
        int data;
        int link_count;
        struct node *links[3];
} LNODE;
```

There may be other node definitions, each with a different number of links. Study `find_int()` to see how it checks all the link fields.

```c
int find_int(LNODE *ptr, int item)
{
        int k,links,found;

        if (ptr == NULL)
             return(FALSE);
        if (ptr->data == item)
             return(TRUE);
        links = ptr->link_count;
        found = FALSE;
        k = 0;
        while((k < links) && !found)
        {
                found = find_int(ptr->links[k]);
```

```
                k++;
        }
        return(found);
}
```

Note the use of the `while()` loop to check each link in the `links` array. Early exits are possible if the `found` variable is set TRUE by a recursive call to `find_int()`.

Conclusion

This section showed the details of searching both binary and generalized trees. Test your understanding of the material with the following section review.

7.5 Section Review

1. Are items in a binary tree required to be in any particular order before a binary search can be performed?
2. How is a queue used in a breadth-first search on a binary tree?
3. What does a depth-first search involve?
4. What are the advantages and disadvantages of the breadth-first search and the depth-first search?

7.6   A C++ TREE Object

When C++ is used to build trees, we are able to take advantage of the object oriented features available within the C++ language. Like the other C++ programs we have examined, C++ can maintain just one tree, or several trees without much additional work on the part of the programmer. Look at Program 7.7.

Program 7.7

```
#include <iostream.h>
#include <iomanip.h>
#include <stdlib.h>

        typedef struct tnode
        {
                int data;
                struct tnode *lchild;
                struct tnode *rchild;
        } TNODE;

class TREE {
public:
        TNODE *ptr;

        TREE::TREE(void);
        void add_node(int item);
        void find_spot(TNODE *p, int n);
        void dfs(TNODE *ptr);
```

```
        } mytree;

        main()
        {
                TNODE *tree;
                int i,numbers[] = {7, 5, 13, 3, 6, 12, 17, 2};

                for(i = 0; i < 8; i++)
                        mytree.add_node(numbers[i]);
                cout << "Depth-First Search    => ";
                mytree.dfs(mytree.ptr);
        }


        TREE::TREE()
        {
                ptr = NULL;
        }

        void TREE::add_node(int item)
        {
                if (ptr == NULL)
                {
                        ptr = new TNODE;
                        ptr->data = item;
                        ptr->lchild = NULL;
                        ptr->rchild = NULL;
                }
                else
                        find_spot(ptr,item);
        }

        void TREE::find_spot(TNODE *p, int n)
        {
                TNODE *np;
                int found;

                if (n < p->data)
                {
                        if (p->lchild == NULL)
                        {
                                np = new TNODE;
                                np->data = n;
                                np->lchild = NULL;
                                np->rchild = NULL;
                                p->lchild = np;
                        }
                        else
                                find_spot(p->lchild,n);
                }
                else
```

```
                 {
                         if (p->rchild == NULL)
                         {
                                 np = new TNODE;
                                 np->data = n;
                                 np->lchild = NULL;
                                 np->rchild = NULL;
                                 p->rchild = np;
                         }
                         else
                                 find_spot(p->rchild,n);
                 }
        }

        void TREE::dfs(TNODE *ptr)
        {
                 if(ptr != NULL)
                 {
                         cout << setw(4) << ptr->data;
                         dfs(ptr->lchild);
                         dfs(ptr->rchild);
                 }
        }
```

In Program 7.7, the TREE class is used to define all of the functions required by the object. The TNODE definition includes both a data field and two link fields. There are four functions defined by the TREE class. A constructor, TREE(), is used to initialize the tree pointer to NULL. Three other functions—add_node(), find_spot(), and dfs()—are used to add a node to the tree, find a suitable location to add the node, and perform a depth-first search of the nodes, respectively.

Look at the definition for each of the functions and try to determine what types of changes are necessary for Program 7.7 to work with multiple objects of the TREE class.

To use multiple trees, simply instantiate multiple objects of the TREE class, as in:

```
TREE tree1, tree2, tree3
```

and then use the standard C++ syntax to use them.

Conclusion

The tree is a very powerful data structure when used to maintain data that is structured in a certain way. Test your knowledge of this material by trying the following section review.

7.6 Section Review

1. What advantage does C++ offer when working with trees?
2. Why is it necessary to initialize the tree pointer to NULL?
3. How many recursive functions does Program 7.7 contain?

Study Questions

General Concepts

Section 7.1
1. What is a binary tree?
2. Can a tree contain any cycles?
3. Explain how a post-order search is performed.
4. What type of application are binary trees best suited for?

Section 7.2
5. What is the difference between a skewed binary tree and an unbalanced tree?
6. When is a tree balanced?
7. How is recursion used to search a tree?

Section 7.3
8. What are the link fields called in a binary tree?
9. What three places can a link field point to?
10. What steps are performed at each node during an in-order traversal?

Section 7.4
11. How do we keep track of a variable number of link fields in a node?
12. Is it necessary to use a doubly linked-list to represent a tree? Why?

Section 7.5
13. What is the difference between searching a generalized tree and a binary tree?
14. If a balanced tree contains 1,024 elements, how many comparisons are necessary to search for an item in the tree?
15. What are the two methods used to search a tree?

Section 7.6
16. How does the `find_spot()` function determine the correct location to add a new node?
17. Does it matter where a new node gets added to the tree? Explain.

Program Design
For each of the following programming exercises, write a C or C++ program that performs the indicated task. Be sure to fully test each program.

18. Write a function that determines if a binary tree is balanced.
19. Write a function that balances a binary tree containing a sorted group of numbers. Test your function with the tree of Figures 7.3(a) and 7.4.
20. Write a function that determines if a binary tree is skewed. Return the following results:

    0 Not skewed
    1 Skewed left
    2 Skewed right

21. Write a depth-first traversal function for a binary tree that does not use recursion.
22. Write a program to test the operation of the `find_it()` function from Section 7.5.
23. Modify Program 7.7 to perform a breadth-first search. What are the results?
24. Write a program to build and maintain two binary trees, one for odd numbers and one for even numbers. The user can search for specific values in the trees. If the value is not found, the program user is given the opportunity to add it to the tree.

25. Modify the TREE class used in Program 7.7 to include a destructor function that will free all associated memory used during program execution.
26. Write a C++ program to implement the generalized tree shown in Figure 7.5.
27. Modify Program 7.4 so that each new subdirectory is indented three spaces.
28. Write a function that actually evaluates the expression contained in a binary tree, using a post-order traversal.
29. Develop a C++ program that builds a binary tree out of a user-supplied string. Store one character from the string in each node. An in-order traversal should display the original input string.
30. Write a prune() function that removes the entire subtree, beginning at a specified node.

8   Graphs

Objectives

This chapter gives you the opportunity to learn:

1. About the different types of graphs.
2. How nodes are connected in a graph.
3. How to distinguish between an undirected graph and a directed graph.
4. A method to traverse a graph.
5. How to determine if the graph contains any cycles.
6. How to use C++ to create a graph object.

Key Terms

Paths   Shortest Path
Fully-Connected Graph   Adjacency Matrix
Link   Vertex
Edge   Undirected Graph
Partially-Connected Graph   Directed Graph
Directed Edge   Graph Traversal
Undirected Edge   Routers
Spanning Tree   Routing Tables
Traveling Salesperson Problem   Prune

Outline

Introduction

The graph data structure has many practical uses, as you will see in this chapter. The **paths** between nodes in a graph can operate in one or both directions. Individual nodes can also be connected to themselves. Unlike the tree, a graph provides a great deal of additional flexibility. Let us begin by reviewing some of the basic details.

8.1   Terminology

A graph is a data structure that contains nodes that are linked together in any combination. For example, a graph can have connections that cause it to resemble a tree as shown in Figure 8.1(a). It could be connected to all other nodes in the graph, in which case it is called a **fully-connected graph,** as illustrated in Figure 8.1(c). The advantage of a fully-connected graph is the ability to get from one node to another using a single **link** (called an **edge**).

A graph could also contain no links to other nodes. Figure 8.1(b) shows a **partially-connected graph.** Notice the direction of the arrowheads shown in Figure 8.1(b). These

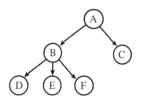

(a) A six-node graph with no cycles
(also passes as a tree)

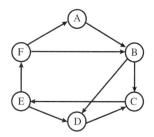

(b) A six-node graph containing cycles

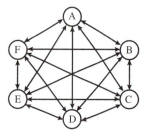

(c) A six-node fully-connected graph

Figure 8.1   Different Types of Graphs

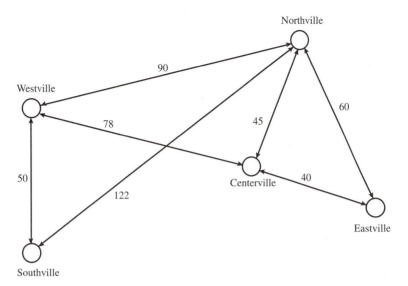

Figure 8.2   Graph of Highways Between Five Cities

arrows show the direction of the edge between two nodes. An edge may or may not be used to travel in both directions. An arrow going only in one direction is called a *unidirectional* (or **directed**) **edge,** allowing travel in only that one direction. A path allowing travel in both directions is called *bidirectional* (or **undirected**), as shown in Figure 8.1(c). Generally, bidirectional links do not show any arrowheads. They are shown here for contrast.

It is also useful to find the **spanning tree** of a graph. This is a tree connecting all nodes of the graph with the fewest number of paths.

Graphs are useful tools with many applications in the areas of communications networks, language processing, process control, and state machine design, to name a few. A telephone network or a computer network uses graphs to control routing of data from node to node. Another example of a graph is shown in Figure 8.2. This graph represents distances between five different cities. The bidirectional links indicate the various paths between them. The relationship between the distances to these cities is quite involved. It is sometimes referred to as a **Traveling Salesperson problem,** because its objective is to find the **shortest path** between all five cities without traveling the same road twice.

Conclusion

In this section you were introduced to some of the terminology associated with graphs. Check your understanding of the material with the following section review.

8.1 Section Review

1. Can a tree be a graph?
2. Can a graph be a tree?
3. What is an advantage of a fully-connected graph?
4. How many ways can a graph be connected?
5. What is the shortest path between all five cities in Figure 8.2?

8.2   Representing a Graph

A graph may be represented in any number of ways. Figure 8.3(a) shows a four-node graph containing both undirected and directed edges.

The **adjacency matrix** in Figure 8.3(b) is organized in such a way that there is one in any element that contains an edge. For example, the first row (row zero) contains 0 1 1 0. This indicates that from node 0 there are edges to nodes 1 and 2 (and no edges to nodes 0 and 3). The last row (row 3) is 1 1 0 0. This indicates edges from node 3 to nodes 0 and 1. The adjacency matrix is a simple structure for representing a graph whose edges do not have weights (as in Figure 8.2).

A nice feature of the adjacency matrix is that, when multiplied by itself, it gives a new adjacency matrix that indicates where there are paths containing *two* edges between nodes. Figure 8.4 shows the result of multiplying adjacency matrix A by itself (resulting in A^2).

0	1	1	0
0	0	0	1
0	0	1	0
1	1	0	0

(a) Graph   (b) Adjacency matrix

Figure 8.3   A Graph and Its Adjacency Matrix

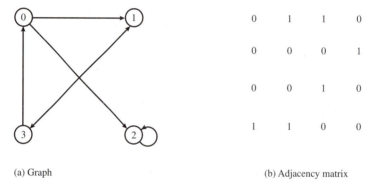

Figure 8.4   Squaring the Adjacency Matrix

The first row of the result (0 0 1 1) indicates that there are paths of two edges between node 0 and nodes 2 and 3. This is verified by examining the original graph in Figure 8.3(a). Program 8.1 shows how the adjacency matrix is multiplied by itself and then scanned to report on all possible paths containing two edges.

Program 8.1

```c
#include <stdio.h>

#define MSIZE 4

void show_matrix(int mat[][MSIZE]);
void multiply(int ma[][MSIZE], int mb[][MSIZE], int mc[][MSIZE]);
void show_paths(int mat[][MSIZE]);

main()
{
        int A[MSIZE][MSIZE] = {{0,1,1,0},
                               {0,0,0,1},
                               {0,0,1,0},
                               {1,1,0,0}};
        int A2[MSIZE][MSIZE];

        printf("The original adjacency matrix is:\n\n");
        show_matrix(A);
        multiply(A,A,A2);
        printf("\nThe squared adjacency matrix is:\n\n");
        show_matrix(A2);
        printf("\nHere are the paths containing two edges:\n\n");
        show_paths(A2);
}

void show_matrix(int mat[][MSIZE])
{
        int r,c;

        for(r = 0; r < MSIZE; r++)
        {
                for(c = 0; c < MSIZE; c++)
                        printf("%3d",mat[r][c]);
                printf("\n");
        }
}

void multiply(int ma[][MSIZE], int mb[][MSIZE], int mc[][MSIZE])
{
        int r,c,k,temp;

        for(r = 0; r < MSIZE; r++)
                for(c = 0; c < MSIZE; c++)
                {
                        temp = 0;
```

```
                               for(k = 0; k < MSIZE; k++)
                                       temp += ma[r][k] * mb[k][c];
                               mc[r][c] = temp;
                       }
        }

void show_paths(int mat[][MSIZE])
{
        int r,c;

        for(r = 0; r < MSIZE; r++)
                for(c = 0; c < MSIZE; c++)
                        if (mat[r][c])
                                printf("From %d to %d\n",r,c);
}
```

Notice how the adjacency matrix is defined:

```
int A[MSIZE][MSIZE] = {{0,1,1,0},
                       {0,0,0,1},
                       {0,0,1,0},
                       {1,1,0,0}};
```

For larger (or smaller) graphs, only the #define for MSIZE has to be changed, along with the initial matrix values.

The execution of Program 8.1 looks like this:

```
The original adjacency matrix is:

    0   1   1   0
    0   0   0   1
    0   0   1   0
    1   1   0   0

The squared adjacency matrix is:

    0   0   1   1
    1   1   0   0
    0   0   1   0
    0   1   1   1

Here are the paths containing two edges:

From 0 to 2
From 0 to 3
From 1 to 0
From 1 to 1
From 2 to 2
From 3 to 1
From 3 to 2
From 3 to 3
```

You should be able to verify that the results are correct.

A graph may also be represented as a list of edges, where an edge is specified by a pair of nodes. The edge list for the graph in Figure 8.3 is (0,1), (0,2), (1,3), (2,2), (3,0), (3,1). This can easily be implemented as a two-dimensional array:

```
int edge_list[6][2] = {{0,1},
                       {0,2},
                       {1,3},
                       {2,2},
                       {3,0},
                       {3,1}};
```

For comparison purposes, the adjacency matrix requires more storage space to represent the same graph as the edge list. This may not always be the case, which suggests that the method used to represent a graph should take its storage requirements into account.

Linked-lists can also be used to represent a graph. Each **vertex** in the graph has its own linked-list to store its edge-connected vertices. Now, however, the once simple task of checking for an edge between two vertices is complicated by the need to search the linked-list of the first vertex to see if it contains an edge to the second vertex. The advantage is that the graph can be built during run time, and not statically allocated as in the previous two

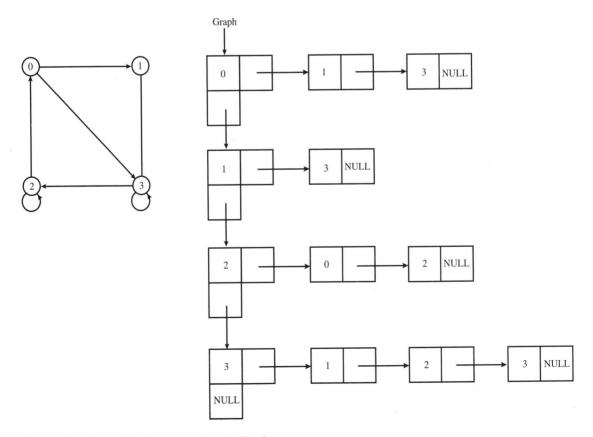

Figure 8.5   Linked-List Representation of a Graph

examples. Figure 8.5 shows a linked-list representation of a graph. Even the vertices of the graph are stored as a linked-list. If the number of nodes is known in advance, an array of pointers to the vertex lists can be used instead.

Conclusion

In this section you were exposed to three methods used to represent a graph. Check your understanding of this material with the following section review.

8.2 Section Review

1. What is an adjacency matrix?
2. Why do we square the adjacency matrix?
3. Can a graph be represented by a list of edges?
4. What is the disadvantage of implementing a graph with a linked-list?

8.3   Directed and Undirected Graphs

The differences between an **undirected graph** and a **directed graph** are illustrated in Figure 8.6. The same set of three nodes is used in Figure 8.6, but the associated adjacency matrices are different due to the use of undirected and directed edges. It is not uncommon to see both types of edges used in graphs. For instance, a program developed to control

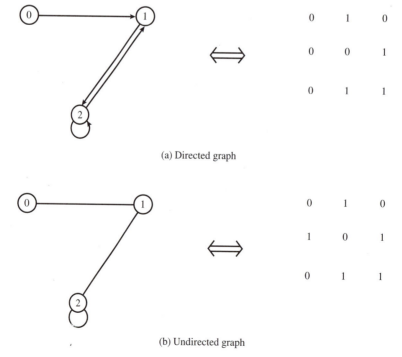

(a) Directed graph

(b) Undirected graph

Figure 8.6   Comparing Directed and Undirected Graphs

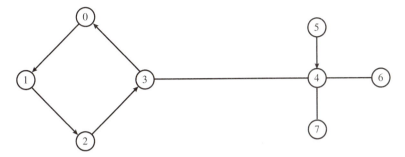

Figure 8.7   Connecting Computers in a LAN

traffic patterns may represent the various intersections and streets in a city as nodes and edges in a graph. Some streets may be one-way (directed). If we are **traversing the graph,** or trying to find a spanning tree or subgraph, we must pay attention to the type of edge encountered at every step.

Figure 8.7 shows a practical example of a graph used to represent interconnections between several computers in a local area network (LAN). Do you see that it is possible to reach any node from any other node (except node 5, which can only talk to all the other nodes, but not listen)? The graph in Figure 8.7 uses both directed and undirected edges. Furthermore, there are only eight edges (three are bidirectional), which suggests a small edge_list array, whereas an adjacency matrix would need to be an 8-by-8 matrix (64 elements). So, an edge_list array seems like a better choice this time as well.

Program 8.2 shows how the edge_list for the graph in Figure 8.7 can be used to determine if a given node is part of a *cycle*. No edges may be traveled more than once in the round trip back to the starting node.

Program 8.2

```
#include <stdio.h>

#define FALSE 0
#define TRUE  1
#define NODES 8
#define EDGES 11

        int edge_list[EDGES][2] = {{0,1}, {1,2}, {2,3}, {3,0},
                                    {3,4}, {4,3}, {4,6}, {4,7},
                                    {5,4}, {6,4}, {7,4}};
        int adjmat[NODES][NODES];

void make_adjmat(void);
int got_cycle(int va, int vb);

main()
{
        int i;

        for(i = 0; i < NODES; i++)
```

```
                {
                        printf("Node %d is ",i);
                        make_adjmat();
                        if (!got_cycle(i,i))
                                printf("not ");
                        printf("part of a cycle.\n");
                }
        }

void make_adjmat(void)
{
        int k;

        for(k = 0;  k < EDGES;  k++)
                adjmat[edge_list[k][0]][edge_list[k][1]] = TRUE;
}

int got_cycle(int va, int vb)
{
        int k, found;

        if (adjmat[va][vb] > 0)
                return(TRUE);
        found = FALSE;
        k = 0;
        while ((k < NODES) && !found)
        {
                if (adjmat[va][k] > 0)
                {
                        adjmat[va][k] *= -1;
                        if (adjmat[k][va] > 0)
                                adjmat[k][va] *= -1;
                        found = got_cycle(k,vb);
                        if (!found)
                        {
                                adjmat[va][k] *= -1;
                                if (adjmat[k][va] < 0)
                                        adjmat[k][va] *= -1;
                        }
                }
                k++;
        }
        return(found);
}
```

The `got_cycle()` function recursively determines if a specified node is part of a cycle. The `make_adjmat()` function builds a new copy of the adjacency matrix from the `edge_list` for each new vertex tested.

A sample execution is as follows:

```
Node 0 is part of a cycle.
Node 1 is part of a cycle.
Node 2 is part of a cycle.
Node 3 is part of a cycle.
Node 4 is not part of a cycle.
Node 5 is not part of a cycle.
Node 6 is not part of a cycle.
Node 7 is not part of a cycle.
```

Why do you think that nodes 4 through 7 are not part of any cycles?

Conclusion

In this section we examined graphs containing directed and undirected edges. Check your understanding of the material with the following section review.

8.3   **Section Review**

1. What is a cycle?
2. When does recursion stop in Program 8.2?
3. What is an undirected edge?
4. Why is it important to identify cycles?

8.4   Traversing a Graph

When working with graphs, the question often arises: Is there a path from vertex A to vertex B? This is a very important question, since the path might be an important communication channel in a computer network. Special network devices called **routers** pick and choose from the possible paths through a network, using **routing tables** that contain information about how the network is connected.

In the last section we saw how a cycle was searched for in a graph containing both directed and undirected edges. Figure 8.8 shows a directed graph that contains no cycles. This allows some simplification of the traversal function. The `got_cycle()` function from Program 8.2 is similar to the approach we will take here. Take a few minutes to study the `is_path()` function from Program 8.3.

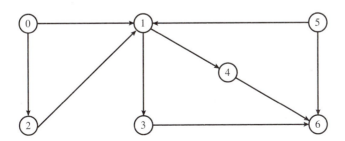

Figure 8.8   Directed Graph Containing No Cycles

Program 8.3

```
#include <stdio.h>

#define FALSE 0
#define TRUE  1
#define NODES 7
#define EDGES 9

        int edge_list[EDGES][2] = {{0,1}, {0,2}, {1,3}, {1,4},
                                    {2,1}, {3,6}, {4,6}, {5,1},
                                    {5,6}};
        int adjmat[NODES][NODES];

void make_adjmat(void);
int is_path(int va, int vb);

main()
{
        int src,dst;

        for(dst = 0; dst < NODES; dst++)
                printf("%4d",dst);
        printf("\n");
        for(src = 0; src < NODES; src++)
        {
                printf("%d: ",src);
                for(dst = 0; dst < NODES; dst++)
                {
                        make_adjmat();
                        if (is_path(src,dst))
                                printf("Yes ");
                        else
                                printf("No  ");
                }
                printf("\n");
        }
}

void make_adjmat(void)
{
        int k;

        for(k = 0; k < EDGES; k++)
                adjmat[edge_list[k][0]][edge_list[k][1]] = TRUE;
}

int is_path(int va, int vb)
{
        int k, found;

        if (adjmat[va][vb] > 0)
                return(TRUE);
        found = FALSE;
```

```
        k = 0;
        while ((k < NODES) && !found)
        {
                if (adjmat[va][k] > 0)
                {
                        adjmat[va][k] *= -1;
                        found = is_path(k,vb);
                        if (!found)
                                adjmat[va][k] *= -1;
                }
                k++;
        }
        return(found);
}
```

The is_path() returns a TRUE value if there is a directed path between va and vb. Note that there may be more than one path. Right now, all we care about is the existence of *any* path between vertices.

The execution of Program 8.3 looks like this:

```
     0    1    2    3    4    5    6
0: No  Yes  Yes  Yes  Yes  No   Yes
1: No  No   No   Yes  Yes  No   Yes
2: No  Yes  No   Yes  Yes  No   Yes
3: No  No   No   No   No   No   Yes
4: No  No   No   No   No   No   Yes
5: No  Yes  No   Yes  Yes  No   Yes
6: No  No   No   No   No   No   No
```

Referring back to Figure 8.8, you should be able to find the paths from vertex to vertex everywhere a 'Yes' appears in the result. Furthermore, do you see that there are four different paths from vertex 0 to vertex 6? They are:

```
0 - 1 - 4 - 6
0 - 1 - 3 - 6
0 - 2 - 1 - 4 - 6
0 - 2 - 1 - 3 - 6
```

The output of Program 8.3 says 'Yes' in row 0, column 6, meaning that there is a path between vertices 0 and 6, when there are actually four. In the next section, we will add weights to the edges and look for the *shortest* path between two vertices.

Conclusion

The directed graph of Figure 8.8 was traversed by the recursive is_path() function. Test your understanding of its operation with the following section review.

8.4 Section Review

1. Why is the path between nodes an important consideration?
2. How does is_path() determine if a path exists between nodes in a graph?
3. What is the function of a router?

8.5   Finding the Shortest Path

In Figure 8.2 we saw a graph of highways (all bidirectional) between five cities, with distances included. In this section, we are concerned with finding the shortest of all possible paths between two vertices (cities in Figure 8.2).

One way to do this is to find all of the paths, add up their respective distances, and select the path with the smallest distance. While this solution produces correct results, it is not recommended for the simple fact that it could be very time consuming to find the shortest path this way if the graph is large. However, for the purposes of this discussion, examine Program 8.4, which displays the distance associated with each edge for all possible paths between two cities in Figure 8.2.

Program 8.4

```
#include <stdio.h>

#define FALSE 0
#define TRUE  1
#define NODES 7
#define EDGES 9

        enum {southville, westville, northville, centerville, eastville};
        int adjmat[NODES][NODES] = {{   0, 50,122,   0,   0},
                                    { 50,   0, 90, 78,   0},
                                    {122, 90,   0, 45, 60},
                                    {   0, 78, 45,   0, 40},
                                    {   0,   0, 60, 40,   0}};
        int path[EDGES], path_ptr, path_count, which, shortest = 3e4;

void all_paths(int va, int vb);

main()
{
        printf("The paths are:\n");
        all_paths(southville, eastville);
        printf("Path %d is the shortest.\n",which);
}

void all_paths(int va, int vb)
{
        int k, total = 0;
        if (adjmat[va][vb] > 0)
        {
                path[path_ptr] = adjmat[va][vb];
                printf("%2d: ",++path_count);
                for(k = 0; k <= path_ptr; k++)
                {
                        total += path[k];
                        printf("%4d",path[k]);
                }
                printf(", Total: %d\n",total);
```

```
             if (total < shortest)
             {
                     shortest = total;
                     which = path_count;
             }
     }
     for(k = 0;  k < NODES;  k++)
             if (adjmat[va][k] > 0)
             {
                     path[path_ptr++] = adjmat[va][k];
                     adjmat[va][k]  *= -1;
                     adjmat[k][va]  *= -1;
                     all_paths(k,vb);
                     adjmat[va][k]  *= -1;
                     adjmat[k][va]  *= -1;
                     path_ptr--;
             }
}
```

Two cities, Southville and Eastville, have nine different paths between them, as illustrated by the sample execution:

```
The paths are:
  1:    50  90  60, Total: 200
  2:    50  90  45  40, Total: 225
  3:    50  78  40, Total: 168
  4:    50  78  45  60, Total: 233
  5:   122  60, Total: 182
  6:   122  90  78  40, Total: 330
  7:   122  90  78  45  60, Total: 395
  8:   122  45  40, Total: 207
  9:   122  45  78  90  60, Total: 395
Path 3 is the shortest.
```

Another approach is to maintain several subpaths at the same time. If one of the subpaths has a shorter distance than the others, the others may be thrown out. For example, if two paths both start at node X and end up at node Y on their way to node Z, the longer path from X to Y can be discarded. As Program 8.4 demonstrated, there are many ways to go from Southville to Eastville. Path 3, from Southville to Westville (50) to Centerville (78) to Eastville (40), is the shortest. This means that the first two paths can be disregarded, and any new paths whose length exceeds path 3's can also be thrown out. Program 8.5 uses a function called shortest_path() to automatically stop a path when its length is greater than the shortest path found so far.

Program 8.5

```
#include <stdio.h>

#define FALSE 0
#define TRUE  1
#define NODES 7
```

```
#define EDGES 9

        enum {southville, westville, northville, centerville, eastville};
        int adjmat[NODES][NODES] = {{  0, 50, 122,  0,  0},
                                    { 50,  0,  90, 78,  0},
                                    {122, 90,   0, 45, 60},
                                    {  0, 78,  45,  0, 40},
                                    {  0,  0,  60, 40,  0}};
        int path[EDGES], spath[EDGES], path_ptr, sptr;
        int total, shortest = 3e4;

void shortest_path(int va, int vb);
void save_path(void);
void show_path(void);

main()
{
        printf("The shortest path is: ");
        shortest_path(southville, eastville);
        show_path();
}

void shortest_path(int va, int vb)
{
        int k;
        if (adjmat[va][vb] > 0)
        {
                path[path_ptr] = adjmat[va][vb];
                total += adjmat[va][vb];
                if (total < shortest)
                {
                        shortest = total;
                        save_path();
                }
                total -= adjmat[va][vb];
        }
        for(k = 0; k < NODES; k++)
                if (adjmat[va][k] > 0)
                {
                        path[path_ptr++] = adjmat[va][k];
                        total += adjmat[va][k];
                        if (total < shortest)
                        {
                                adjmat[va][k] *= -1;
                                adjmat[k][va] *= -1;
                                shortest_path(k,vb);
                                adjmat[va][k] *= -1;
                                adjmat[k][va] *= -1;
                        }
                        total -= adjmat[va][k];
                        path_ptr--;
```

```
            }
}

void save_path()
{
        for(sptr = 0; sptr <= path_ptr; sptr++)
                spath[sptr] = path[sptr];
}

void show_path()
{
        int i;

        for(i = 0; i < sptr; i++)
                printf("%4d",spath[i]);
        printf(", Total: %d\n",shortest);
}
```

The shortest_path() function is very similar to the all_paths() function used in Program 8.4. One big difference is that the current path length is always known (stored in the global variable total), and any path that exceeds the shortest found so far is terminated. This is accomplished with this if statement:

```
if (total < shortest)
{
        adjmat[va][k] *= -1;
        adjmat[k][va] *= -1;
        shortest_path(k,vb);
        adjmat[va][k] *= -1;
        adjmat[k][va] *= -1;
}
```

The number of paths checked by Program 8.5 is significantly smaller than those of Program 8.4, all thanks to this one if statement. A good programming exercise would be to add path counters to Programs 8.4 and 8.5 to compare how much work each program does.

The length of the shortest path is saved in the global variable shortest. The initial value (3e4) is chosen to be significantly greater than any possible path through the cities. In general, choosing a "big" number like this is not the proper way to initialize a variable used in comparisons. Some users may wish to run the program with very large distances (such as a global shipping company). A better way to do the initialization of the shortest variable would be to add the distance of every edge together, then add one more to that sum. This guarantees that any path we find is shorter than the initial path length (because no cycles are allowed to artifically inflate the length). This is left for you to devise on your own.

Conclusion

The more-efficient shortest-path method was examined in this section. Paths whose length could never be smaller than the smallest path found so far are **pruned.** Check your understanding of the material with the following section review.

1. Can there be more than one path between nodes during a traversal?
2. What happens when we search for the shortest path and the number of nodes is large?
3. What is the best method to initialize the `shortest` path variable before the search is started?

8.6   A C++ GRAPH Object

In this section we will see how a C++ graph class is designed so that it implements the graph using linked-lists. The graph from Figure 8.7 is used as the test graph, and is specified by an edge list. Program 8.6 uses its GRAPH class to instantiate a graph object (cities), build the graph, and then steps through the vertex array and displays the contents of the linked-list storing the connecting nodes (if any).

Program 8.6

```
#include <iostream.h>
#include <iomanip.h>

#define NODES 8
#define EDGES 11

        int edge_list[EDGES][2] = {{0,1}, {1,2}, {2,3}, {3,0},
                                   {3,4}, {4,3}, {4,6}, {4,7},
                                   {5,4}, {6,4}, {7,4}};

        typedef struct node
        {
                int dst;
                struct node *link;
        } LNODE;

class GRAPH {
public:
        LNODE *vertex[NODES];

        GRAPH(void);
        void build_graph(void);
        void add_node(int va, int vb);
        void show_graph(void);
};

main()
{
        int i;
        GRAPH cities;
        LNODE *ptr;

        cities.build_graph();
        cities.show_graph();
}

GRAPH::GRAPH()
```

```
{
        int i;

        for(i = 0; i < NODES; i++)
                vertex[i] = NULL;
}

void GRAPH::build_graph()
{
        int i;

        for(i = 0; i < EDGES; i++)
                add_node(edge_list[i][0], edge_list[i][1]);
}

void GRAPH::add_node(int va, int vb)
{
        LNODE *p1, *p2;

        p1 = new LNODE;
        p1->dst = vb;
        p1->link = NULL;
        if (vertex[va] == NULL)
                vertex[va] = p1;
        else
        {
                p2 = vertex[va];
                while (p2->link != NULL)
                        p2 = p2->link;
                p2->link = p1;
        }
}

void GRAPH::show_graph()
{
        int i;
        LNODE *ptr;

        for(i = 0; i < NODES; i++)
        {
                ptr = vertex[i];
                cout << "Node " << i << " connects to ";
                if (ptr == NULL)
                        cout << "nothing";
                else
                while (ptr != NULL)
                {
                        cout << setw(3) << ptr->dst;
                        ptr = ptr->link;
                }
                cout << "\n";
        }
}
```

The constructor GRAPH() is necessary because a vertex in the graph may have directed edges into it, but not out of it (as we saw with node 5 in Figure 8.7). NULL pointers are assigned to each element of the vertex array, to guarantee that there is an empty list present for nodes with no outgoing edges.

Program 8.6 displays the following when executed:

```
Node 0 connects to    1
Node 1 connects to    2
Node 2 connects to    3
Node 3 connects to    0   4
Node 4 connects to    3   6   7
Node 5 connects to    4
Node 6 connects to    4
Node 7 connects to    4
```

Refer back to Figure 8.7 to verify that these results are correct.

Conclusion

In this section we saw the beginning of a C++ class for graph objects. Check your understanding of the material with the following section review.

8.6 Section Review

1. How is the graph initialized?
2. Where does add_node() place a newly allocated node?
3. What is one limitation of the GRAPH class?

Study Questions

General Concepts

Section 8.1

1. When is a graph fully connected?
2. What is a spanning tree?
3. Name three applications that use a graph data structure.

Section 8.2

4. When do we use an adjacency matrix?
5. What happens when we multiply an adjacency matrix by itself?
6. Explain the advantage of implementing a graph using a linked-list.

Section 8.3

7. How do we test for cycles?
8. Why is it common to see both directed and undirected edges in a graph?
9. Is the adjacency matrix built only one time?

Section 8.4

10. How do we determine if one node is connected to another?
11. How is recursion used to check for a path between nodes in the graph?

Section 8.5

12. Explain one method to determine the shortest distance between two nodes.
13. When do we disregard a path between nodes?
14. What is the initial value of the `shortest` variable in Program 8.4? Why is it so large? Is it large enough?

Section 8.6

15. How is the edge list used to build a graph object?
16. What is the job of the constructor in the `GRAPH` class?
17. What is the advantage of using a C++ graph object?

Program Design

For each of the following programming exercises, write a C or C++ program that performs the indicated task.

18. Write a function that builds an adjacency matrix from an edge list.
19. Write a function that creates an edge list using an adjacency matrix.
20. Modify Program 8.2 so that it tests the graph in Figure 8.9.
21. Complete the design of Program 8.6 by adding C++ member functions `shortest_path()` and `all_paths()`.
22. Modify Program 8.4 so that it finds all the paths between cities L and C in Figure 8.10.

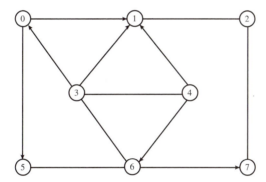

Figure 8.9   Graph for Question 20

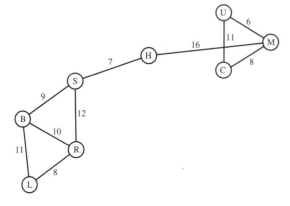

Figure 8.10   Intercity Distance Graph for Questions 22 and 23

23. Modify Program 8.4 so that it finds the shortest path between cities L and C in Figure 8.10.

24. Modify Programs 8.4 and 8.5 so that they keep track of the total number of paths checked. Compare the results of both executions.

25. Write a function called `init_shortest()` that initializes the global variable `shortest` to the sum of every edge distance in the graph, plus one.

26. Write a function that creates an edge list from a linked-list-based graph.

9   Hash Tables

Objectives

This chapter gives you the opportunity to learn:

1. The terminology associated with hash tables.
2. When to use a hash table.
3. How to write a hash function.
4. The various ways to handle collisions.
5. About ways to improve the hash function.
6. Methods available to handle any level of collision.
7. How to implement a hash table object in C++.

Key Terms

Hashing Function

Access

Collision Resolution

Collision Detection

Level of Collision

Hash Table Policy

HASH

Hash Table Objects

Outline

Introduction

The **hash table** is a data structure that we use when we want to eliminate the time it takes to search for an item. An ideal hash table will eliminate search time all together, providing direct access to the data. Let's begin by identifying what a hash table is and why it is useful.

9.1   Terminology

The term hash table is an exotic name for a rather simple data structure. We turn to hash tables when we need efficient storage and retrieval of data. A hash table utilizes a *hash* function, or **hashing function,** that creates unique indexes for the data items stored in the hash table.

A practical use for the hash table lies in the internal operation of a compiler. When a source file is compiled, a symbol table is generated. Every function name and variable name a programmer uses occupies a space in the symbol table. The compiler needs to read and write the symbol table frequently while it converts the source file into an executable program.

A large source file may contain several hundred symbol table entries. A linear search of the symbol table for a particular name could take a lot of time and significantly affect the time required to compile the program. This is where the hash table comes to the rescue. The search time for a hash table is designed to be the same for any name, and generally requires a single **access** into the hash table.

Consider a 64-element hash table, shown in Figure 9.1. This hash table is implemented using a rectangular array of eight element strings. A hash function converts input strings into 6-bit index values for the hash table. So, searching the hash table is a simple matter of running a string name through the hash function to get the index. This is demonstrated in Figure 9.2. The hash function can be designed to produce the 6-bit index in the same amount of time no matter how many characters are in the input string. This provides a nice solution to the problem we have with the compiler and its frequent use of the symbol table.

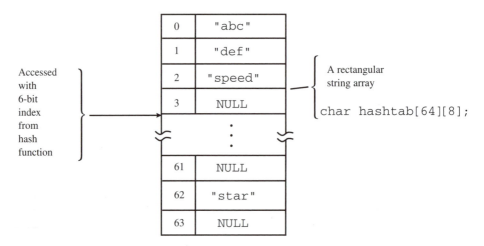

Figure 9.1   A 64-Element Hash Table

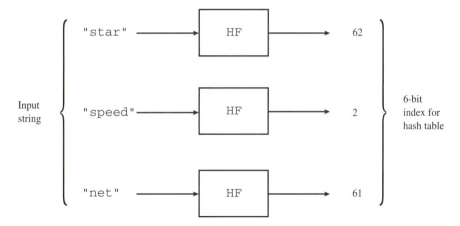

Figure 9.2 Operation of a Hash Function (HF)

One drawback in the use of a hash table is the unpredictability of the hash function. As a consequence of designing our own hash functions, we are left with a degree of uncertainty about what kinds of strings generate what kinds of indexes. For example, in Figure 9.2, notice that the input string "net" hashes to an index value of 61. There is currently an empty string in element 61 of the hash table (refer back to Figure 9.1). This means we can store "net" in location 61.

Because there is uncertainty in the hash function, it is not uncommon for two strings to hash to the same index. For example, "group" may hash to an index value of 62, just as "star" has already done. This is called a *collision*. How the programmer deals with collisions (**collision resolution**) is an important topic that will require detailed treatment.

Conclusion

In this section you were introduced to the terminology associated with hash tables. Check your understanding of the material with the following section review.

9.1 Section Review

1. What is the main advantage of using a hash table?
2. What does a hash function do?
3. What is a collision?
4. What is the drawback to using a hash table?

9.2   Why Use a Hash Table?

A hash table should be used whenever fast access to stored data is required. As we saw in the compiler example, when the number of symbols in the symbol table gets large, the time required for a sequential search for a specific symbol becomes significant. For instance, a sequential search of 1,024 elements requires, worst case, 1,024 comparisons. Even a binary tree storing the same 1,024 elements (in order) still has a worst case of ten comparisons.

The beauty of the hash table is that *all accesses take the same amount of time.* No matter how large the hash table, all that is necessary is the correct index, which is supplied quickly by the hash function. Ideally, the hash element selected by the index is the one we are looking for (there are no collisions), so we require a *single* comparison to find the correct element stored in a hash table. The time required to access any element is then based solely on the time necessary to generate an index with the hash function.

Another example of where a hash table would be useful has to do with counting words in a document. Many spell checkers regularly report the number of different words in a document, or allow custom user dictionaries to be built. As the size of these structures grows large, the problem of worst-case sequential search time comes up again. A hash table would eliminate this problem as well.

Hash functions may be designed in such a way that the same number of steps are used to generate an index, regardless of the size of the variable name being hashed. This will be demonstrated in the next section.

Conclusion

In this section you were provided with one example of why a hash table should be used in a few specific applications. Check your understanding of this material with the following section review.

9.2 Section Review

1. When do we want to use a hash table?
2. Why do we need to worry about worst case search time?
3. Explain how all accesses to a hash table can take the same time.
4. How is the compiler's symbol table similar to the spell checker's word counter?
5. What problem does a hash table eliminate?

9.3   Hash Functions

The hash function lies at the core of a hash table. It is the job of a hash function to produce the unique index into the hash table. Usually, a hash function reads a string of characters and then manipulates the values of the characters in a special way to generate the index. One way to do this is to add the ASCII values of all the string characters together. The index for a 64-element hash table could then be the lower 6 bits of the ASCII sum.

The problem with this hash function is that it takes longer to generate the index value as the size of the string increases. Even though we may get a better distribution of index values, we get them at the expense of extra computation time. Recall that we want to access stored data quickly, so we must be able to generate the index value quickly as well. A method to do this is as follows: Add the ASCII code of the first character in the string to the ASCII codes of the middle character and the last character in the string. Figure 9.3 shows a few examples of how the characters are chosen.

An ideal hashing function would generate a unique index for each character string encountered. In actual practice, we end up throwing away some of the hashing information when the index is generated. Since the hash table size is a power of 2, the index typically requires fewer bits than the hash value generated from the input string. As previously discussed, the

Input Strings	First	Middle	Last	Hash Value
"D"	'D'	'D'	'D'	12
"DB"	'D'	'D'	'B'	10
or				
	'D'	'B'	'B'	8
"INDEX"	'I'	'D'	'X'	37
"CAPTURE"	'C'	'T'	'E'	28

Figure 9.3   Choosing Characters to Hash

hash function may use only the lower 6 bits of the ASCII sum to make the index. When you throw bits away it is difficult to predict the index value a string will hash to, so it is necessary to test the hash function with a wide variety of input strings to see how well the index values get distributed. In the worst case the hash function produces the same index value for every input string. Hopefully, the number of collisions produced by the hash function is small compared to the number of items stored.

The following four programs illustrate the concepts and principles just described. Program 9.1 gets an input string from the user and passes it to a hash function that implements the three-character sum method. The value of the hash index is then displayed.

Program 9.1

```
#include <stdio.h>
#include <string.h>

int hash(char *name);

main()
{
        char input[32];

        do
        {
                printf("Enter a string => ");
                gets(input);
                if (strlen(input))
                        printf("%s hashes to an index value of %d\n\n",
                                input, hash(input));
        } while (strlen(input));
}

int hash(char *name)
{
        int middle, hash_value;
```

```
    middle = strlen(name) / 2;
    hash_value = name[0] + name[middle] + name[strlen(name) - 1];
    hash_value &= 0x3f;
    return hash_value;
}
```

Let us examine the hash function used in Program 9.1.

```
int hash(char *name)
{
    int middle, hash_value;

    middle = strlen(name) / 2;
    hash_value = name[0] + name[middle] + name[strlen(name) - 1];
    hash_value &= 0x3f;
    return hash_value;
}
```

Notice how the middle position of the string is found. The length of the string is divided by 2. The integer result is the index for the middle character in the string. The first, middle, and last character values are added together and then bitwise ANDed with 0x3F to preserve only the lower 6 bits. This six-bit result is the value returned to main(). With only 6 bits we always see a value from 0 to 63 for the index.

A sample execution of Program 9.1 looks like this:

```
Enter a string => ABC
ABC hashes to an index value of 6

Enter a string => DEF
DEF hashes to an index value of 15

Enter a string => TURNER
TURNER hashes to an index value of 52

Enter a string => VICTORIA
VICTORIA hashes to an index value of 38

Enter a string => ASHLEY
ASHLEY hashes to an index value of 38

Enter a string => KENNY
KENNY hashes to an index value of 50

Enter a string => KRISTEN
KRISTEN hashes to an index value of 44

Enter a string => KIMBERLY
KIMBERLY hashes to an index value of 41

Enter a string => QIL
QIL hashes to an index value of 38
```

There is a nice distribution of index values in this short list of names, but also notice that VICTORIA, ASHLEY, and QIL all hash to an index value of 38. This is unfortunate as well as unpredictable, but is a consequence of using a hash function that has to throw away information. Even so, for a simple hash function, it still does a good job. It executes quickly, taking the same amount of time, no matter how long the input string.

Program 9.2 expands Program 9.1 into a complete hashing application. A function called make_string() generates random length strings of one to five characters of uppercase letters. The main() function calls make_string() 64 times to see how many collisions are generated. The hash table is displayed at the end of the program and indicates the number of times each location was accessed.

Program 9.2

```
#include <stdio.h>
#include <string.h>
#include <stdlib.h>

void make_string(char *str);
int hash(char *name);

        int hash_table[64];
        int free_hash = 64;

main()
{
        int j,index;
        char input[6];

        printf("64 random strings...\n\n");
        for(j = 0; j < 64; j++)
        {
                make_string(input);
                index = hash(input);
                if (!hash_table[index])
                        free_hash--;
                hash_table[index]++;
        }
        printf("\n\n");
        printf("Hash Table...\n\n");
        for(j = 0; j < 64; j++)
        {
                printf("%02d ",hash_table[j]);
                if(7 == j % 8)
                        printf("\n");
        }
        printf("\n");
        printf("The number of free locations is %d\n",free_hash);
}

void make_string(char *str)
```

```
{
        int i,k;

        do
        {
                k = rand() % 6;
        } while(!k);
        for(i = 0; i < k; i++)
                str[i] = 'A' + rand() % 26;
        str[i] = '\0';
        printf("%s\t",str);
}


int hash(char *name)
{
        int middle;
        int hash_value;
        static int ccount;

        middle = strlen(name) / 2;
        hash_value = name[0] + name[middle] + name[strlen(name) - 1];
        printf("hash = %X\t",hash_value);
        if (++ccount == 3)
        {
                ccount = 0;
                printf("\n");
        }
        hash_value &= 0x3f;
        return hash_value;
}
```

A sample execution of Program 9.2 follows:

```
64 random strings
AKYI     hash = E3     T        hash = FC     Q        hash = F3
IYJZ     hash = ED     ETZJ     hash = E9     HOXOB    hash = E2
LEX      hash = E9     D        hash = CC     Q        hash = F3
BZ       hash = F6     YDE      hash = E2     GQ       hash = E9
QIL      hash = E6     R        hash = F6     DYCE     hash = CC
KORZT    hash = F1     AAT      hash = D6     STB      hash = E9
X        hash = 108    NJOI     hash = E6     KUWM     hash = EF
NKY      hash = F2     PGZJ     hash = F4     LXHYM    hash = E1
PRL      hash = EE     S        hash = F9     L        hash = E4
Q        hash = F3     CEQ      hash = D9     QWFB     hash = D9
KS       hash = F1     W        hash = 105    TUK      hash = F4
OM       hash = E9     Y        hash = 10B    KPUTW    hash = F7
WHEQ     hash = ED     FVHZ     hash = E8     JTO      hash = ED
RM       hash = EC     C        hash = C9     HIADI    hash = D2
D        hash = CC     O        hash = ED     TJRM     hash = F3
J        hash = DE     FUK      hash = E6     XHHCG    hash = E7
```

```
A           hash = C3      FEJ      hash = D5      S        hash = F9
UFH         hash = E3      PRFPR    hash = E8      QEIQJ    hash = E4
LWCAA       hash = D0      NBICT    hash = EB      EYMS     hash = E5
YT          hash = 101     H        hash = D8      OR       hash = F3
XKDH        hash = E4      ACBU     hash = D8      DDO      hash = D7
Y           hash = 10B
```

```
Hash Table...

00 01 00 01 00 01 00 00
01 01 00 02 03 00 00 00
01 00 01 00 00 01 01 01
02 02 00 00 00 00 01 00
00 01 02 02 03 01 03 01
02 05 00 01 01 04 01 01
00 02 01 05 02 00 02 01
00 02 00 00 01 00 00 00
```

```
The number of free locations is 27
```

Examine the set of 64 random strings. Notice that many of them have identical hash values. This indicates the presence of collisions, and accounts for the hash table values of 2 or more. For example, two sets of strings all hash to the same two index values. Strings LEX, OM, ETZJ, GQ, and STB all hash to a value of 0xE9 (of which we only use the lower 6 bits). Three other strings, Q, TJRM, and OR all hash to an index value of 0xF3. As a matter of fact, the Q string is actually generated three times by make_string().

The number of free locations is a good measure of how well your hash function distributes index values. There are 27 free locations left when Program 9.2 completes execution. So, we have filled slightly more than half of the hash table. This implies we get a collision almost half of the time. Let us experiment with the hash function to see if we can improve on this behavior.

Suppose we try to distinguish between strings based on more than the first, middle, and last positions of the characters. For instance, the single string "D" hashes to the same index as "DDD" and "DIDAD" and many other multicharacter strings. To distinguish between these types of strings we can try adding the string *length* to the hash value. Strings that previously hashed to the same index will now hash to different index values if their lengths are different.

Program 9.3 contains an additional statement in the hash() function that adds the string length to the hash value. This is the only change from Program 9.2.

Program 9.3

```c
#include <stdio.h>
#include <string.h>
#include <stdlib.h>

void make_string(char *str);
int hash(char *name);

        int hash_table[64];
```

```
        int free_hash = 64;

main()
{
        int j,index;
        char input[6];

        printf("64 random strings...\n\n");
        for(j = 0; j < 64; j++)
        {
                make_string(input);
                index = hash(input);
                if (!hash_table[index])
                        free_hash--;
                hash_table[index]++;
        }
        printf("\n\n");
        printf("Hash Table...\n\n");
        for(j = 0; j < 64; j++)
        {
                printf("%02d ",hash_table[j]);
                if(7 == j % 8)
                        printf("\n");
        }
        printf("\n");
        printf("The number of free locations is %d\n",free_hash);
}

void make_string(char *str)
{
        int i,k;

        do
        {
                k = rand() % 6;
        } while(!k);
        for(i = 0; i < k; i++)
                str[i] = 'A' + rand() % 26;
        str[i] = '\0';
        printf("%s\t",str);
}


int hash(char *name)
{
        int middle;
        int hash_value;
        static int ccount;

        middle = strlen(name) / 2;
        hash_value = name[0] + name[middle] + name[strlen(name) - 1];
```

```
hash_value += strlen(name);
printf("hash = %X\t",hash_value);
if (++ccount == 3)
{
        ccount = 0;
        printf("\n");
}
hash_value &= 0x3f;
return hash_value;
}
```

A sample execution of Program 9.3 gives the following results:

```
64 random strings...

AKYI     hash = E7      T       hash = FD      Q         hash = F4
IYJZ     hash = F1      ETZJ    hash = ED      HOXOB     hash = E7
LEX      hash = EC      D       hash = CD      Q         hash = F4
BZ       hash = F8      YDE     hash = E5      GQ        hash = EB
QIL      hash = E9      R       hash = F7      DYCE      hash = D0
KORZT    hash = F6      AAT     hash = D9      STB       hash = EC
X        hash = 109     NJOI    hash = EA      KUWM      hash = F3
NKY      hash = F5      PGZJ    hash = F8      LXHYM     hash = E6
PRL      hash = F1      S       hash = FA      L         hash = E5
Q        hash = F4      CEQ     hash = DC      QWFB      hash = DD
KS       hash = F3      W       hash = 106     TUK       hash = F7
OM       hash = EB      Y       hash = 10C     KPUTW     hash = FC
WHEQ     hash = F1      FVHZ    hash = EC      JTO       hash = F0
RM       hash = EE      C       hash = CA      HIADI     hash = D7
D        hash = CD      O       hash = EE      TJRM      hash = F7
J        hash = DF      FUK     hash = E9      XHHCG     hash = EC
A        hash = C4      FEJ     hash = D8      S         hash = FA
UFH      hash = E6      PRFPR   hash = ED      QEIQJ     hash = E9
LWCAA    hash = D5      NBICT   hash = F0      EYMS      hash = E9
YT       hash = 103     H       hash = D9      OR        hash = F5
XKDH     hash = E8      ACBU    hash = DC      DDO       hash = DA
Y        hash = 10C

Hash Table...

00 00 00 01 01 00 01 00
00 01 01 00 02 02 00 00
01 00 00 00 00 01 00 01
01 02 01 00 02 01 00 01
00 00 00 00 00 02 02 02
01 04 01 02 04 02 02 00
02 03 00 02 03 02 01 03
02 00 02 00 01 01 00 00

The number of free locations is 27
```

Although the same number of entries are made in the hash table as in Program 9.2, notice that the hash table no longer contains two 05 entries (indicating 5 accesses to the same location). Instead, there are now two 04 entries. This indicates that by adding the string length we have managed to redistribute the collisions. This will have a beneficial effect on the search time when resolving collisions (which we will do in the next two sections).

Another point to consider is that each of the 64 random strings now hashes to different index values. Remember, OR and Q used to hash to an index value of 0xF3. Now, both of these strings hash to completely different indexes, 0xF4 and 0xF5. Notice that both of these indexes are different from the original.

One last attempt at improving the hash function is made in Program 9.4. The hash() function now adds *all* the characters in the string to create the hash value.

Program 9.4

```
#include <stdio.h>
#include <string.h>
#include <stdlib.h>

void make_string(char *str);
int hash(char *name);

        int hash_table[64];
        int free_hash = 64;

main()
{
        int j,index;
        char input[6];

        printf("64 random strings...\n\n");
        for(j = 0; j < 64; j++)
        {
                make_string(input);
                index = hash(input);
                if (!hash_table[index])
                        free_hash--;
                hash_table[index]++;
        }
        printf("\n\n");
        printf("Hash Table...\n\n");
        for(j = 0; j < 64; j++)
        {
                printf("%02d ",hash_table[j]);
                if(7 == j % 8)
                        printf("\n");
        }
        printf("\n");
        printf("The number of free locations is %d\n",free_hash);
}

void make_string(char *str)
{
```

```
        int i,k;

        do
        {
                k = rand() % 6;
        } while(!k);
        for(i = 0; i < k; i++)
                str[i] = 'A' + rand() % 26;
        str[i] = '\0';
        printf("%s\t",str);
}


int hash(char *name)
{
        int k,hash_value;
        static int ccount;

        hash_value = name[0];
        for(k = 1; k < strlen(name); k++)
                hash_value += name[k];
        printf("hash = %X\t",hash_value);
        if (++ccount == 3)
        {
                ccount = 0;
                printf("\n");
        }
        hash_value &= 0x3f;
        return hash_value;
}
```

As shown in the following sample execution, we get a good improvement in the number of different indexes generated, dropping from 27 to 23 free locations. This means that four new indexes were generated by the hash function. Also, the hash table now contains four 03 values, and no 04s or 05s. This is another benefit of the new hash function.

```
64 random strings...

AKYI    hash = 12E      T       hash = 54       Q       hash = 51
IYJZ    hash = 146      ETZJ    hash = 13D      HOXOB   hash = 180
LEX     hash = E9       D       hash = 44       Q       hash = 51
BZ      hash = 9C       YDE     hash = E2       GQ      hash = 98
QIL     hash = E6       R       hash = 52       DYCE    hash = 125
KORZT   hash = 19A      AAT     hash = D6       STB     hash = E9
X       hash = 58       NJOI    hash = 130      KUWM    hash = 144
NKY     hash = F2       PGZJ    hash = 13B      LXHYM   hash = 192
PRL     hash = EE       S       hash = 53       L       hash = 4C
Q       hash = 51       CEQ     hash = D9       QWFB    hash = 130
KS      hash = 9E       W       hash = 57       TUK     hash = F4
OM      hash = 9C       Y       hash = 59       KPUTW   hash = 19B
WHEQ    hash = 135      FVHZ    hash = 13E      JTO     hash = ED
```

```
RM        hash = 9F    C        hash = 43    HIADI    hash = 15F
D         hash = 44    O        hash = 4F    TJRM     hash = 13D
J         hash = 4A    FUK      hash = E6    XHHCG    hash = 172
A         hash = 41    FEJ      hash = D5    S        hash = 53
UFH       hash = E3    PRFPR    hash = 18A   QEIQJ    hash = 17A
LWCAA     hash = 168   NBICT    hash = 170   EYMS     hash = 13E
YT        hash = AD    H        hash = 48    OR       hash = A1
XKDH      hash = 12F   ACBU     hash = 11B   DDO      hash = D7
Y         hash = 59
```

```
Hash Table...

01 01 00 01 03 00 01 00
01 00 02 00 01 00 00 01
00 03 02 02 01 01 01 02
02 03 01 02 02 00 01 02
00 01 01 01 00 01 02 00
01 02 00 00 00 02 02 01
03 00 02 00 01 01 00 00
00 00 01 01 00 02 02 00
```

```
The number of free locations is 23
```

We must still pay a price for getting a better distribution from the hash function. In this case, we give up the need for speed. If the user enters a 30-character string, `hash()` will have to add all 30 character values together, a very time-consuming job if that particular string is popular and is searched for often. If speed is not an issue, the reduction in collisions is worth the added effort.

Conclusion

In this section we examined a number of methods for converting an input string into a unique hash table index. Check your understanding of this material with the following section review.

9.3 Section Review

1. What is the significant property of an ideal hash function?
2. What is the worst-case behavior of a hash function?
3. What is one reason why a hash function may be unpredictable?
4. Explain why a lower number of free locations in a hash table is better than a higher number of free locations.
5. Why is index generation time such an important issue?

9.4   Collision Detection

An ideal hash function would take 64 different strings and generate 64 different index values (0 through 63). As we saw in the executions of Programs 9.2 through 9.4, many locations in the hash table had counts greater than 01. This indicates that there are collisions occurring when the strings are processed. In this case, it is easy to **detect a collision.** If we access the hash table with a new index and the location contains 00, the index is brand new. If the location does not contain 00, then it has been accessed at least once in the past. This means that our index value has been generated before, either by the current input string or by some other input string.

It is important to determine which type of situation we have encountered when we determine we have already accessed a certain hash table location. If we are hashing the same string that we hashed before, everything is OK, and we really have not had a collision. On the other hand, if we have a different input string hashing to the same index value, a collision has actually occurred. The programs we have looked at so far have not needed to deal with these details. Now that it is of interest, we must implement a method to keep track of the names used to hash the index values. In the case of a string, this simply means we need to store each input string in the hash table. Now, when a location is accessed, we compare the string stored at the location with the current string. If they match, there is no collision. Otherwise, further work must be performed to resolve the collision (which we will examine in the next section).

Program 9.5 uses an array of strings to represent the new hash table, rather than the integer array used in Programs 9.2, 9.3, and 9.4.

Program 9.5

```c
#include <stdio.h>
#include <string.h>
#include <stdlib.h>

void make_string(char *str);
int hash(char *name);

        char hash_table[64][6];
        int accesses[64];
        int collisions[64];
        int free_hash = 64;

main()
{
        int j,index;
        char input[6];

        printf("64 random strings...\n\n");
        for(j = 0; j < 64; j++)
        {
                make_string(input);
                index = hash(input);
                accesses[index]++;
                if (!strlen(hash_table[index]))
                {
                        free_hash--;
                        strcat(hash_table[index],input);
                }
                else
                if (strcmp(input,hash_table[index]))
                        collisions[index]++;
        }
```

```
            printf("\n\n");
            printf("Hash Table...\n\n");
            for(j = 0;  j < 64;  j++)
            {
                    printf("%6s -> %2d,%2d    ",hash_table[j],accesses[j],
                            collisions[j]);
                    if(3 == j % 4)
                            printf("\n");
            }
            printf("\n");
            printf("The number of free locations is %d\n",free_hash);
}

void make_string(char *str)
{
            int i,k;

            do
            {
                    k = rand() % 6;
            } while(!k);
            for(i = 0;  i < k;  i++)
                    str[i] = 'A' + rand() % 26;
            str[i] = '\0';
            printf("%s\t",str);
}


int hash(char *name)
{
            int k,hash_value;
            static int ccount;

            hash_value = name[0];
            for(k = 1;  k < strlen(name);  k++)
                    hash_value += name[k];
            printf("hash = %X\t",hash_value);
            if (++ccount == 3)
            {
                    ccount = 0;
                    printf("\n");
            }
            hash_value &= 0x3f;
            return hash_value;
}
```

Initially, each string stored in the hash table has a length of 0, due to the method used to initialize global variables. When an input string hashes to an index that selects an empty string, we have the *initial* hash string for that location. The input string is then stored in the hash table at the specified index.

If the hash string found at the index location is not empty, we must *compare* the input string with the string stored in the hash table. If they are identical, there is no collision.

The `strlen()`, `strcmp()`, and `strcat()` functions are used to perform the various checks and operations on the hash table elements.

A sample execution of Program 9.5 looks like this:

```
64 random strings

AKYI      hash = 12E    T      hash = 54    Q        hash = 51
IYJZ      hash = 146    ETZJ   hash = 13D   HOXOB    hash = 180
LEX       hash = E9     D      hash = 44    Q        hash = 51
BZ        hash = 9C     YDE    hash = E2    GQ       hash = 98
QIL       hash = E6     R      hash = 52    DYCE     hash = 125
KORZT     hash = 19A    AAT    hash = D6    STB      hash = E9
X         hash = 58     NJOI   hash = 130   KUWM     hash = 144
NKY       hash = F2     PGZJ   hash = 13B   LXHYM    hash = 192
PRL       hash = EE     S      hash = 53    L        hash = 4C
Q         hash = 51     CEQ    hash = D9    QWFB     hash = 130
KS        hash = 9E     W      hash = 57    TUK      hash = F4
OM        hash = 9C     Y      hash = 59    KPUTW    hash = 19B
WHEQ      hash = 135    FVHZ   hash = 13E   JTO      hash = ED
RM        hash = 9F     C      hash = 43    HIADI    hash = 15F
D         hash = 44     O      hash = 4F    TJRM     hash = 13D
J         hash = 4A     FUK    hash = E6    XHHCG    hash = 172
A         hash = 41     FEJ    hash = D5    S        hash = 53
UFH       hash = E3     PRFPR  hash = 18A   QEIQJ    hash = 17A
LWCAA     hash = 168    NBICT  hash = 170   EYMS     hash = 13E
YT        hash = AD     H      hash = 48    OR       hash = A1
XKDH      hash = 12F    ACBU   hash = 11B   DDO      hash = D7
Y         hash = 59


Hash Table...

HOXOB ->  1, 0        A ->  1, 0              ->  0, 0        C ->  1, 0
    D ->  3, 1          ->  0, 0      IYJZ ->  1, 0              ->  0, 0
    H ->  1, 0          ->  0, 0         J ->  2, 1              ->  0, 0
    L ->  1, 0          ->  0, 0          ->  0, 0        O ->  1, 0
      ->  0, 0        Q ->  3, 0         R ->  2, 1        S ->  2, 0
    T ->  1, 0      FEJ ->  1, 0       AAT ->  1, 0        W ->  2, 1
   GQ ->  2, 1      CEQ ->  3, 2     KORZT ->  1, 0    KPUTW ->  2, 1
   BZ ->  2, 1          ->  0, 0        KS ->  1, 0       RM ->  2, 1
      ->  0, 0       OR ->  1, 0       YDE ->  1, 0      UFH ->  1, 0
      ->  0, 0     DYCE ->  1, 0       QIL ->  2, 1          ->  0, 0
LWCAA ->  1, 0      LEX ->  2, 1          ->  0, 0          ->  0, 0
      ->  0, 0      JTO ->  2, 1      AKYI ->  2, 1     XKDH ->  1, 0
 NJOI ->  3, 2          ->  0, 0       NKY ->  2, 1          ->  0, 0
  TUK ->  1, 0     WHEQ ->  1, 0          ->  0, 0          ->  0, 0
      ->  0, 0          ->  0, 0     QEIQJ ->  1, 0     PGZJ ->  1, 0
      ->  0, 0     ETZJ ->  2, 1      FVHZ ->  2, 1          ->  0, 0


The number of free locations is 23
```

The sample execution displays each element of the hash table in the following manner:

Hash String -> Accesses, Collisions

You may notice that many of the strings in the "`random strings...`" section of the execution are not shown at all in the hash table output. This is the result of their having collided with the initial hash string stored at the same index location. For example, hash string `D` hashes to location 4 before `KUWM` does, so we do not see `KUWM` in the hash table. The same is true for the strings `NJOI`, `QWFB`, and `NBICT`, which all hash to location 48, although only `NJOI` is stored there. This is because `NJOI` is generated *before* the other two strings.

Obviously, we do not want to lose this information. *Resolving* the collision (storing the colliding string as well) will be covered in the next section.

Conclusion

In this section we saw how a newly structured hash table was used to store strings at hashed locations. String comparison provided an easy collision detection method. Check your understanding of this material with the following section review.

9.4 Section Review

1. What is stored at a new hash table location?
2. How is a collision determined?
3. Explain how the strings `D` and `KUWM` hash to location 4.
4. Explain how `NJOI`, `QWFB`, and `NBICT` all hash to location 48.
5. Why store the first string to hash to a location? Why not store the second, or third?

9.5   Resolving Collisions

Ideally, we would never have to worry about resolving a hash table collision, because there would be none. Our hash function would generate unique indexes for each input string.

The sample execution of Program 9.5 clearly demonstrated that strings that collided with stored hash strings were not displayed or stored in the hash table, which only had room for one string at each location.

An easy way to resolve collisions is to increase the number of strings that can be stored at each location. This increases the size of the hash table, but is a small price to pay for getting collision resolution.

The new hash table is organized as shown in Figure 9.4. As indicated, each index generated by the hash function is used to select a group of *two* hash strings. The policy for accessing the new hash table is as follows:

1. If the first string of the group is empty, store the current hash string in it.
2. If the first string is not empty, compare it with the current hash string. If they are the same, there is no collision.
3. If the two strings are different, examine the second string in the group. If it is empty, store the current hash string there. This resolves one **level of collision.**
4. If the second string is not empty, compare it with the current hash string. If they are the same, there is no collision.
5. If the strings are not the same, increment the collision counter for that index.

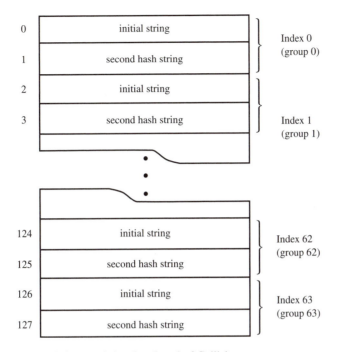

Figure 9.4   Resolving One Level of Collision

Program 9.6 implements this hash table policy and uses the hash table organization shown in Figure 9.4.

Program 9.6

```
#include <stdio.h>
#include <string.h>
#include <stdlib.h>

void make_string(char *str);
int hash(char *name);

        char hash_table[64*2][6];
        int accesses[64*2];
        int collisions[64];
        int free_hash = 64*2;

main()
{
        int c,j,index,offset;
        char input[6];

        printf("64 random strings...\n\n");
        for(j = 0; j < 64; j++)
        {
                make_string(input);
```

```
                index = hash(input);
                offset = index * 2;
                if (!strlen(hash_table[offset]))
                {
                        free_hash--;
                        strcat(hash_table[offset],input);
                        accesses[offset]++;
                }
                else
                if (!strcmp(input,hash_table[offset]))
                        accesses[offset]++;
                else
                if (!strlen(hash_table[offset+1]))
                {
                        free_hash--;
                        strcat(hash_table[offset+1],input);
                        accesses[offset+1]++;
                }
                else
                if (!strcmp(hash_table[offset+1],input))
                        accesses[offset+1]++;
                else
                        collisions[index]++;
        }
        printf("\n\n");
        printf("Hash Table...\n\n");
        for(j = 0; j < 64; j += 4)
        {
                for (c = 0; c < 8; c += 2)
                        printf("%6s ->    %2d    ",hash_table[j+j+c],
                                accesses[j+j+c]);
                printf("\n");
                for (c = 0; c < 8; c += 2)
                        printf("%6s ->    %2d    ",hash_table[j+j+c+1],
                                accesses[j+j+c+1]);
                printf("\n");
                for (c = 0; c < 8; c += 2)
                        printf("Collisions: %2d    ",collisions[j + c/2]);
                printf("\n\n");
        }
        printf("\n");
        printf("The number of free locations is %d\n",free_hash);
}

void make_string(char *str)
{
        int i,k;

        do
        {
                k = rand() % 6;
        } while (!k);
        for(i = 0; i < k; i++)
```

```
                str[i] = 'A' + rand() % 26;
        str[i] = '\0';
        printf("%s\t",str);
}


int hash(char *name)
{
        int k,hash_value;
        static int ccount;

        hash_value = name[0];
        for(k = 1; k < strlen(name); k++)
                hash_value += name[k];
        printf("hash = %X\t",hash_value);
        if (++ccount == 3)
        {
                ccount = 0;
                printf("\n");
        }
        hash_value &= 0x3f;
        return hash_value;
}
```

The **hash table policy** is controlled by these statements:

1. If the first string of the group is empty, store the current hash string in it.

```
offset = index * 2;
if (!strlen(hash_table[offset]))
{
        free_hash--;
        strcat(hash_table[offset],input);
        accesses[offset]++;
}
```

2. If the first string is not empty, compare it with the current hash string. If they are the same, there is no collision.

```
else
if (!strcmp(input,hash_table[offset]))
        accesses[offset]++;
```

3. If the two strings are different, examine the second string in the group. If it is empty, store the current hash string there. This resolves one level of collision.

```
else
if (!strlen(hash_table[offset+1]))
{
        free_hash--;
        strcat(hash_table[offset+1],input);
        accesses[offset+1]++;
}
```

4. If the second string is not empty, compare it with the current hash string. If they are the same, there is no collision.

```
else
if (!strcmp(hash_table[offset+1],input))
      accesses[offset+1]++;
```

5. If the strings are not the same, increment the collision counter for that index.

```
else
      collisions[index]++;
}
```

The formatting of the output on the display is written to help visualize the hashing policy using the following coding:

```
printf("Hash Table...\n\n");
for(j = 0; j < 64; j += 4)
      {
            for (c = 0; c < 8; c += 2)
                  printf("%6s ->     %2d      ",hash_table[j+j+c],
                              accesses[j+j+c]);
            printf("\n");
            for (c = 0; c < 8; c += 2)
                  printf("%6s ->     %2d      ",hash_table[j+j+c+1],
                              accesses[j+j+c+1]);
            printf("\n");
            for (c = 0; c < 8; c += 2)
                  printf("Collisions: %2d      ",collisions[j + c/2]);
            printf("\n\n");
}
```

Groups of four hash table entries are displayed simultaneously. The j+j+c terms are used to generate the proper index values.

A sample execution of Program 9.6 follows:

```
64 random strings...
```

AKYI	hash = 12E	T	hash = 54	Q	hash = 51
IYJZ	hash = 146	ETZJ	hash = 13D	HOXOB	hash = 180
LEX	hash = E9	D	hash = 44	Q	hash = 51
BZ	hash = 9C	YDE	hash = E2	GQ	hash = 98
QIL	hash = E6	R	hash = 52	DYCE	hash = 125
KORZT	hash = 19A	AAT	hash = D6	STB	hash = E9
X	hash = 58	NJOI	hash = 130	KUWM	hash = 144
NKY	hash = F2	PGZJ	hash = 13B	LXHYM	hash = 192
PRL	hash = EE	S	hash = 53	L	hash = 4C
Q	hash = 51	CEQ	hash = D9	QWFB	hash = 130
KS	hash = 9E	W	hash = 57	TUK	hash = F4
OM	hash = 9C	Y	hash = 59	KPUTW	hash = 19B
WHEQ	hash = 135	FVHZ	hash = 13E	JTO	hash = ED

```
RM       hash = 9F     C       hash = 43     HIADI   hash = 15F
D        hash = 44     O       hash = 4F     TJRM    hash = 13D
J        hash = 4A     FUK     hash = E6     XHHCG   hash = 172
A        hash = 41     FEJ     hash = D5     S       hash = 53
UFH      hash = E3     PRFPR   hash = 18A    QEIQJ   hash = 17A
LWCAA    hash = 168    NBICT   hash = 170    EYMS    hash = 13E
YT       hash = AD     H       hash = 48     OR      hash = A1
XKDH     hash = 12F    ACBU    hash = 11B    DDO     hash = D7
Y        hash = 59
```

```
Hash Table...

  HOXOB ->    1         A ->    1            ->    0         C ->    1
        ->    0           ->    0            ->    0           ->    0
Collisions:   0     Collisions:   0     Collisions:   0     Collisions:   0


      D ->    2           ->    0       IYJZ ->    1            ->    0
  KUWM ->    1            ->    0           ->    0            ->    0
Collisions:   0     Collisions:   0     Collisions:   0     Collisions:   0


      H ->    1           ->    0          J ->    1            ->    0
        ->    0           ->    0      PRFPR ->    1            ->    0
Collisions:   0     Collisions:   0     Collisions:   0     Collisions:   0


      L ->    1           ->    0           ->    0          O ->    1
        ->    0           ->    0           ->    0            ->    0
Collisions:   0     Collisions:   0     Collisions:   0     Collisions:   0


        ->    0         Q ->    3          R ->    1          S ->    2
        ->    0           ->    0      LXHYM ->    1            ->    0
Collisions:   0     Collisions:   0     Collisions:   0     Collisions:   0


      T ->    1       FEJ ->    1        AAT ->    1          W ->    1
        ->    0           ->    0           ->    0        DDO ->    1
Collisions:   0     Collisions:   0     Collisions:   0     Collisions:   0


     GQ ->    1       CEQ ->    1      KORZT ->    1      KPUTW ->    1
      X ->    1         Y ->    2           ->    0       ACBU ->    1
Collisions:   0     Collisions:   0     Collisions:   0     Collisions:   0


     BZ ->    1           ->    0         KS ->    1         RM ->    1
     OM ->    1           ->    0           ->    0      HIADI ->    1
Collisions:   0     Collisions:   0     Collisions:   0     Collisions:   0


        ->    0        OR ->    1        YDE ->    1        UFH ->    1
        ->    0           ->    0           ->    0            ->    0
Collisions:   0     Collisions:   0     Collisions:   0     Collisions:   0


        ->    0      DYCE ->    1        QIL ->    1            ->    0
        ->    0           ->    0        FUK ->    1            ->    0
Collisions:   0     Collisions:   0     Collisions:   0     Collisions:   0
```

```
 LWCAA ->    1         LEX ->    1              ->    0               ->    0
       ->    0         STB ->    1              ->    0               ->    0
Collisions:  0    Collisions:    0    Collisions:    0    Collisions:    0

       ->    0         JTO ->    1        AKYI ->    1         XKDH ->    1
       ->    0          YT ->    1         PRL ->    1               ->    0
Collisions:  0    Collisions:    0    Collisions:    0    Collisions:    0

  NJOI ->    1              ->    0         NKY ->    1               ->    0
  QWFB ->    1              ->    0       XHHCG ->    1               ->    0
Collisions:  1    Collisions:    0    Collisions:    0    Collisions:    0

   TUK ->    1        WHEQ ->    1              ->    0               ->    0
       ->    0              ->    0              ->    0               ->    0
Collisions:  0    Collisions:    0    Collisions:    0    Collisions:    0

       ->    0              ->    0        QEIQJ ->   1         PGZJ ->    1
       ->    0              ->    0              ->    0               ->    0
Collisions:  0    Collisions:    0    Collisions:    0    Collisions:    0

       ->    0        ETZJ ->    1        FVHZ ->    1               ->    0
       ->    0        TJRM ->    1        EYMS ->    1               ->    0
Collisions:  0    Collisions:    0    Collisions:    0    Collisions:    0


The number of free locations is 70
```

Notice how each group is displayed. The format is as follows:

Initial Hash String -> Accesses
Second Hash String -> Accesses
Collisions

In the entire display, there is only a *single* collision. It is in the group containing NJOI and QWFB. Recall from the previous section that the third string was NBICT (all three strings had to index 48).

It is tempting to think that we should now increase the size of the hash table again, allowing for three strings in each index group. This may actually be wasteful, as we have only a single string that cannot be stored under the existing policy. Instead, we could modify the policy so that, after two misses, we simply advance to the next index in the hash table. If it is empty, we use it as if we hashed there in the first place. We may also wish to go backwards one index, or check both positions, depending on which is available.

An altogether different approach would be to use the hash table detailed in Figure 9.5. Figure 9.5 shows a very efficient way to implement a hash table using linked-lists. By changing the array from an array of strings to an array of pointers, we can handle any number of collisions without wasting any space. For example, location 0 contains a pointer to a node containing "ABC". The pointer field of this node is NULL, indicating no collisions have occurred at index value 0. Index value 1, on the other hand, contains a pointer to the node containing "DSC". This link field of this node points to another node containing "GLOF". The link field in this node is NULL. Another collision on index value 1 would be resolved by

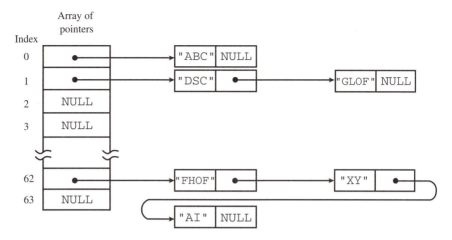

Figure 9.5   Hash Table as an Array of Linked-Lists

simply adding an additional node to the linked-list pointed to by the node containing "GLOF". The actual implementation of this approach is left for you to discover on your own.

Conclusion

In this section we examined how to resolve collisions in a hash table by doubling the number of strings that can be stored at each index location. Other space-efficient methods (using the next/previous entry, linked-lists) were presented as well. Check your understanding of this material with the following section review.

9.5 Section Review

1. Why is it necessary to check both strings stored at an index?
2. What are the limitations of Program 9.6?
3. How do linked-lists save on storage space in the pointer-based hash table of Figure 9.5?
4. How is the string AI found in the pointer-based hash table?

9.6   The C++ HASH Class

In this section we will examine the components of a class of hash table functions and variables called **HASH.** In keeping with the features available in C++, everything we need to work with a hash table will be contained in objects instantiated from the HASH class.

The definition of the HASH class begins like this:

```
#define HASHsize 64
#define SYMBOLsize 6

class HASH {
public:
    char symbol[SYMBOLsize];
```

```
        char table[HASHsize][SYMBOLsize];
        int index;

        HASH(void);
        int hashfn(char name[]);
        int collide(char name[], int index);
        void addsymbol(char name[], int index);
        void showtable(void);
};
```

All of the variables and functions necessary to support a hash table are contained in this definition. Let us examine each of the functions and see what use they make of the symbol, table, and index variables.

The first function is the *constructor* HASH(). This function automatically executes when a HASH object is instantiated. It is used to initialize the hash table with empty strings.

```
HASH::HASH()
{
        int i;

        for(i = 0; i < HASHsize; i++)
                table[i][0] = '\0';
}
```

The next function is the hash function hashfn(), which finds the sum of the first, middle, and last ASCII characters in the symbol string, and returns the lower 6 bits of the sum as the index.

```
int HASH::hashfn(char name[])
{
        int mid, hashval;

        mid = strlen(name) / 2;
        hashval = name[0] + name[mid] + name[strlen(name) - 1];
        hashval &= 0x3f;
        return hashval;
}
```

It may be useful to have a function that determines if the current index is colliding with a previously generated index of the same value. The collide() function returns a TRUE value if a collision is present, and FALSE if there is no collision.

```
int HASH::collide(char name[], int index)
{
        int empty, samesymbol;

        empty = (0 == strlen(table[index]));
        samesymbol = (0 == strcmp(table[index],name));
        return (!empty && !samesymbol);
}
```

The addsymbol() function is called when we know the new index points to a free hash table location. The symbol string is copied into the selected location.

```
void HASH::addsymbol(char name[], int index)
{
    strcat(table[index],name);
}
```

The HASH object would not be complete without a function to display the contents of the hash table. That is what showtable() does. Groups of eight strings are displayed one line at a time.

```
void HASH::showtable()
{
    int i,ccount = 0;

    cout << "Hash Table...\n";
    for(i = 0; i < HASHsize; i++)
    {
        cout << table[i] << "\t";
        if (++ccount == 8)
        {
            ccount = 0;
            cout << "\n";
        }
    }
    cout << "\n";
}
```

Program 9.7 shows how the HASH class member functions are used to implement a working hash table.

Program 9.7

```
#include <iostream.h>
#include <string.h>
#include <stdlib.h>

#define HASHsize 64
#define SYMBOLsize 6

class HASH {
public:
    char symbol[SYMBOLsize];
    char table[HASHsize][SYMBOLsize];
    int index;

    HASH(void);
    int hashfn(char name[]);
    int collide(char name[], int index);
    void addsymbol(char name[], int index);
    void showtable(void);
};

HASH::HASH()
{
```

```
        int i;

        for(i = 0; i < HASHsize; i++)
                table[i][0] = '\0';
}

int HASH::hashfn(char name[])
{
        int mid, hashval;

        mid = strlen(name) / 2;
        hashval = name[0] + name[mid] + name[strlen(name) - 1];
        hashval &= 0x3f;
        return hashval;
}

int HASH::collide(char name[], int index)
{
        int empty, samesymbol;

        empty = (0 == strlen(table[index]));
        samesymbol = (0 == strcmp(table[index],name));
        return (!empty && !samesymbol);
}

void HASH::addsymbol(char name[], int index)
{
        strcat(table[index],name);
}

void HASH::showtable()
{
        int i,ccount = 0;

        cout << "Hash Table...\n";
        for(i = 0; i < HASHsize; i++)
        {
                cout << table[i] << "\t";
                if (++ccount == 8)
                {
                        ccount = 0;
                        cout << "\n";
                }
        }
        cout << "\n";
}

void makesymbol(char name[])
{
        int i,j;
```

```
        do
        {
                i = rand() % SYMBOLsize;
        } while (!i);
        for(j = 0; j < i; j++)
                name[j] = 'A' + rand() % 26;
        name[i] = '\0';
}

main()
{
        HASH myhash;
        int i,collisions = 0;

        cout << "64 random strings...\n";
        for(i = 0; i < HASHsize; i++)
        {
                makesymbol(myhash.symbol);
                cout << myhash.symbol << "\t";
                myhash.index = myhash.hashfn(myhash.symbol);
                if (!myhash.collide(myhash.symbol,myhash.index))
                        myhash.addsymbol(myhash.symbol,myhash.index);
                else
                        collisions++;
                if (7 == (i % 8))
                        cout << "\n";
        }
        cout << "\n";
        myhash.showtable();
        cout << "There were " << collisions << " collisions.\n";
}
```

As with the previous examples presented in this chapter, 64 random strings are generated and hashed. The program keeps track of the number of collisions, and displays the final hash table. A sample execution is as follows:

```
64 random strings
AKYI     T         Q        IYJZ     ETZJ     HOXOB    LEX      D
Q        BZ        YDE       GQ       QIL      R        DYCE     KORZT
AAT      STB       X         NJOI     KUWM     NKY      PGZJ     LXHYM
PRL      S         L         Q        CEQ      QWFB     KS       W
TUK      OM        Y         KPUTW    WHEQ     FVHZ     JTO      RM
C        HIADI     D         O        TJRM     J        FUK      XHHCG
A        FEJ       S         UFH      PRFPR    QEIQJ    LWCAA    NBICT
EYMS     YT        H         OR       XKDH     ACBU     DDO      Y

Hash Table...
         YT                  A                 W
X        C                   YY       DD
```

LWCAA			HIADI			FEJ	AAT	DDO
H	CEQ						J	
	LXHYM	HOXOB		AKYI	L	EYMS	QIL	XHHCG
FVHZ	ETZJ			NBICT	RM	IYJZ	PRL	KUWM
	KORZT	NKY		QQ	PGZJ		BZ	KPUTW
	SS				T			

```
There were 23 collisions.
```

This sample execution is similar to those we have seen before, although the underlying process is now completely different, being object oriented. This allows handling of multiple **hash table objects** if necessary, with far less effort and program coding in C++ than what is possible with C.

Conclusion

It would be a good exercise to expand the HASH class to support linked-list collision resolution, or some other suitable collision resolution method. For now, test your understanding of the HASH class with the following section review.

9.6 Section Review

1. Why bother writing a C++ HASH class? Why not just use C?
2. Why do we need to initialize the hash table with the constructor?
3. When does the collide() function return a FALSE condition?

Study Questions

General Concepts

Section 9.1

1. What is involved in searching a hash table?
2. When is a hash function unpredictable?
3. Does search time have to be the same for each hash table element?

Section 9.2

4. Why use a hash table?
5. What is a characteristic of an ideal hash function?
6. Compare worst-case search times for a 4,096-element block of data. How many comparisons are required for sequential, binary, and ideal hash functions?

Section 9.3

7. How does a hash function generate hashing information?
8. When do we throw away hashing information?
9. What does the number of free locations in a hash table measure?
10. How is the length of the string used to redistribute collisions?

Section 9.4

11. How many different conditions exist when a location is accessed?
12. Why store the hash string in the hash table?
13. How is strcmp() used to check for collisions?

Section 9.5

14.   When is the hashing policy used?

15.   How is a linked-list used to resolve a collision?

16.   Why not just store 64 strings at each hash location, instead of 2 (as in Figure 9.4)?

Section 9.6

17.   What changes need to be made to Program 9.7 to allow three additional hash tables to be instantiated?

18.   What controls the size of the hash table and hash symbol string in Program 9.7?

19.   Why are all the members of the HASH class public members?

Program Design

For each of the following programming exercises write a C or C++ program that performs the indicated task. Be sure to fully test each program with a wide variety of input data.

20.   Show how a word counter can be implemented using a hash table. For example, the following text contains four words: "The cat in the hat." One word ("the") occurs twice. The hash table should store each word and its frequency of occurrence.

21.   Modify the hash function in Program 9.2 to improve the free locations left after hashing all of the strings. This means there should be fewer free locations if you improve the hash function.

22.   Add the changes used to improve the hash function in Program 9.2 from Question 21 to Programs 9.3, 9.4, and 9.5. Describe the results.

23.   Some operating systems store their file names as unique binary signatures rather than the individual characters of the file name. Design a hash function that generates indexes for MS-DOS file names (8 character name + 3 character extension).

24.   Show how a *self-modifying* hash function could be implemented that adjusts the way it generates indexes based on the length of the input strings.

25.   Design a hash function that hashes strings of local seven-digit phone numbers.

26.   Show how a hash table could store a mailing list. Address the table using the street name.

27.   Design a data structure containing a hash table of hash tables. The main hash table contains 64 elements. Each element is an eight-element hash table. Use one hash function to select one of 64 locations in the main hash table, and a *different* hash function to choose one of eight locations in the secondary hash tables.

28.   Design a hash table that uses linked-lists for collision resolution.

29.   Redesign Program 9.7 so that no parameters are passed to member functions hashfn(), collide(), and addsymbol(). Restrict access to index and symbol by making then private, main() must be redesigned since it will no longer have access to index and symbol.

30.   Write a C++ class for a hash table that is capable of storing four eight-character strings in each of 128 locations.

31.   Write a C++ class for a hash table of 64 locations that uses linked-list collision resolution. The strings being hashed are nine-digit ZIP codes.

10   Other Data Structures

Objectives

This chapter gives you the opportunity to learn:

1. What a heap is and how to use it.
2. How a file can be viewed as a data structure.
3. How to view the directory as a data structure.
4. How to work with and perform operations on a set.
5. About the structure and use of a lookup table.

Key Terms

Heap

Fragmented

Heap Sort

File

Text Files

Binary Files

.COM File

.EXE File

.PCX File

Directory Entry

Clusters

Sets

Empty Set

Union

Intersection

Power Set

Lookup Tables

Color Palette

Output Lookup Table

Finite State Machine

Outline

Introduction

In this chapter we will examine several other interesting data structures. They may not be used as often as the data structures we have already examined, but they are just as important. The usefulness of these structures allow for some very powerful applications to be developed.

10.1   The Heap

The **heap** is a name given to two different data structures. First, a heap is the memory located between high memory used by the stack and low memory, which is used by the program to create local variables. This is illustrated in Figure 10.1. As shown in Figure 10.1,

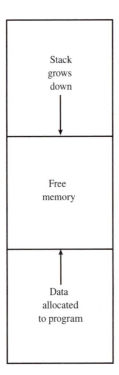

Figure 10.1   A Memory Heap

(a) Array   (b) Tree

1.   25

2.   16

3.   15

4.   35

5.   14

6.   7

7.   2

8.   11

9.   3

10.   6

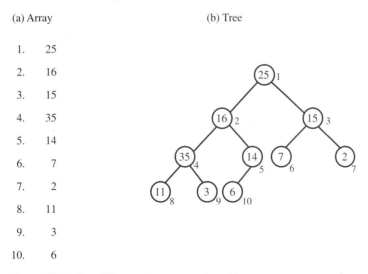

Figure 10.2   Two Ways to Represent a Set of Integers

the region of memory known as the heap is a dynamic structure. As a program executes, contents of the stack and memory are constantly changing due to the coding of the program. As a result of this environment, maintenance of the heap is of interest in terms of program and operating system efficiency.

As a program executes, it causes the heap to become **fragmented.** Unless dealt with properly, memory resources will be exhausted and program execution may fail. It is therefore necessary for the operating system to deal with the heap.

The second heap data structure deals with a binary tree with restrictions on how nodes can be ordered in the tree. The restriction simply requires the value of the data in the parent node to be larger than its children. These restrictions on a heap provide for an efficient implementation of a priority queue. The highest priority node is the root node of the tree. Examine Figure 10.2. With a data element size of 10, it is easy to view how the tree is formed from the array, adding nodes in the tree and completing each level before moving to the next lower level. The only requirement of a heap is that the parent node is larger that its children. If the heap rules are broken, it is possible to perform a **heap sort** to shuffle the data around inside of the tree to satisfy the heap condition. In Figure 10.2(a), it is hard to tell that elements 2 and 4 are not conforming to the restriction of a heap. In Figure 10.2(b), it is obvious that node 4 containing 35 should be swapped with element 2 to conform. Then, nodes 4 and 2 must be swapped because the first swap between nodes 2 and 4 now causes a problem with nodes 1 and 2.

Examine Figure 10.3 to verify the data stored in the array and the tree do satisfy the heap conditions.

Conclusion

In this section, we examined data structures known as heaps. Test your understanding of the material by trying the following section review.

(a) Array   (b) Tree

1.   25

2.   16

3.   15

4.   35

5.   14

6.   7

7.   2

8.   11

9.   3

10.   6

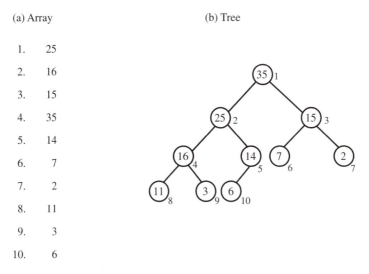

Figure 10.3   Two Representations of a Heap of Integers

10.1 Section Review

1. What is a heap?
2. What rule determines if the data is in the form of a heap?
3. Can any array be arranged into the form of a heap?
4. In what type of application is a heap useful?

10.2   The File as a Data Structure

Consider the variety of data structures that can be stored in a **file.** The type of structure depends on the requirements of the application using the file. Data files can be stored as **text files** or as **binary files.** Inside of the text file or binary file, anything goes. We will examine some different types of file formats to identify the underlying structure. For example, consider the three types of files listed in Figure 10.4. As shown in Figure 10.4(a), a **.COM file** is a DOS executable file. The structure of the file overlays the code, data, and stack segments in the same 64KB memory segment. Inside of this one 64KB segment, the execution of the .COM file occurs.

Figure 10.4(b) describes the structure of an **.EXE file.** The structure of the file includes header information located at the beginning of the file (including the relocation table), stack segments, code segments, and data segments. As indicated in the figure, the contents of an .EXE file can be placed anywhere in memory because of the relocation information.

The **.PCX file** structure shown in Figure 10.4(c) identifies a structure consisting of a header containing control data such as image dimensions, version information, and flags (optional palette present/not present) followed by run length encoded data, and an optional 256-color palette.

Some applications run into trouble when working with old, outdated files that contain incompatible or unrecognizable structures.

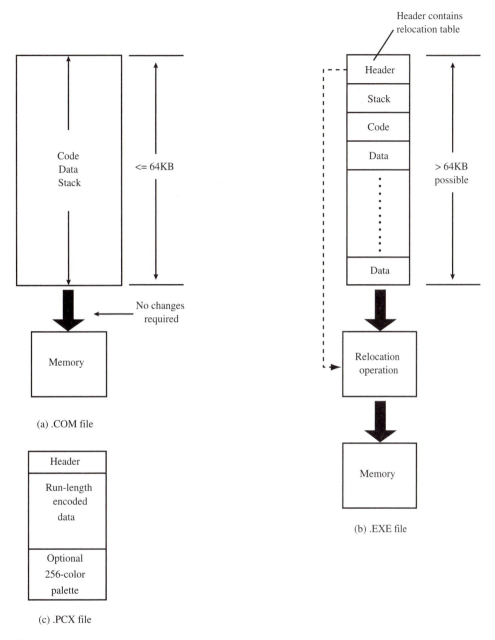

(a) .COM file

(c) .PCX file

(b) .EXE file

Figure 10.4   Three Different File Data Structures

Conclusion

In this section, we examined a few types of file formats and their structures. Test your understanding of this material by trying the following section review.

10.2 Section Review

1. What determines the structure of data stored in a file?
2. What are two ways to think of data stored in a file?

10.3   The Directory as a Data Structure

The directory structure of a computer disk is itself a data structure. Reexamine Figure 7.2, where we stored a directory structure as a tree. In DOS, a 32-byte **directory entry** stores all of the necessary file information. The format of the directory entry looks like this:

- File name (8 bytes)
- Extension (3 bytes)
- Attributes (1 byte)
- Reserved (10 bytes)
- Time (2 bytes)
- Date (2 bytes)
- First cluster (2 bytes)
- File size (4 bytes)

Consider a `struct` to define this data structure:

```
struct DOSFILE
{
    char name[8];
    char extension[3];
    unsigned char attributes;
    char reservedarea[10];
    unsigned int time;
    unsigned int date;
    unsigned int start_cluster;
    unsigned long file_size;
}
```

Although the directory structure can be viewed as a tree, the physical location of files on a disk are stored using the FAT, or File Allocation Table.

Consider the fact that the operating system must account for each block of data on a disk. If a certain block is available, it might be allocated on the next request for storage. Many different conditions can occur that affect the directory structure and the FAT, such as a new file being created, an existing file needing to allocate more space, or possibly, a file being deleted and needing to free all of the allocated blocks of disk space. The FAT stores information about the usage of the storage available on the disk. The FAT entries for a particular file form a chain (similar to a linked-list) that connects all of the dynamically allocated **clusters** of the file. Consider the simplified FAT shown in Figure 10.5. The FAT contains entries for two files. The first file begins with cluster 2, giving this cluster chain:

2   3   4   5

The chain ends at cluster 5 due to the `0xFFF` entry.

*	*	3	4
0	1	2	3
5	FFF	14	0
4	5	6	7
9	12	0	FFF
8	9	10	11
11	0	8	0
12	13	14	15

* Reserved

Figure 10.5   Simplified FAT with Cluster Chains

The starting cluster for the second file is 6. The resulting cluster chain is:

$$6 \quad 14 \quad 8 \quad 9 \quad 12 \quad 11$$

This illustrates an important point: Files may be physically stored all over the disk (fragmented) and still be logically connected, through their associated cluster chain. Clearly, any damage to a disk's FAT may result in a catastrophic loss of data.

Conclusion

In this section we examined how the directory structure of a disk can be viewed as a data structure. Test your understanding of this material by trying the following section review.

10.3 Section Review

1. What is the FAT?
2. What type of information does the directory entry contain?
3. What is fragmentation?

10.4   Sets

Sets are important data structures, having a wide range of applications in graph theory, artificial intelligence, and problem solving.

A set may contain zero (the **empty set**) or more elements. Furthermore, any element of a set could be a set itself. In this section we only consider sets of basic elements, such as characters or numbers.

Two operations typically performed on sets are:

Union: The union of two sets is a third set containing all elements of each set, with no duplicates. For example,

```
{abc} union {cd} = {abcd}
```

Intersection: The intersection of two sets is a third set containing only those elements that appear in both sets. An example is:

```
{abc} intersection {cd} = {c}
```

It is possible that the intersection results in the empty set.

How should we represent the set? A set of characters can be easily represented using a string. A set of integers can use an integer array. Both of these types of sets would be static, fixed in size, and therefore limited in their application. Program 10.1 uses fixed size character strings to keep the set_union() and set_intersection() functions simple. In Section 10.6 you will see how a linked-list is used to store a set of elements.

Program 10.1

```c
#include <stdio.h>
#include <string.h>

#define FALSE 0
#define TRUE  1

int is_member(char element, char set[]);
void set_union(char setA[], char setB[], char setC[]);
void set_intersection(char setA[], char setB[], char setC[]);

main()
{
        char s1[] = "abcd";
        char s2[] = "cdef";
        char s3[10],s4[10];

        printf("Set 1 = {%s}\n",s1);
        printf("Set 2 = {%s}\n",s2);
        set_union(s1,s2,s3);
        printf("Set 1 UNION Set 2 = {%s}\n",s3);
        set_intersection(s1,s2,s4);
        printf("Set 1 INTERSECTION Set 2 = {%s}\n",s4);
}

int is_member(char element, char set[])
{
        if (0 != strchr(set,element))
                return(TRUE);
        else
                return(FALSE);
}
```

```
void set_union(char setA[], char setB[], char setC[])
{
        int i,k;

        strcpy(setC,setA);
        k = strlen(setA);
        for(i = 0; i < strlen(setB); i++)
                if (!is_member(setB[i],setC))
                {
                        setC[k] = setB[i];
                        k++;
                        setC[k] = '\0';
                }
}

void set_intersection(char setA[], char setB[], char setC[])
{
        int i,p;

        p = 0;
        for(i = 0; i < strlen(setA); i++)
                if (is_member(setA[i],setB))
                {
                        setC[p] = setA[i];
                        p++;
                        setC[p] = '\0';
                }
}
```

When Program 10.1 executes, we get the following:

```
Set 1 = {abcd}
Set 2 = {cdef}
Set 1 UNION Set 2 = {abcdef}
Set 1 INTERSECTION Set 2 = {cd}
```

A third, more challenging set operation involves creating a **power set.** A power set is the set of all possible sets that can be generated from the elements of the original set. For example, if the original set is {ab}, the power set is:

```
{ {}, {a}, {b}, {ab} }
```

Note that the elements of a power set are sets themselves. This will require some thinking to come up with a good representation.

Conclusion

The union and intersection operations for sets were covered in this section. Test your knowledge of the material with the following section review.

10.4 Section Review

1. What is the result of {123} union {456}?
2. What is the result of {123} intersection {456}?
3. What is a limitation of a string-based set?

10.5   Lookup Tables

Lookup tables are data structures that contain predetermined data in a group of locations, accessed according to the user's wishes. For example, the graphics card on the personal computer uses a lookup table called the **color palette,** which maps pixel values in the range 0 to 255 to a predetermined set of color values. The pixel value read from image memory is used as an index into the color palette (or **output lookup table**), where the actual pixel color value is read out and sent to the display hardware. Figure 10.6 shows an example of how an output lookup table is used to convert a 256 gray level image into a negative image, in real time. The output lookup table is loaded with a set of numbers so that the 8-bit inverse of each index is stored in each location (255 stored at 0, 0 stored at

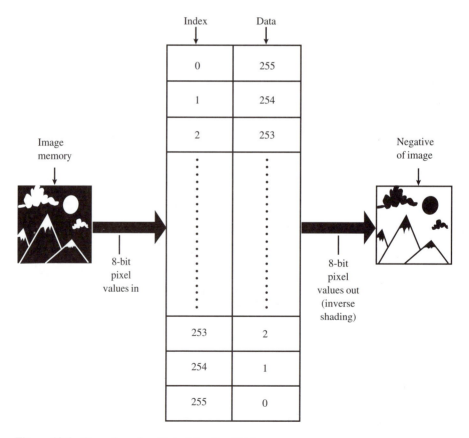

Figure 10.6   Operation of an Output Lookup Table

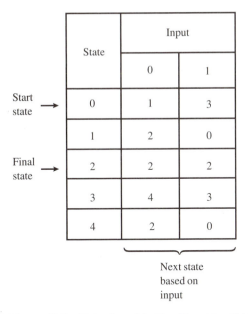

	State	Input	
		0	1
Start state →	0	1	3
	1	2	0
Final state →	2	2	2
	3	4	3
	4	2	0

Next state
based on
input

Figure 10.7 Finite State Machine Transition Table

255, etc.). The correct pixel value for the negative image comes out of the table as it is accessed by pixels from the image memory. If a function is used to mathematically change all of the pixel values stored in the image memory, the negative would not be produced in real time.

Lookup tables are also useful when trying to speed up a program. For example, a number-intensive program that performs trig operations on a limited range of angles may slow down due to the processing time required for the trig operations. If, however, a suitable set of trig values a precomputed and stored in a lookup table (at the beginning of execution), the program can obtain the trig results much quicker by just reading the lookup table.

Lookup tables can also contain data such as the transitions between states in a control application. Figure 10.7 shows a transition table for a **finite state machine** that recognizes any number of ones followed by two zeros. Running the machine is as simple as moving from row to row in the lookup table.

Conclusion

Lookup tables conclude our detailed examination of data structures. Test your knowledge of the material with the following section review.

10.5 Section Review

1. How does a lookup table work?
2. How can a lookup table be used to false color an image?
3. How can lookup tables be used to control a process?

10.6   A C++ SET Object

We conclude this last chapter on new data structures with a look at how a set object can be used. Program 10.2 uses the class SET to instantiate three set objects (odd, even, and both).

Program 10.2

```cpp
#include <iostream.h>
#include <iomanip.h>
#include <string.h>

        typedef struct node
        {
                char data;
                struct node *link;
        } LNODE;

class SET {
public:
        LNODE *set_ptr;

        SET(void);
        void build_set(char set[]);
        void add_node(char item);
        void show_set(void);
};

main()
{
        SET odd, even, both;

        odd.build_set("13579");
        even.build_set("2468");
        both.build_set("369");
        odd.show_set();
        even.show_set();
        both.show_set();
}

SET::SET()
{
        set_ptr = NULL;
}

void SET::build_set(char set[])
{
        int i;

        for(i = 0; i < strlen(set); i++)
                add_node(set[i]);
}
```

```
void SET::add_node(char item)
{
        LNODE *p1, *p2;

        p1 = new LNODE;
        p1->data = item;
        p1->link = NULL;
        if (set_ptr == NULL)
                set_ptr = p1;
        else
        {
                p2 = set_ptr;
                while (p2->link != NULL)
                        p2 = p2->link;
                p2->link = p1;
        }
}

void SET::show_set()
{
        LNODE *ptr;

        cout << "The set is {";
        ptr = set_ptr;
        while (ptr != NULL)
        {
                cout << ptr->data;
                ptr = ptr->link;
        }
        cout << "}\n";
}
```

The new feature presented in Program 10.2 is the representation of each set as a linked-list. This allows the sets to be as large as desired. The function build_set() constructs a linked-list from the input string passed to it. The show_set() function traverses the list, displaying each character as it is encountered.

A sample execution of Program 10.2 is as follows:

```
The set is {13579}
The set is {2468}
The set is {369}
```

You are encouraged to add the other required member functions for union and intersection on your own.

Conclusion

The initial portion of a C++ SET class was presented in this section. As always, multiple copies of the data structure are possible using instantiation. Test your knowledge of the material with the following section review.

10.6 Section Review

1. Why use a linked-list instead of a string to represent a character set?
2. What is the SET() constructor used for?

Study Questions

General Concepts

Section 10.1

1. Why is it useful to arrange data in the form of a heap?
2. When using an array to create a heap, why is it difficult to determine if the heap condition is satisfied?
3. Why is a heap suited to implement a priority queue?

Section 10.2

4. What are two differences between .COM and .EXE files?
5. How does an application working with a .PCX file know if the color palette is included in the file?

Section 10.3

6. What does the FAT contain?
7. What is a cluster chain?
8. How are FAT entries logically connected?

Section 10.4

9. What are the typical operations performed on sets?
10. What advantage does a linked-list set representation have over a string-based or array-based set?

Section 10.5

11. How can a lookup table be used to speed up an application?
12. Explain how a lookup table maps one set of data items to another.
13. How can a finite state machine be represented using a lookup table?

Section 10.6

14. With Program 10.2 using linked-lists for set representation, how is the is_member() function from Program 10.1 affected?
15. What type of structure is needed for a power set?

Program Design

16. Add the set_union() and set_intersection() functions to Program 10.2.
17. Modify Program 10.2 so that integer sets can be instantiated.
18. Write a function called power_set() that creates the power set of the input set.
19. The FAT shown in Figure 10.5 contains at least one erroneous *(lost)* cluster entry. Write a function that will find lost clusters and free them.
20. Implement the finite state machine whose transition table is shown in Figure 10.7.
21. Extend the C++ SET class to contain a member function called base_two() that generates a set containing powers of 2 from zero to 15 (1, 2, 4, 8, ..., 32768).

11 Application Program: Virtual Maze

Objectives

This chapter gives you the opportunity to learn:

1. How ray casting works.
2. The differences between ray casting and ray tracing.
3. How to use precomputed data tables.
4. How to represent a virtual world with a handful of data structures.
5. How to perform texture mapping.
6. Methods to minimize execution time.

Key Terms

Ray Casting
Field of View
Ray Tracing
Walls
Cells

Game Grid
Pixels
Virtual World
Scale
Texture Mapping

Outline

Figure 11.1   Virtual Maze Screen Shot

Introduction

The popularity of first-person virtual reality games (such as DOOM) is largely due to their realistic real-time color graphics. The player actually moves around in the game world, as if the game world were seen through the player's eyes. Simulating a three-dimensional room or landscape can be a very time-consuming and computationally complex exercise. Doing the simulation in real time is even harder. The programmers behind these types of games know how to squeeze the most performance out of the processor. Attention must be paid to execution time at every step. In addition, it is also necessary to have a good understanding of algebra and trigonometry (as well as physics) to write the necessary graphic routines. Furthermore, representing all of the information required to simulate the 3D-game world requires the use of several different types of data structures.

In this chapter we will examine the development, and theory behind, a simple 3D, first-person game called **Virtual Maze.** The player "walks" through the maze by pressing the arrow keys or by moving the mouse. The goal is to reach an "Exit" door.

The Virtual Maze game changes the computer's video mode to VGA and uses a 320-by-200 pixel resolution, with 256 colors. Figure 11.1 shows a screen shot of the game in action. The technique used to draw the game screen is called ray casting. The ray casting must be done as fast as possible so that the screen updates in real time. Let us see how ray casting works, and the data structures needed to support it.

11.1   What Is Ray Casting?

Ray casting is the process of generating an image on the computer screen based on rays of "light" cast out of the player's eye (a central viewpoint) for a **field of view** similar to what our own eyes would see if looking at the same scene in the real world. This process is similar to a technique known as **ray tracing,** which mathematically models all the possible rays that will enter the user's "eye," complete with rays that reflect off multiple surfaces in the scene. Ray tracing produces photorealistic images but unfortunately requires significant computation time, making it a poor choice for real-time imaging applications. Ray casting attempts to achieve some of the visual aspects of ray tracing, but at a much faster speed.

The basic method behind ray casting follows this sequence of steps:

1. Pick a direction for the ray.
2. Find the distance to the first horizontal intersection of the ray with an object.
3. Find the distance to the first vertical intersection of the ray with an object.
4. Pick the intersection with the smallest distance.
5. Use the distance to calculate the height of a vertical strip to draw on the screen.
6. Draw the strip.

Let us examine the entire process.

Seeing the Walls

The objects in Virtual Maze are **walls.** So, steps 2 and 3 are actually finding the distance to the closest wall in front of the player. The height of the wall is based on its distance from the player. The larger the distance, the smaller the height. Figure 11.2 shows a sample ray being cast.

The ray begins at the player's position and extends outward until it eventually hits the edge of the game world, which is composed of a rectangular grid of **cells,** where each cell represents a 64-by-64 section of the overall game world. The 8-by-8 **game grid** in Figure 11.2 actually represents a 512-by-512 world. Managing 64 game cells is easier than managing 512^2 (or over 250,000) cells.

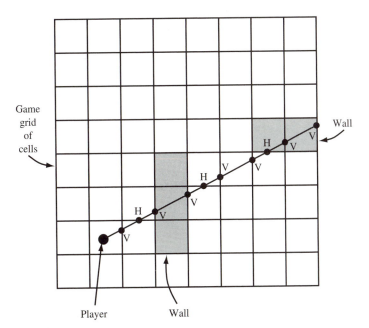

Figure 11.2   Casting a Ray

Each cell contains one of three things: the player, a floor section, or a wall section. Different characters are used to represent each object. Walls use the characters '1' through '4' and 'E' (for the Exit). The player is represented by 'P' and the floor by '.'. The rectangular grid of cells is easily represented by a two-dimensional global character array:

```
unsigned char game_map[MAPROWS][MAPCOLS];
```

where MAPROWS and MAPCOLS are #defines that specify the size of the grid.

Finding the intersection of a ray involves checking horizontal intersections (H in Figure 11.2) and vertical intersections (V) against the value of the game cell at the intersection. If any of the wall characters are found, a wall has been hit.

The code to find the closest horizontal intersection looks like this:

```
/* Look for first horizontal intersection with a wall */

float hit_hwall()
{
    float rpos,rstep,cpos,cstep;
    int found;

    rpos = (player.cellr * CELLSIZE) - 1;
    cstep = CELLSIZE * invtan[tptr];
    if (angle < 180)
        rstep = -CELLSIZE;
    else
    {
        rstep = CELLSIZE;
        rpos += (1+CELLSIZE);
        cstep *= -1;
    }
    cpos = player.c + (player.r - rpos) * invtan[tptr];
    hcolor = cellval(rpos,cpos);
    if (is_wall(hcolor))
    {
        if (hcolor == 'E')
            hcolor = NUMWALLS - 1;
        else
            hcolor -= '1';
        hslice = ((int)cpos) % CELLSIZE;
        return dist(player.r,player.c,rpos,cpos);
    }
    found = 0;
    while ((cpos >= 0) && (cpos < CMAX) && !found)
    {
        rpos += rstep;
        cpos += cstep;
        hcolor = cellval(rpos,cpos);
        if (is_wall(hcolor))
        {
```

```
                    found = 1;
                    if (hcolor == 'E')
                        hcolor = NUMWALLS - 1;
                    else
                        hcolor -= '1';
                    hslice = ((int)cpos) % CELLSIZE;
            }
    }
    if (found)
        return dist(player.r,player.c,rpos,cpos);
    else
    {
        hcolor = 0;
        hslice = -1;
        return INFINITY;
    }
}
```

The hit_hwall() function is quite complex and requires a good deal of explanation, algebra, and trignometry to fully grasp its operation. You are encouraged to investigate its operation on your own, based on your own intuition.

The code for finding the closest vertical intersection is very similar to the code in hit_hwall().

```
/* Look for first vertical intersection with a wall */

float hit_vwall()
{
    float rpos,rstep,cpos,cstep;
    int found;

    cpos = (player.cellc * CELLSIZE) - 1;
    rstep = CELLSIZE * tantab[tptr];
    if ((angle >= 90) && (angle < 270))
        cstep = -CELLSIZE;
    else
    {
        cstep = CELLSIZE;
        cpos += (1+CELLSIZE);
    }
    if ((angle < 90) || (angle >= 270))
        rstep *= -1;
    rpos = player.r + (player.c - cpos) * tantab[tptr];
    vcolor = cellval(rpos,cpos);
    if (is_wall(vcolor))
    {
        if (vcolor == 'E')
            vcolor = NUMWALLS - 1;
        else
            vcolor -= '1';
```

```
            vslice = ((int)rpos) % CELLSIZE;
            return dist(player.r,player.c,rpos,cpos);
    }
    found = 0;
    while ((rpos >= 0) && (rpos < RMAX) && !found)
    {
            rpos += rstep;
            cpos += cstep;
            vcolor = cellval(rpos,cpos);
            if (is_wall(vcolor))
            {
                    found = 1;
                    if (vcolor == 'E')
                        vcolor = NUMWALLS-1;
                    else
                        vcolor -= '1';
                    vslice = ((int)rpos) % CELLSIZE;
            }
    }
    if (found)
            return dist(player.r,player.c,rpos,cpos);
    else
    {
            vcolor = 0;
            vslice = -1;
            return INFINITY;
    }
}
```

After `hit_hwall()` and `hit_vwall()` have done their jobs, there are two sets of inter-section information. The closer of the two intersections (H and V) is used to draw a slice of the wall that was hit.

Notice that there are only three horizontal intersections in Figure 11.2, and seven ver-tical ones. Some of these intersections hit cells that contain wall sections. The second ver-tical intersection (the first to hit a wall) is closer to the player than the third horizontal intersection (also the first to hit a wall). A strip from the wall associated with the closer vertical intersection is drawn.

Drawing an Entire Scene

To generate an entire screen, 320 rays are cast. The player's direction is used to cast out rays beginning at 30 degrees minus the player's direction, and going to 30 degrees plus the player's direction. This sweeps a 60-degree arc over the game field. Each ray cast results in one column of **pixels** drawn on the screen (the strip from steps 5 and 6), casting 320 rays results in an entire screen of the game world being drawn. Since the screen is actually a 320-by-200 array of pixels, a large block of screen memory (1 byte per pixel) must be ma-nipulated when drawing the strips. As we will see, it is necessary to efficiently write to the screen memory so that screen updates are performed very quickly.

The ray casting function in Virtual Maze is as follows:

```
/* Ray cast an entire scene (320 columns) */

void ray_cast()
{
    float xdist,ydist,dist,temp;
    int i,r,c,ray,size;
    unsigned char color;

    color = 0;
    for(ray = 0; ray < 320; ray++)
    {
        angle = player.dir - ray*ANGLEINC + 30;
        if (angle < 0)
            angle += 360;
        if (angle > 360)
            angle -= 360;
        ta = (angle/ANGLEINC);
        tptr = ta;
        xdist = hit_hwall();
        ydist = hit_vwall();
        if (xdist < ydist)
        {
            dist = xdist;
            color = hcolor;
            wall = color;
            slice = hslice;
        }
        else
        {
            dist = ydist;
            color = vcolor;
            wall = color;
            slice = vslice;
        }
        temp = (SCALE/(dist + NOTZERO)*corr[ray]);
        size = (int)(temp + 0.5);
        if (slice == -1) slice = 0;
        draw_strip(ray,size,slice);
    }
}
```

A number of #defines are used to control the activities in ray_cast(). These are ANGLEINC, SCALE, and NOTZERO. ANGLEINC is the incremental angle added or subtracted from the current viewing angle to step one pixel to the right or left. Its value is 60/320 (0.1875). SCALE is an arbitrary value used to control how large objects appear (set to 14000). Its value is based on how many pixels tall an object will be when viewed from the farthest distance possible. NOTZERO is set to a very small value (1e-10) and is used to guarantee that a division-by-zero never occurs when scaling the size of an object.

The `draw_strip()` function is responsible for drawing the intersected texture-mapped wall strip. `Draw_strip()` is covered in Section 11.5.

Conclusion

Check your understanding of ray casting with the following section review.

11.1 Section Review

1. What is ray casting?
2. What are the differences between ray casting and ray tracing?
3. How is the final distance to a wall determined?
4. How is the height of a wall strip determined?
5. What is a cell?
6. What type of data structure is used to store the game grid?

11.2   Using Precomputed Data Tables

The functions that find the horizontal and vertical intersections use a prearranged line equation to solve for the next horizontal or vertical intercept. The equations use the tangent (and inverse tangent) of the ray's angle in their solution. Calculating a trigonometric function during ray casting will slow things down significantly. To eliminate this problem, an array of precomputed tan and inv-tan values are used as a lookup table during ray tracing. The tables are computed for a specific set of angles at the beginning of the game, before ray casting begins. The set of angles begins at 0 degrees and goes up in fixed increments (`ANGLEINC`, which equals 0.1875) all the way to 360 degrees. The size (in angles) of the player's field of view and the number of columns in the game screen determine the size of the increments between angles. Rays are only cast out at angles that are represented in the tables.

Some of the angles in the data table need special attention, due to the nature of the tan and inv-tan functions. Specifically, at 90 and 270, the value of the tangent function goes to infinity, so we must be careful when initializing the data tables.

Another data table that is used during ray casting stores a range of inv-cos values that are used to correct the distance to each intersection. Objects are actually farther away than they appear as a result of the relationship between the polar and rectangular coordinates used in the ray casting mathematics. This data table, called `corr`, contains 320 correction values, one for each column of pixels on the display screen (which correspond to all 320 angles in the current field of view).

The `build_tables()` function precomputes all the required tan, inv-tan, and inv-cos values.

```
/* Precompute tangent and distance-correction tables */

void build_tables()
{
    int k;
    double angle;

    for(k = 0; k < TSIZE; k++)
```

```
        {
                angle = k*ANGLEINC*PI/180.0;
                switch(k)
                {
                case     0: tantab[k] = 0;
                        invtan[k] = INFINITY;
                        break;
                case  D90: tantab[k] = INFINITY;
                        invtan[k] = 0;
                        break;
                case D180: tantab[k] = 0;
                        invtan[k] = INFINITY;
                        break;
                case D270: tantab[k] = INFINITY;
                        invtan[k] = 0;
                        break;
                default:    tantab[k] = (float)tan(angle);
                        invtan[k] = (float)(1.0/tantab[k]);
                }
        }
        angle = -30.0*PI/180.0;
        for(k = 0; k < 320; k++)
        {
                corr[k] = (float)1.0/cos(angle);
                angle += 2*30/320.0*PI/180.0;
        }
}
```

The value of TSIZE is #defined to be 1920. This is the result of choosing a 60-degree field of view (what the player can see at any time) and having a horizontal screen resolution of 320.

Conclusion

This section introduced the advantages of using precomputed data tables. Test your understanding of the material with the following section review.

11.2 Section Review

1. What is the advantage of using precomputed data tables?
2. What type of special considerations must be taken when computing the tan function?
3. Why is the inv-cos table smaller than the other tables?
4. How many increments of ANGLEINC are required to get to a value of 90 degrees? This is the value of D90. What do you think the value of D180 and D270 are?

11.3   Avoiding the Run-Time Stack

In this section we examine a technique that involves the use of a #define, rather than a function, to actually plot a pixel on the screen. A pixel-plotting function would require three parameters (row, column, and color) to be pushed onto the run-time stack, along with other necessary information. A run-time stack is used during execution of a C/C++ program to maintain information about the `main()` function and other functions that are called, such as return address, input and output parameters, and return values, as well as pointers to other areas within the run-time stack. The code to create and maintain the run-time stack is automatically generated by the compiler. So, if every call to a pixel-plotting function requires the use of the run-time stack, we have a problem trying to do everything in real time. There are actually 64,000 sets of pushes (and pops) for an entire game screen. To speed things up, a `#define` is used instead of a function. The `#define` will be expanded into code *in place,* and not require use of the run-time stack for parameter passing. The `#define` code is essentially the same code that would be in the pixel-plotting function—we have just eliminated the need to call the function.

The `#define` that plots pixels in the Virtual Maze program is as follows:

```
#define pp(r,c,color) vbuff[(((int)r<<8)+((int)r<<6))+(int)c]=(unsigned char)color;
```

Note the use of type casting. This is necessary with the `r` and `c` variables, which are declared as floats to more accurately keep track of the pixels' position.

`vbuff` is a pointer initialized to the base address of the VGA display memory. This address is typically `0xA0000000` on a DOS machine.

Conclusion

In this section we examined a technique to eliminate accesses to the run-time stack. Check your understanding of this material with the following section review.

11.3 Section Review

1. How does use of the run-time stack affect execution time?
2. What kind of information is stored on the run-time stack?
3. How does `pp()` eliminate accesses to the run-time stack?

11.4   Representing the Virtual World

As previously mentioned, the **virtual world** is represented by a rectangular grid of cells, each of which contains information about a specific 64-by-64 section of the virtual world. The 3D world rendered by Virtual Maze is stored in an ASCII file called GAMEMAP.DAT, which looks like this:

```
1111111111111111111111111111111111444444444444444444444444444
1............................................4............................4
1............................................4............................4
1............................................4............................4
1...222222...222222222222222...222222222222222222222....44444
1........2.......4.........2...2................................1
1........2.......4.........2...2.............................11111
1....1...2...22222222222.........222222222222222222....13E33
1....1...2.................................................2....1...3
144441...2...............................P.......................244441...3
4....1...2.................................................2....1...3
```

```
4....1...2222222222222222..........22222222222.......2....1...3
4..........4.............2...2...........................1...3
4..........4.............2...2...........................1...3
4...44444...2222222222222222...22222222222222222222222221...3
4.....4..............1.......1......3.......3........3...3
4.....4..............1111111111......3.......3........3...3
4.....4.......................3.......3.......3........3
4.....4.......................3.......3.......3........3
4444444411111111111111111111111111113333333333333333333333333333
```

where the map characters have the following meaning:

```
.               Floor
1-4             Wall patterns
P               Player
E               Exit
```

Virtual Maze reads in the GAMEMAP.DAT file at the beginning of the game. The cell containing P is the initial player position. The player is only allowed to move into cells that are floor cells, or into the Exit cell (which ends the game).

   The game grid is stored in ASCII so that you may create your own virtual maze with a simple text editor, such as the EDIT utility supplied with DOS and Windows. As we saw before, the game grid is defined like this:

```
unsigned char game_map[MAPROWS][MAPCOLS];
```

The game grid is stored in an external file so that the user may design his or her own game grid without having to modify the program. In addition, the small size of the game grid (64 by 20 in our case) allows it to be read in very quickly through the use of the getc() function. The code to do this is as follows:

```c
/* Read the game map into memory */

void load_map()
{
    FILE *fp, *fopen();
    int r,c;
    unsigned char mdat;

    fp = fopen("gamemap.dat","rb");
    for(r = 0; r < MAPROWS; r++)
    {
        for(c = 0; c < MAPCOLS; c++)
        {
            mdat = getc(fp);
            game_map[r][c] = mdat;
        }
        mdat = getc(fp); /* eat cr */
        mdat = getc(fp); /* eat lf */
    }
    fclose(fp);
}
```

The actual `load_map()` function in the Virtual Maze program contains additional statements that examine `mdat` to determine if the player's position should be initialized.

The Walls

The patterns for the walls are stored in the `WALLPATT.DAT` file. Each wall (there are five) is represented by a block of 4,096 bytes, organized into a two-dimensional array that contains data for a 64-by-64 pixel pattern. One column of the array specifies one column of pixels (a strip) on the screen. Each pixel can be one of the 256 standard VGA colors.

The array used to store all the wall patterns is a global three-dimensional array defined like this:

```
unsigned char wall_maps[NUMWALLS][CELLSIZE][CELLSIZE];
```

where `NUMWALLS` represents the number of walls (five) and `CELLSIZE` has a value of 64.

The wall patterns can be modified, or new patterns created, using the `TILEEDIT.EXE` utility supplied on the companion disk. `TILEEDIT.EXE` creates and stores a single wall pattern into a data file. Use this command line to edit or create a pattern:

```
C> TILEEDIT P1.DAT
```

where `P1.DAT` is a pattern file. When you have five pattern files, create a new `WALLPATT.DAT` file with this DOS command:

```
C> COPY P1.DAT + P2.DAT + P3.DAT + P4.DAT + P5.DAT    WALLPATT.DAT
```

The five wall patterns are loaded into `wall_maps` at the beginning of the game. The fifth pattern is always the Exit wall. The code to load the wall maps looks like this:

```
/* Read the wall patterns into memory */

void load_walls()
{
    FILE *fp, *fopen();
    int wall,r,c;

    fp = fopen("wallpatt.dat","rb");
    for(wall = 0; wall < NUMWALLS; wall++)
        for(r = 0; r < CELLSIZE; r++)
            for(c = 0; c < CELLSIZE; c++)
                wall_maps[wall][r][c] = getc(fp);
    fclose(fp);
}
```

Both `game_map` and `wall_maps` are defined as global arrays to make them easily accessible by every function in the Virtual Maze program. Note that no error checking is provided to guarantee that the `WALLPATT.DAT` file exists.

Conclusion

In this section you saw how the game world is represented and stored in a number of multidimensional arrays. Check your understanding of the material with the following section review.

11.4 Section Review

1. How can a 3D world be simulated by the use of a 2D game grid?
2. Why not use an integer or float array to store the game grid, instead of an `unsigned char` array?
3. How many bytes of storage are needed for the five walls and the game grid?
4. How are the `game_map` and `wall_maps` arrays defined? Why not pass pointers to these arrays in the function calls?

11.5   Texture Mapping

Drawing a strip of a wall is done after the nearest intersection is found and the distance to it has been calculated. The distance is used to **scale** the height of the strip so that its height changes in proportion to distance. The maximum height is limited to 200 pixels, since the resolution of the game screen is 320 by 200.

When the height of the strip is known, a technique called **texture mapping** is used to transfer the graphical strip data from the global pattern array `wall_maps` to the screen. The character stored in the `game_map` cell that is associated with the intersection specifies the wall pattern to use.

There are three cases to consider when drawing a strip:

1. The height of the strip is less than 64.
2. The height of the strip equals 64.
3. The height of the strip is greater than 64.

Figure 11.3 shows how strips are mapped in each case. As Figure 11.3(a) shows, when the strip is scaled down, pixels in the original strip (stored in the global `wall_maps` array) are skipped at regular intervals. Instead of skipping pixel values, Figure 11.3(c) shows pixel values being duplicated in the scaled strip, the essential technique behind a zoom operation. In each case we are actually controlling how indexes into the `wall_maps` array are generated.

To draw the scaled strip as fast as possible, a custom function is used, rather than one of the built-in graphic functions (which do not perform texture mapping either). This function is called `draw_strip()` and contains the following statements:

```
/* Draw a scaled, texture-mapped vertical strip */

void draw_strip(int col, int size, int pos)
{
    int i,j,k;
    float pixel_inc,pixel_row;
    unsigned char color;

    pixel_inc = (float)CELLSIZE / size;
    if (size > STRIP_SIZE)
    {
        pixel_row = ((size - STRIP_SIZE) / 2) * pixel_inc;
        size = STRIP_SIZE;
    }
    else
```

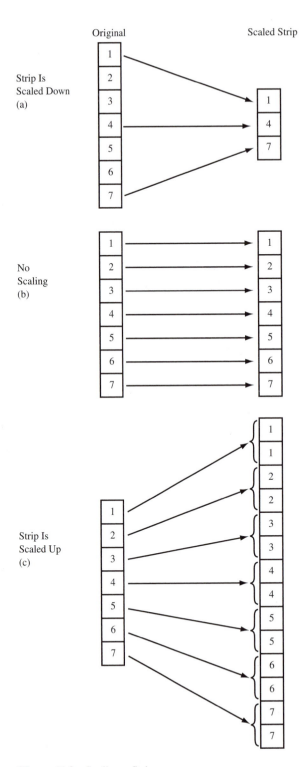

Figure 11.3   Scaling a Strip

```
        pixel_row = 0;
  j = (STRIP_SIZE - size) / 2;
  for(i = 0; i < j; i++)
        pp(i,col,CEILING);
  for(k = 0; k < size; k++)
  {
        color = wall_maps[wall][(int)pixel_row][pos];
        pixel_row += pixel_inc;
        pp(j,col,color);
        j++;
  }
  for(i = j; i < STRIP_SIZE; i++)
        pp(i,col,FLOOR);
}
```

Note the pp() function. In order to draw the strip as fast as possible, pp() is implemented as a #define, rather than an actual function, to avoid use of the run-time stack. Since 200 pixels are always plotted for a single strip, the real-time aspect of the game would most likely be lost if pp()'s three parameters were constantly pushed onto the run-time stack. By #defining pp(), its function call is expanded in place into the appropriate code without having to use the run-time stack for anything.

For every pixel written to the screen, a calculation must be performed to find its address within the video display memory used by the VGA hardware. The 320-by-200 pixel resolution requires a display memory of 64,000 bytes. So, pixels have addresses between 0 and 63999. One way to generate the address looks like this:

```
pixel_address = (row * 320) + column;
```

This method requires a multiply operation, which really means 64,000 multiply operations when drawing an entire screen. This could be very time consuming. Instead, pixel addresses are generated like this:

```
pixel_address = (row << 8) + (row << 6) + column;
```

This equation takes advantage of the fact that the sum of 64 and 256 is 320. In addition, shifting a binary number to the left 6 bits (or 8) is equivalent to multiplying the number by 64 (or 256). The shift left operation is much faster than the multiply, and helps keep the address generation time to a minimum.

The Floor and Ceiling

To add to the overall sense that we are looking at a real environment, it is necessary to simulate the floor and ceiling as well. Texture mapping can be used to map lights onto the ceiling and panels onto the floor (or carpeting, or pools of radioactive material). In Virtual Maze, two different colors are used to create the effect of a floor and ceiling. No additional texture mapping is performed. Figure 11.4 illustrates the components of an entire column of pixels in the game screen.

In this example, the 100-pixel wall strip is centered around line 100. The remaining 100 pixels of the column are divided equally, giving 50 pixels each for the ceiling and floor colors. Every strip has its height centered around line 100 to create the illusion of a horizon far off in the distance.

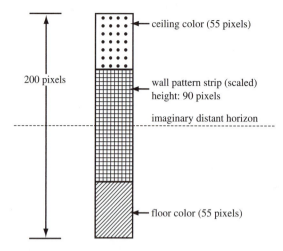

Figure 11.4   One Column of Pixels in the Game Screen

Conclusion

In this section you were introduced to a graphical technique called texture mapping. Check your understanding of this technique with the following section review.

11.5 Section Review

1. What is texture mapping?
2. Why are there three cases to consider when drawing a strip?
3. How many parameter pushes are saved by implementing `pp()` as a `#define`?
4. What is the address of the pixel at row 100 and column 100?
5. Why do we try to avoid using the run-time stack during texture mapping?
6. How are the floor and ceilings represented?
7. What data structures are involved in texture mapping?

11.6   Virtual Maze

To turn our set of ray casting functions and data structures into a working game program. it is necessary to add some functions and structures to take care of such things as legally moving the player (with keyboard or mouse), switching video modes, and keeping track of the game time. The operation of these additional functions is left for you to discover on your own.

The Overall Game Loop

Virtual Maze uses a very simple loop:

1. Get player movements.
2. Ray cast the new scene.

Player movements are controlled by the arrow keys on the keyboard, or by moving the mouse. The up arrow moves the player forward, the down arrow backwards. The left and right arrows rotate the player counterclockwise and clockwise, respectively. Similar movements on the mouse have the same effect.

Once the player's new position and direction have been calculated (assuming the player has not tried to walk through a wall), a new scene is rendered. If the player stands still, the ray caster does not render a new scene. This helps to reduce flicker and is acceptable since Virtual Maze is a static environment. A dynamic environment contains things that move, lights that flash, and so on, and must be continuously rendered.

The Program

Program 11.1 is the Virtual Maze game. It is quite lengthy and will require a good deal of time to examine. A number of sections utilize interrupts and 80x86 microprocessor architecture. These sections of code are kept very small and should be straightforward if you read the comments and think about what the game is doing while the code is executing.

Program 11.1

```
/* Virtual Maze */

#include <bios.h>
#include <conio.h>
#include <dos.h>
#include <fcntl.h>
#include <io.h>
#include <math.h>
#include <memory.h>
#include <stdio.h>
#include <stdlib.h>
#include <string.h>


/* ------------------------------------------------------------------- */
/* Various constants */

/* Boolean */

#define FALSE       0
#define TRUE        1

/* Video */

#define VGA         0x13
#define TEXT        0x03
#define FLOOR       66
#define CEILING     34
#define STRIP_SIZE  200

/* Math */
```

```
#define PI              3.1415926536
#define TSIZE           1920
#define ANGLEINC        ((double)360/TSIZE)
#define D90             TSIZE/120*90/3
#define D180            2*D90
#define D270            3*D90
#define INFINITY        1e10
#define NOTZERO         1e-10
#define SCALE           14000

/* Keyboard */

#define UP              72
#define DN              80
#define LT              75
#define RT              77

/* Mouse */

#define RESET_MOUSE 0
#define GET_STATUS  3
#define READ_MOUSE  0x0B
#define MOUSE_INT   0x33

/* Time */

#define READ_TIME   0x2c
#define DOS_INT     0x21

/* Game */

#define MAPCOLS     64
#define MAPROWS     20
#define CELLSIZE    64
#define RMAX        MAPROWS*CELLSIZE
#define CMAX        MAPCOLS*CELLSIZE
#define NUMWALLS    5

/* Stuff to do on-the-fly */

#define shl(r,n) ((int)r << n)
#define pp(r,c,color) vbuff[shl(r,8)+shl(r,6)+(int)c]=(unsigned char)color
#define cellval(x,y) game_map[(int)x/CELLSIZE][(int)y/CELLSIZE]
#define sqr(z) (z)*(z)
#define is_wall(cell) ((('1' <= cell) && (cell <= '4')) || (cell == 'E'))
#define dist(x1,y1,x2,y2) sqrt(sqr(x1-x2) + sqr(y1-y2))

/* ---------------------------------------------------------------- */
/* Define player info. */

typedef struct
{
        int cellr, cellc;
```

```
        float r,c;
        float dir;
} player_type;

        player_type player;

/* Precomputed tables */

        float tantab[TSIZE];
        float invtan[TSIZE];
        float corr[320];

/* Wall variables */

        unsigned char wall_maps[NUMWALLS][CELLSIZE][CELLSIZE];
        int tptr,slice,hslice,vslice,wall;
        unsigned char hcolor,vcolor;

/* Game control */

        unsigned char game_map[MAPROWS][MAPCOLS];
        int stopped;
        long starttime;
        int gotdir;
        int mousedr,mousedc;
        unsigned char oldfloor;
        float angle,ta;

/* Pointer to base of video RAM */

unsigned char far *vbuff = (char far *)0xA00000001;

/* ----------------------------------------------------------------- */
/* Function Prototypes */

float hit_hwall(void);
float hit_vwall(void);
void ray_cast(void);
void draw_strip(int col, int size, int pos);
int move_player(void);
void build_tables(void);
void load_map(void);
void load_walls(void);
int use_mouse(int op);
void video_mode(int mode);

/* ----------------------------------------------------------------- */
/* Here we go... */

void main()
{
        int k,still_playing,mins,secs;
        long stoptime,gametime;
```

```
        union REGS regs;

        regs.h.ah = READ_TIME;
        int86(DOS_INT, &regs, &regs);
        starttime = regs.h.ch * 3600 + regs.h.cl * 60 + regs.h.dh;
        video_mode(VGA);
        load_map();
        load_walls();
        build_tables();
        use_mouse(RESET_MOUSE);
        ray_cast();
        stopped = FALSE;
        still_playing = TRUE;
        while (!stopped && still_playing)
        {
                still_playing = move_player();
                ray_cast();
        }
        video_mode(TEXT);
        regs.h.ah = READ_TIME;
        int86(DOS_INT, &regs, &regs);
        stoptime = regs.h.ch * 3600 + regs.h.cl * 60 + regs.h.dh;
        gametime = stoptime - starttime;
        if (gametime < 0)
                gametime += 24*3600;
        mins = gametime / 60;
        secs = gametime % 60;
        printf("You played for %d minutes and %d seconds.\n",mins,secs);
}

/* ------------------------------------------------------------------ */
/* Set the video mode (using inline assembly language) */

void video_mode(int mode)
{
        asm mov ah,0
        asm mov al, byte ptr mode
        asm int 0x10
}

/* ------------------------------------------------------------------ */
/* Read the game map into memory */

void load_map()
{
        FILE *fp, *fopen();
        int r,c;
        unsigned char mdat;

        fp = fopen("gamemap.dat","rb");
        for(r = 0; r < MAPROWS; r++)
```

```
        {
                for(c = 0; c < MAPCOLS; c++)
                {
                        mdat = getc(fp);
                        game_map[r][c] = mdat;
                        if (mdat == 'P')
                        {
                                player.cellr = r;
                                player.cellc = c;
                                player.r = r*CELLSIZE + CELLSIZE/2;
                                player.c = c*CELLSIZE + CELLSIZE/2;
                                player.dir = (starttime % 8) * 45;
                                oldfloor = game_map[r][c-1];
                        }
                }
                mdat = getc(fp); /* eat cr */
                mdat = getc(fp); /* eat lf */
        }
        fclose(fp);
}


/* ------------------------------------------------------------------ */
/* Precompute tangent and distance-correction tables */

void build_tables()
{
        int k;
        double angle;

        for(k = 0; k < TSIZE; k++)
        {
                angle = k*ANGLEINC*PI/180.0;
                switch(k)
                {
                case    0: tantab[k] = 0;
                           invtan[k] = INFINITY;
                           break;
                case  D90: tantab[k] = INFINITY;
                           invtan[k] = 0;
                           break;
                case D180: tantab[k] = 0;
                           invtan[k] = INFINITY;
                           break;
                case D270: tantab[k] = INFINITY;
                           invtan[k] = 0;
                           break;
                default:   tantab[k] = (float)tan(angle);
                           invtan[k] = (float)(1.0/tantab[k]);
                }
        }
        angle = -30.0*PI/180.0;
```

```
        for(k = 0; k < 320; k++)
        {
                corr[k] = (float)1.0/cos(angle);
                angle += 2*30/320.0*PI/180.0;
        }
}

/* ------------------------------------------------------------------ */
/* Calculate new player position based on keyboard/mouse inputs */

int move_player()
{
        int mr,mc,left_click,button;
        player_type temp;
        char kyb;
        unsigned char spot;

        left_click = use_mouse(READ_MOUSE);
        if (left_click)
                stopped = TRUE;
        temp.r = player.r;
        temp.c = player.c;
        temp.dir = player.dir;
        gotdir = FALSE;
        if (kbhit())
        {
                kyb = getch();
                if (!kyb)
                {
                        kyb = getch();
                        gotdir = TRUE;
                        switch(kyb)
                        {
                                case UP: temp.r -= 24*sin(temp.dir*PI/180.0);
                                         temp.c += 32*cos(temp.dir*PI/180.0);
                                         break;
                                case DN: temp.r += 24*sin(temp.dir*PI/180.0);
                                         temp.c -= 32*cos(temp.dir*PI/180.0);
                                         break;
                                case LT: temp.dir += 3; break;
                                case RT: temp.dir -= 3; break;
                                default: gotdir = FALSE;
                        }
                }
        }
        if (mousedr || mousedc)
        {
                temp.r += mousedr*sin(temp.dir*PI/180.0);
                temp.c -= mousedr*cos(temp.dir*PI/180.0);
                temp.dir -= mousedc/12.0;
                button = use_mouse(RESET_MOUSE);
```

```
                        gotdir = TRUE;
              }
              if(temp.r < 0) temp.r = 0;
              if(temp.r > RMAX) temp.r = RMAX;
              if(temp.c < 0) temp.c = 0;
              if(temp.c > CMAX) temp.c = CMAX;
              if(temp.dir < 0)
                        temp.dir += 360;
              if(temp.dir > 360)
                        temp.dir -= 360;
              temp.cellr = temp.r / CELLSIZE;
              temp.cellc = temp.c / CELLSIZE;
              spot = game_map[temp.cellr][temp.cellc];
              if((spot == '.') || (spot == 'P') && gotdir)
              {
                        game_map[player.cellr][player.cellc] = oldfloor;
                        player.cellr = temp.cellr;
                        player.cellc = temp.cellc;
                        player.r = temp.r;
                        player.c = temp.c;
                        player.dir = temp.dir;
                        oldfloor = game_map[player.cellr][player.cellc];
                        game_map[player.cellr][player.cellc] = 'P';
              }
              else
              if ((spot == 'E') && gotdir)
                        stopped = TRUE;
              return(kyb != 'q');
}


/* ------------------------------------------------------------------- */
/* Reset/Read the mouse */

int use_mouse(int op)
{
        union REGS regs;

        switch(op)
        {
                case RESET_MOUSE: regs.h.ah = RESET_MOUSE;
                        int86(MOUSE_INT, &regs, &regs);
                        return(0);
                case READ_MOUSE: regs.x.ax = READ_MOUSE;
                        int86(MOUSE_INT, &regs, &regs);
                        mousedr = regs.x.dx;
                        if (mousedr > 50) mousedr = 50;
                        if (mousedr < -50) mousedr = -50;
                        mousedc = regs.x.cx;
                        if (mousedc > 50) mousedc = 50;
                        if (mousedc < -50) mousedc = -50;
                        regs.x.ax = GET_STATUS;
```

```
                              int86(MOUSE_INT, &regs, &regs);
                              return(regs.x.bx & 1);
                      default:
                              return(0);
              }


}

/* ------------------------------------------------------------------ */
/* Look for first horizontal intersection with a wall */

float hit_hwall()
{
        float rpos,rstep,cpos,cstep;
        int found;

        rpos = (player.cellr * CELLSIZE) - 1;
        cstep = CELLSIZE * invtan[tptr];
        if (angle < 180)
                rstep = -CELLSIZE;
        else
        {
                rstep = CELLSIZE;
                rpos += (1+CELLSIZE);
                cstep *= -1;
        }
        cpos = player.c + (player.r - rpos) * invtan[tptr];
        hcolor = cellval(rpos,cpos);
        if (is_wall(hcolor))
        {
                if (hcolor == 'E')
                        hcolor = NUMWALLS - 1;
                else
                        hcolor -= '1';
                hslice = ((int)cpos) % CELLSIZE;
                return dist(player.r,player.c,rpos,cpos);
        }
        found = 0;
        while ((cpos >= 0) && (cpos < CMAX) && !found)
        {
                rpos += rstep;
                cpos += cstep;
                hcolor = cellval(rpos,cpos);
                if (is_wall(hcolor))
                {
                        found = 1;
                        if (hcolor == 'E')
                                hcolor = NUMWALLS - 1;
                        else
                                hcolor -= '1';
                        hslice = ((int)cpos) % CELLSIZE;
```

```
                }
        }
        if (found)
                return dist(player.r,player.c,rpos,cpos);
        else
        {
                hcolor = 0;
                hslice = -1;
                return INFINITY;
        }
}

/* -------------------------------------------------------------- */
/* Look for first vertical intersection with a wall */

float hit_vwall()
{
        float rpos,rstep,cpos,cstep;
        int found;

        cpos = (player.cellc * CELLSIZE) - 1;
        rstep = CELLSIZE * tantab[tptr];
        if ((angle >= 90) && (angle < 270))
                cstep = -CELLSIZE;
        else
        {
                cstep = CELLSIZE;
                cpos += (1+CELLSIZE);
        }
        if ((angle < 90) || (angle >= 270))
                rstep *= -1;
        rpos = player.r + (player.c - cpos) * tantab[tptr];
        vcolor = cellval(rpos,cpos);
        if (is_wall(vcolor))
        {
                if (vcolor == 'E')
                        vcolor = NUMWALLS - 1;
                else
                        vcolor -= '1';
                vslice = ((int)rpos) % CELLSIZE;
                return dist(player.r,player.c,rpos,cpos);
        }
        found = 0;
        while ((rpos >= 0) && (rpos < RMAX) && !found)
        {
                rpos += rstep;
                cpos += cstep;
                vcolor = cellval(rpos,cpos);
                if (is_wall(vcolor))
                {
                        found = 1;
```

```
                    if (vcolor == 'E')
                            vcolor = NUMWALLS-1;
                    else
                            vcolor -= '1';
                    vslice = ((int)rpos) % CELLSIZE;
            }
    }
    if (found)
            return dist(player.r,player.c,rpos,cpos);
    else
    {
            vcolor = 0;
            vslice = -1;
            return INFINITY;
    }
}

/* ---------------------------------------------------------------- */
/* Ray cast an entire scene (320 columns) */

void ray_cast()
{
    float xdist,ydist,dist,temp;
    int i,r,c,ray,size;
    unsigned char color;

    color = 0;
    for(ray = 0; ray < 320; ray++)
    {
            angle = player.dir - ray*ANGLEINC + 30;
            if (angle < 0)
                    angle += 360;
            if (angle > 360)
                    angle -= 360;
            ta = (angle/ANGLEINC);
            tptr = ta;
            xdist = hit_hwall();
            ydist = hit_vwall();
            if (xdist < ydist)
            {
                    dist = xdist;
                    color = hcolor;
                    wall = color;
                    slice = hslice;
            }
            else
            {
                    dist = ydist;
                    color = vcolor;
                    wall = color;
                    slice = vslice;
```

```
                }
                temp = (SCALE/(dist + NOTZERO)*corr[ray]);
                size = (int)(temp + 0.5);
                if (slice == -1) slice = 0;
                draw_strip(ray,size,slice);
        }
}

/* ------------------------------------------------------------------ */
/* Draw a scaled, texture-mapped vertical strip */

void draw_strip(int col, int size, int pos)
{
        int i,j,k;
        float pixel_inc,pixel_row;
        unsigned char color;

        pixel_inc = (float)CELLSIZE / size;
        if (size > STRIP_SIZE)
        {
                pixel_row = ((size - STRIP_SIZE) / 2) * pixel_inc;
                size = STRIP_SIZE;
        }
        else
                pixel_row = 0;
        j = (STRIP_SIZE - size) / 2;
        for(i = 0; i < j; i++)
                pp(i,col,CEILING);
        for(k = 0; k < size; k++)
        {
                color = wall_maps[wall][(int)pixel_row][pos];
                pixel_row += pixel_inc;
                pp(j,col,color);
                j++;
        }
        for(i = j; i < STRIP_SIZE; i++)
                pp(i,col,FLOOR);
}

/* ------------------------------------------------------------------ */
/* Read the wall patterns into memory */

void load_walls()
{
        FILE *fp, *fopen();
        int wall,r,c;

        fp = fopen("wallpatt.dat","rb");
        for(wall = 0; wall < NUMWALLS; wall++)
                for(r = 0; r < CELLSIZE; r++)
                        for(c = 0; c < CELLSIZE; c++)
```

```
                              wall_maps[wall][r][c] = getc(fp);
        fclose(fp);
}
```

A large number of global variables are used to pass information back and forth between various functions. While it is good to keep global variable usage to a minimum, in this case we take advantage of the global accessibility to avoid time-consuming parameter passing on the run-time stack.

What's Next?

Many improvements can be made to the Virtual Maze program, which was written in a simple format to allow each part of the ray casting process to be coded in a straight forward manner. Once you have a complete understanding of how the program works, you can make manyadditions to challenge your programming skills. Here is a short list of features you might try to add:

- Textured ceilings and floors
- Flashing lights
- Other objects (people, robots, monsters) to interact with the player
- Transporters
- Doors that open and close
- Stairs and elevators to different levels (almost a true 3D world)
- Furniture
- A view of the sky

These new features will require additional data structures and functions to implement. If you are interested in further details of game design, there are a large number of books available to satisfy your needs. The inspiration for this material was an excellent chapter in *Tricks of the GAME Programming Gurus.* Chapter 6, "The Third Dimension," written by Andre LaMothe, is a detailed introduction to ray casting, with many illustrations to help you understand the material.

Conclusion

This section completed a brief introduction to a simple first-person virtual reality game. Many of the topics presented in this book are employed in the Virtual Maze program. Test your understanding of this material with the following section review.

11.6 Section Review

1. What is a first-person game?
2. Describe the ray casting technique.
3. Why is it important to cast every ray as fast as possible?
4. How is the game world represented?
5. How are walls represented?
6. What is texture mapping?
7. Why are the trig tables built at the beginning of the game?

Study Questions

General Concepts

Section 11.1

1. Why is ray tracing a poor choice for real-time imaging?
2. What is the basic method behind ray casting?
3. What is stored in a game cell?

Section 11.2

4. Why use precomputed data tables?
5. How is the size of a precomputed data table determined?

Section 11.3

6. How can a #define be used in place of a function?
7. How many pixels need to be written to screen memory to display an entire screen?

Section 11.4

8. Explain how several new objects, such as pieces of furniture, can be represented in the 2D game map array.
9. What are the overall dimensions of the Virtual Maze game world?
10. Why does the wall_maps array have three indexes?

Section 11.5

11. What are the three cases to consider when drawing a strip of the wall?
12. Explain why a wall strip would be scaled down. How is this accomplished?
13. What technique is used to keep the pixel_address generation time to a minimum?

Section 11.6

14. How are the player's movements controlled?
15. What is a dynamic environment?
16. How is the initial player direction chosen?
17. How is the player prevented from walking through a wall?

Program Design

The following programming problems all involve modifications to the Virtual Maze program. In addition to writing the code to implement each new feature, explain the reasoning behind your choice of a particular data structure in your solution.

18. Add a transporter to the Virtual Maze program. A transporter consists of a transmitting cell and a receiving cell. Use a 'T' to indicate a transmitting cell and an 'R' for the receiving cell. The player's current position (and view) is instantly changed to that of the receiving cell when the player walks into the transmitting cell.
19. Add flashing lights to the Virtual Maze program by picking one texture color (out of the 256 available) to represent a flashing light code. When this color code is encountered during draw_strip(), the actual pixel color written to the screen should be one of two shades that alternate at a predetermined rate (white for one half of a second, black for the other half second).
20. Add transparency to the texture-mapping code in draw_strip(). In a method similar to adding flashing lights, choose a texture color to represent transparent pixels. Transparency is implemented by skipping writes to display memory whenever the transparent pixel color is encountered. This allows the background color to remain visible (since it is not overwritten).

21. Change the way the ceiling is drawn so that a 360-degree view of the sky is available. This can be accomplished by creating an image of the sky in a buffer that wraps around in the horizontal direction.

22. Add a second floor pattern that causes the player to move in slow motion as if moving through quicksand, thereby requiring more effort to move through it.

23. Add an invisible wall that cannot be walked through.

24. Devise your own data structure (or structures) for representing the Virtual Maze game world. What changes are necessary to the ray caster to utilize your new data structure?

25. Add the necessary statements to the Virtual Maze program to determine the average number of display screens cast out in 1 second. Do this by counting how many screens are cast while the game is being played. Divide the screen count by the total game time (in seconds).

26. Modify Virtual Maze so that two different walls may be designated as exits.

27. Add a *radar* screen to Virtual Maze that displays a low-resolution view of the game world as seen from above. The player can be a single pixel of a certain color, located at the proper place in the 2D display. Walls may be optionally displayed.

28. Add a "demo" feature to Virtual Maze that has the game play itself for 5 seconds, pause for 5 seconds, and start a new 5-second game (over and over). The player can press any key at any time to start a new game.

29. Add a "trip camera" to Virtual Maze by storing all player movements to a data file as the game is being played. Allow Virtual Maze to "view" the data file at startup and show a replay of a saved game.

30. Add a new wall pattern to Virtual Maze that looks like a key. The player must touch the wall in order to use the Exit wall to end the game. Modify WALLPATT.DAT, GAMEMAP.DAT, and associated game structures and functions as necessary.

Appendix A:
C/C++ Reference

The C/C++ Environment

The C/C++ environment contains an **editor, compiler, include files, library files, linker,** and much more. The functions of these components are as follows:

Editor Allows you to enter and modify your source code.

Compiler A program that converts the program you have developed into the code understood by the computer.

Include Files Files that consist of many separate definitions and instructions that may be useful to a programmer in certain instances.

Library Files These files contain previously compiled programs that perform specific functions. These functions can be used to help you develop your programs.

Linker Essentially, the linker combines all of the necessary parts (such as library files) of your program to produce the final executable code. Linkers play an important and necessary role in all of your programs. In larger programs, it is general practice to break the program down into smaller parts, each of which is developed and tested separately. The linker will then combine all of these parts together to form your final executable program code.

The main parts of the C/C++ environment are shown in Figure A.1.

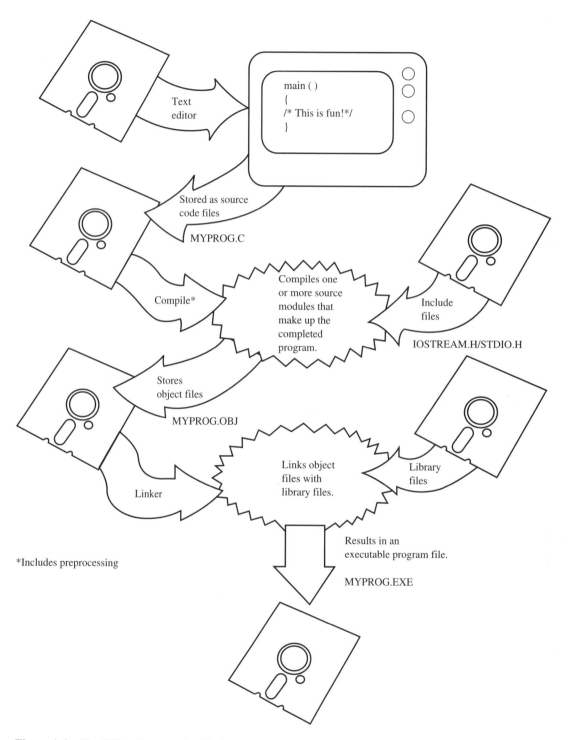

Figure A.1   The C/C++ Programming Environment

The Programmer's Block

Every well-documented program will start with a block called the **programmer's block.** It consists of **remarks** that contain the following information:

1. Program name
2. Developer
3. Description of the program
4. Explanation of all variables
5. Explanation of all constants

Elements of C/C++

To write a program, you use a set of characters. This set includes the uppercase and lowercase letters of the English alphabet, the ten decimal digits of the Arabic number system, and the underscore (_) character. White space characters (such as the spaces between words) are used to separate the items in a program, much the same as they are used to separate words in this book. These white space characters also include the tab and carriage return, as well as other control characters that produce white spaces.

Tokens.   In every source program, the most basic element recognized by the compiler is a single character or group of characters known as a **token.** Essentially, a token is source program text that the compiler will not break down any further—it is treated as a fundamental unit. As an example, in main() is a token; so are the required opening brace ({) as well as the plus sign (+).

Keywords.   **Keywords** are predefined tokens that have special meanings to the compiler. Their definitions cannot be changed; thus, they cannot be used for anything else except the intended action they have on the program in which they are used. These keywords are as follows:

```
auto       double     int        struct     break      else
long       switch     case       enum       register   typedef
char       extern     return     union      const      float
short      unsigned   continue   for        signed     void
default    goto       sizeof     volatile   do         if
static     while
```

Types of Data.   There are three major types of data: numbers, characters, and strings. A **character** is any item from the set of characters used. A **string** is a combination of these characters.

Types of Numbers.   Numbers fall into two general categories: **integer** (whole numbers) and **float** (numbers with decimal points). These two main categories can be further divided as shown in Table A.1.

As you can see in Table A.1, C/C++ offers a rich variety of **data types.** Generally speaking, the larger the value range of the data type, the more computer memory it takes to store it. As a general rule, you want to use the data type that conserves memory and still accomplishes the desired purpose.

Table A.1   Subdivisions of Data Types

Type Identifier	Meaning	Range of Values (80x86)
char	character	–128 to 127
int	integer	–32,768 to 32,767
short	short integer	–32,768 to 32,767
long	long integer	–2,147,483,648 to 2,147,483,647
unsigned char	unsigned character	0 to 255
unsigned	unsigned integer	0 to 65,535
unsigned short	unsigned short integer	0 to 65,535
unsigned long	unsigned long integer	0 to 4,294,967,295
enum	enumerated	0 to 65,535
float	floating point	3.4E +/– 38 (7 digits)
double	double floating point	1.7E +/– 308 (15 digits)
long double	long double floating point	1.7E +/– 4932 (15 digits)

As you may note in Table A.1, some of the data types produce the same range of values (such as int and short). This is because on other computer systems, short and int may actually have different ranges.

C/C++ Statements

A C/C++ **statement** controls the flow of the execution of a program. It consists of keywords, **expressions,** and other statements. An expression is a combination of operands and operators that expresses a single value (such as answer = 3 + 5;).

There are two types of statements. These are **single statements** and **compound statements.** A *compound statement* is delimited by braces ({ }), whereas a single statement ends with a semicolon (;).

Examine the program shown in Figure A.2 for the elements presented in this section (plus others still to come).

The printf() Function

The printf() function is used to write information to **standard output** (normally your monitor screen). The structure of this function is

```
printf(character strings with format specifiers, variables or values);
```

Characters are set off by single quotes (such as 'a'), and strings are set off by double quotes (such as "This is a string."). A **format specifier** instructs the printf() function how to convert, format, and print its **arguments.** For now, think of an argument as the actual values that are within the parentheses of the function. A format specifier begins with a percent (%) character. As an example,

```
printf("This is a C statement.\n");
```

Preprocessor
directives ——▶

```
#include <stdio.h>
#include <math.h>
#define PI 3.14159
#define SQUARE(x) ((x) * (x))
```

Programmer's
block

Definition
of each
function

```
/*
Program:  Circle Area
Developed by: A. G. Programmer

Description:  This program will solve for the area of a circle.  The
              programmer need only enter the radius.  Value returned
              is in square units.

Variables:

        input_value = Value entered by the user.
        radius      = Radius of the circle.
        area        = Area of the circle.

Constants:

        PI = 3.14159

Function Prototypes:
*/

void explain_program(void);
float get_value(void);
float circle_area(float radius);
void display_answer(float area);
```

Explanation
of variables

Main
function ——▶

```
main()
{
    float radius;          /* Radius of the circle. */
    float area;            /* Area of the circle.   */

    explain_program();                /* Explains program to user.*/
    radius = get_value();             /* Get radius from user.     */
    area = circle_area(radius);       /* Compute the circle area.  */
    display_answer(area);             /* Display the answer.       */
}
```

Other
functions ——▶

```
void explain_program()               /* Explains the program.     */
{
    printf("This program calculates the area of a circle.\n");
    printf("Just enter the value of the radius and press -RETURN-\n");
    printf("\n");       /* Put in a blank line. */
}

float get_value()                    /* Gets radius from user.    */
{
    float input_value;               /* Value entered by the user. */

    printf("Value of the radius ==> ");
    scanf("%f",&input_value);
    return(input_value);
}

float circle_area(float radius)      /* Compute the circle area.  */
{
    float area;                      /* Area of the circle.       */

    area = PI * SQUARE(radius);
    return(area);
}

void display_answer(float area)      /* Display the answer.       */
{
    printf("\n\n");                          /* Print two blank lines.    */
    printf("The area of the circle is %f units.",area);
}
```

Figure A.2 Structure of a C Program

when executed produces

```
This is a C statement.
```

The \n characters represent the "new line" *escape sequence* that outputs a carriage return and a line feed to the display (more on this shortly). With a format specifier and an argument,

```
printf("The number 92 in decimal is %d.",92);
```

when executed produces

```
The number 92 in decimal is 92.
```

Another way of producing the same output is

```
printf("The number %d in decimal is %d.",92,92);
```

Table A.2 lists the various type fields used by the `printf()` function in format specifiers.

Escape Sequences

The \n is an example of an **escape sequence** that can be used by the `printf()` function. The backslash symbol (\) is referred to as the escape character. You can think of an escape sequence used in the `printf()` function as an escape from the normal interpretation of a string. This means that the next character used after the \ will have a special meaning, as listed in Table A.3.

Table A.2 Field Type Format Specifiers Used by `printf()`

Character	Argument	Resulting Output
d	integer	Signed decimal integer.
i	integer	Signed decimal integer.
o	integer	Unsigned octal integer.
u	integer	Unsigned decimal integer.
x	integer	Unsigned hexadecimal integer using lowercase letters.
X	integer	Unsigned hexadecimal integer using uppercase letters.
f	floating point	Signed floating-point number.
e	floating point	Signed floating-point number using e notation.
E	floating point	Signed floating-point number using E notation.
g	floating point	Signed decimal number in either e form or f form, whichever is shorter.
G	floating point	Signed decimal number in either E form or f form, whichever is shorter.
c	character	A single character.
s	string	Prints character strings.
%	none	Prints the % sign.

Note: Use an l prefix with %d, %u, %x, %o, to specify long integer (for example, %ld).

Table A.3   Escape Sequences

Sequence	Meaning
\n	New line
\t	Tab
\b	Backspace
\r	Carriage return
\f	Form feed
\'	Single quote
\"	Double quote
\\	Backslash
\xdd	ASCII code in hexadecimal
\ddd	ASCII code in octal

Note: The double quote and the backslash can be printed by preceding them with the backslash.

Field Width Specifiers

The `printf()` function allows you to format your output. When you print the output of a type `float`, it will appear as: `16.000000`; even though you do not need the six trailing zeros, they are still printed. The `printf()` function provides **field width specifiers** so that you can control how printed values will appear on the display. The syntax is:

```
%<width>.<digits>F
```
Where

`%`	=	The format specification.
`<width>`	=	The width of the field.
`<digits>`	=	Number of digits to the right of the decimal.
`F`	=	The format specifier.

As an example, the statement

```
printf("The number %5.2f uses them.",6.0);
```

would display

```
The number   6.00 uses them.
```

Note that the width first indicates how the number is justified (five spaces), and then the number of digits following the decimal point is specified.

In C++, the `cout` function is also available to display output. More information about C++ is presented at the end of this Appendix.

More Than One Specifier

You can use more than one format specifier in a `printf()` function. However, you must have at least as many arguments as format specifiers; if not, the results will be unpredictable. You can have more arguments than format specifiers; however, the extra arguments will just be ignored.

An example of using more than one format specifier is

```
printf("A character is %c and a number is %d.",'a',53);
```

Note that the arguments are separated by commas.

Identifying and Declaring Things

What Is a Function?

A **function** is an independent collection of **declarations** and statements. A declaration states the relationship between the name and type of a variable or other function. It is important that you realize a function is usually designed to perform one task. Every program must have one function called `main()`, but it may also have many other functions. Dividing tasks into separate parts in a program makes programs easier to design, correct, understand, and modify.

What Needs Identification?

When you create a function, it's best to give it a descriptive name. As an example, a function that would calculate the total power dissipated in a resistor could be named

```
resistor_power()
```

This is more descriptive than naming it

```
function_1()
```

These two examples both use **identifiers** to distinguish one function from the other. An identifier is nothing more than the name you give to a part of your program. Identifiers can be used to name parts of a formula, such as

```
total = resistor_1 + resistor_2;
```

An identifier can be used to assign a constant value that describes the value and can then be used in your program:

```
PI = 3.14159;
circle_area = PI * radius * radius;
```

As you can see from these examples, identifiers play an important role in every program.

Creating Your Own Identifiers

There are some rules to follow when making your own identifiers. First, every identifier must start with a letter of the alphabet (uppercase or lowercase) or the underscore _. The remainder of the identifier may use any arrangement of letters (uppercase or lowercase), digits (0 through 9), and the underscore—and that's it—no other characters are allowed. This means that spaces are not allowed in identifiers. Most compilers will distinguish among at least the first 31 characters of an identifier.

Case Sensitivity

Identifiers are case sensitive. This means that the compiler makes a distinction between uppercase and lowercase letters in an identifier. Thus, as far as the compiler is concerned, the following identifiers are not equal:

```
pi PI Pi pI
```

Neither are the following:

```
This_One THIS_ONE this_one
```

All of the identifiers above are legal; it is just that they are not equal. What this means is that you must be careful with your use of identifiers. As an example, if you define the identifier `pi` to be equal to 3.14159, you must use the lowercase letters `pi` anywhere in the program you expect the identifier to equal 3.14159. If you use `PI` or `Pi`, neither of which you assigned a value to, then the program will contain errors.

Keywords

An identifier cannot have the same spelling and case as a keyword.

Variables

All variables must be declared. This means that you must let the compiler know ahead of time, before you use the variables, the identifier that will be used for each variable as well as the type of variable you will be using. At first, this may seem like a lot of extra work. But you will find that by doing this you will actually reduce the chances for program errors.

What Is a Variable?

You can think of a variable as a specific memory location set aside for a specific kind of data and given a name for easy reference. Essentially, you use variables so that the same memory space can hold different values of the same type at different times. As an example, if you were calculating the voltage across a fixed value of resistance as the current changed, the voltage variable would have a different value each time the current changed.

Declaring Variables

You must declare all variables before using them. To declare a variable, you must declare its type and identifier. Table A.4 presents the fundamental **type specifiers** that will be used for variables.

Initializing Variables

You can combine a variable declaration with the **assignment operator(=),** thus giving the variable a value at the same time that it is declared. This is shown in Program A.1.

Table A.4 Fundamental Type Specifiers

Integers	Floating Point	Other Types
char	double	const
enum	float	void
int	long double	volatile
long		
short		
signed		
unsigned		

Program A.1

```
#include <stdio.h>

main()
{
    char a_character = 'a';    /* This declares/assigns a character.  */
    int an_integer = 15;       /* This declares/assigns an integer.   */
    float floating_point = 27.62; /* This declares/assigns a float point.*/

    printf("%c is the character.\n",a_character);
    printf("%d is the integer.\n",an_integer);
    printf("%f is the floating point.\n",floating_point);
}
```

Note that, in each case, the variable declaration is followed by a comment that states the purpose of each variable. It's good to get in the habit of doing this kind of program documentation.

Declaring Multiple Variables

If you have multiple variables of the same data type, you can declare them as follows:

```
int number_1, number_2, number_3;
```

Even though this definition is legal, this practice will not be used because it discourages you from commenting on each variable used in the program.

Why Declare?

When you declare variables, you gather all the information about them at one place in the program. This allows everyone reading your source code to quickly identify the data that will be used (assuming that you add comments that give good explanations). Doing this also forces you to do some planning before leaping into the program code. Another important reason for doing this is that it prevents you from misspelling a variable within the program. If there were no requirements to declare, then you could create a new identifier without knowing it. This could cause disastrous problems that are very difficult to find and correct. The more you program, and the more complex and practical your programs are, the more thankful you will be that variables must be declared before you can use them.

Operators

An operator causes the program to do something to variables. Specifically, an **arithmetic operator** allows an arithmetic operation (such as addition, +) to be performed on variables. We will discuss the most commonly used arithmetic operators.

Arithmetic Operators

The common arithmetic operators used by C/C++ are listed in Table A.5.
Program A.2 illustrates the use of the first four arithmetic operators.

Program A.2

```c
#include <stdio.h>

main()
{
    float number_1 = 15.0;    /* First arithmetic operator.          */
    float number_2 = 3.0;     /* Second arithmetic operator.         */
    float addition_answer;    /* Answer to addition problem.         */
    float subtraction_answer; /* Answer to subtraction problem.      */
    float multi_answer;       /* Answer to multiplication problem.   */
    float division_answer;    /* Answer to division problem.         */

    addition_answer = number_1 + number_2;
    subtraction_answer = number_1 - number_2;
    multi_answer = number_1 * number_2;
    division_answer = number_1 / number_2;

    printf("15 + 3 = %f\n",addition_answer);
    printf("15 - 3 = %f\n",subtraction_answer);
    printf("15 * 3 = %f\n",multi_answer);
    printf("15 / 3 = %f\n",division_answer);
}
```

Table A.5   Common Arithmetic Operators

Symbol	Meaning	Example
+	Addition	answer = 3 + 5 (answer → 8)
−	Subtraction	answer = 5 − 3 (answer → 2)
*	Multiplication	answer = 5 * 3 (answer → 15)
/	Division	answer = 10 / 2 (answer → 5)
%	Remainder	answer = 3 % 2 (answer → 1)

Execution of Program A.2 produces

```
15  +  3  =  18.000000
15  -  3  =  12.000000
15  *  3  =  45.000000
15  /  3  =  5.000000
```

Note that all of the numbers used in Program A.2 were of type `float`. It's important to note that division of type `int` variables will truncate the answer. This means that 5/2 = 2 and that 2/3 = 0. The remainder operator (`%`) requires the use of whole numbers. This operator is also called the *modulo* operator.

Precedence of Operations

Precedence of operations is simply the order in which arithmetic operations are performed. As an example, consider the expression

```
X = 5 + 4/2;
```

Precedence of operations requires that division be done before addition. If this were not the case, then the operation above could be interpreted in two different ways. If the division were performed first, it would yield (5 + 2 = 7). If addition were performed first, 5 would be added to 4 and then the sum would be divided by 2 (9/2 = 4.5). The interpretation of any expression must be consistent for reliable and predictable program results. For example, if you want to indicate that 5 is to be added to 4 first and the result then divided by 2, parentheses must be used:

```
X = (5 + 4)/2;
```

Table A.6 indicates the precedence of operations for C/C++. In all cases, operations proceed from left to right.

Compound Assignment Operators

Compound assignment operators combine the simple assignment operator with another operator. For example, consider the statement:

```
answer = answer + 5;
```

Table A.6   Precedence of Operations

Priority	Operation
First	( )
Second	Negation (assigning a negative number)
Third	Multiplication *, Division /
Fourth	Addition +, Subtraction –

Table A.7   Common Compound Assignments

Symbol	Example	Meaning
+=	X += Y;	X = X + Y;
−=	X −= Y;	X = X − Y;
*=	X *= Y;	X = X * Y;
/=	X /= Y;	X = X / Y;
%=	X %= Y;	X = X % Y;

What this statement means is that the memory location called "answer" will be assigned the new value of its old value plus 5. The = sign means *assigned to* and is called the assignment operator. Thus, if `answer` had the value of 10, then

```
answer = answer + 5;
```

would cause the new value of `answer` to be 15.

This expression can be shortened by using the compound assignment

```
answer += 5;
```

Table A.7 lists the compound assignments of the arithmetic operators presented at the beginning of this section.

Getting User Input

The `scanf()` Function

The `scanf()` function is a built-in function that allows your program to get user input from the keyboard. You can think of it as doing the opposite of the `printf()` function. Its use is illustrated in Program A.3.

Program A.3

```c
#include <stdio.h>

/*                  Getting user input.                  */
main()
{
     float value;     /* A number inputted by the program user. */

     printf("Input a number => ");
     scanf("%f", &value);

     printf("The value is => %f", value);
}
```

When Program A.3 is executed, the output will appear as follows (assuming the program user inputs the value of 23.6):

```
Input a number => 23.6
The value is => 23.600000
```

Note that the `scanf()` function has a similar format to that of the `printf()` function. First, it contains the `%f`, enclosed in quotation marks. This tells the program that a value will be entered that will be a floating-point type. Next, it indicates the variable identifier where this value will be stored. It indicates this by using a comma outside the quotes and then an `&` (ampersand sign) immediately followed by the name of the variable identifier (`&value`). Now the value that the user inputs will be the value of the variable `value`.

Format Specifiers

The format specifiers for the `scanf()` function are similar to those for the `printf()` function. This is illustrated in Table A.8.

It should be noted that either the `%f` or the `%e` format specifier may be used for accepting either exponential or decimal notation.

The `scanf()` function can accept more than one input with just one statement, as shown below:

```
scanf("%f%d%c",&number1, &number2, &character);
```

In the preceding case, the variable `number1` will accept a type `float`, the variable `number2` a type `int`, and `character` a type `char`. In this case, the program user would have to type in three separate values separated by spaces. As an example:

```
52.7 18 t
```

Using C++, the `cin` function is also available to get data from the user. More information about C++ is presented at the end of this Appendix.

Some Important Rules

What is important in a structured program is that there is no jumping around. If you don't know how to do this (if you have never used a GOTO), then consider yourself lucky! People can

Table A.8   `scanf()` Format Specifiers

Specifier	Meaning
%c	A single character.
%d	Signed decimal integer.
%e	Exponential notation.
%f	Floating-point notation.
%o	Unsigned octal integer.
%u	Unsigned decimal integer.
%x	Unsigned hexadecimal integer.

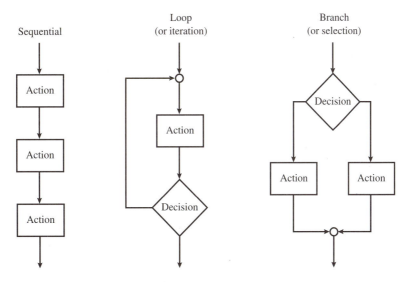

Figure A.3   Concepts of the Three Kinds of Programming Blocks

understand things a lot easier if they can follow them logically from one step to another. Hence, you should always follow these important rules when doing block structured programming:

1. All blocks are entered from the top.
2. All blocks are exited from the bottom.
3. When the computer finishes one block, it goes on to another block or ends.

Can you design every program this way? Yes, you can—with absolutely no exceptions. There is no excuse for writing a program in C/C++ that doesn't contain block structure.

Types of Blocks

No matter what programming language you use, there are only three necessary types of blocks:

1. Sequential block
2. Loop (or iteration) block
3. Branch (or selection) block

What does each of these blocks do? A **sequential block** is the simplest kind of programming block. It is nothing more than a straight sequence of statements, one following the other. A **loop block** can cause the program to go back and repeat a part of the program over again, whereas a **branch block** gives the option of performing a different sequence of instructions. The concepts of these three different kinds of blocks are illustrated in Figure A.3.

Using Functions

A function is an independent collection of source code designed to perform a specific task. All C/C++ programs have at least one function called `main()`.

Making Your Own Functions

You can make your own functions. Doing this allows you to create a function and tell C/C++ what the function is to do. Then you can use it over and over again just like the built-in functions. This means that you could create a function to solve for an electrical series circuit, one to solve for a parallel circuit, or one to solve for the electrical characteristics of a transistor amplifier—to name just a few. Define it only once, give it a name, and then call on it any time you want—just like you call on `puts()` or `printf()` any time you want. As you can see from this, to call a function, you simply use its name.

What Makes a Function?

In C, when you create a **function** other than `main()`, you first declare it and then define it. When you declare a function, you code in what is called the **function prototype.** A function prototype gives the function name plus other important information concerning the function. This appears at the beginning of the program before `main()`.

When you define a function, you again give the name of the function and other information about it (just as you did for the prototype), and you also produce the body of the function, which contains all of the source code to be used by that function.

To illustrate how a function can be used, consider Program A.4.

Program A.4

```
#include <stdio.h>

/* Function prototype. */

float square_it(float number);
/* This is the function that will square the number. */

main()
{
        float value;    /* Number to be squared.    */
        float answer;   /* The square of the number. */

        printf("Give me a number and I'll square it => ");
        scanf("%f", &value);

        answer = square_it(value);      /* Call the function. */

        printf("The square of %f is %f", value, answer);

        exit(0);
}

float square_it(float number)
{
        float answer;                   /* The square of the number. */
```

```
            answer = number * number;

            return(answer);
}
```

Program A.4 has created a separate function called `square_it()`. This new function computes the square of a number. Where does it get this number? It gets it from the main function `main()`. How does it get it? It is passed to it from `main()`. How is it passed to it? It is passed to it through its parameter argument (`float number`). Figure A.4 shows how **value passing** is done.

Note from Figure A.4 that the formal parameter list contains declarations of the function parameters. In this case, the function has only one, called `parameter_1`. This formal parameter is present in the function prototype as well as in the head of the function definition. However, when the function is called (as called from `main()`), its actual parameter need not have the same name as its formal parameter (it must still have the same type). For example, in Program A.4, the actual parameter was `value` and the formal parameter was `number`. Thus the **formal parameters** define the types and numbers of function parameters, whereas the **actual parameters** are used when calling the function.

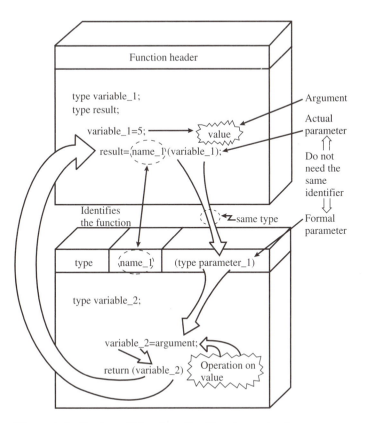

Figure A.4   Passing a Value from One Function to Another

How Functions May Be Called

Figure A.5 illustrates the different ways functions may call other functions. Notice that a function may also call itself. This is called **recursion.** The only restriction is that a function cannot be defined within the body of another function.

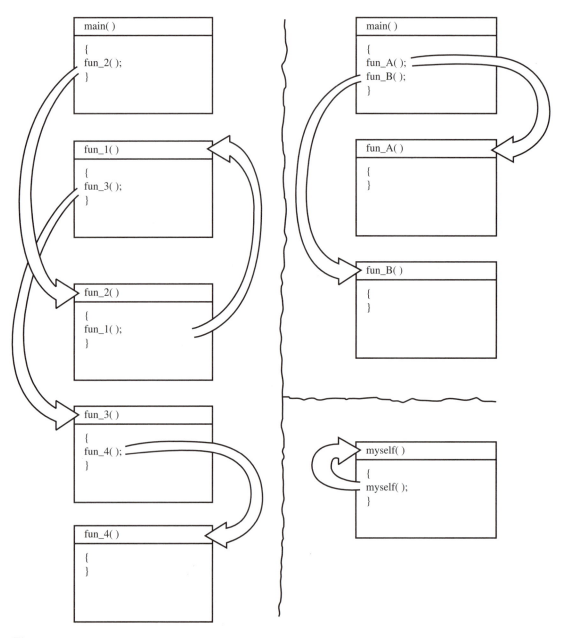

Figure A.5   How Functions May Call Other Functions

Using #define Statements

Look at Program A.5. What it does is take the number 5 and square it. It does this by using the preprocessor command #define, where the identifier square is defined with its parameter (x).

Program A.5

```
#include <stdio.h>
#define square(x) x*x

main()
{
        float number;    /* Square of a number. */

        number = square(5);

        printf("The square of 5 is %f",number);
}
```

Program A.5 uses the preprocessor directive #define. This defines a preprocessor **macro.** A macro, in this sense, is simply a string of tokens that will be substituted for another string of tokens. As an example, in the preprocessor macro for Program A.5

```
#define square(x) x*x
```

when the statement

```
square(x)
```

appears in the program, the compiler will actually substitute

```
x*x
```

Thus, in the above program, when the macro is used

```
number = square(5);
```

the processor actually substitutes

```
number = 5*5;
```

As you can see, the blanks on each side of the preprocessor directive serve to separate the tokens to be substituted. This is shown in Figure A.6.

This preprocessor macro may now be used by any function anywhere in the program. Thus, to square any number (constant or variable), simply use

```
answer = square(number);
```

Defining Constants

The constant PI is defined like this: #define PI 3.1415926. Thus, anywhere that PI appears in the program text, we can simply substitute the value 3.1415926.

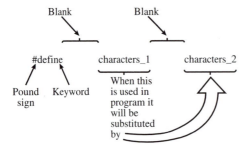

Figure A.6 Construction of the `#define` Statement

Table A.9 Relational Operators Used in C

Symbol	Meaning	TRUE Examples	FALSE Examples
>	Greater than	5 > 3	3 > 5
		(3 + 8) > (5 − 2)	(12/6) > 18
>=	Greater than or equal to	10 > = 10	3 > = 5
		(3*4) > = 8/2	8 + 5 > = 10*15
<	Less than	3 < 5	5 < 3
		12/3 < 12*3	9 − 2 < 3 + 1
<=	Less than or equal to	3 < = 15	15 < = 3
		18/6 < = 9/3	12 + 4 < = 12/4
==	Equal to	5 == 5	10 == 5
		2 + 7 == 18/2	8 − 5 == 2 + 4
!=	Not equal to	8 ! = 5	5 ! = 5
		8−5 ! = 2 + 4	24/6 ! = 12/3

Relational Operators

A **relational operator** is a symbol that indicates a relationship between two quantities. These quantities may be variables, constants, or functions. The important point about these relations is that they are either **TRUE** or **FALSE**—there is nothing in between!

The relational operators used in C/C++ are shown in Table A.9.

For relational operators, the value returned for a TRUE condition is a 1, whereas the value returned for a FALSE condition is a 0. This is illustrated by Program A.6.

Program A.6

```
#include <stdio.h>

main()
{
        float logic_value;        /* Numeric value of relational expression */

        printf("Logic values of the following relations:\n\n");
```

```
logic_value = (3 > 5);
printf("(3 > 5) is %f\n",logic_value);

logic_value = (5 > 3);
printf("(5 > 3) is %f\n",logic_value);

logic_value = (3 >= 5);
printf("(3 >= 5) is %f\n",logic_value);

logic_value = (15 >= 3*5);
printf("(15 >= 3*5) is %f\n",logic_value);

logic_value = (8 < (10-2));
printf("(8 < (10-2)) is %f\n",logic_value);

logic_value = (2*3 < 24/3);
printf("(2*3 < 24/3) is %f\n",logic_value);

logic_value = (10 < 5);
printf("(10 < 5) is %f\n",logic_value);

logic_value = (24 <= 15);
printf("(24 <= 15) is %f\n",logic_value);

logic_value = (36/6 <= 2*3);
printf("(36/6 <= 2*3) is %f\n",logic_value);

logic_value = (8 == 8);
printf("(8 == 8) is %f\n",logic_value);

logic_value = (12+5 == 15);
printf("(12+5 == 15) is %f\n",logic_value);

logic_value = (8 != 5);
printf("(8 != 5) is %f\n",logic_value);

logic_value = (15 != 3*5);
printf("(15 != 3*5) is %f\n",logic_value);
}
```

Execution of Program A.6 yields

```
Logic values of the following relations:
(3 > 5) is 0.000000
(5 > 3) is 1.000000
(3 >= 5) is 0.000000
(15 >= 3*5) is 1.000000
(8 < (10-2)) is 0.000000
(2*3 < 24/3) is 1.000000
(10 < 5) is 0.000000
```

```
(24 <= 15) is 0.000000
(36/6 <= 2*3) is 1.000000
(8 == 8) is 1.000000
(12+5 == 15) is 0.000000
(8 != 5) is 1.000000
(15 != 3*5) is 0.000000
```

As you can see from this output, a relational operation returns a value of either 1 or 0. If the operation is TRUE, a value of 1 is returned, and if the operation is FALSE, a value of 0 is returned.

To illustrate a portion of the program, consider the following program excerpt:

```
logic_value = (3 > 5);
printf("(3 > 5) is %f\n",logic_value);

logic_value = (5 > 3);
printf("(5 > 3) is %f\n",logic_value);
```

The variable logic_value has been declared a type float. You may wish to try this with other types. In the first program line, it is being set to the value of the relational operation (3 > 5). This statement is FALSE; therefore, the value returned will be a 0. This value is displayed on the monitor as a type float (%f), as 0.000000. In the second program line, the variable logic_value is being set to the value of the relational operation (5 > 3). This is a TRUE statement and hence the value returned will be 1. This also is displayed as a type float, producing the display of 1.000000.

The remainder of the program continues with the same type of process.

Equal To

It may at first seem strange to use the == (double equals or "equal-equal") to mean equal to. Understandably, many who are new to C/C++ may have thought that the use of the = (single equals) would mean equal to. The fact is that the = (single equals) does not mean the same as it does in ordinary math. What the = means in C/C++ is **assignment.**

It's important to make the distinction between the assignment operator (=) and the equals operator (==). The assignment operator takes the value on the right side of the assignment statement and puts it in the memory location of the variable on the left side of the assignment. The equals operator does something different. It simply compares the value of one memory location to the value of another memory location. No transfer of data from one memory location to the other takes place.

The Open Branch

The basic idea of an **open branch** is illustrated in Figure A.7.

There are two important points about the open branch. First, the flow of the program always goes forward to new information. Second, the option may or may not be used—but the remainder of the program is always executed. The open branch is accomplished by using the **if statement.**

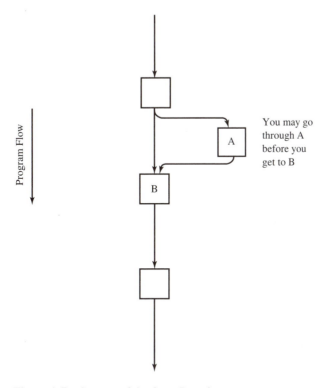

Program Flow

You may go
through A
before you
get to B

A

B

Figure A.7   Concept of the Open Branch

The if() Statement

The if() statement is referred to as a **conditional statement** because its execution will depend on a specific condition. The form of the if() statement is

```
if (expression) statement
```

What this means is that if expression is TRUE, then statement will be executed. If expression is FALSE, statement will not be executed.

Calling a Function

Because the if() statement can be used with a compound statement, it seems natural to ask if it can be used to call another function (which could also contain some more if statements). The answer is yes it can. This is illustrated in Program A.7.

Program A.7

```
#include <stdio.h>

void power_calculation(float voltage);

main()
```

```
{
        float voltage;      /* Voltage measurement in volts. */

        printf("Enter the voltage reading in volts => ");
        scanf("%f",&voltage);

        if (voltage >= 100.0)
                power_calculation(voltage);

        printf("Input value of %f volts is acknowledged.",voltage);
        exit(0);
}

void power_calculation(float voltage)
{
        float resistor;    /* Resistance value in ohms.   */
        float power;       /* Power calculation in watts. */

        printf("Voltage is equal to or greater than 100 V\n");
        printf("Please enter the resistor value => ");
        scanf("%f",&resistor);

        power = voltage*voltage/resistor;

        printf("The power dissipation is %f watts.\n",power);
}
```

Program Analysis

Program A.7 illustrates good programming practice in that it is divided into two separate parts. This doesn't mean that the more parts a program has the better it is. It means that each distinct task should be distinguished within the program.

The Closed Branch

The basic idea of a **closed branch** is illustrated in Figure A.8.

There are two important points about the closed branch. First, the flow of the program always goes forward to new information. Second, the program will do one of two options (not both) and then proceed with the rest of the program. The closed branch is accomplished by the **if...else statement.**

The `if...else` Statement

The `if...else` statement is another conditional statement. It differs from the `if` statement in that the `if` statement represents an open branch whereas the `if...else` statement represents a closed branch. The form of this statement is

```
if (expression) statement₁ else statement₂
```

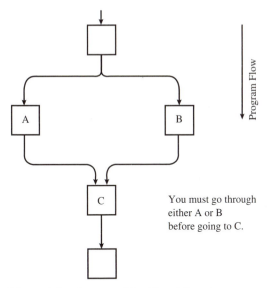

Figure A.8 Concept of the Closed Branch

What this means is that if `expression` is TRUE, then `statement`$_1$ will be executed and `statement`$_2$ will not be executed. If, on the other hand, `expression` is FALSE, then `statement`$_1$ will not be executed and `statement`$_2$ will be executed.

Compound `if...else`

You can add even more power to your program's decision-making capabilities through the use of **compound `if...else` statements.** This is illustrated in Program A.8. The program will compute the area of a square or the area of a circle. The program user selects which computation is to be performed.

All of the compound statements are placed in their own functions. Also notice that the formulas are defined using the `#define` directive at the head of the program.

Program A.8

```
#include <stdio.h>
#define PI 3.141592        /* The constant pi.   */
#define square(x) x*x       /* Area of a square. */
#define circle(r) PI*r*r    /* Area of a circle. */

void user_selection(void);  /* Get selection from user.       */
void circle_data(void);     /* Get circle radius and compute. */
void square_data(void);     /* Get square side and compute.   */
void wrong_selection(void); /* Notify user of wrong selection. */

main()
{
```

```
        printf("\n\nThis program will compute the area of\n");
        printf("a square or the area of a circle.\n");

        user_selection();     /* Get selection from user. */

        printf("\n\nThis concludes the program to calculate\n");
        printf("the area of a circle or a square.");

        exit(0);
}

void user_selection()       /* Get selection from user. */
{
        float selection;    /* User selection.              */

        printf("\nSelect by number:\n");
        printf("1] Area of circle. 2] Area of square.\n");
        printf("Your selection (1 or 2) => ");
        scanf("%f",&selection);

        if (selection == 1)
                circle_data();
        else
        if (selection == 2)
                square_data();
        else
                wrong_selection();
}

void circle_data()          /* Get circle radius and compute. */
{
        float radius;       /* Radius of the circle.          */
        float area;         /* Circle area in square units.   */

        printf("Give me the length of the circle radius => ");
        scanf("%f",&radius);

        area = circle(radius);

        printf("A circle of radius %f has an area of ",radius);
        printf("%f square units.",area);
}

void square_data()          /* Get square side and compute.        */
{
        float side;         /* Side of the square.                 */
        float area;         /* Area of the square in square units. */

        printf("Give me the length of one side of the square => ");
        scanf("%f",&side);
```

```
        area = square(side);

        printf("A square of length %f has an area of ",side);
        printf("%f square units.",area);
}

void wrong_selection()          /* Notify user of wrong selection. */
{
        printf("That was not one of the selections.\n");
        printf("You must run the program again and\n");
        printf("select either a 1 or a 2.\n");
}
```

Bitwise Boolean Operators

When doing **bit manipulation,** you are working with the individual bits of data within the computer. With bit manipulation you should think of all stored data in its binary form of 1s and 0s. Doing this is a great aid to understanding what is to follow. Think of the binary 1 as a Boolean TRUE and the binary 0 as a Boolean FALSE. Table A.10 illustrates the meanings of various **Boolean operators.** Some of these will already be familiar to you.

The following discussion will give you some additional information about each of the bitwise operators presented in Table A.10.

Bitwise Complementing

To get the **bitwise complement** of a number, convert the number to its binary equivalent, then change each 1 to a 0 and each 0 to a 1 (the same as taking the ones complement). Convert the resulting binary number back to the base of the original number. The resulting value is the bitwise complement of the number.

Table A.10 Boolean Operations

Operation	Bitwise Operator	Meaning	With Bits
Bitwise COMPLEMENT	~	Change bit to its opposite	~1 = 0 ~0 = 1
Bitwise AND	&	The result is 1 if both bits are 1	0 & 0 = 0 0 & 1 = 0 1 & 0 = 0 1 & 1 = 1
Bitwise OR	|	The result is 0 if both bits are 0	0 | 0 = 0 0 | 1 = 1 1 | 0 = 1 1 | 1 = 1
Bitwise exclusive OR	^	The result is 1 if both bits are different	0 ^ 0 = 0 0 ^ 1 = 1 1 ^ 0 = 1 1 ^ 1 = 0

Program A.9 is a program excerpt that illustrates the action of the bitwise complement.

Program A.9

```
#include <stdio.h>

main()
{
        int value;

        printf("Input a hex number from 00 to FF =>");
        scanf("%X",&value);
        printf("The bitwise complement is => %X",~value);
}
```

Assuming the program user enters the value A3, execution of Program A.9 yields

```
Input a hex number from 00 to FF => A3
The bitwise complement is => 5C
```

Note that the bitwise complement operator ~ is used on the variable value. This is done in the second printf() function:

```
printf("The bitwise complement is => %X",~value);
```

Bitwise ANDing

To get the **bitwise AND** of a number, convert the number to its binary equivalent, then AND each corresponding bit of the two resulting binary numbers. Convert the resulting binary number back to the base of the original number. The resulting value is the bitwise ANDing of the two numbers.

Program A.10 illustrates the action of bitwise ANDing.

Program A.10

```
#include <stdio.h>

main()
{
        int value1;

        int value2;

        printf("Input a hex number from 00 to FF => ");
        scanf("%X",&value1);
        printf("Input a hex number to be bitwise ANDed => ");
        scanf("%X",&value2);

        printf("Bitwise ANDing of %X and %X produces => ",value1,value2);
        printf("%X",value1 & value2);
}
```

Assuming that the program user enters the values of D3 and 8E, execution of the above program produces

```
Input a hex number from 00 to FF => D3
Input a hex number to be bitwise ANDed => 8E
Bitwise ANDing of D3 and 8E produces => 82
```

Bitwise ORing

To get the **bitwise OR** of a number, convert the number to its binary equivalent, then OR each corresponding bit of the two resulting binary numbers. Convert the resulting binary number back to the base of the original number. The resulting value is the bitwise ORing of the two numbers.

Program A.11 illustrates the action of bitwise ORing.

Program A.11

```
#include <stdio.h>

main()
{
        int value1;
        int value2;

        printf("Input a hex number from 00 to FF => ");
        scanf("%X",&value1);
        printf("Input a hex number to be bitwise ORed => ");
        scanf("%X",&value2);
        printf("Bitwise ORing of %X and %X produces => ",value1,value2);
        printf("%X",value1 | value2);
}
```

Assuming that the program user enters the values of D3 and 8E, execution of Program A.11 produces

```
Input a hex number from 00 to FF => D3
Input a hex number to be bitwise ORed => 8E
Bitwise ORing of D3 and 8E produces => DF
```

Bitwise XORing

To get the **bitwise XOR** (exclusive OR) of a number, convert the number to its binary equivalent, then XOR each corresponding bit of the two resulting binary numbers. Convert the resulting binary number back to the base of the original number. The resulting value is the bitwise XORing of the two numbers.

Program A.12 illustrates the action of bitwise XORing.

Program A.12

```
#include <stdio.h>

main()
```

```
{
        int value1;
        int value2;

        printf("Input a hex number from 00 to FF => ");
        scanf("%X",&value1);
        printf("Input a hex number to be bitwise XORed => ");
        scanf("%X",&value2);

        printf("Bitwise XORing of %X and %X produces => ",value1,value2);
        printf("%X",value1 ^ value2);
}
```

Assuming that the program user enters the values of D3 and 8E, execution of Program A.12 produces

```
Input a hex number from 00 to FF => D3
Input a hex number to be bitwise XORed => 8E
Bitwise XORing of D3 and 8E produces => 5D
```

Shifting Bits

C/C++ also allows for shifting bits left or right. This is accomplished with the shift left operator << or the shift right operator >>. To determine the result of a bitwise shift, convert the value to binary, then shift the binary bits the required number of bits in the indicated direction. Convert the resulting binary number back to the base of the original value. In C++, the << and >> operators are also used to perform other functions. This is known as *operator overloading*.

Program A.13 illustrates a shift left operation.

Program A.13

```
#include <stdio.h>

main()
{
        int value1;
        int shift_left;

        printf("Input a hex number from 00 to FF => ");
        scanf("%X",&value1);
        printf("Input a number of bits to be left shifted => ");
        scanf("%X",&shift_left);
        printf("Shifting %X %d places to the left produces => "
                ,value1,shift_left);
        printf("%X",value1 << shift_left);
}
```

Assuming that the program user enters the value 5C to be shifted to the left 3 bits, execution of Program A.13 yields

```
Input a hex number from 00 to FF => 5C
Input a number of bits to be left shifted => 3
Shifting 5C 3 places to the left produces => 2E0
```

Logical AND

The **logical AND** operation is expressed as

```
(expression₁) && (expression₂)
```

The above operation will be evaluated TRUE only if $expression_1$ is TRUE *and* $expression_2$ is TRUE; otherwise, the operation will be evaluated as FALSE. Keep in mind that in C a FALSE evaluation is actually a 0, whereas a TRUE evaluation is actually a non-zero value. Table A.11 summarizes the AND operation.

Observe that the double && is used to represent this operation. No spaces are allowed between these symbols, although spaces are allowed to the left and right of this double symbol.

Program A.14 illustrates the use of the logical AND operation.

Program A.14

```c
#include <stdio.h>

main()
{
        float result;   /* Result of logical expression. */

        result = 0 && 0;
        printf("0 && 0 = %f\n",result);

        result = 0 && 1;
        printf("0 && 1 = %f\n",result);

        result = 1 && 0;
        printf("1 && 0 = %f\n",result);

        result = 1 && 1;
        printf("1 && 1 = %f\n",result);
}
```

Table A.11   The AND Operation

expression₁	expression₂	Result
FALSE	FALSE	FALSE
FALSE	TRUE	FALSE
TRUE	FALSE	FALSE
TRUE	TRUE	TRUE

Execution of Program A.14 yields

```
0 && 0 = 0.000000
0 && 1 = 0.000000
1 && 0 = 0.000000
1 && 1 = 1.000000
```

Notice the variable `result` is of type `float`. You should try this with other data types as well. It is then used to store the result of each of the AND operations.

The OR Operation

The **logical OR** operation in C is expressed as

(expression₁) || (expression₂)

This operation will be evaluated FALSE only if expression₁ is FALSE *and* expression₂ is FALSE; otherwise. the operation will be evaluated as TRUE. As before, a FALSE evaluation is actually a 0 whereas a TRUE evaluation is actually a non-zero value. Table A.12 summarizes the OR operation.

Observe that the double ‖ is used to represent this operation. No spaces are allowed between these symbols, although spaces are allowed to the left and right of this double symbol.

Program A.15 illustrates the use of the OR operation.

Program A.15

```
#include <stdio.h>

main()
{
        float result;    /* Result of logical expression. */

        result = 0 || 0;
        printf("0 || 0 = %f\n",result);

        result = 0 || 1;
        printf("0 || 1 = %f\n",result);

        result = 1 || 0;
        printf("1 || 0 = %f\n",result);

        result = 1 || 1;
        printf("1 || 1 = %f\n",result);
}
```

Table A.12 The OR Operation

expression₁	expression₂	Result
FALSE	FALSE	FALSE
FALSE	TRUE	TRUE
TRUE	FALSE	TRUE
TRUE	TRUE	TRUE

Execution of Program A.15 yields

```
0 || 0 = 0.000000
0 || 1 = 1.000000
1 || 0 = 1.000000
1 || 1 = 1.000000
```

Notice that the variable result in this case is of type `float`. Again, other types could have been used. It is then used to store the result of each of the OR operations.

Relational and Logical Operations

Relational operations may be used with logical operations. This can be done because a relational operation returns a TRUE or FALSE condition. These are the same conditions used by logical operators. Table A.13 shows the order of *precedence* for the operators presented up to this point. This means that the `!` is evaluated before the `*`, which is evaluated before the `<`, and so on.

There is a new logical operator shown in Table A.13, called the **logical NOT** and represented by the `!`. You will see an example of this shortly. For now, realize that what Table A.13 shows is which of these operations will be done before others in a program line that contains more than one of them.

Program A.16 shows an example of using relational and logical operations together. The program gets a number from the program user and then checks to see if its value is between 1 and 10. If it is, a message is printed to the screen.

Program A.16

```
#include <stdio.h>

main()
{
        float number;       /* User input number. */

        printf("\n\nGive me a number from 1 to 100 => ");
        scanf("%f",&number);

        if ((number >= 1.0)&&(number <= 10.0))
            printf("You gave me a number between 1 and 10.");
}
```

Table A.13   Precedence of Operations

Operators	Name
!	Logical NOT
* /	Multiplication and Division
+ -	Addition and Subtraction
< <= >= >	Less, Less or Equal, Greater or Equal, Greater
== !=	Equal, Not Equal
&&	Logical AND
||	Logical OR

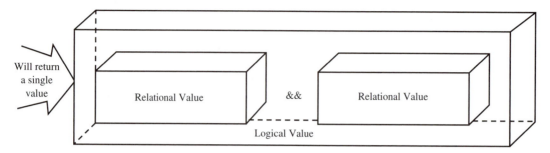

Figure A.9   Relational and Logical Operation

Note the program line that combines a relational and a logical expression:

```
if ((number >= 1.0)&&(number <= 10.0))
```

This statement can be thought of as shown in Figure A.9.

The parentheses around the relational operations may be omitted because the >= and the <= have higher precedence than the &&. However, there is no harm in putting them there, and they should be used if they improve clarity.

Data Types

You will recall that every item of data has a type. It may be an int, char, or other type. The compiler allows you to add a type int to a type float. Doing this is called *mixing types.*

When data types are mixed in an expression, the compiler will convert all of the variables to a single compatible type. Then the operation will be carried out. This is done according to the **rank** of the data type. Variables of a lower rank are converted to the types of variables with a higher rank. The ranking of variables is

Low Rank <= char, int, long, float, double => High Rank

This means that if an operation with a char and an int takes place, the resulting value will be of type int. If an operation with a float and an int takes place, the resulting output will be of type float. A good rule to follow is not to mix data types. If it is necessary to do so, use the method of **type casting.**

Type Casting

Type casting provides a method for converting a variable to a particular type. To do this, simply precede the variable by the desired type. As an example, if value were originally declared as a type int, it would be converted to a type float as follows:

```
result = (float)value;
```

The variable result will now be of type float.

You should be cautious when demoting a variable from a higher rank to a lower rank. In doing this, you are asking a larger value to fit into a smaller value, and this usually results in lost data.

You cannot use the cast on a type `void`. You can cast any type to `void`, but you cannot cast a type `void` to any other type.

lvalue

There are times in programming when you will see the term **lvalue.** It literally means left-handed value because an assignment operation assigns the value of the right-hand operand to the memory location indicated by the left-hand operand. As an example: `value = 3+5;` is a legal statement, but `3+5 = value;` is not because the left-hand value is not an lvalue.

The `switch` Statement

The `switch` statement is an easier way to code multiple `if...else if...else` statements. The `switch` statement has the form shown below:

```
switch (expression₁)
{
  case constant-expression : (expression₁)
  default : (expression₂)
}
```

Where

switch	=	Reserved word indicating that a `switch` statement is about to take place.
expression₁	=	Any legal expression.
{		Defines the beginning of the `switch` body.
case	=	Reserved word indicating that what follows is the constant-expression required for a match.
constant-expression		Identifies what is required for a match. This must be of the same data type as `expression₁` (sometimes called the case label).
default	=	a reserved word indicating the option to be exercised if no match is made.
}		Defines the ending of the `switch` body.

The construction of the `switch()` statement requires the introduction of two other keywords: `case` and `break`. Essentially the `switch()` statement identifies a variable whose value will determine which `case` will be activated. The `break` lets the compiler know when the selected program code is to end.

Compounding the `switch`

You may use compound statements with the `switch()`. This is illustrated in Program A.17. This program is an expansion of the previous ones in this section. The program actually performs a calculation with the selected form of Ohm's Law.

Program A.17

```
#include <stdio.h>

main()
{
```

```
char selection;    /* Item to be selected by program user. */
float voltage;     /* Circuit voltage in volts.            */
float current;     /* Circuit current in amps.             */
float resistance;  /* Circuit resistance in ohms.          */

printf("\n\nSelect the form of Ohm's Law needed by letter:\n");
printf("A] Voltage B] Current C] Resistance\n");
printf("Your selection (A, B, or C) => ");
scanf("%c",&selection);

switch(selection)
{
        case 'A' : {  /* Solve for voltage. */
                      printf("Input the current in amperes => ");
                      scanf("%f",&current);
                      printf("Value of the resistance in ohms => ");
                      scanf("%f",&resistance);
                      voltage = current*resistance;
                      printf("The voltage is %f volts.",voltage);
                   }
                   break;
        case 'B' : {  /* Solve for current. */
                      printf("Input the voltage in volts => ");
                      scanf("%f",&voltage);
                      printf("Value of the resistance in ohms => ");
                      scanf("%f",&resistance);
                      current = voltage/resistance;
                      printf("The current is %f amperes.",current);
                   }
                   break;
        case 'C' : {  /* Solve for resistance. */
                      printf("Input the voltage in volts => ");
                      scanf("%f",&voltage);
                      printf("Value of the current in amperes => ");
                      scanf("%f",&current);
                      resistance = voltage/current;
                      printf("The resistance is %f ohms.",resistance);
                   }
                   break;
        default  : printf("That was not a correct selection.\n");
                   printf("Please go back and select A, B, or C");
} /* End of switch. */
}
```

Observe the block structure used in the switch() statement. This structure makes it easier to read and understand the program code. Notice that the compound statement is indented and how its beginning and closing are clearly defined with the { and }. Also note the location of the `break`. It lets you clearly see where the body of the option ends. Again, structure makes very little difference to the program user. Program structure is for you and others who will be modifying or trying to understand your program.

What May Be Switched

In the `switch()` statement, $expression_1$ may be of type `int` as well as `char`. A type `float` is not permitted as an $expression_1$ type in a `switch` statement.

Switching Within Switches

You may have multiple `switch()` statements within other `switch()` statements. This concept is illustrated in Figure A.10.

The Conditional Operator

The conditional operator has the form of an `if...else` statement. It is

$expression_1$? $expression_2$: $expression_3$

What happens is that when $expression_1$ is TRUE (any value other than zero), the whole operation becomes the value of $expression_2$. If, on the other hand, $expression_1$ is FALSE (equal to zero), the whole operation becomes the value of $expression_3$. A simple illustration is presented in Program A.18.

Program A.18

```
#include <stdio.h>

main()
{
        int selection;      /* User input selection */

        printf("Enter a 1 or a 0 => ");
        scanf("%d",&selection);

        selection? printf("A one.") : printf("A zero.");
}
```

In Program A.18, if the program user inputs a 0, the second `printf()` will be evaluated, and the monitor will display

```
A zero.
```

If the program user inputs a 1 (or any non-zero value), the first `printf()` will be evaluated, and the monitor will display

```
A one.
```

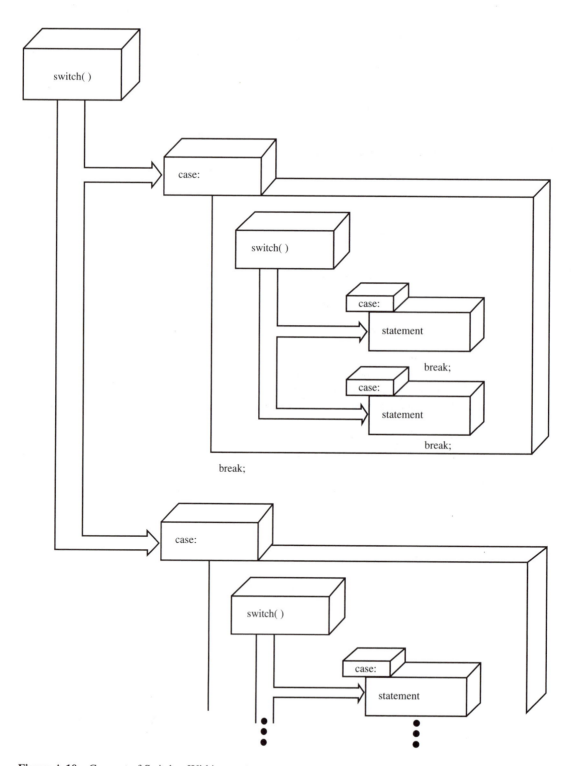

Figure A.10   Concept of Switches Within a `switch()`

The `for` Loop

The **for loop** contains four major parts:

1. The value at which the loop starts.
2. The condition under which the loop is to continue.
3. The changes that are to take place for each loop.
4. The loop instructions.

These parts are put together in the `for` loop as follows:

```
for(initial-expression; conditional-expression; loop-expression)
        {loop instructions};
```

The structure of the `for()` loop is shown in Figure A.11.

Program A.19 computes the distance a body falls in feet per second, for the first 5 seconds of free fall, as given by the equation

$$S = 1/2\ at^2$$

Where

S = The distance in feet.
a = Acceleration due to gravity (32 ft/sec^2).
t = Time in seconds.

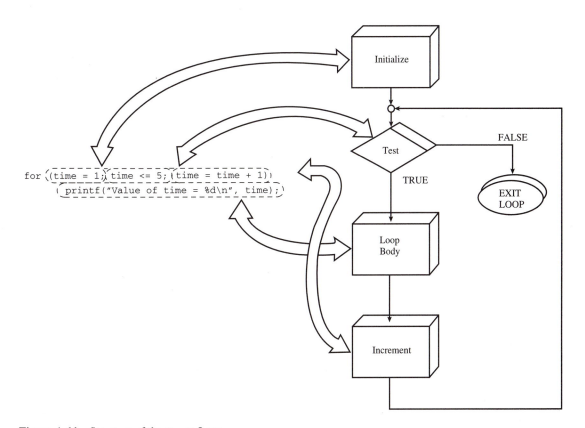

Figure A.11 Structure of the `for()` Loop

Program A.19

```c
#include <stdio.h>
#define a 32.0

main()
{
        int time;       /* Counter variable. */
        int distance;   /* Distance covered by the falling body. */

        /* The loop starts here. */

        for(time = 1; time <= 5; time = time + 1)
        {
                distance = 0.5*a*time*time;
                printf("Distance at the end of %d seconds is %d feet.\n"
                        ,time,distance);
        }
        /* The loop stops here. */

        printf("This is the end of the loop.");
}
```

Execution of Program A.19 produces

```
Distance at the end of 1 seconds is 16 feet.
Distance at the end of 2 seconds is 64 feet.
Distance at the end of 3 seconds is 144 feet.
Distance at the end of 4 seconds is 256 feet.
Distance at the end of 5 seconds is 400 feet.
This is the end of the loop.
```

Note that each of the statements within the {} ends with a semicolon. This is because each is a complete statement. Also note that the ending brace of the compound statement does not require a semicolon.

The Increment and Decrement Operators

C/C++ offers a shorthand notation for a common programming operation. This is the ability to increment or to decrement a value. The for() loop of the previous program uses time = time + 1 to increment the variable time. This could have been condensed to time++. The meanings of the increment and decrement operators are given in Table A.14.

The while Loop

Another kind of loop structure is called the **while loop.** As you will see, this loop has the same elements as the for() loop. The difference is that its elements are distributed throughout the loop. You will find that it's best to use the while() loop in situations where you don't know ahead of time how many times the loop will be repeated (such

Table A.14 Increment and Decrement Operators

Operator	Meaning
X++	Increment *X* after any operation with it (called **post-incrementing**).
++*X*	Increment *X* before any operation with it (called **pre-incrementing**).
X– –	Decrement *X* after any operation with it (called **post-decrementing**).
– –*X*	Decrement *X* before any operation with it (called **pre-decrementing**).

as creating a loop in your program that lets the program user automatically repeat the program).

Structure of the `while` Loop

The structure of the `while()` loop is

```
while(expression)
        statement;
```

The statement may be a single statement or a compound statement (enclosed in braces { }). The statement is executed zero or more times until the expression becomes FALSE.

In the operation of the `while()` loop, `expression` is first evaluated. If this evaluation is FALSE (0), then `statement` is never executed, and control passes from the `while` statement to the rest of the program. If the evaluation is TRUE (not zero), then `statement` is executed and the process is repeated again.

Program A.20 illustrates the `while` loop. It evaluates a variable called `time` for five different values.

Program A.20

```
#include <stdio.h>

main()
{
        int time = 1;          /* Counter variable. */

        while(time <= 5)
        {
                printf("Value of time = %d\n",time);
                time++;
        } /* End of while. */

        printf("End of the loop.");
}
```

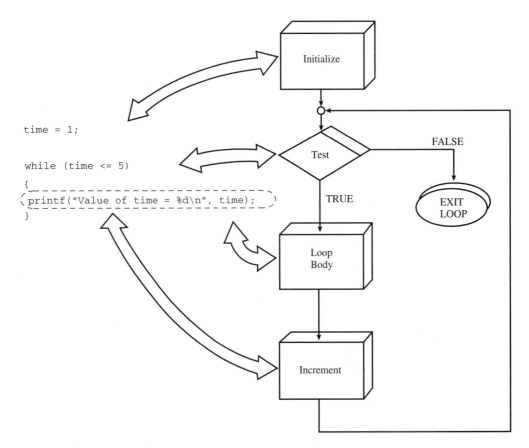

```
time = 1;

while (time <= 5)
{
printf("Value of time = %d\n", time);
}
```

Figure A.12   Structure of the `while()` Loop

Execution of Program A.20 produces

```
Value of time = 1
Value of time = 2
Value of time = 3
Value of time = 4
Value of time = 5
End of the loop.
```

The operation of the `while()` loop does the test before execution. The logic diagram for Program A.20 is illustrated in Figure A.12.

The `do while` Loop

The last of the three loop types is the **`do while` loop.** As you will see, this loop structure is similar to the `while()` loop, the difference being that the test condition is evaluated *after* the loop is executed. Recall that the `while()` loop tests the condition *before* the loop is executed.

What the `do while` Loop Looks Like

The `do while()` loop has the form

```
do
   statement
while(expression);
```

where `statement` may be a single or a compound statement. `statement` is executed one or more times until `expression` becomes FALSE (a value of 0). Execution is done by first executing `statement`, then testing `expression`. If `expression` is FALSE, the do statement terminates, and control passes to the next statement in the program. Otherwise, if `expression` is TRUE, `statement` is repeated, and the process starts over again.

Using the `do while`

Program A.21 illustrates the action of the do loop. Note that it is a counting loop. The counting variable is `time`. The program simply increments the counter from 1 to 5 in steps of 1.

Program A.21

```
#include <stdio.h>

main()
{
        int time;          /* Counter variable. */

        time = 1;

        do {
                printf("Value of time = %d\n",time);
                time++;
        }while(time <= 5);

        printf("End of the loop. ");
}
```

Program output is

```
Value of time = 1
Value of time = 2
Value of time = 3
Value of time = 4
Value of time = 5
End of the loop.
```

Note that the output is no different from the similar program using the `while()` loop (Program A.20). The program logic is different in that the action part of the loop is done before the test. Figure A.13 illustrates the operation of the `do while()` loop.

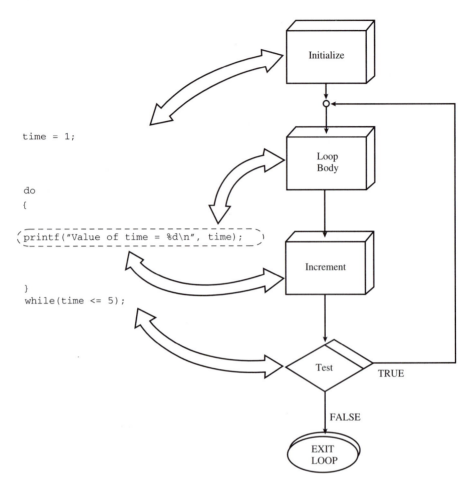

Figure A.13 Structure of the do while() Loop

Recursion

A program that uses **recursion** contains a function that calls itself. As Figure A.14 shows, a programmer may use *direct recursion* or *indirect recursion* (or both). In Figure A.14(a), the myself() function calls itself directly. In Figure A.14(b), the first() and second() functions form a recursive cycle, which repeats itself. A program that contains a recursive function works in a similar fashion to one that contains a loop. However, each time a recursive function calls itself, another complete *copy* of the function is placed into memory. This is not what happens during a pass through a loop.

Run-Time Stack

The C/C++ programming environment supports recursion by careful use of a **run-time stack,** a special data structure used to store variable and parameter values for each function in a program. As a program calls function after function, the run-time stack grows. When

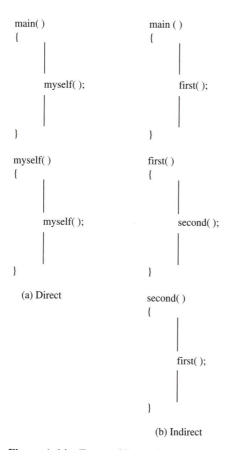

```
main( )                          main ( )
{                                {
     |                                |
     |                                |
     |                                |
     myself( );                       first( );
     |                                |
     |                                |
}                                }

myself( )                        first( )
{                                {
     |                                |
     |                                |
     |                                |
     myself( );                       second( );
     |                                |
     |                                |
}                                }

    (a) Direct                   second( )
                                 {
                                      |
                                      |
                                      |
                                      first( );
                                      |
                                      |
                                 }

                                    (b) Indirect
```

Figure A.14   Types of Recursion

a function terminates, the run-time stack gets smaller. The run-time stack is automatically managed for the programmer. What the programmer has to do is write the code in such a way that the recursion stops at some level. Otherwise, the run-time stack will grow so large that it runs out of memory, and the program crashes.

A Sample Program

Program A.22 shows one way the level of recursion can be controlled.

Program A.22

```
#include <stdio.h>

int fact(int num);

main()
{
        int N;

        printf("Enter the value of N => ");
```

```
        scanf("%d",&N);
        printf("\nN! equals %5d",fact(N));
}

int fact(int num)
{
        if (num == 0)
                return 1;
        else
                return num * fact(num - 1);
}
```

The `fact()` function computes the *factorial* of a non-negative integer. For example, 4 factorial (which we write in mathematical shorthand as 4!) equals 4 * 3 * 2 * 1, or 24. The `fact()` function is recursive, because of the `return` statement

```
return num * fact(num - 1);
```

which represents a direct call to `fact()`. But this is the second of two `return` statements. The first `return` statement

```
return 1;
```

does not call `fact()`. This is where the recursion will stop. Because each new call to `fact()` is done with a smaller value of `num`, eventually `fact()` will be called with `num` equal to zero, as in `fact(0)`. The test within the `if()` statement

```
if (num == 0)
    return 1;
else
    return num * fact(num - 1);
```

determines when to stop recursion.

Using Pointers

Program A.23 shows the significance of the * (called the **indirection operator**) or **pointer** operator and the & (address operator).

Program A.23

```
#include <stdio.h>

main()
{
        char value;     /* A memory location to hold a character.   */
        char *pointer;  /* A pointer. */

        value = 97;
        printf("%u => | %d | <= address and data of value.\n",&value,value);

        pointer = &value;
```

```
printf("%u => | %d | <= address and data of pointer.\n"
                ,&pointer,pointer);

printf("\n Value stored in pointer = %d\n",pointer);
printf(" Address of pointer : &pointer = %u\n",&pointer);
printf(" Value pointed to: *pointer = %d\n",*pointer);
}
```

Execution of Program A.23 yields

```
1204 => | 97 | <= address and data of value.
4562 => |1204| <= address and data of pointer.
Value stored in pointer = 1204
Address of pointer: &pointer = 4562
Value pointed to: *pointer = 97
```

What is happening in Program A.23 is illustrated in Figure A.15.

As you can see from the figure, the variable *pointer will have exactly the same value as the address of the variable to which it is pointing. What is important is to understand the meaning of the following when it comes to using pointers:

pointer → Contains the value stored in the variable pointer.
&pointer → Will give the address of the variable pointer.
*pointer → Will give the value stored at the memory location whose address is stored in the variable pointer.

Using Pointers to Pass Variables

A pointer will now be used to return a single value back to the calling function. What will happen here is that a value of 5 will be assigned to a variable of the calling function by the called function. What happens now is that the same thing will be done using a pointer instead of a return().

To do this, the function callme() will use a pointer in its formal argument:

```
void callme(int *p);
```

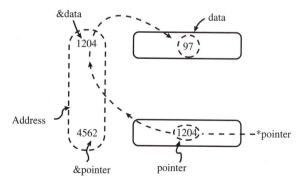

Figure A.15 Concept of a Pointer

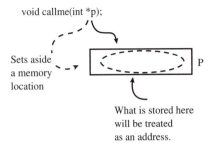

void callme(int *p);

Sets aside
a memory
location

P

What is stored here
will be treated
as an address.

Figure A.16   Setting a Pointer Argument

It is helpful to think of this as if it sets up a memory location to act as a pointer—meaning that what will be stored there will be the address (memory location) of another variable. This concept is shown in Figure A.16.

When the function `callme()` is called, the address of the variable to be changed will be passed to it:

```
main()
{
    int x;
    callme(&x);
```

What has happened is shown in Figure A.17.

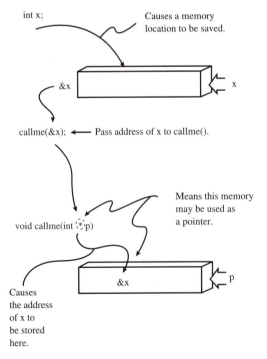

int x;

Causes a memory
location to be saved.

&x

x

callme(&x); ◄─── Pass address of x to callme().

void callme(int *p)

Means this memory
may be used as
a pointer.

&x

p

Causes
the address
of x to
be stored
here.

Figure A.17   Action of Calling the Function

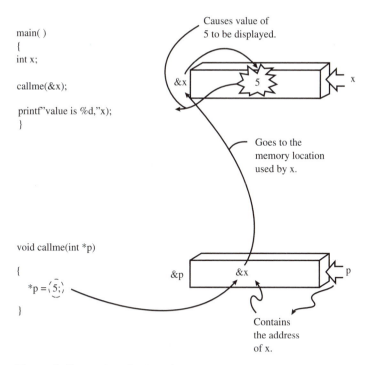

```
main( )
{
int x;

callme(&x);

printf"value is %d,"x);
}
```

Causes value of
5 to be displayed.

&x

5

x

Goes to the
memory location
used by x.

```
void callme(int *p)

{
  *p = 5;

}
```

&p   &x   p

Contains
the address
of x.

Figure A.18   Action of a Called Function

When the function is called, it places the value 5 at the address pointed to by the pointer:

```
void callme(int *p)
{
     *p = 5;
}
```

This is shown in Figure A.18.

The program that makes all of this happen is shown in Program A.24. Execution of Program A.24 yields

```
The value of x is 0
The new value of x is 5
```

Program A.24

```
#include <stdio.h>

void callme(int *p);

main()
{
     int x;

     x = 0;
     printf("The value of x is %d\n",x);
```

```
        callme(&x);
        printf("The new value of x is %d",x);
}

void callme(int *p)
{
        *p = 5;
}
```

This seems like a lot of effort just to assign a value of 5 to the variable x. However, this example demonstrates the passing of a value from one function to another using a pointer.

Scope of Variables

Local Variables

All of the variables declared in the programs up to this point have been local. The concept of a **local variable** is illustrated in Program A.25. This program is attempting to use a variable in other_function() that was declared in the main() function.

Program A.25

```
#include <stdio.h>

void other_function(void);

main()
{
        int a_variable;

        a_variable = 5;

        printf("The value of a_variable is %d\n",a_variable);
        other_function();
}

void other_function()
{
        printf("The value of a_variable in this function is %d",a_variable);
}
```

Program A.25 will not compile because other_function() does not know the meaning of the variable a_variable declared in main(). The reason for this is that when a variable is declared within a function, it is known only to that function and to none of the others. This means that the variable is local to the function in which it is declared. Another way of saying this is that the **scope** of a local variable is only within the function in which it is declared and the **life** of that variable lasts only while the function in which it is declared is active.

Global Variables

In order to make a variable known to all the functions in your C program, it must be declared ahead of `main()`. This is illustrated in Program A.26. This program will compile because the variable is now known to both functions.

Program A.26

```
#include <stdio.h>

void other_function(void);
int a_variable;

main()
{
        a_variable = 5;

        printf("The value of a_variable is %d\n",a_variable);
        other_function();
}

void other_function()
{
        printf("The value of a_variable in this function is %d",a_variable);
}
```

When a variable is declared in this fashion it is called a **global variable.** The scope of a global variable is every function within the program. The life of a global variable lasts as long as any part of the program is active. Figure A.19 illustrates.

Caution with Global Variables

Using global variables can sometimes lead to unexpected results because any function can change the value of a global variable. Thus, when another function uses a global variable it may now have a value different from what you might expect. This is especially true when a recursive function uses a global variable.

It is considered good programming practice to keep your variables as local as possible. In this manner you are protecting these variables from being changed by other functions. This is why variables are passed between functions as arguments. When this is done, the value of each of these variables is protected.

Static Variables

In C, a **static variable** is a variable that is local. But, unlike a local, its life lasts as long as the program is active—even though its scope is only within the function that declared it. What this means is that a "normal" (automatic) local variable is completely forgotten by the computer once the function in which it was declared is no longer active. When the function is called again, the automatic variable no longer has the value it was left with when the function terminated.

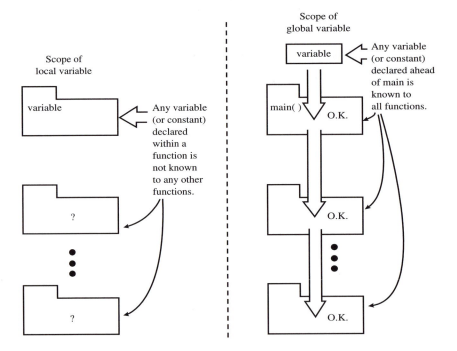

Figure A.19   Concept of Scope

This is not the case with a static variable. Its value is retained by the computer so that when the function that declared it is called again, its previous value is used. This concept is illustrated by Program A.27.

Program A.27

```
#include <stdio.h>

void second_function(void);

main()
{
        second_function();
        second_function();
        second_function();
}

void second_function()
{

        static int number;

        number++;
        printf("This function has been called %d times.\n",number);
}
```

Execution of Program A.27 yields

```
This function has been called 1 times.
This function has been called 2 times.
This function has been called 3 times.
```

The important point about Program A.27 is that the value of the `static` variable is remembered between calls to the function. It makes no difference from how many different functions this is done within the same program; its value will still be retained as long as the program is active. However, it is still a local variable known only to the function in which it was defined. In addition, any variable declared as a static variable is automatically initialized to zero the first time it is used.

Creating a Disk File

In order to store user input data on the computer disk, a file must be created on the disk for storing the data. This can be done in many different ways. One way is to have the program create the disk file automatically. In order to do this, you must observe the rules for the operating system (**OS**) used by your system. The OS used by the IBM PC and compatibles contains specific rules concerning the naming of a disk file. What follows is a summary of legal file names.

A DOS Review

A legal DOS file name has the form

```
[Drive:]FileName[.EXT]
```

Where

      Drive = The optional name of the drive that contains the disk you want to access.

      FileName = The name of the file (up to eight characters).

      .EXT = An optional extension to the file name (up to three characters).

Check your operating system manual for legal file names available on your system.

Saving a Character String

Program A.28 illustrates a method of saving a character string to a disk file. In this case, the program user may input any string of characters from the keyboard and have them automatically saved to a file called `MYFILE.DAT`. The program will continue getting characters from the program user until a carriage return is entered.

Program A.28

```c
#include <stdio.h>

main()
{
        FILE *file_pointer;      /* This is the file pointer.        */
        char file_character;     /* Character to be read from the file. */
```

```
        /* Create a file called MYFILE.DAT and assign its address
           to the file_pointer: */

        file_pointer = fopen("MYFILE.DAT","w");

        /* Put a stream of data into the opened file: */

        while((file_character = getche()) != '\r')
               file_character = putc(file_character, file_pointer);

        /* Close the created file. */

        fclose(file_pointer);
}
```

Note that like the other file programs, Program A.28 uses the built-in function `fopen()`, which includes the w character meaning that the file is being opened for writing into. When all file activity is completed, the file is closed with the built-in function `fclose()`.

Reading a Character Stream

A **character stream** is a sequence of bytes of data being sent from one place to another (such as from computer memory to the disk).

To read a character stream from a disk file, you use the same tactics as these for reading characters from the keyboard. The difference is that your program will continue to read a stream of characters until it encounters an end-of-file marker (EOF). This is automatically placed at the end of a disk file when the file is created. When this marker is read by the program, it indicates that the end of the file has been reached and there is nothing further to read. Program A.29 illustrates.

Program A.29

```
#include <stdio.h>

main()
{
        FILE *file_pointer;    /* This is the file pointer.           */
        char file_character;   /* Character to be read from the file. */

        /* Open an existing file called MYFILE.DAT and assign its address
           to the file_pointer: */

        file_pointer = fopen("MYFILE.DAT","r");

        /* Get a stream of characters from the opened file
           and display them on the screen.                 */

        while((file_character = getc(file_pointer)) != EOF)
```

```
        printf("%c",file_character);

/* Close the created file. */

    fclose(file_pointer);
}
```

Program A.29 is very similar to Program A.28. The `fopen()` function is used with the `r` character directive, meaning that the file is being opened for reading. The main difference is in the `while` loop:

```
while((file_character = getc(file_pointer)) != EOF)
        printf("%c",file_character);
```

Here, the `while` loop continues until an EOF marker is reached, indicating the end of the file. While the loop is active, the characters received from the disk file are directed to the monitor screen for display.

Disk File Status

Table A.15 shows the possible conditions you can encounter when working with disk data. As you can see from Table A.15, there are four possibilities when working with disk information.

Besides the considerations presented in Table A.15, there are four different ways of reading and writing data. These are listed in Table A.16.

You have already used the first two methods in Table A.16. These allow you to perform simple I/O where you can store and retrieve characters or strings. The programs in this section will concentrate on the last two methods: mixed data types and structure or blocks of data.

File Format

A C program designed for disk I/O uses the type `FILE` with a corresponding file pointer. The type `FILE` is a predefined structure declared in the header file `<stdio.h>`. This file must be included in all of your C programs designed for disk I/O. This predefined `FILE` structure helps establish the necessary link between your program and the disk operating system. In C++, we use the header file `<iostream.h>`.

Table A.15 Disk File Conditions

Condition	Meaning
1	The disk file does not exist, and you want to create it on the disk and add some information.
2	The disk file already exists, and you want to get information from it.
3	The disk file already exists, and you want to add more information to it while preserving the old information that was already there.
4	The disk file already exists, and you want to get rid of all of the old information and add new information.

Table A.16   Different Methods of Reading and Writing Data

Method	Comments
One character at a time	Inputs and outputs one character to the disk at a time.
Read and write data and strings	Inputs and outputs a string of characters to the disk.
Mixed mode	Used for I/O of characters, strings, floating points, and integers.
Structure or block method	Used for I/O of array elements and structures.

Table A.17   C File Type Commands

String Command	Meaning
"a"	Open for appending. New data is added to existing file data or a new file is created.
"r"	Open for reading. File must already exist.
"w"	Open for writing. Contents written over or new file created.
"a+"	Open for reading and appending. If file does not exist, it will be created.
"r+"	Open for both reading and writing—file must exist.
"w+"	Open for both reading and writing. Contents written over.

Examine Table A.17. Note in Table A.17 how these file directives relate to the different ways you can treat a disk file.

Example File Program

Program A.30 demonstrates several important points about disk files. This program allows the user one of the following options for creating and reading from a simple message file:

1. Create a new file by a user-supplied file name.
2. Create a new file by a user-supplied file name and place a message in it.
3. Read a message from an existing file.
4. Append a message to an existing file.
5. The user is told if a given file for reading or appending does not exist.

Program A.30

```
#include <stdio.h>

main()
{
        char selection[2];        /* User file selection.         */
        char file_name[13];       /* Name of the disk file.       */
        char user_choice[2];      /* User choice for file activity. */
        int selection_value;      /* User selection number.       */
        int file_character;       /* File character to be saved.  */
        FILE *file_pointer;       /* File pointer.                */
```

```
/* Display user options. */

printf("Select one of the following by number:\n");
printf("1] Create a new file.    2] Write over an existing file.\n");
printf("3] Add new data to an existing file.\n");
printf("4] Get data from an existing file.\n");

/* Get and act on user input. */

do
{
        printf("Your selection => ");
        gets(user_choice);
        selection_value = atoi(user_choice);

        switch(selection_value)
        {

                case 1  :
                case 2  : strcpy(selection, "w");
                          break;
                case 3  : strcpy(selection, "a");
                          break;
                case 4  : strcpy(selection, "r");
                          break;
                default : {
                                  printf("That was not one of the "
                                      "choices./n");
                                  selection_value = 0;
                          }
        }
} while(selection_value == 0);

/* Get the file from the user. */

printf("Enter the name of the file => ");
gets(file_name);

/* Open the file for action. */

if((file_pointer = fopen(file_name, selection)) == NULL)
{
        printf("Cannot open file %s!", file_name);
        exit(-1);
}

/* Write to or read from the file. */

switch(selection_value)
{
        case 1 : break;
        case 2 :
```

```
            case 3 : {
                                 printf("Enter string to be saved:\n");
                                 while((file_character = getche()) != '\r')
                                        file_character = putc(file_character,
                                                       file_pointer);
                         }
                         break;
            case 4 : {
                                 while((file_character = getc(file_pointer)) !=
                                        EOF)
                                       printf("%c",file_character);
                         }
                         break;
      }

      /* Close the opened file. */

      fclose(file_pointer);
}
```

Note: The function `getch()` gets a character from the keyboard and does not echo it to the screen. The function `getche()` does the same thing except it does echo the character to the screen.

Execution of Program A.30 produces

```
Select one of the following by number:
1] Create a new file.    2] Write over an existing file.
3] Add new data to an existing file.
4] Get data from an existing file.
Your selection => 2
Enter the name of the file => MYFILE.01
Enter string to be saved: Saved by a C program.
```

The message above can be retrieved at a later date, added to, or written over. Note that the program will tell the user if the desired file does not exist. With this program, any new file must first be created by the user.

Mixed File Data

The previous file programs were limited to working with strings. Program A.31 illustrates a method of working with files that allows you to input numerical as well as string data. The program illustrates a process of entering the mixed data from the parts structure program of the previous sections. This is accomplished with a new function called `fprintf()`.

Program A.31

```
#include <stdio.h>

main()
{
```

```
char part_name[15];      /* Type of part.          */
int quantity;            /* Number of parts left. */
float cost_each;         /* Cost of each part.     */
FILE *file_pointer;      /* File pointer.          */

/* Open a file for writing. */

file_pointer = fopen("B:PARTS.DAT","w");

/* Get data from program user. */

printf("Enter part type, quantity, cost each, separated by spaces:\n");
printf("Press -RETURN- to terminate input.\n");
scanf("%s %d %f", part_name, &quantity, &cost_each);
fprintf(file_pointer, "%s %d %f", part_name, quantity, cost_each);

/* Close the opened file. */

fclose(file_pointer);
}
```

Execution of Program A.31 produces:

```
Enter part type, quantity, cost each, separated by spaces:
Press -RETURN- to terminate input.
Resistor, 12, 0.05
```

Assuming that the program user carefully follows instructions, the scanf() function will receive the required data and the fprintf() function will store it in the opened file. The fprintf() function has the form:

```
fprintf(FILE *stream, const char *format..argument);
```

This function accepts a series of arguments, and outputs the formatted stream as specified by the format string. This is similar to printf().

Program A.31 has several weaknesses. It doesn't protect user input (the scanf() function is used). It also doesn't let the user know if there was a problem opening the file. However, it does illustrate a simple program that enters mixed data types into a file. The key to the program is the fprintf() function, which allows the user to format the input data to the disk in many different ways—in this case as a string, then as an integer, and finally as a float.

Retrieving Mixed Data

Program A.32 demonstrates how the mixed data stored on the disk may be retrieved and sent to the monitor screen.

The key to this program is the fscanf() function. This function is similar to the scanf() function except that a pointer to FILE is used as its first argument.

Program A.32

```
#include <stdio.h>

main()
{
        char part_name[15];     /* Type of part.        */
        int quantity;           /* Number of parts left. */
        float cost_each;        /* Cost of each part.    */
        FILE *file_pointer;     /* File pointer.         */

        /* Open a file for reading. */

        file_pointer = fopen("B:PARTS.DAT","r");

        /* Get data from disk file. */

        while(fscanf(file_pointer, "%s %d %f", part_name, &quantity,
                &cost_each) != EOF)
            printf("%s %d %f\n", part_name, quantity, cost_each);

        /* Close the opened file. */

        fclose(file_pointer);
}
```

Assuming that the file contained the data entered by the previous program, execution of Program A.32 would yield:

```
Resistor 12 0.050000
```

Text vs. Binary Files

All of the file I/O you have been using up to this point has been what is called **text files**. Numbers stored on the disk in string format are stored as strings instead of as numerical values. Because of this, the storage of numerical data as strings does not use disk space efficiently. One way to increase the disk storage efficiency is to use what is called the **binary mode** of disk I/O rather than the **text mode.** The **binary file** does not store numbers as a string of characters (as is done with text files). Instead, they are stored as they are in memory—2 bytes for an integer, 4 for a floating point, and so on for the rest. The only restriction is that a file stored in binary mode must also be retrieved in binary mode, or what you get will not make sense. All that you need to do is add the letter b after the file directive. Thus fopen("MYFILE.01","wb") means to open (or create) a file called MYFILE.01 for writing in binary format. Likewise, fopen("MYFILE.01","rb") means to open the file MYFILE.01 for reading in binary format. As you may have guessed, fopen("MYFILE.01","ab") means to open the file MYFILE.01 for appending in binary format.

The "ws" directive could have been used to indicate that a file was to be opened for writing in string format. For the previous programs, the s could have been added to all of the file directives, resulting in a string format file. However, this is redundant, because, by default, files are opened for string format unless the directive is modified with the b for binary format.

Record Input

Program A.33 shows an example of saving data structures to a file. This is a powerful and important method of saving complex data to disk files. Observe that this program is similar to that of the mixed data type. However, the important difference is that it stores a data structure to the file. This is done using a new function called `fwrite`.

Program A.33

```
#include <stdio.h>

typedef struct
{
        char part_name[15];      /* Type of part.        */
        int quantity;            /* Number of parts left. */
        float cost_each;         /* Cost of each part.   */
} parts_structure;

main()
{
        parts_structure parts_data;     /* Parts structure variable. */
        FILE *file_pointer;             /* File pointer.            */

        /* Open a file for writing. */

        file_pointer = fopen("B:PARTS.DAT","wb");

        /* Get data from program user. */

        do
        {
                printf("\nName of part => ");
                gets(parts_data.part_name);
                printf("Number of parts => ");
                scanf("%d",&parts_data.quantity);
                printf("Cost per part => ");
                scanf("%f",&parts_data.cost_each);

                /* Write structure to opened file. */

                fwrite(&parts_data, sizeof(parts_data), 1, file_pointer);

                /* Prompt user for more input. */

                printf("Add more parts (y/n)? => ");
        } while (getche() == 'y');
```

```
        /* Close the opened file. */

        fclose(file_pointer);
}
```

Assuming that the user enters the given value, execution of Program A.33 will yield

```
Name of part => Resistor
Number of parts => 12
Cost per part => 0.05
```

This data will now be saved to the disk as a block of information in a binary format under the file name of PARTS.DAT on drive B:.

Record Output

Program A.34 illustrates the retrieval of the block of data entered by Program A.33. Note that this program uses the same type definition of the parts structure as did Program A.33.

Program A.34

```
#include <stdio.h>

typedef struct
{
        char part_name[15];    /* Type of part.        */
        int quantity;          /* Number of parts left. */
        float cost_each;       /* Cost of each part.    */
} parts_structure;

main()
{
        parts_structure parts_data;    /* Parts structure variable. */
        FILE *file_pointer;            /* File pointer.             */

        /* Open a file for reading. */

        file_pointer = fopen("B:PARTS.DAT","rb");

        /* Get data from file and display. */

        while(fread(&parts_data, sizeof(parts_data), 1, file_pointer) == 1)
        {
                printf("\nPart name => %s\n",parts_data.part_name);
                printf("Number of parts => %d\n",parts_data.quantity);
                printf("Cost of part => %f\n",parts_data.cost_each);
        }

        /* Close the opened file. */

        fclose(file_pointer);
}
```

When executed, Program A.34 will look for the file PARTS.DAT on drive B: and open it in the binary mode for reading (the file must already exist). The data is read using the fread() function, which has the form

```
fread(buffer, size, n, pointer)
```

This is very similar to the fwrite() function. Again, buffer is a pointer to the data, size is the size of the data in bytes, n is the number of items of this size, and pointer points to the file to be written to.

The fread() function will return the number of items actually written to the disk. In the input program (Program A.33) the value of n is 1. If this value differs in the output program, the file will no longer be read. This is accomplished by having the file read in a while() loop as long as this function is equal to 1.

Streams

You have actually worked with two kinds of streams—a text stream and a binary stream (text files and binary files). A text stream consists of lines of characters. Each line of characters ends with a terminating newline character (\n). The important point about text streams (such as those stored to a disk file) is that they may not all be stored in the same way your program stores them. This is the case with DOS, where, unlike C/C++, the end of a line is terminated with both a newline character and a carriage return character (\n\r). This is not the case with a binary stream. The only requirement here is that you know the size of what was stored in the file.

The Buffered Stream

When a file I/O is performed, an association needs to be made between the stream and the file. This is done by using a section of memory referred to as a **buffer.** Think of a buffer as a reserved section of memory that will hold data. This acts as a temporary storage place in memory. The bytes being read from or written to the file are stored here. In this way, when a file is read from the disk, it is first stored in the buffer as a fixed "chunk" of data. Each of these "chunks" is the same size. What happens is that a process that reads or writes data from or to the disk is actually first communicating with the buffer. Hence the name **buffered stream** for a stream of data that is stored in this buffer. Only when the buffer is **flushed** (data transferred from the buffer to the disk) is data actually stored to the disk from the buffer. Doing this reduces the amount of access time between the disk and the program.

A buffer may not be flushed if the program is abnormally terminated. It's of interest to note that the file pointer you declare and use in your disk file programs is actually a pointer to this buffer. Thus, for stream files, the file pointer replaces all references to the file after it has been opened.

In the standard header file <stdio.h>, the following constants are defined:

```
EOF = 1

NULL = 0

BUFSIZE = 512
```

As you may recall, EOF is the end-of-file marker placed at the end of a disk file. NULL is assigned to a file pointer if an error has occurred, and BUFSIZE is the size assigned to the I/O stream. You can redefine BUFSIZE from its assigned optimum value.

Standard Files

When you run your program, it automatically opens three **standard files.** These are the standard input, standard output, and standard error files. On your PC, these files represent the keyboard (for standard input) and the monitor (for standard output and error). This idea is illustrated in Figure A.20.

The reason for having a standard error output is to ensure that the program always has access to your monitor. This is necessary in case you have directed your standard output somewhere else (such as to the disk). Thus, if you have an error during this process, the program still has access to your monitor to let you know that an error has taken place.

Redirecting Files

You can use DOS commands to carry out **file redirection** on your disk. As an example, suppose you have the following two disk files:

READFILE.EXE <= A program that normally gets data from the keyboard (standard input).

DATAFILE <= A character file that contains data from the keyboard—this file could have been produced when a word processor was being used.

If you then enter the following from the DOS prompt (A>):

```
A> READFILE < DATAFILE
```

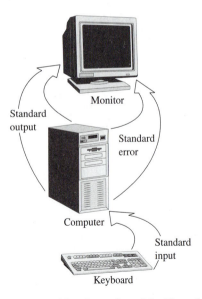

Figure A.20   Illustration of the Three Standard Files

(the .EXE extension is omitted), this will redirect standard input for the `READFILE` to get its data from `DATAFILE` rather than from the keyboard.

The converse can also be done. Suppose that you have a program called `DATAMAKE.EXE` that produces data (say, the results of some calculations) and normally outputs the results to the monitor. Then

```
A> DATAMAKE > NEWDATA
```

will redirect the standard output so that instead of the data from the program `DATAMAKE.EXE` going to the monitor, it goes to the file called `NEWDATA`.

Piping of Files

Piping of a file simply means to cause two or more separate disk files to act as if they were joined together. The DOS piping command is the `|`. As an example, MS-DOS contains a utility program that will do an alphabetical sort (called `SORT.COM`). If you want to see your disk directory displayed alphabetically sorted you would enter

```
A> DIR | SORT
```

(The extension `.COM` is not entered.)

Filtering

Filtering is the process of modifying data in some fashion while it is in the process of being transferred from one file to another. As an example, if you have a file that contains a list of words called `WORDFILE.OLD`, you can copy it to another file called `WORDFILE.NEW` and alphabetize the words in the process. To do this, you need to have the MS-DOS `SORT.COM` file on your disk. Then do the following:

```
A> SORT < WORDFILE.OLD > WORDFILE.NEW
```

This will cause the information in `WORDFILE.OLD` to be stored alphabetically in the file called `WORDFILE.NEW`. What you have done here is filter the data through the `SORT` program in the process of copying it from one file to another. A helpful aid employed by many programmers is the use of filtering to display an alphabetically sorted disk directory one screen at a time. For this to be done, both of the MS-DOS programs `SORT.COM` and `MORE.COM` must be accessible. From the DOS prompt, you would enter

```
A> DIR | SORT | MORE
```

I/O Levels

There are actually two levels of I/O. The one you have been working with is called the **standard I/O.** The other is called the low-level I/O. The advantage of the standard I/O is that it requires less programming detail on your part. Its disadvantage is that you have less control over the details of the I/O process, and it is slower than low-level I/O. For most programming tasks, standard I/O will meet the I/O requirements. The standard I/O functions actually use the low-level I/O. Low-level I/O is usually referred to as **system I/O** and is the topic of the next discussion.

Random Access Files

Up to this point, the types of files you have worked with have been **sequential access files.**
This means that when you work with file data, you get all of the data in one chunk from the
disk. In a **random access file,** a particular data item may be accessed while the rest of the
file is ignored. Program A.35 illustrates a random access file that uses the parts inventory
program. To understand this program, you must first know what is meant by a file pointer.

Program A.35

```c
#include <stdio.h>

typedef struct
{
        char part_name[15];        /* Type of part.          */
        int quantity;              /* Number of parts left. */
        float cost_each;           /* Cost of each part.     */
} parts_structure;

main()
{
        parts_structure parts_data;    /* Parts structure variable. */
        FILE *file_pointer;            /* File pointer.              */
        int record_number;             /* Number of the record.      */
        long int offset;               /* Offset of the record.      */

        /* Open the file for reading. */

        if((file_pointer = fopen("B:PARTS.DAT","r")) == NULL) /* Error check */
        {
                printf("Unable to open file B:PARTS.DAT");
                exit(-1);
        }

        /* Get record number from the user. */

        printf("Enter the record number => ");
        scanf("%d",&record_number);

        /* Compute the offset value of the selected record. */

        offset = record_number * sizeof(parts_data);

        /* Go to the required file. */

        if(fseek(file_pointer, offset, 0) != 0)    /* Error check */
        {
                printf("Pointer moved beyond file boundary.");
                exit();
        }
```

```
/* Read the selected file data. */

fread(&parts_data, sizeof(parts_data), 1, file_pointer);

/* Display the file data. */

printf("\nName of part => %s\n",parts_data.part_name);
printf("Number of parts => %d\n",parts_data.quantity);
printf("Cost of each part => %f\n",parts_data.cost_each);

/* Close the opened file. */

fclose(file_pointer);
}
```

File Pointers

The **file pointer** is simply a pointer to a particular place in the file. What a file pointer does is to point to the byte in the file where the next access to the file will take place. As an example, every time you access a disk file, the file pointer starts at position 0, the beginning of the file. Every time you write data to the file, the file pointer ends up at the end of the file. When you do an append operation to a file, the file pointer is first set to the end of the file before new data is written to the file.

There is a built-in function called fseek() that moves the file pointer. This function will move the file pointer to the position in the file where the next file access will occur. It is used in Program A.35 in order to access a single record from any place within the file.

The fseek() contains three arguments. The first is the file pointer, next is the value of the offset, and last is the mode. There are three values for the fseek() function mode. These are:

> 0 => Count from the beginning of the file.
> 1 => Start from the current pointer position.
> 2 => Start from the end of the file.

These values are defined as

> 0 => SEEK_SET,
> 1 => SEEK_CUR,
> 2 => SEEK_END.

The fseek() function returns a non-zero value only if it fails to perform its required operation.

Additional Reference Material for C++ Users

The C++ language retains all of the features and functionality of the C language. Much of the differences that set these two languages apart stem from the object-oriented capabilities found only within C++, but there are some other important features as well. The following material is applicable for C++ users only.

The cout Function

The cout function is used to write information to **standard output** (normally your monitor screen). A typical structure for this function is

```
cout << "character string" << variable << '.' ;
```

where the << symbols represent the insertor function. This function is used to insert characters or numbers into the standard output stream.

Characters are set off by single quotes (such as 'a' or '.'), and strings are set off by double quotes (such as "This is a string."). An **I/O manipulator** instructs the cout function how to convert, format, and print its **arguments.** For now, think of an argument as the actual values that are within the parentheses of the function. As an example,

```
cout << "This is a C++ statement.";
```

when executed produces

```
This is a C++ statement.
```

With an I/O manipulator, the execution of

```
cout.setf(ios::hex);
cout << "The number 92 in hexadecimal is" << 92 << ".\n";
```

produces

```
The number 92 in hexadecimal is 5c.
```

I/O manipulators are used to control the way numbers are formatted and displayed by cout and the I/O operators. Here, we used the ios::hex manipulator to force cout to display a number in hexadecimal format. These manipulators are found in the iomanip.h file.

Table A.18 lists the various I/O manipulators used by cout.

Program A.36 illustrates the use of the different I/O manipulators.

Program A.36

```
#include <iostream.h>
#include <iomanip.h>

main()
{
     cout << "The value 92 displayed as an integer is " << 92 << ".\n";
     cout.setf(ios::oct);
     cout << "The value 92 displayed in octal is " << 92 << ".\n";
     cout.setf(ios::hex);
     cout << "The value 92 displayed in hexadecimal is " << 92 << ".\n";
     cout.setf(ios::uppercase);
     cout << "The value 92 displayed in HEXADECIMAL is " << 92 << ".\n";
     cout << "The value 92.5 displayed as a float is " << 92.5 << ".\n";
     cout.setf(ios::scientific);
     cout << "The value 92.5 displayed in SCIENTIFIC notation is " << 92.5 << ".\n";
     cout.setf(ios::uppercase);
     cout << "The value 92.5 displayed in scientific notation is " << 92.5 << ".\n";
}
```

Table A.18   I/O Manipulators Used by `cout`

Manipulator Flag	Bit Value	Resulting Output
`ios::skipws`	0x0001	Skip white space
`ios::left`	0x0002	Left-align output
`ios::right`	0x0004	Right-align output
`ios::internal`	0x0008	Pad number with spaces
`ios::dec`	0x0010	Output decimal number
`ios::oct`	0x0020	Output octal number
`ios::hex`	0x0040	Output hexadecimal number
`ios::showbase`	0x0080	Show base indicator
`ios::showpoint`	0x0100	Show decimal point on float
`ios::uppercase`	0x0200	Use A..F in hexadecimal output
`ios::showpos`	0x0400	Output plus sign on integers
`ios::scientific`	0x0800	Output in scientific notation
`ios::fixed`	0x1000	Output with fixed decimal point
`ios::unitbuf`	0x2000	Flush streams after insertion
`ios::stdio`	0x4000	Flush `stdout`, `stderr` after insertion

Execution of Program A.36 results in the following output:

```
The value 92 displayed as an integer is 92.
The value 92 displayed in octal is 134.
The value 92 displayed in hexadecimal is 5c.
The value 92 displayed in HEXADECIMAL is 5C.
The value 92.5 displayed as a float is 92.5.
The value 92.5 displayed in SCIENTIFIC notation is 9.25E+01.
The value 92.5 displayed in scientific notation is 9.25e+01.
```

As output shows, the formats used to display the two numbers 92 and 92.5 are different in each line. The format used by `cout` can be modified through the use of the `cout.setf()` and `cout.unsetf()` functions. Each manipulator in Table A.18 has a unique binary value that corresponds with a bit in a special area called `ios::flags`. So, when you use `cout.setf(ios::uppercase)`, you are actually setting a specific bit in `ios::flags` that is in turn used by `cout` to control formatting.

Notice how the change made to the `uppercase` flag affects the output of Program A.36.

Escape Sequences

The `\n` is an example of an **escape sequence** that can be used by the `cout` function. The backslash symbol (\) is referred to as the escape character. You can think of an escape sequence used in the `cout` function as an escape from the normal interpretation of a string. This means that the next character used after the \ will have a special meaning, as listed in Table A.3.

I/O Manipulators

The `cout` function allows you to format your output. For example, the output of a type `float` might appear as: `16.000000`. Even though you do not need the six trailing zeros, they are still printed. The `cout` function provides I/O manipulators that allow you to control how printed values will appear on the monitor.

We have already seen a few examples of how I/O manipulators work in Program A.36. Two more useful manipulators are `setw()` and `setprecision()`. `setw()` is the set-width function, which controls how many spaces wide the field is for a number. For example, the three statements

```
cout << "The count is " << counter << "\n";
cout << "The count is " << setw(4) << counter << "\n";
cout << "The count is " << counter << "\n";
```

produce the following output when executed:

```
The count is 25
The count is    25
The count is 25
```

Notice that the output from the second `cout` statement contains two additional blank spaces before the number 25. This is the result of the `setw(4)` manipulator. Also, the output of the third `cout` statement is the same as the first. This is because the `setw()` function affects the way only the next number output with `cout` is displayed. It is necessary to use `setw()` more than once to format a group of numbers.

The `setprecision()` function controls the number of digits that follow the decimal point when displaying a `float`. Examine the following four statements:

```
cout << "The interest is " << 123.456 << "\n";
cout << "The interest is " << setw(10) << 123.456 << "\n";
cout << "The interest is " << setprecision(2) << 123.456 << "\n";
cout << "The interest is " << 123.456 << "\n";
```

The cin Function

The `cin` function is a built-in C++ function that allows your program to get user input from the keyboard. You can think of it as doing the opposite of the `cout` function. Its use is illustrated in Program A.37.

Program A.37

```
#include <iostream.h>

// Getting user input.

main()
{
    float value;     // A number supplied by the program user.

    cout << "Input a number => ";
    cin >> value;
    cout << "The value is => " << value << "\n";
}
```

When Program A.37 is executed, the output will appear as follows (assuming the program user inputs the value of 23.4:

```
Input a number => 23.4
The value is => 23.4
```

Note that the `cin` function has a similar format to that of the `cout` function. Instead of `<<`, we use the `>>` operator to direct information from the standard input to our variable. The `>>` operator is called an *extractor*. It is used to extract information from the input stream.

The type of variable used in the `cin` statement controls how the input stream is scanned and converted. In Program A.37, since `value` is defined as a `float`, the `cin` statement knows what to look for in the input stream. A carriage return is used to terminate the input number.

The `cin` function can accept more than one input with just one statement, as follows:

```
cin >> number1 >> number2 >> character;
```

where the variable `number1` has been defined as a `float`, the variable `number2` a type `int`, and `character` a type `char`. In this case, the program user could type in three separate values separated by spaces. As an example:

```
52.7 18 t
```

Because it is easy for the program user to make errors entering data in this manner, multiple inputs with the `cin` function will be done one variable at a time.

Appendix B:
ASCII Table

Character*	Code	Character	Code	Character	Code	Character	Code
NUL	0 ($00)	blank	32 ($20)	@	64 ($40)	`	96 ($60)
SOH	1	!	33	A	65	a	97
STX	2	"	34	B	66	b	98
ETX	3	#	35	C	67	c	99
EOT	4	$	36	D	68	d	100
ENQ	5	%	37	E	69	e	101
ACK	6	&	38	F	70	f	102
BEL	7	'	39	G	71	g	103
BS	8	(	40	H	72	h	104
HT	9	)	41	I	73	i	105
LF	10	*	42	J	74	j	106
VT	11	+	43	K	75	k	107
FF	12	,	44	L	76	l	108
CR	13	–	45	M	77	m	109
SO	14	.	46	N	78	n	110
SI	15	/	47	O	79	o	111
DLE	16 ($10)	0	48 ($30)	P	80 ($50)	p	112 ($70)
DC1	17	1	49	Q	81	q	113
DC2	18	2	50	R	82	r	114
DC3	19	3	51	S	83	s	115
DC4	20	4	52	T	84	t	116
NAK	21	5	53	U	85	u	117
SYN	22	6	54	V	86	v	118
ETB	23	7	55	W	87	w	119
CAN	24	8	56	X	88	x	120
EM	25	9	57	Y	89	y	121
SUB	26	:	58	Z	90	z	122
ESC	27	;	59	[	91	{	123
FS	28	<	60	\	92			124
GS	29	=	61	]	93	}	125
RS	30	>	62	↑	94	-	126
US	31	?	63	_	95	DEL	127 ($7F)

*These 32 characters (code numbers 0 through 31) are known as **control characters.**

Index